THE CONSTRUCTION LAW LIBRARY FROM WILEY LAW PUBLICATIONS

ARCHITECT AND ENGINEER LIABILITY: CLAIMS AGAINST DESIGN PROFESSIONALS
    Robert F. Cushman and Thomas G. Bottum, Editors

CONDOMINIUM AND COMMUNITY ASSOCIATION LITIGATION
    Wayne S. Hyatt and Philip S. Downer, Editors

CONSTRUCTION ACCIDENT PLEADING AND PRACTICE
    Turner W. Branch, Editor

CONSTRUCTION CLAIMS AND LIABILITY
    Michael S. Simon

CONSTRUCTION DEFAULTS: RIGHTS, DUTIES, AND LIABILITIES
    Robert F. Cushman and Charles A. Meeker, Editors

CONSTRUCTION DELAY CLAIMS
    Barry B. Bramble and Michael T. Callahan

CONSTRUCTION ENGINEERING EVIDENCE
    Loren W. Peters

CONSTRUCTION FAILURES
    Robert F. Cushman, Irvin E. Richter, and Lester E. Rivelis, Editors

CONSTRUCTION INDUSTRY CONTRACTS: LEGAL CITATOR AND CASE DIGEST
    Wiley Law Publications Editorial Staff

CONSTRUCTION INDUSTRY FORMS (TWO VOLUMES)
    Robert F. Cushman and George L. Blick, Editors

CONSTRUCTION LITIGATION: REPRESENTING THE CONTRACTOR
    Robert F. Cushman, John D. Carter, and Alan Silverman, Editors

CONSTRUCTION LITIGATION: REPRESENTING THE OWNER
    Robert F. Cushman and Kenneth M. Cushman, Editors

CONSTRUCTION LITIGATION: STRATEGIES AND TECHNIQUES
    Barry B. Bramble and Albert E. Phillips, Editors

DIRECTORY OF CONSTRUCTION INDUSTRY CONSULTANTS
    Robert F. Cushman and George L. Blick, Editors

HANDLING FIDELITY AND SUSETY CLAIMS
    Robert F. Cushman and Charles H. Stamm, Editors

HAZARDOUS WASTE DISPOSAL AND UNDERGROUND CONSTRUCTION LAW
    Robert F. Cushman and Bruce W. Ficken, Editors

SWEET ON CONSTRUCTION INDUSTRY CONTRACTS
    Justin Sweet

CONSTRUCTION LITIGATION: STRATEGIES AND TECHNIQUES

CONSTRUCTION LITIGATION: STRATEGIES AND TECHNIQUES

BARRY B. BRAMBLE, Esquire

ALBERT E. PHILLIPS, Esquire
Editors

WILEY

Wiley Law Publications
JOHN WILEY & SONS
New York • Chichester • Brisbane • Toronto • Singapore

Copyright © 1989 by John Wiley & Sons, Inc.

All rights reserved. Published simultaneously in Canada.

Reproduction or translation of any part of this work
beyond that permitted by Section 107 or 108 of the
1976 United States Copyright Act without the permission
of the copyright owner is unlawful. Requests for
permission or further information should be addressed to
the Permissions Department, John Wiley & Sons, Inc.

This publication is designed to provide accurate and
authoritative information in regard to the subject
matter covered. It is sold with the understanding that
the publisher is not engaged in rendering legal, accounting,
or other professional service. If legal advice or other
expert assistance is required, the services of a competent
professional person should be sought. *From a Declaration
of Principles jointly adopted by a Committee of the
American Bar Association and a Committee of Publishers.*

Library of Congress Cataloging in Publication Data

Construction litigation : strategies and techniques/Barry B.
    Bramble, Albert E. Phillips, editors.
       p. cm. — (Construction law library)
    ISBN 0-471-61371-1
    1. Building—Contracts and specifications—United States
—Trial practice. 2. Construction industry—Law and
legislation—United States—Trial practice. 3. Liability
(Law)—United States—Trial practice. 4. Trial practice—
United States. I. Bramble, Barry B. II. Phillips, Albert E.,
1940–   . III.   Series.
KF8925.B84C664   1989
343.73′07869′00269—dc20
[347.3037869002269]
                                           89-31897
                                              CIP

Printed in the United States of America

10 9 8 7 6 5 4 3 2 1

PREFACE

The purpose of this book is to make you more effective in advocating and presenting your client's interests in construction litigation. Therefore, we provide the perspectives and experiences of more than a dozen seasoned lawyers, engineers, and accountants. These professionals have grappled with the difficult challenges of presenting and refuting complex construction claims to factfinders of all types. In this book, the authors generously dispense experienced insight and practical advice.

We identify the most serious obstacles in presenting your construction case, and propose specific ways to deal with them. The challenges for the advocate include simplifying complex technical issues, control and management of voluminous construction documents, realistically evaluating the case, use and misuse of experts, and effective presentation techniques. We provide insight into the most difficult technical issues: construction delay, lost productivity, and damages. Specific advocacy strategies are necessary for the forum, whether it is a jury trial, bench trial, arbitration, board of contract appeals, court of claims, or appellate courts. In addition to these forums, we discuss maximizing your client's advantage through settlement and alternative disputes resolution techniques such as minitrials, mediation, and summary trials.

We thoroughly examine these topics with frankness, practical suggestions, and illustrations. We share examples to enlighten the transition from the general to specific. Although we provide numerous case citations, we emphasize the practical wisdom of experienced professionals.

This book is for anyone in the construction industry who must present a construction claim or dispute. Commonly the advocate is the attorney, but today other professionals in the construction industry are called upon to present their case.

We gratefully acknowledge the efforts of the many busy attorneys and other professionals who contributed to this book. Their dedication to this treatise will be appreciated by our readers.

March 1989

BARRY B. BRAMBLE
Philadelphia, Pennsylvania

ALBERT E. PHILLIPS
Atlanta, Georgia

ABOUT THE EDITORS

Barry B. Bramble is executive counsel of the construction management and consulting firm, MDC Systems Corp. of Philadelphia, the Construction Services Division of Day & Zimmermann, Inc. He is a recognized expert in the area of construction claims and a frequent speaker for professional societies, trade organizations, legal associations, and civic groups. Mr. Bramble has written numerous articles on construction industry topics and is a co-author of *Construction Delay Claims, Deskbook of Construction Contract Law, Discovery in Construction Litigation,* and *Avoiding and Resolving Construction Claims.* Mr. Bramble is a member of the Bar of the Commonwealth of Pennsylvania and the Bar of the State of New Jersey. He is a member of several committees of the American Bar Association, including the Forum Committee on the Construction Industry, Fidelity and Surety Law Committee, and the Public Contract Law Section. He also serves as a member of the American Arbitration Association's Panel of Construction Arbitrators.

Albert E. Phillips is a senior partner of Phillips, Hinchey & Reid, an Atlanta law firm specializing in construction matters. Mr. Phillips is a frequent seminar speaker and lecturer on the prevention, handling, and resolution of construction disputes. He currently serves as a member of the Forum Committee on the Construction Industry of the American Bar Association, the Public Contract Law Section, and the Construction Litigation Committee. He is vice-chairman of its Committee on Fidelity and Surety Law. Mr. Phillips is an advisor to the National Association of Attorneys General Committee on Construction Contracts and is chairman of the National Institute of Municipal Law Officers Section on Public Contracts. Mr. Phillips also serves as a member of the American Arbitration Association's panel of Construction Arbitrators.

SUMMARY CONTENTS

PART I	PRETRIAL ACTIVITY	
Chapter 1	Making the Complex Simple	3
Chapter 2	Case Management	19
Chapter 3	Discovery	35
Chapter 4	Use of Consultants and Experts	63
PART II	EVIDENTIARY ISSUES	
Chapter 5	Presentation of Delay and Acceleration Claims	79
Chapter 6	Lost Productivity Claims	105
Chapter 7	Establishing Damages	141
PART III	FORUM ISSUES	
Chapter 8	Advocacy in Construction Arbitration	165
Chapter 9	Federal Contract Disputes and Forums	195
Chapter 10	Alternative Disputes Resolution	239
Chapter 11	Court Trials	267
PART IV	TRIAL ISSUES	
Chapter 12	The Affirmative Case	301
Chapter 13	Defense and Cross-Examination	321
Chapter 14	Settling Construction Cases	347
Chapter 15	The Decision to Appeal	375
Table of Cases		381
Index		393

DETAILED CONTENTS

PART I   **PRETRIAL ACTIVITY**

Chapter 1   **Making the Complex Simple**
Albert E. Phillips, Esquire
Phillips, Hinchey & Reid
Atlanta, Georgia

§ 1.1   Introduction
§ 1.2   Complex Challenges for the Attorney
§ 1.3   Identify the Central Parties
§ 1.4   Focus on the Key Issues
§ 1.5   Understand the Technical Issues
§ 1.6   Develop Straightforward Explanations
§ 1.7   Steer through Procedures
§ 1.8   Conclusion

Chapter 2   **Case Management**
M. Michael Egan, Jr., Esquire
Hurt, Richardson, Garner, Todd & Cadenhead
Atlanta, Georgia

§ 2.1   Litigation Support Systems
§ 2.2   Why Use Litigation Support?
§ 2.3   Designing the Litigation Support System
§ 2.4   —Key Phrases versus Full Text
§ 2.5   —Developing Key Phrases
§ 2.6   —The Review Process
§ 2.7   Updating the System
§ 2.8   Uses of a Litigation Support System
§ 2.9   Marshalling Resources for Trial
§ 2.10 —Witness Availability
§ 2.11 —Document Availability
§ 2.12 —Location of the Trial
§ 2.13 Budget and Cost Control
§ 2.14 —Predicting Litigation Costs
§ 2.15 —Practical Aspects of Litigation Budgets
§ 2.16 —The True Cost of Litigation

Chapter 3   Discovery

Suzanne H. Charles, Esquire
Fox & Charles
Clifton Park, New York

§ 3.1	Introduction
§ 3.2	Purpose
§ 3.3	The Discovery Plan
§ 3.4	Scope
§ 3.5	Devices
§ 3.6	—Interrogatories
§ 3.7	—Depositions
§ 3.8	—Production of Documents
§ 3.9	—Requests for Inspection
§ 3.10	—Requests for Admissions
§ 3.11	Targeting Information
§ 3.12	Privileges
§ 3.13	Organization and Management
§ 3.14	Targeting Witnesses
§ 3.15	Motion Practice
§ 3.16	Conclusion

Chapter 4   Use of Consultants and Experts

Anthony M. Noce, Jr., P.E., Esquire
Lisbon Contractors, Inc.
Danboro, Pennsylvania

§ 4.1	Introduction
§ 4.2	Decision to Retain an Expert
§ 4.3	The Selection Process
§ 4.4	Roles of the Expert
§ 4.5	Interrogatories and Depositions of Opposing Experts
§ 4.6	Cross-Examination of Opposing Experts
§ 4.7	—Foundations of Expert's Opinion
§ 4.8	—Prior Opinions
§ 4.9	—Expert versus Staff Time
§ 4.10	—Compensation
§ 4.11	—Learned Treatises
§ 4.12	Conclusion

PART II   EVIDENTIARY ISSUES

Chapter 5   Presentation of Delay and Acceleration Claims

Barry B. Bramble, Esquire
MDC Systems Corp.
Philadelphia, Pennsylvania

DETAILED CONTENTS

§ 5.1	Introduction
§ 5.2	What Is Delay?
§ 5.3	What Is Acceleration?
§ 5.4	Need for Reliable Analysis
§ 5.5	—Scheduling Techniques to Demonstrate Delay
§ 5.6	Approaching the Forum
§ 5.7	Explaining CPM Scheduling
§ 5.8	Explaining Delays
§ 5.9	Explaining Acceleration
§ 5.10	Using Graphics
§ 5.11	Developing Themes for Presentation
§ 5.12	Defenses to Delay Claims
§ 5.13	Conclusion

Chapter 6 Lost Productivity Claims

Stephen M. Rymal, P.E.
Cozen & O'Connor
Philadelphia, Pennsylvania

§ 6.1	Introduction
§ 6.2	Definition of Loss of Efficiency
§ 6.3	Obstacles to Recovery for Lost Productivity Claims
§ 6.4	Judicial Recognition of Lost Productivity Claims
§ 6.5	Causes of Loss of Efficiency
§ 6.6	—Increased Labor Forces
§ 6.7	—Trade Stacking
§ 6.8	—Overtime
§ 6.9	—Adverse Weather
§ 6.10	—Out-of-Sequence Work
§ 6.11	—Acceleration
§ 6.12	—Change Orders
§ 6.13	—Constructive Changes
§ 6.14	—Disruption
§ 6.15	Proving Lost Productivity Claims
§ 6.16	Liability
§ 6.17	Causation and Injury
§ 6.18	—Experts
§ 6.19	—Trade Publications
§ 6.20	—Historical Data
§ 6.21	—Job-Specific Data
§ 6.22	Damages
§ 6.23	Conclusion

Chapter 7   Establishing Damages
Frederic R. Miller, C.P.A.
Paul W. Pocalyko, C.P.A.
Coopers & Lybrand
Washington, D.C.
Philadelphia, Pennsylvania

§ 7.1   Introduction
§ 7.2   Basic Elements of Damages Presentations
§ 7.3   —Quantifying Incremental Impacts
§ 7.4   —Linking the Liability and Damage Aspects of Claims
§ 7.5   —Importance of Well-Supported Documentation
§ 7.6   —Simplicity and Clarity of Damages Presentation
§ 7.7   General Damage Theories
§ 7.8   —Total Cost Claims
§ 7.9   —Specific Identification Claims (Cause and Effect Method)
§ 7.10   —Modified Total Cost Claims
§ 7.11   —Quantum Meruit Claims
§ 7.12   Presentation of Specific Types of Damages
§ 7.13   —Change Orders and Extra Work
§ 7.14   —Defective Work
§ 7.15   —Delay and Disruptions
§ 7.16   —Overhead
§ 7.17   —Cost Overruns and Related Documentation
§ 7.18   —Interest
§ 7.19   —Labor, Material, and Equipment Escalation during Construction
§ 7.20   Conclusion

PART III   FORUM ISSUES

Chapter 8   Advocacy in Construction Arbitration
Peter Goetz, Esquire
Goetz, Fitzpatrick & Flynn
New York, New York

§ 8.1   Introduction
§ 8.2   Agreement to Arbitrate
§ 8.3   Types of Arbitration
§ 8.4   Arbitration under the American Arbitration Association
§ 8.5   —Selection of Arbitrators from AAA Panel Lists
§ 8.6   —Arbitrator Categories
§ 8.7   —Sole Arbitrator Selection
§ 8.8   —Selecting the Right Arbitrators
§ 8.9   —Arbitrator Disclosure and Disqualification

DETAILED CONTENTS

§ 8.10	—Special Arbitrator Selection Procedures
§ 8.11	Tripartite Arbitration
§ 8.12	Consolidation of Arbitrations
§ 8.13	—Elements Necessary for Consolidation
§ 8.14	Alternatives to Consolidation
§ 8.15	Advocacy Style
§ 8.16	Conduct at Hearings
§ 8.17	Opening Statements
§ 8.18	The Evidence
§ 8.19	Closing Statements
§ 8.20	Hearing Format
§ 8.21	Hearing Transcript
§ 8.22	Post-Hearing Briefs
§ 8.23	Site Visits
§ 8.24	Adjournments
§ 8.25	Demonstrative Evidence
§ 8.26	The Award
§ 8.27	Punitive Damages
§ 8.28	Other Elements of an Award
§ 8.29	Vacating the Award
§ 8.30	Conclusion

Chapter 9 **Federal Contract Disputes and Forums**

Alvin A. Schall, Esquire
United States Department of Justice
Washington, D.C.

§ 9.1	Introduction
§ 9.2	Scope of the Contract Disputes Act
§ 9.3	Contractor Claims
§ 9.4	—Who May Submit a Claim
§ 9.5	—What Constitutes a Claim
§ 9.6	—Certification Requirement
§ 9.7	—Contracting Officer's Decision
§ 9.8	Government Claims
§ 9.9	Appealing the Contracting Officer's Decision
§ 9.10	—Necessity of a Decision
§ 9.11	—Time for Appealing the Decision
§ 9.12	—Election Doctrine
§ 9.13	—Decisions Not Involving Money Claims
§ 9.14	Review of Decisions of Boards of Contract Appeals and the Claims Court

§ 9.15	Small Claims
§ 9.16	Interest
§ 9.17	Payment of Claims
§ 9.18	Fraudulent Claims
§ 9.19	Agency Boards of Contract Appeals
§ 9.20	—Practice before the Boards
§ 9.21	—Bringing an Appeal
§ 9.22	—Discovery, Prehearing Procedures, and Motions
§ 9.23	—Hearings and Post-Hearing Matters
§ 9.24	—Small Claims Procedures
§ 9.25	United States Claims Court
§ 9.26	—Bringing Suit in the Claims Court
§ 9.27	—Discovery, Pretrial Procedures, and Motions
§ 9.28	—Trials and Post-Trial Matters
§ 9.29	Transfer and Consolidation of Cases
§ 9.30	Attorneys' Fees
§ 9.31	Selecting a Forum
§ 9.32	The Miller Act

Chapter 10   **Alternative Disputes Resolution**

John Anthony Wolf, Esquire
Ober, Kaler, Grimes & Shriver
Baltimore, Maryland
Washington, D.C.
New York, New York

§ 10.1	Introduction
§ 10.2	Benefits of Alternative Disputes Resolution
§ 10.3	Criticisms of Alternative Disputes Resolution

MINITRIAL

§ 10.4	Elements of the Minitrial
§ 10.5	History of the Minitrial
§ 10.6	Types of Disputes Resolved by Minitrial
§ 10.7	The Minitrial Agreement
§ 10.8	—Status of the Pending Dispute
§ 10.9	—Discovery before the Minitrial
§ 10.10	—Procedures to Govern the Information Exchange
§ 10.11	—Logistics at the Information Exchange
§ 10.12	—The Role of the Neutral
§ 10.13	—Confidentiality
§ 10.14	Minitrial Case Study

DETAILED CONTENTS

MEDIATION
- § 10.15 Definition
- § 10.16 Benefits of Mediation
- § 10.17 Mediation Rules
- § 10.18 Role of the Mediator
- § 10.19 Mediation Case Study

SUMMARY JURY TRIAL
- § 10.20 Historical Perspective
- § 10.21 When to Use Summary Jury Trials
- § 10.22 Pretrial Conference
- § 10.23 Jury Selection and Presentation
- § 10.24 Post-Trial Discussion and Negotiation
- § 10.25 Public Access to Summary Jury Trials

Chapter 11 Court Trials
Walter T. Wolf, Esquire
Farr, Wolf & Lyons
Bellmawr, New Jersey

- § 11.1 Introduction
- § 11.2 Unique Characteristics of Construction Claims
- § 11.3 Forum Selection
- § 11.4 —Consideration of Site Viewing
- § 11.5 Advocating a Construction Claim to a Jury
- § 11.6 Jury Selection
- § 11.7 —Professional Assistance
- § 11.8 —Voir Dire
- § 11.9 Opening Statement
- § 11.10 Direct Examination
- § 11.11 Fact Witnesses
- § 11.12 Expert Witnesses
- § 11.13 Documents and Demonstrative Evidence
- § 11.14 Closing Arguments and Jury Charges
- § 11.15 Advocating a Construction Claim to a Judge
- § 11.16 Use of Special Masters
- § 11.17 —Sample Order for Appointment of Special Master
- § 11.18 Conclusion

PART IV TRIAL ISSUES

Chapter 12 The Affirmative Case
John W. Hinchey, Esquire
Phillips, Hinchey & Reid
Atlanta, Georgia

DETAILED CONTENTS

§ 12.1	Reconstructing the Past
§ 12.2	Developing the Theme
§ 12.3	Introducing the Case
§ 12.4	—Keep It Simple
§ 12.5	—Use the Dramatic Method
§ 12.6	—Reach Out and Grip Someone
§ 12.7	—Be and Appear Sincere
§ 12.8	—Develop Your Talents to Best Advantage
§ 12.9	—Be Accurate, but Don't Argue
§ 12.10	—Use Visuals
§ 12.11	—Confront Problems with the Case
§ 12.12	—Rehearse
§ 12.13	—The Best and Last Chance
§ 12.14	Presenting the Case
§ 12.15	—Proof Strategies
§ 12.16	—Typical Proof Strategy
§ 12.17	—General Tips in Witness Presentation
§ 12.18	—Expert Testimony
§ 12.19	—Real and Demonstrative Evidence
§ 12.20	—Redirect Testimony
§ 12.21	—Summarizing the Case

Chapter 13 **Defense and Cross-Examination**
David T. Knight, Esquire
Jeanne T. Tate, Esquire
Shackleford, Farrior, Stallings & Evans
Tampa, Florida

§ 13.1	Introduction
§ 13.2	Risk Allocation
§ 13.3	Perfecting Rights by Timely Notice
§ 13.4	Preserving the Facts
§ 13.5	Indemnification Clauses
§ 13.6	Do You Want a Jury?
§ 13.7	—Types of Jury Selection
§ 13.8	—Goals of Jury Selection
§ 13.9	Opening Statement
§ 13.10	—Goals of Opening
§ 13.11	—Typical Opening in a Construction Case
§ 13.12	Responding to the Plaintiff's Case
§ 13.13	—Objecting during Direct Examination
§ 13.14	Cross-Examination
§ 13.15	—Impeachment

DETAILED CONTENTS

§ 13.16	—Discrediting Direct Examination
§ 13.17	—Expert Witnesses
§ 13.18	—Records Witnesses
§ 13.19	Mounting the Attack on Damages
§ 13.20	Defendant's Case
§ 13.21	—Fact Witnesses
§ 13.22	—Expert Witnesses
§ 13.23	—Charts and Documentation
§ 13.24	Jury Instructions and Verdicts
§ 13.25	Conclusion

Chapter 14   **Settling Construction Cases**
M. Hamilton Whitman, Jr., Esquire
Ober, Kaler, Grimes & Shriver
Baltimore, Maryland

§ 14.1	Introduction
§ 14.2	Principles Underlying Settlement: Control and Cost
§ 14.3	Good Reasons to Settle
§ 14.4	Bad Reasons to Settle
§ 14.5	Considerations of Confidentiality
§ 14.6	Initiating Settlement
§ 14.7	—Offers of Judgment
§ 14.8	—Settlement Conferences
§ 14.9	Documenting Settlement
§ 14.10	—Liquidating Agreements
§ 14.11	—Mary Carter Agreements
§ 14.12	Negotiating toward Settlement
§ 14.13	—Negotiating Style
§ 14.14	—Timing of Negotiations
§ 14.15	Dealing with the Players
§ 14.16	Conclusion

Chapter 15   **The Decision to Appeal**
Albert E. Phillips, Esquire
Phillips, Hinchey & Reid
Atlanta, Georgia

§ 15.1	Introduction
§ 15.2	Is the Decision Appealable?
§ 15.3	Should the Case Be Appealed?

Table of Cases

Index

PART I
PRETRIAL ACTIVITY

CHAPTER 1

MAKING THE COMPLEX SIMPLE

Albert E. Phillips, Esquire

Albert E. Phillips is a senior partner of Phillips, Hinchey & Reid, an Atlanta law firm specializing in construction matters. Mr. Phillips is a frequent seminar speaker and lecturer on the prevention, handling, and resolution of construction disputes. He currently serves as a member of the Forum Committee on the Construction Industry of the American Bar Association, the Public Contract Law Section, and the Construction Litigation Committee. He is vice-chairman of its Committee on Fidelity and Surety Law. Mr. Phillips is an advisor to the National Association of Attorneys General Committee on Construction Contracts and is chairman of the National Institute of Municipal Law Officers Section on Public Contracts. Mr. Phillips also serves as a member of the American Arbitration Association's Panel of Construction Arbitrators.

§ 1.1 Introduction
§ 1.2 Complex Challenges for the Attorney
§ 1.3 Identify the Central Parties
§ 1.4 Focus on the Key Issues
§ 1.5 Understand the Technical Issues
§ 1.6 Develop Straightforward Explanations
§ 1.7 Steer through Procedures
§ 1.8 Conclusion

§ 1.1 Introduction

Complexity is the most difficult challenge facing attorneys in design and construction litigation. In 1981 one court noted:

> [E]xcept in the middle of a battlefield, nowhere must men coordinate the movement of other men and materials in the midst of such chaos and with such limited certainty of present facts and future occurrences as in a huge construction project. . . . Even the most painstaking planning frequently turns out to be mere conjecture and accommodation to changes must necessarily be of the rough, quick and *ad hoc* sort, analogous to everchanging commands on the battlefield.[1]

It is often idyllically reported that there was a time when the construction process was relatively simple. Local owners, contractors, and architects worked together in harmony, recognizing that their business and professional reputations were always at stake. A solid set of plans and specifications, coupled with the personal attention of the contractor, usually meant a project built on time and within budget. Significant claims and disputes were the exception, and when they did arise, they were usually resolved without resorting to expensive litigation.

Suffice to say, things have changed! Personal relationships among the principal parties are no longer the norm. The handshake has been replaced by volumes of contracts. Competitive pressures are intense, and there is usually little room in the owner's budget, or the contractor's estimate, for mistakes. As expected, these and other trends have resulted in a dramatic increase in both the number and magnitude of construction claims and disputes. All too often the economic viability of a project is threatened by the contractor's claim for extras. On the other hand, the financial future of the contractor may be in jeopardy from delays caused by defective plans and specifications. Sadly, not only are the claims themselves mushrooming, but the cost and expense associated with their resolution are escalating wildly out of control. The complexity of the construction process often contributes to this cost.

A construction contract, broadly speaking, is nothing more than a written agreement between two parties. Therefore, what is special about a claim or dispute arising on a construction project? At least four aspects readily appear: (1) construction disputes usually involve more parties and more contracts than the owner, the general contractor, and the agreement between the two; (2) the issues commonly raised are complex, diverse, and numerous, though interwoven; (3) the events leading to the claim may take place over many months, or even years; and (4) the dispute often arises during, not after, construction, thereby requiring immediate decisions and action rather than affording the parties or their representatives extensive periods of time for study, review, and consideration. The failure to act or react promptly may constitute a decision in itself—a decision that can yield disastrous results and lead to litigation.

---

[1] Blake Constr. Co. v. C.J. Coakley Co., 431 A.2d 569, 575 (D.C. 1981).

§ 1.2 Complex Challenges for the Attorney

When representing one of the parties to a construction dispute, the attorney is faced with several challenges that serve to complicate the task. The facts and circumstances pertaining to construction disputes are more numerous and complex than those pertaining to most other disputes. This can be attributed to a number of factors. Construction is a dynamic process, not a static event. The construction process requires close coordination of many varied and difficult tasks. Changes in the project are inevitable, and lengthy periods of time are required to complete a project, frequently two years or more.

The construction process also involves multiple parties, many of whom may be parties to the dispute. A typical construction claim generally involves several issues and disputes, not one single problem. Moreover, these issues are often multifaceted, involving diverse technical aspects of engineering, construction, management, accounting, and scheduling. One of the complexities is often the difficulty of demonstrating cause and effect relationships. When causation is proved, the resulting losses may be difficult to analyze and prove. Finally, the attorney may be overwhelmed by the amount of documentation generated by the construction process. Other chapters of this book examine how the attorney can handle these challenges. Here, we address one main goal of the attorney—to make the complex simple.

Making the complex simple involves distilling the essence from the universe of facts, circumstances, problems, issues, and technicalities, and making them understandable. As we discuss in **Chapter 5**, this does not mean resorting to simplemindedness. A simpleminded approach lacks evaluation, analysis, and consideration. Making the complex simple in construction-related disputes requires a concerted level of analysis from each of the required professional disciplines.

There are many ways that attorneys can simplify complex construction disputes without resorting to simplemindedness. They include (1) identifying the central parties to the dispute; (2) identifying and focusing upon the key issues and events; (3) working to understand the technical issues in order to clarify them for others; (4) focusing upon the causative linkage between the parties, events, and losses; (5) developing a straightforward explanation of the dispute; and (6) channeling the dispute through the procedural maze, directing it toward the resolution most favorable to the client.

In approaching a construction claim, the attorney must have a solid appreciation of the factual orientation of construction claims. Construction disputes, like most other contract disputes, involve facts and circumstances, the contractual agreement of the parties, and the principles of applicable law. However, in construction disputes the applicable law is seldom seriously contested. Construction law is based upon fairly well settled principles of basic contract law. Further, though some aspects remain to receive universal application, the law governing construction disputes is reaching a level of maturity.

In many claims, the contract provisions do not serve as the primary battleground. Most construction contracts consist of familiar standard forms. Even though many of the forms are revised periodically, most of the terms are relatively clear and straightforward. Further, even when standard forms are not used, they may nevertheless be used as the basis of the contract terms. It is not unusual for parties to utilize provisions adapted from standard form contracts when drafting clauses concerning time extensions, differing site conditions, and changes.

The facts and related circumstances typically govern the resolution of construction disputes. Relevant facts should be discovered, marshalled, properly analyzed, distilled, simplified, and well presented. Facts that are never discovered are useless at best. Facts that are discovered but not understood (or worse, misunderstood) are not only useless, they are potentially disastrous.

The attorney must endeavor to uncover all of the relevant facts and circumstances, either pro or con. Once uncovered, the attorney must undertake to understand the significance of the facts, both standing alone and within the context of the entire project. Further, the attorney must be able to distinguish the facts that are important from those that are not. Finally, the attorney must be able to organize the important facts for internal use, negotiation, and formal presentation in a concise, understandable, persuasive, and cost-effective manner.

§ 1.3 Identify the Central Parties

The construction process requires that many parties come together in a coordinated and cooperative effort to produce the finished product. The number of parties directly involved may vary with the size and complexity of the project. The list below, though not all-inclusive, demonstrates the breadth and diversity of the work force often needed in a construction project.

Developer	Consulting Professionals
Owner	Construction Manager
Construction Lender	Contractors
Permanent Lender	Subcontractors
Design Professionals	Lower-Tier Subcontractors

§ 1.3 IDENTIFY CENTRAL PARTIES

Suppliers
Equipment Renters
Laborers
Unions

Sureties
Insurers
Government Agencies

Each of these parties has its own unique function to perform—and its own interest to serve. For example, the architect/engineer designs an office building for the owner, who employs a general contractor to build it. The general contractor in turn subcontracts the concrete work to another, who obtains concrete from a local supplier. Each party constitutes a link in the chain. If the supplier is late, the concrete subcontractor may be delayed, thereby disrupting and delaying the general contractor, other subcontractors, and thus, the entire project. The owner, needing timely completion to fulfill its leasing commitments, may receive a request from the general contractor for an extension of time to seek a concrete supplier other than the one originally approved. The owner may pass the request on to its designer for approval. The failure of any one party to properly and promptly fulfill its role can adversely impact the entire project. Therefore, the role played by each participant is vital to the ultimate success of the venture.

Taken singularly, there is nothing unique about most construction tasks. Given application of the requisite skill by each person involved, almost every single task can be performed over and over without difficulty or mistake. Why then do problems invariably arise? Construction of even the smallest project involves a process rather than an event, a process of constructing something that has never before been built by the same people in the same location for the same price under the precise same circumstances. Because there are so many parties involved on a project and because construction is an interwoven process, when a dispute arises, multiple parties are usually involved. This translates to multiparty litigation, and many parties' records to be discovered and people to be deposed. Consequently, the litigation process becomes complicated and attorneys are often distracted from what should be the focus of their case.

When choosing parties to be named as defendants to a construction contract action, the claimant's choices may be limited by the principle of privity of contract. One may generally sue only the parties to the contract. However, the defendants, in naming third-party defendants, may expand the network of contractual relationships to include many of the parties listed above.

If the dispute resolution forum is arbitration, the number of parties before the arbitration panel may be limited by contractual provisions prohibiting consolidation. Separation arbitrations may be instituted and may proceed concurrently. However, separate arbitration panels may only serve to further complicate the resolution of a dispute that involves several parties.

The principles of privity and no consolidation of arbitration seldom serve to simplify the number of parties involved in the resolution of a construction dispute. Therefore, the attorney must endeavor to identify the central parties to the dispute by identifying the breached relationships.[2] The immediate parties are generally determined by the contract. But the contractual chain must be examined to determine the potential "culprits" for the failure or problem. Then the appropriate parties can be named, and the documentation and witnesses of the "culprit" party can be examined. The contractual party and the "culprit" party are not always the same.

For example, a contractor may contend it has encountered delay because of design errors. The contractor has an agreement with the owner, but not with the designer. In some jurisdictions, the contractor may not sue the designer directly. The person responsible is the designer who breached the owner-designer contract, which in turn resulted in a breach of the owner-contractor agreement. The attorney representing the contractor may only be able to sue the owner, but must examine the relevant records of both the owner and designer in preparing for trial. The owner faces the same tasks when the one to blame is not actually the contractor but one of the subcontractors.

Because of the interwoven fabric of the construction process and the numerous issues that arise, it is often possible to identify more than one potential party to blame for problems. This leads to multiparty litigation, which in many instances unnecessarily complicates construction cases. The task then is to identify the key issues in dispute (§ 1.4) or the big ticket losses, and identify the related parties. The focus of discovery, analysis, and pretrial preparation should be on those matters. This is not a suggestion to ignore other issues and parties. However, limiting the central actors and issues allows the attorney to simplify the complexities of multiparty construction litigation.

§ 1.4 Focus on the Key Issues

Another way to simplify the complex is to identify and focus on the key issues in dispute. Because of the overwhelming number of potential issues in a construction case, the attorney may be enticed by an opponent into chasing the red herring issues and being distracted from the real issues.

---

[2] M. Callahan & B. Bramble, Discovery in Construction Litigation, 2 (2d ed. 1988).

§ 1.4 FOCUS ON KEY ISSUES

Even without the encouragement of the opponent, the attorney may flounder through pretrial preparation, examining too many issues or the wrong issues. Either way this can be disastrous for both the attorney and client. Thus, early goals should be identifying all possible issues and then ranking them in order of importance.

The first step in this process is to develop a checklist of all potential issues. This may include legal, contractual, and factual issues. Although many of the central issues will be factual, the legal and contractual issues must not be overlooked. The checklist may be the product of brainstorming in which every conceivable matter is listed. This will help avoid the possibility of overlooking issues.

The attorney may need the assistance of various persons in developing the issues list, such as the client, its consultant, and any cooperative parties. In construction litigation, the client generally is not one individual, but a company or firm that may have representatives in the field, in the office, and in various management tiers, thus providing other sources of ideas.

After developing the checklist of issues, the next step is to separate the wheat from the chaff. As from any brainstorming session, many ideas will prove to be creative but not applicable. Thus, the attorney must now endeavor to focus on important issues. A separation process begins: issues and non-issues; major issues and minor issues; issues easily proved and issues with difficult proof requirements. It is possible to eliminate some matters as non-issues after discussions with the client. Other small matters that appear to be non-issues may be tied together into larger issues. Often many of the specific breaches will be mere symptoms of underlying problems. For example, numerous change order requests, requests for field revisions, items of shoddy workmanship, and repeated delays all may be indicative of a poor performance by the subcontractor. The attorney should look for patterns, trends, and related events. Not only will this define fundamental issues, but it may also provide the attorney with a theme for presenting the client's case to the factfinder.

After eliminating the non-issues, the remaining list of real issues must be ranked by importance. Three factors may be helpful in this regard. First, identify the big ticket losses. The issues with the largest dollar losses should attract a larger proportion of the attorney's pretrial preparation. Often the client will be able to identify the areas with the largest direct or out-of-pocket losses. However, in construction there are many indirect and impact costs which can be enormous. Determining these impact losses is not always readily apparent. As we discuss in **Chapter 7**, the involvement of an accountant or cost engineer may be appropriate at an early stage. The identification of the big ticket losses may involve a study in itself by such a professional.

Second, many of the disputes in construction are time-related. The longer the duration of the problem, the longer the possible delay to the project. For example, the attorney will want to focus on a six-month project shutdown, rather than a two-day strike. We further discuss the challenges of analyzing delay claims in **Chapter 5**.

Third, recurring problems and similar disputes indicate another area of focus for the attorney in pretrial preparation. Recurring problems often indicate a fundamental breach, or perhaps even bad faith by one or more parties. Further, one may be able to establish a common thread or common denominator to the origin of problems and disputes, allowing an accurate identification of their cause (which may have been unknown to the project participants).

§ 1.5 Understand the Technical Issues

In order to simplify the issues for the trier of fact, the attorney must first understand the issues. Ultimately, a relatively small number of documents and witnesses will become the core case. This core will provide the winning, or unfortunately, the losing edge. The attorney must fully understand this core. But the challenge of construction litigation for the attorney involves more than just understanding the essence of the case that has been compiled by others. The attorney must take the lead and marshall the process to develop and understand the issues and facts that compose the core of the case.

Understanding the issues involves the recognition and selection of the most important documents, facts, and witnesses. This is a continuing process that begins with the initial discussions with the client. The process continues in file review, detailed document review, witness interviews, formal discovery, negotiation, preparation for the hearing, and the hearing itself.

The attorney must recognize that most of such facts and circumstances will never be conveyed to the factfinder. Most of the reviewed documents and witnesses' stories will never be introduced into evidence by either side. Nor should they be.

The construction attorney's goals are to simplify the complex, boil down the mass of facts into its essence, persuade the factfinder with clarity of presentation, and achieve the best possible result for the client. The construction attorney's goal is not to:

1. Inundate the factfinder with paper and witnesses;
2. Support the court reporting industry with thousands of transcript pages; or
3. Impress bystanders by demonstrating an ability to speak complexese.

§ 1.5 UNDERSTAND TECHNICAL ISSUES

The primary issues in most construction cases are usually framed by the facts of the dispute. Frequently, the factual issues are difficult to assess, involving combinations of complex facts and highly technical considerations. Often the evaluation of these issues will involve technical criteria, specialized applications, or processes outside the knowledge of either the client or the attorney. Further, the issues are not often subject to black and white answers, even with a full understanding of the technical considerations.

Moreover, as noted in § **1.4**, many construction disputes involve concepts that are time-related. This includes claims of delay, disruption, acceleration, lost productivity, increased costs, and extended overhead. Often the causes of delay originate or are claimed to originate in problems of engineering, management, and construction procedures. To gain an understanding of these technical matters, attorneys must often retain experts in these fields. These experts are not retained solely to provide expert testimony, but to assist in the evaluation of technical issues, to sort out the bulk of the facts, to develop an understanding of the issues, and to help educate the attorney.

The subject of experts in construction litigation is more fully discussed in **Chapter 4**. However, some discussion is warranted here because experts are important resources for attorneys in understanding the issues of the case.

The attorney must choose the right expert; as to experts generally, many will call, but few should be chosen. Initially, the attorney must identify the issues in order to determine the extent to which specialized fields of learning are the subject of the issues in dispute. Then the attorney must determine the needed fields of expertise. There may be several important technical issues, and they may need to be addressed by more than one professional, either hired individually or collectively from a single broad-based firm. If the issues are concentrated within a particular field, a specialized firm or individual may serve the need. The expertise must be matched to the needs of the client and the issues in dispute.

Consulting firms may also provide support to the attorney in the pretrial process, especially in the area of fact collection and analysis. Whether to engage an expert to assist in this regard may depend upon two factors. The first is whether the attorney has the personnel resources to handle a document-intensive dispute. Second, even if the attorney has the personnel and resources, they may be inexperienced in the subject matter of the dispute and in construction disputes in general. An extensive legal and paralegal staff without expertise in construction litigation may be inadequate for the task. Of the two factors, often the extent of the attorney's resources will be the deciding factor.

A major construction dispute will involve, at least initially, thousands, and sometimes millions of documents. A preliminary review by paralegals or technically oriented staff may be desirable. The preliminary review should be geared to identify relevant documents for evaluation by more senior technical and legal professionals. Perhaps more importantly, the goal of the preliminary review should be to eliminate irrelevant documents, so as not to divert the focus of the analysis. This can be done by comparing the checklist of issues against the document inventory and eliminating certain files altogether. For example, if there are no issues relating to concrete, then the boxes of concrete delivery tickets and test reports can be set aside. Other documents will have to be examined on an individual basis to determine relevancy to the issues. In some instances, as we discuss in **Chapter 2**, a computerized document base may be appropriate.

The review, evaluation, and management of the project documentation is an important function that can lead to understanding the issues of the case. This process must not be taken lightly. It can often be undertaken in a cost-effective and thorough manner by using personnel available from the attorney's staff and from the client's in-house resources, as well as from consulting firms.

Often the technical professionals have the experience in record-keeping to know what documents should exist in the project record. Key documents and even entire categories of documents may be overlooked in the discovery process. The expert can direct the attorney to the specific types of documents that should be obtained to analyze certain technical issues. The absence of such records from documents produced by the parties in discovery will have important repercussions and compound the problems for the attorney.

Similarly, the expert will know what to look for in the relevant field of expertise. This will not only include documents, but other pieces of evidence such as signs of fatigue and failure in materials. Important pieces of nondocumentary evidence may otherwise be overlooked.

Experts may recognize immediately the significance of documents and other important pieces of a complex puzzle. This will often serve to expedite the analysis and understanding of the issues. Nontechnical staff may routinely process such critical evidence along with more mundane elements, failing to recognize its importance and thereby slowing down the analytical process.

Experts are often valuable in interpreting combinations of apparently innocuous facts and circumstances so that they can be used in supportable and useful conclusions. This is part of the analytical process. For example, the project documentation relating to the application of labor forces may be computerized and plotted into graphics indicating the peaks and valleys of labor utilization and productivity. Study of these graphics may reveal important causes of delay, disruption, and resulting damages. In the raw state, the labor records may appear to be a dusty pile of documents. Analyzed by an expert, the records may provide the key to a dispute.

§ 1.6 DEVELOP STRAIGHTFORWARD EXPLANATIONS 13

Technical professionals may also be employed to assist in evaluating and demonstrating the crucial element of causation. Especially in the areas of design malpractice, construction delay, and lost labor productivity, the causation element is often overlooked, misunderstood, or inadequately presented by the attorney. Causation may be left to inference; more often it is inadequately linked to the facts and evidence. Experts can be helpful in establishing or disproving the causal tie between the events and the results. But this must not be glossed over. Unfortunately, some experts and attorneys believe that the mere opinion of the expert can serve as the sole proof of causation, without a specific tie to project documentation and other evidence. In this regard, the attorney must clearly take control to assure that the expert understands the proof requirements of causation and the need for a factual basis in the specific project. The expert may know he is right, but the attorney must prove it with the facts.

Other experts may be helpful in quantifying recoverable damages or defenses thereto. This process is discussed in **Chapter 7**. Accountants, cost engineers, and others knowledgeable in construction costs are often indispensable to the claimant's attorney in understanding the elements and categories of losses that can result from the issues in dispute. Similarly, they assist the defense counsel in refuting such claims under appropriate circumstances.

Overall, the most important functions that the experts provide are analytical and educational. Experts can analyze the technical information in such a way as to provide an important understanding of the technical issues in dispute. They can then impart that understanding to the attorney. It is not enough for the expert to understand the issues. The attorney must then apply the facts to the law and direct the matter through the dispute resolution process. In order to properly represent the client in negotiation, presentation, and other aspects, the attorney must have a thorough understanding of the factual, technical, contractual, and legal issues relating to the dispute.

§ 1.6 Develop Straightforward Explanations

Only if the attorney thoroughly understands the pertinent facts and how those facts apply to the law and the contractual context, can a theory of the case be developed. Once the facts and issues are understood individually, they must be put together as a whole. This requires the attorney to think through the case, piecing the puzzle together. An overall guiding theory of the case can be used to pursue the case to the best possible resolution for the client, and can serve as the basis for negotiation or litigation. The development of a straightforward explanation for the client's position will serve as a springboard for the advocate's skills.

Straightforward explanations for the individual issues are also important. Although the attorney understands the issues, this understanding must be clearly and succinctly conveyed to the trier of fact, whether it is a jury, judge, arbitration panel, or administrative board. The explanations of individual issues fit the overall theory of the case, and vice versa.

In developing explanations, the attorney must endeavor to reduce complexity without distorting the meaning. Often important aspects are glossed over in an attempt to force the facts to fit the explanation. Attorneys insisting upon this approach may find the opposing counsel exposing the distortion and presenting contrary facts. Such distortions are especially dangerous if the proponent is the expert witness. In that regard, one way of reducing the complexity of technical issues is by analogy or reference to everyday experiences. As we discuss in **Chapter 5**, attorneys have developed network schedules for events like cooking dinner, fixing a flat tire, and cleaning house to explain critical path method scheduling. Again, if an inappropriate analogy is utilized, the opponent may pick up on the theme to demonstrate distortions and weaknesses, and perhaps even turn the analogy back on its maker.

Technical issues are often depicted by charts, graphs, photographs, slides, models, and even videos. Visual demonstrations may provide a welcome relief to the trier of fact who is subject to a barrage of verbal testimony, documentary evidence, and oral argument. These aids, if accurately and clearly prepared, go a long way toward assisting the factfinder in visualizing and understanding the situation that the attorney attempts to convey in words. Complex facts can be summed up and the image driven home with color and illustration. The science of the graphic arts should indeed come to play in making the complex construction issue more understandable. See **Chapter 5** on delay and **Chapter 7** on damages for ideas on how these complex concepts may be illustrated and presented.

Another effective technique in developing straightforward explanations is to eliminate the use of unnecessary technical terminology (complexese) and legal jargon (legalese). Resort to such terms may be a mask for a lack of true technical knowledge, or worse yet, a substitute for thorough analysis or straightforward explanation. Frequently such terms detract from an understandable explanation by diverting attention to terms. The terms may add to confusion rather than creating understanding.

Concerning straightforward explanations, however, four warnings are appropriate. First, explanations that are too simplistic may only insult the factfinder. Remember: simplification does not involve simplemindedness.

Second, an overly complex explanation will bore the trier of fact. Frequently, this dilemma is the result of an "overly-prepared" attorney who does not really understand the essence of the case. Too much attention was paid to detail and not enough to understanding. Recounting detail is not a substitute for effective advocacy.

Third, the above warning concerning complexity should not be interpreted so as to minimize the presentation of the detailed factual basis required in construction litigation. All of the explanations, theories, and expert opinions must be painstakingly linked to facts put into evidence. This is especially true of the causation element in delay and disruption claims. But other elements in issue may succumb to inadequate proof. Despite the overwhelming amount of project documentation and facts, the attorney may be faced with a lack of available proof to establish certain aspects of construction claims. Discerning this lack of critical evidence early is important to subsequent handling and preparation of the claim or defense.

Finally, the construction attorney should be wary of resorting to the use of shortcut theories like total cost damages (see **Chapter 7**). Rather than proving each element of damages, this theory purports that the overall recoverable damages may be calculated by subtracting the bid costs from the actual project costs. In some instances, courts have allowed this method where an adequate foundation is laid.[3] However, there is always a danger of a lack of factual basis for the application of the theory. Further, such a theory is not necessarily a shortcut to an effective explanation, but may be a short circuit in logic. This type of shortcoming may be detected and rejected by a jury, as well as by the more experienced factfinders on an arbitration panel or in a bench trial.

§ 1.7 Steer through Procedures

Successful resolution of construction disputes is often hampered by procedural complexities in addition to the factual and technical complexities involved in the merits of the dispute. In effective representation, the attorney must endeavor to simplify the complex procedures. The goal of the attorney is to channel the dispute through the procedural maze, directing the dispute toward a prompt resolution most favorable to the client.

In some instances, the interests of the defending party may be to prevent attempts by the claimant to expedite the presentation of the matter to the factfinder for final determination. This may occur when the claimant has garnered all of the facts, analyzed its case, and acted to prevent the defending party from obtaining the information it needs for a defense. Many

---

[3] The foundations for the total cost theory may include the following premises: (1) there exists no other way to demonstrate the losses, and this is not due to negligent recordkeeping by the claimant; (2) there are no significant errors in the bid or estimate; (3) the claimant is able to distinguish and account for any of its own inefficiencies or problems; and (4) the actual costs are reasonable. *See* B. Bramble & M. Callahan, Construction Delay Claims § 10.6 (1987).

owners are opposed to arbitration of construction claims filed by contractors, especially when owners are precluded from access to the contractor's records before the start of the hearings. However, in most cases, attempts to stall the prehearing procedures are not in the interests of either party. A prolonged pretrial process will usually divert from a concerted analytical effort, result in an on-again/off-again defense, and drive up legal and other costs.

The procedural maze in construction disputes often begins during contract administration. Many construction contracts contain clauses requiring notice, submission of documentation, and even a forum for resolving construction disputes during the construction process. Contracts with public owners may require administrative dispute resolution procedures before the contracting agencies. Failure to comply with these administrative steps may preclude the claimant from resorting to litigation. Courts may dismiss the claimant's suit for failure to exhaust administrative remedies. Once a lawsuit is properly filed, the discovery and other pretrial procedures may prolong the formal resolution for several years. Even arbitration hearings may be delayed by such matters as exchange of documents, selecting arbitrators, determination of hearing locale, motions to stay arbitration proceedings, and establishing available hearing dates. As a result, construction disputes often languish awaiting formal resolution. Without the threat of immediate trial or hearing, the parties may not be motivated to resolve the dispute informally through negotiation.

Thus, the construction attorney must endeavor to guide the dispute through the various procedures. Too often, the attorney becomes embroiled in subsidiary disputes that divert attention from the central issues. The client's need to promptly conclude the case is set aside, and time and resources are squandered. One goal is to simplify the process so as to minimize the client's resources devoted to the process as opposed to the analysis and resolution of the issues in dispute. Another is to resort to the pretrial procedures to the extent necessary to allow an adequate investigation of the merits. These may be conflicting goals, in that minimizing the costs of the pretrial procedures may serve to thwart an adequate preparation. But maximizing the procedural costs will rarely result in effective representation.

§ 1.8 Conclusion

It is almost universally true that formal resolution (trial or arbitration) of a construction dispute turns upon the resolution of a small handful of issues, not a detailed resolution of every minute controversy presented. Indeed, the construction attorney who looks back on personal experience will agree that many disputes were left unresolved when the final decision was made. Therefore, the goal of the successful construction attorney is to determine the identity of the central issues in advance and to present the client's case on these issues in its most forceful, effective light. That is not to suggest that other details should be ignored. It is merely to state that the factfinder, whether it be an arbitration panel, a judge, or a jury, is far more likely to keep its attention focused on the important issues if counsel does likewise.

In focusing the attention of the factfinder on the important issues, the attorney must be careful not to have as a goal the exhaustion of every fact known by every witness before the trial is over. Judges and jurors have slept through the testimony of many important witnesses because the attorney failed to recognize what was important and what was not.

Remember that it is not the attorney or the expert who is expected to benefit from the presentation, it is the factfinder. Thus it is important that the case be conceptualized and presented as something that must be understood by the least knowledgeable of the factfinders. Simplicity must be the order of the day.

The only way that simplicity can be achieved is through mastering the complex. That is to say that the attorney and the attorney's consultants must plumb the depths of the complex facts, seeking the thread of simplicity that can be convincingly presented in the most effective and persuasive manner.

CHAPTER 2

CASE MANAGEMENT

M. Michael Egan, Jr., Esquire

M. Michael Egan, Jr., is a partner in the Atlanta law firm of Hurt, Richardson, Garner, Todd & Cadenhead where he practices in the construction law area on behalf of contractors, owners, architects, and sureties. He is a member of the American Bar Association's Forum Committee on the Construction Industry and the Fidelity & Surety Committee of the Torts and Insurance Practice Section. He also serves as an arbitrator for the American Arbitration Association. He holds an undergraduate degree and a masters degree in economics from Duke University. He has a J.D. from the University of Georgia Law School where he was Notes Editor of the *Georgia Law Review*.

§ 2.1   Litigation Support Systems
§ 2.2   Why Use Litigation Support?
§ 2.3   Designing the Litigation Support System
§ 2.4   —Key Phrases versus Full Text
§ 2.5   —Developing Key Phrases
§ 2.6   —The Review Process
§ 2.7   Updating the System
§ 2.8   Uses of a Litigation Support System
§ 2.9   Marshalling Resources for Trial
§ 2.10 —Witness Availability
§ 2.11 —Document Availability
§ 2.12 —Location of the Trial
§ 2.13 Budget and Cost Control
§ 2.14 —Predicting Litigation Costs
§ 2.15 —Practical Aspects of Litigation Budgets
§ 2.16 —The True Cost of Litigation

§ 2.1 Litigation Support Systems

Construction disputes are ideally suited for litigation support systems. Construction litigation typically involves a multitude of persons who have generated a large number of documents over a lengthy period of time. Single issue cases are the exception, not the rule. The problem, therefore, is how to correlate the facts, the witnesses, and the documents so that some sense can be made of the case and so that the attorney understands every important aspect of the dispute.

No matter what the size of the case or the number of documents involved, the answer to this organizational problem is a litigation support system.[1] Although to many this has come to mean computers, a computer is only a tool by which a great deal of well organized data can be obtained quickly. In truth, a computer is merely one aspect of implementing the litigation support system, and not everyone agrees that it is a necessary tool.[2] However, a computer is ideally suited to the task at hand—the reference and cross-reference of data in a logical framework.[3] The key to success of the litigation support system is to have the attorneys who are in charge of the case design the system and actively use it.

§ 2.2 Why Use Litigation Support?

A litigation support system can accomplish several important tasks for a lawyer involved in a construction dispute. First, a litigation support system forces the attorney to identify the legal and factual issues of the case at the beginning and to redefine and sharpen those issues as more becomes known about the case. Hence, the very process of designing the litigation support system for a specific case requires the attorney to focus squarely on the major legal and factual questions presented by the dispute.

Second, a litigation support system saves clients' money and attorneys' time. In a well-designed support system, all of the documents in the case are reviewed extensively only one time. Suppose, for example, that there are 3,000 separate documents in a case. This is not an unusual number for

---

[1] Dombroff, *Litidex: A Computer-Compatible Manual Litigation Organization System,* 1981 Trial Lawyers Guide 417; A. Seimer & D. Land, Wilmer, Cutler & Pickering Manual on Litigation Support Databases (2d ed. 1989).

[2] *See* Trowbridge vom Baur & Simmons, *How to Manage the Big Case Without a Computer,* 29 Prac. Law. 45 (1983).

[3] Feiler, *Computer Aided Litigation Support in Patent Litigation,* 25 Idea 177 (1984).

a construction dispute. Furthermore, suppose that, after the attorney has obtained all of these documents from the client and from the opponent, the attorney decides to depose a certain witness, Mr. Jones. A paralegal or associate dutifully goes through all 3,000 documents to identify every document received by or written by Mr. Jones. Assume that, later in the case, the attorney decides to depose a second witness, Mr. Smith. The same paralegal or associate is required again to sort through all 3,000 documents to identify every document written by or received by Mr. Smith. This is an obvious duplication of effort and clearly a waste of time. If the reviewers record who received the documents and who wrote them the first time all documents are reviewed, then this information is readily accessible for the remainder of the case, either through a manual card system or through a computerized arrangement of the data.

Third, in a large construction case that takes place over a number of years and in which a number of attorneys are involved, the litigation support system, in essence, "remembers" all documents and issues in the case in a way that is not possible for any one attorney.[4] For example, if in the first year of a case one attorney attends a document production and obtains a certain number of documents, the attorney records in the system the fact that those documents were produced, how many were produced, who produced them, and the ordinary fact that the documents are now contained within that case's file. Over a period of years, documents are frequently moved about in a law office, such as during remodeling and office relocations. The litigation support system thus enables the attorneys handling a case to retain continuity as to the source and content of documents, which is not otherwise possible when multiple attorneys are involved in a case over a number of years. The human memory is unable to keep up with all the details of a complex case over an extended period of time. The litigation support system solves this problem. Using the above example, in the third year of the case the computer can identify all documents produced by a specific party from the beginning of the case.

Finally, if the support system has been well planned and well implemented, it can be a very effective tool both in preparing for trial and in actually trying the case. The mass of information representing the significant facts in the case is placed at the effective disposal of the attorney trying the case in a way that does not require the memorization of every conceivable document. In the end, the litigation support system cannot replace ordinary judgment as to what is important and what is convincing. However, it is a safety net under a construction attorney to prevent the loss of important, convincing papers in the mass of data.

---

[4] *See* Snyder, *Stop Playing Hide & Seek With Your Documents,* 72 A.B.A. J. 54 (1986).

§ 2.3 Designing the Litigation Support System

Evidence is presented in court or in arbitration through witnesses and documents. The legal and factual issues in the case determine which documents and which witnesses will be presented. Thus, in its simplest form, a litigation support system can be thought of in three terms: (1) the witness, (2) the document, and (3) the legal and factual issues referred to by either the witness or the document. The purpose of a litigation support system is to rapidly connect a legal or factual issue with a specific witness or document.

In construction cases, as in all cases, the file organization should be clearly divided into three groups of documents. The first group is composed of documents created by the parties during the course of the dispute. The second group is composed of documents created by the attorneys for the parties during the course of handling the dispute. As a general proposition, the first group is discoverable and the second group is not. Finally, there is a third group of documents, such as depositions and pleadings, that are created during the course of the case and are shared by all parties.

In general, litigation support systems can likewise be divided into three kinds. The first kind attempts only to categorize and make manageable the original documents created by the parties before the dispute went to litigation. The second kind ties together not only the parties' original documents but also the depositions and pleadings created by the parties during the course of litigation. The third kind of litigation support system is all-encompassing, because it places the entire file, including internal law firm memoranda, research memoranda, and ordinary correspondence into the system.

Frequently, the most effective litigation support systems for construction cases are those that are simple and least expensive. Accordingly, the ideal litigation support system does not attempt to encompass the entire case file into the system. Instead, the case file is broken down into two separate indexes. The first index contains references and cross-references to the original documents created by the parties during the course of their dispute and the documents shared by all parties during the course of the litigation—pleadings and depositions. As we describe in the following sections, the references and cross-references pertain mainly to the documents' dates, authors, recipients, subject matter, and description.

The second index is for keeping up with the documents created by the lawyers in the case, such as legal research memoranda, correspondence to clients, and other matters which generally are either not discoverable or not relevant. Because it is simpler than the first index and contains less data, it normally can be kept manually. This second index does not attempt to reference all documents; it is merely a quick reference to file organization. However, through these two indexes, the attorney can quickly find truly important documents.

§ 2.4 —Key Phrases versus Full Text

The first step in designing the system is for the attorney to identify key phrases that describe the significant legal and factual issues in the case. Each document is then reviewed by paralegals or other technical support staff and assigned one or more key phrases in order to succinctly record the subject matter of the document. Although it is possible to enter the full text of all documents into a computer, either through optical scanners or retyping, such a task is enormously expensive in terms of labor and computer costs.[5] More importantly, it does not accomplish the fundamental task at hand, which is that a person with judgment and an understanding of the case read each document and record, once and for all, its significance. Mechanically putting an entire document into a computer system makes it no more useful in a case than photocopying a case report makes that case useful to an attorney arguing before a court. Not until the case is read, understood, and correlated to the issue at hand can that case be useful. Likewise, not until a document is read, understood, and correlated to the issues in a case can it be useful. The key phrase method forces the accomplishment of this task at an early stage in the design of the litigation support system.

§ 2.5 —Developing Key Phrases

The development of key phrases is a multistep process. First, the attorney learns, in general, the legal and factual subject matter of the case through the pleadings in the case, discussions with the other side and the client, and interviews of key witnesses. The next step is to read a carefully chosen sampling of the documents from key files, such as the correspondence file, transmittal file, job meeting minutes, and test files, to understand the case further. After those first steps, the attorney is ready to create the key phrases by identifying factual and legal issues in the case. For example, suppose that the case involves concrete foundation walls which allegedly were not poured within the tolerances allowed by the specifications. Suppose also that one party claims that, even if the foundation walls were out of tolerance, the walls were fully surveyed and accepted by the opposing party. In this scenario, the key phrases suggested from a factual point of view are foundations, tolerances, specifications, and surveying. From a legal point of view, the questions are waiver, inspection, acceptance, and contract performance.

---

[5] Potash, *Litigation Support for Small Firms,* 71 A.B.A. J. 68, 71 (1985); *see also* Reich, *Building a Litigation Support System to Organize Documents,* 32 Prac. Law. 59 (1986).

The more specific and detailed the key phrases, the more useful they are. Key phrases that are tailored to the specific facts of a case will help the attorney find documents pertaining to a narrow, sharply defined subject matter. However, the wording of the phrases must be broad enough to capture the different ways that the factual and legal issues may be stated in the project documentation. For example, the term "concrete" may be referenced in documents in different ways. The writer of the document may discuss "bad pours," may mention the concrete subcontractor by name, or may reference Division 3 of the Uniform Construction Index pertaining to concrete work. All of these may refer to defective concrete work, but not mention the word concrete. The persons reviewing the documents should be fully briefed on construction industry jargon, technical considerations, and the legal issues.

The next step is to create an index form to use in analyzing every document in the construction case. The form should have a place to record the following information:

1. Number of the document
2. Source of the document
3. Date of the document
4. Deposition exhibit number, if any, of the document
5. Relative importance of the document (0–4, with 4 the most significant and 0 irrelevant to the dispute)
6. Description of the document (check, letter, pay requests)
7. Very short abstract of the document
8. Author of the document
9. Recipient of the document, including copies
10. Persons discussed in the document
11. Documents discussed in the document
12. Key phrases to identify the subject matter.

§ 2.6 —The Review Process

Assume that lawyers have already attended a document production and arranged for the copying of certain files. A winnowing process is already underway by virtue of the decision as to what is worth copying. After copying, each document is stamped with a number on its first page. In cases involving a large number of documents, the process of stamping itself can take several days. To save time, only the first page of every document should be stamped, except in the rare instance of extremely lengthy documents dealing with a myriad of subjects. Through the stamping process, every document is assigned a number. These numbers are used with the computer software that has been chosen to manipulate the recorded data.

The next step is for paralegals and attorneys to begin the process of reviewing each of the documents in detail. In undertaking this process, the reviewer should have the index form and the key phrases described in detail on a definition sheet. If there is a group of several reviewers, the definition sheet assures uniformity in the review process. In addition, to save room in the computer memory, a number is assigned to each author and each recipient as well as to each subject. Hence, when the form is filled out, everything but the short abstract of the document will be a number. The reviewer records the number of a document, who wrote it, who received it, the subject matter (reduced to the key phrases), and what kind of document it is. Every category of information is important, including the ordinary description of the document. The information on the form is then entered into the computer.

Depositions and pleadings should also be entered into the system in nearly the same fashion as other documents. However, certain adjustments must be made, because, in a deposition, it is no longer important who the author or recipient of the deposition is per se. Rather, the subject matter, documents discussed, and pertinent page numbers constitute the truly important information. Accordingly, a deposition index must be done in order to effectively incorporate the deposition into the litigation support system.

Most court reporters now offer a full text search capability whereby, through the use of certain words or phrases, the entire text of a deposition can be searched by computer. While this is certainly useful, finding a witness's discussion of a particular subject depends upon the searcher's ability to use exactly the same words that witness used in describing a specific event or document. Using the earlier foundation wall/tolerance example, the attorney may have simply specified "concrete walls" or "poured-in-place concrete" in the computer search instead of the phrase the witness actually used, "concrete wall." Accordingly, the computer search would fail. Furthermore, the mere fact that a deposition is stored in its entirety in the memory of a computer does not make the deposition useful by an attorney at trial. A deposition's true usefulness arises from a careful reading, followed by the incorporation of its pertinent information into the key phrase index of the entire case. The traditional deposition summary as such is not utilized. Instead, the deposition is indexed page by page using the same form with which the other documents are indexed.

In reviewing a deposition and putting its contents into the litigation support system, the most important items again are the documents discussed, the persons discussed, and the key subjects discussed. In addition, the document number system must be adopted to the page of the deposition.

Pleadings should also be integrated into the litigation support system as they are received. The most important pleadings in this category, of course, are answers to interrogatories or admissions made in answers. In addition, affidavits filed in support of various motions are also important. These kinds of pleadings contain facts which may be used at trial, and they should be indexed using the same form used for other documents.

§ 2.7 Updating the System

During the course of litigation, new legal and factual issues are suggested by the witnesses, the documents, or the attorneys. In addition, some issues gain in importance, while others lose significance. Therefore, the litigation support system must be updated as the case develops. Occasionally, the documents must be reviewed with respect to a new issue not previously identified. In addition, as the trained and experienced reviewers go through the files, new subjects might occur to them. They must be constantly alert to add new key phrases and to clarify the meaning of certain technical matters. The process of reviewing the documents and entering them into the computer system is critical and, hence, should be monitored daily by an attorney. A familiar, recurring problem is large groups of documents which will seemingly not fit any category and yet are clearly important. These must be worked into the system, perhaps through new key phrases. Furthermore, the work of the reviewers must be checked in order to determine that they are all using the key phrases in the same fashion.

In the event that new subjects are suggested during the course of litigation, the documents must be examined again to determine which of them contain these subjects. It is best to discover any serious omission in the key word index as soon as possible. If the omission is caught in the early stages of the initial review of documents, an expensive and time-consuming re-examination of all documents will be prevented.

§ 2.8 Uses of a Litigation Support System

Once the system is created, it can be used in a number of effective ways to help the attorney understand the case and prepare for trial. An example is the preparation of an expert witness.[6] Assume that an issue in the case is the cost of completing a construction project and that an expert has been retained to estimate that cost. If one of the key phrases is "cost of

---

[6] *See* DuBowe, *Automated Litigation Support: A Litigator's Primer,* 68 A.B.A. J. 1118, 1121 (1982).

completion," the computer will identify for the attorney, out of all of the many thousands of documents, those documents which speak about the cost of completing the project. By running the key phrase "cost of completion" through the computer, it will generate references to documents which no attorney, using memory alone, could possibly have kept in mind. Furthermore, because these documents are identified by number, a paralegal can readily retrieve the documents from the file, copy them, and refile them. Thus, the expert is given a copy of all documents pertaining to the issue of cost of completion. The expert witness can then be prepared to testify, free from fear that opposing counsel will confront the witness at trial with a document which is seemingly contradictory to the witness's testimony.

The system can also be used to help decide what witnesses and documents will be used at trial. Taking the earlier example of "foundation walls," the computer can identify every document and every deposition page where foundation walls are discussed. Furthermore, it can list chronologically the documents that discuss the issue. The documents can be pulled from the file in the same order in which the computer identifies them and stacked chronologically. Inevitably, a chronological review of documents that have been assembled from several sources reveals interrelationships between the parties and the events on the project that previously either were not known or were little understood. Sometimes a revelation from this process can be startling and very important. In any event, from a chronological review of all documents on a particular subject, the attorney can determine what witnesses and what documents relate significantly to a particular subject.

The computer can also generate a printed list of all documents that have been produced in the case. The computer will further refine that list to all documents that became deposition exhibits in the case. From these lists, an attorney can choose which documents will appear as trial exhibits on a pretrial order. The listing of exhibits is frequently required in both state and federal courts. A computer printout of the trial exhibit list saves the laborious and time-consuming process of dictating a description of every document to be used at the trial. The printout also provides the attorney with a checklist, in essence, of all documents in the case so that no critical documents are overlooked.

Finally, the subject matter index can be very helpful in cross-examining witnesses at trial. For example, if you know that a specific witness is to testify the next day in court, you can have the computer prepare a list of every subject which that witness has discussed either in a document or in depositions. If the witness brings up the question of acceptance of foundation walls, the lawyer will have a quick and immediate reference to every page of the witness's deposition on which the subject of "foundation wall acceptance" was discussed.

§ 2.9 Marshalling Resources for Trial

It is never too early to begin thinking about what resources will be necessary for trial of a construction case. Once the trial begins, it is too late to marshall the necessary resources. Essentially, the problem can be reduced to three categories: people, paper, and place. As simple as it may seem, the pretrial orchestration in a construction case is all directed toward having the right witness with the right documents on the appointed day in the right place. The number of documents in a construction case is so large that it is usually impractical to have all documents at the place where the trial is to be held. Additionally, a construction case normally involves several witnesses that must be contacted and scheduled to testify. Therefore, for the attorney trying the case, the question is one of practical logistics. In order to keep the case moving at all times, one must have a team already in place to assure that the documents and witnesses are waiting nearby.

§ 2.10 —Witness Availability

Early on in the case, a notebook should be devoted solely to information about potential witnesses. The notebook should be arranged alphabetically. Each witness information sheet should contain the witness's home and work telephone numbers, address, place of employment, and whether the witness is to be subpoenaed to testify at trial. In addition, the witness information sheet should contain a description of any problems with the witness's availability. It is also helpful to describe, in summary form, the witness's involvement on the construction project at issue.

As soon as a trial date is known, an attendance plan should be adopted for every witness, including experts. When possible and suitable, the witnesses should be notified immediately through a form letter that tells them the date and time of their anticipated appearance and of any meetings with the attorneys before that appearance. If there are any hostile witnesses who must be subpoenaed, the date and method of service should be established as soon as a trial date is known. Inevitably, some witnesses will have schedule problems that make appearance at the trial inconvenient for them. Every trial attorney has experienced the frustration and difficulty of getting witnesses to lay aside their ordinary business in order to come to either a trial or an arbitration hearing. Keeping witness attendance information available in one convenient location and using it to coordinate schedules is very helpful. The attorney can then concentrate on the case. In a recent construction arbitration hearing, the claimant presented 14 witnesses, and the respondent presented 11 witnesses. The logistics of keeping up with this many people and having them present at the right time was readily accomplished with a written plan in the witness notebook.

One person should be assigned to witness coordination because the lead attorney seldom has sufficient time, as the weeks and days close in toward final presentation of the case, to make all of the arrangements with all of the witnesses. Hence, it is critical to establish a "witness person" who handles all the problems of having the witnesses present at the right place and time. It is best if this person is also attending the trial because of the possibility of changes in adjournment times, out-of-order proofs, and schedules. Such changes seem to be the rule in construction cases, rather than the exception.

§ 2.11 —Document Availability

The final, most important step in managing a construction case is identifying and having readily available those documents which will be necessary for either the direct or cross-examination of witnesses. The key to effective use of documents in a construction case is a reference and cross-reference index which permits the attorney to quickly find documents. This can only be accomplished if a litigation support system has been implemented, even if it is a very simple manual system.

If the case has been managed through a computerized litigation support system, then marshalling one's resources for trial means being certain that the computerized information is readily available during the course of the trial. One way is to print hard copy (printouts) in the form of two lists of documents for each witness that is expected to testify. The first list contains all the documents that a particular witness wrote, received, or discussed, in chronological order. Sometimes during the course of trial, it is easier to remember when something occurred in conjunction with a witness's testimony than it is to correlate the information in any other way. The second list for each witness should be sorted by subject matter; it is perhaps the more important of the two lists.

In construction cases, nonexpert witnesses are prone to make broad, partisan pronouncements which amount to no more than sweeping generalizations about the way the work proceeded at the project. The problem is that, in the compressed time frame of a trial or an arbitration hearing, a witness's gross generalizations may seem as important to the factfinder as any of the other evidence in the case. The day can only be saved by either a specific document or a specific deposition text which is contrary to the witness's broad generalization. An example of this is a general contractor's project superintendent who testifies on the stand that, "As far as I can remember, we never did delay any of the work, and so as far as I am concerned, we didn't put the owner behind time at all." In trial, and particularly in arbitration hearings, statements like this are made all the time. By examining the subject matter listing of documents for the project superintendent, one can find, under the key phrase "causes for delay," letters either received by or authored by the project superintendent that discuss delay on the project. The list would also identify the general subject matter of the letter. Thus, when time comes for cross-examination, the attorney can find those documents and those portions of depositions where the project superintendent discussed delay. In some instances, this simply helps one find familiar documents quickly. However, in the pressure of trial, it is easy to forget pertinent evidence. The list provides a very quick checklist to defeat the superintendent's unexpected and harmful generalization that the general contractor caused no delay on the project.

Perhaps even more important, remembering that individual pages of depositions can be treated by the computerized litigation support system as if they are individual documents, the hard copy list will contain those portions of the project superintendent's deposition where he was asked about the subject of delay. In the more relaxed atmosphere of the deposition before trial, the project superintendent may have stated that there were a few instances in which delay was caused by the general contractor. However, quickly finding a statement like that in a 300- or 400-page deposition is difficult at best when one uses a traditional deposition summary that is based solely on a first-to-last page organization. The subject matter index solves this problem.

In addition, all of the documents that have been listed as exhibits on either party's pretrial order can be sorted by author, recipient, subject matter, and key phrase. This also will help in preparing for trial.

Finally, particularly with respect to one's own witnesses, there is, of course, no replacement for the old-fashioned witness file containing those documents which counsel intends to introduce through the witness and the proposed order of introduction. The witness file can also contain all of those documents which counsel intends to use in cross-examination. An effective litigation support system can help the attorney in deciding what documents will be in that file. However, particularly in the instance of cross-examination, a witness may speak on an issue about which the attorney did not expect testimony. The computer generated subject matter listing can help the attorney to quickly respond to the witness in this situation.

§ 2.12 —Location of the Trial

Wherever the trial is to be held, the attorney must think in terms of how the documents can be made readily available during the course of trial. If there is more than a box or two of documents, arrangements must be made so that the main set of documents can be kept relatively near the courthouse or the arbitration hearing room so that the documents necessary for that day are immediately available. Generally, the actual management of documents and the responsibility for having them available to the lead attorney is delegated to a paralegal or associate who is familiar with the litigation support system, the order of witnesses, and the trial exhibit list.

It is time consuming and cumbersome to transport a large number of documents to and from the courthouse every day. Normally, either through the court or the arbitrators, the attorneys can obtain an agreement that they will disclose to one another which witnesses will testify the next day. This greatly aids in assuring that the documents likely to be used the next day are available to the attorneys without bringing the entire file. (One minor advantage of arbitration is that the arbitrators are usually flexible with respect to bringing documents in and out of hearings, making space available for the storage of documents near the hearing room, and other amenities.) In general, one must realistically examine what documents are likely to be necessary during the course of a trial and make early arrangements for the convenient availability of the documents. One cannot simply bring everything to the hearing every day; this is cumbersome and distracts the attorney from the case.

§ 2.13 Budget and Cost Control

One of the most difficult problems in construction litigation is keeping the cost of litigation within an acceptable limit, given the amount in controversy. It is our experience in construction disputes that the dollar amount of a claim or controversy does not necessarily correspond to the effort and cost involved in litigating the case. Rather, the cost of litigating a specific case hinges more upon the number of issues presented in the case and the need for experts pertaining to those issues than upon any other factors. In addition, the number of litigating parties in the case can also significantly increase costs. It can take just as much money to litigate a $100,000 dispute made up of 20 construction-related issues as it can to litigate a $1 million case comprised of only one or two construction-related issues.

§ 2.14 —Predicting Litigation Costs

Construction disputes are among the most expensive matters to litigate. The facts of a construction dispute usually evolve over an extended period of time and can occasionally involve extremely technical issues. Furthermore, the contract between the parties normally includes references to specifications, drawings, addenda, general conditions, and special conditions, all of which are elaborate and complex. A construction project also usually involves a multitude of parties in the form of general contractors, subcontractors, suppliers, sureties, owners, lenders, architects, construction managers, and engineers. All of this is a prescription for extremely expensive litigation.

Given that the costs of litigation can possibly consume the amount in controversy, the client and the attorney should attempt to establish a budget at the beginning of a case. The budget estimate must take into account the number and complexity of the issues to be litigated. The budget should include estimates for attorney fees, deposition costs, travel costs, copying costs, and expert witness costs. However, it is extremely difficult to predict the litigation costs of a specific dispute. Among other things, one cannot predict the number or nature of legal maneuvers of the other side, such as motions to dismiss and motions for summary judgment. One also cannot control the extent to which the opposition will engage in expensive deposition discovery. Furthermore, it is very difficult to estimate how long it will take to review, organize, and analyze all of the documents in a case. Usually, one does not even know at the beginning how many documents there are. Finally, how long the case will last is seldom a known factor. This can be influenced by the court docket, by the availability of time of arbitrators, by the period of time it takes to accomplish discovery in the case, and, by whether the case will ultimately settle. Some of the greatest expense in construction disputes arises during the final preparation and actual trial, when extremely long hours are logged. Without knowing if the case will settle, it is impossible to budget for that kind of expense.

Despite these many hurdles, an imperfect budget is better than no cost control at all. The budget process can sometimes reveal a greater merit to what previously appeared to be a poor settlement. It can also help prevent the inevitable frustration that both client and lawyer feel when litigation costs exceed the amount in controversy.

By far, the most important question concerning litigation costs is whether the case will involve a complex delay issue. If the project has been seriously delayed and delay damages are an important part of the claim from either party's point of view, then the cost of the litigation will be very large. This is a function of the simple principle that a delay claim cannot be proven or disproven unless virtually all the time involved in the actual construction of a project is accounted for by a witness, usually an expert. To account for all the time on the project requires the expert to review all major construction activities. This will, in turn, involve a review of all documents pertaining to the construction project by the delay expert retained either to prosecute or to defend the case. Inevitably, this is extremely expensive. Therefore, in considering budget and cost control, the first question an attorney must ask is whether the case involves delay claims. We discuss delay claims in **Chapter 5**.

§ 2.15 —Practical Aspects of Litigation Budgets

Perhaps in construction litigation more so than in any other area of the law, clients should be billed not less than monthly for all expenses and fees, unless, of course, the case is a contingency fee arrangement. A record of all fees and costs, including experts' fees, should be kept continuously. In the event that the budget is exceeded, one can identify why and when an overrun occurred on a monthly basis (when memories are still fresh).

A typical example of a budget-busting event is a production of documents under the Federal Rules of Civil Procedure. One party prepares a very well crafted, tailored request for specific documents, and the other side then produces the entire file en masse in a jumbled, disorganized fashion. The party seeking the documents has the option of going to court to attempt to force a different kind of production, a step which will inevitably take considerable time and money. The other option is to go through the unorganized documents. In either event, the budget made on the basis of parties cooperating in accordance with the Federal Rules of Civil Procedure is suddenly no longer accurate. At least with a budget, one can identify what has caused greater expense and decide whether the overall strategy of the case must change in order to deal with the greater expense.

Litigation budgets can also help assess the costs of pursuing alternative strategies in complex cases. Without question, various forums for dispute resolution and various methods of litigating have differing costs. We discuss these various forums and methods in **Chapters 8** through **11**. A budget should not be an end in itself, but rather a means of helping to assure cost-effective strategies. In the end, only a lawyer who knows and can control costs can obtain happy, repeat clients. Costs cannot always be controlled, but if they are not at least known by the attorney, then they will surely control the attorney, the case, and the client.

Finally, in any discussion of the budget for a case, the attorney and the client should not confuse a budget with a clear and written understanding of their fee arrangement. A budget is an estimate and, unless it is clearly intended as a fee arrangement by both the attorney and the client, it should not become a lump sum or a fixed price. Unfortunately, attorneys hesitate to discuss budgets at all because of the propensity of the client to turn the estimate into a guaranteed cost of litigation. An attorney who engages in serious budgeting with a client must take steps, in both the fee agreement and frank discussions, to guard against any misunderstanding of the relationship between actual fees and the projected budget.

§ 2.16 —The True Cost of Litigation

The true cost of litigation for any business organization greatly exceeds the actual out-of-pocket expenses. Of course, encompassed within the definition of costs must be payments to attorneys and consultants, deposition expense, expert witness fees, copying costs, travel and courier services, and other miscellaneous costs.

The costs that many clients tend to omit in their calculations, however, are the opportunity costs of their own time and attention. Presumably, construction companies or building owners are in business to make a certain profit. In deciding whether a particular construction project is worth pursuing, they calculate a rate of return, and, within that calculation, they incorporate the value of their time. It is rare, however, for litigants to think of the case in this fashion. Accordingly, they often fail to include the cost of their own time and attention, which can be very large in a construction dispute. The opportunity cost of litigation, therefore, must be examined by any potential litigant in terms of how this time and money might alternatively be spent on other matters which might yield a higher rate of return.

Furthermore, as a prospective matter, because the outcome of litigation is rarely known, analyzing the true cost of litigation often means also assessing probable outcomes. While this is very difficult to do, it is far better to examine at the beginning, and throughout the litigation, what the probable outcome may be. This probability must then be weighed along with the total cost of pursuing litigation, including the lost opportunity cost, in order to determine whether the litigation is worth pursuing.

CHAPTER 3

DISCOVERY

Suzanne H. Charles, Esquire

Suzanne H. Charles is a member of the firm of Fox and Charles in Clifton Park, New York. She is a magna cum laude graduate of the State University of New York at Albany and of Albany Law School, where she was a member of the Albany Law Review. Prior to entering the private sector, she spent 12 years in the field of public contract law and litigation representing the State of New York, its agencies, and public benefit corporations engaged in building and highway construction. Ms. Charles is a member of the American Bar Association, the Forum Committee on the Construction Industry, the New York State Bar Association, the Women's Bar Association of the State of New York, and the American Arbitration Association's panel of arbitrators for the construction industry.

- § 3.1 Introduction
- § 3.2 Purpose
- § 3.3 The Discovery Plan
- § 3.4 Scope
- § 3.5 Devices
- § 3.6 —Interrogatories
- § 3.7 —Depositions
- § 3.8 —Production of Documents
- § 3.9 —Requests for Inspection
- § 3.10 —Requests for Admissions
- § 3.11 Targeting Information
- § 3.12 Privileges
- § 3.13 Organization and Management
- § 3.14 Targeting Witnesses
- § 3.15 Motion Practice
- § 3.16 Conclusion

§ 3.1 Introduction

Discovery in construction litigation has been compared to the search for a needle in a haystack "complicated by the reality that the fields are large and the haystacks are many."[1] Unlike a simple negligence case that usually involves limited issues and parties, a multimillion dollar construction project may go on for years and involve multiple parties, each with different contractual and implied duties or professional standards of care.

Similarly, records in a simple negligence case might consist of a few pages of documents, while the records kept during the course of a major construction project often seem to exceed the height of the building or the length of the highway. Construction records are not usually neatly filed and easily accessible. If records exist at all, they are often tossed in boxes in an unheated job-site trailer or they are gathering dust in a storage warehouse under a pile of rejected materials. Construction projects, by their very nature, are seasonal and sporadic. Employees may go to work on other jobs or leave a company altogether to work in another state or even in another country. Sometimes they even die.[2]

The unique language of the construction industry makes asking the right questions in discovery much more important. Such terms as CPM schedule, shop drawings, foreman's daily reports, and job cost ledger may seem foreign to the uninitiated, but access to these documents, and others like them, is vital to preparation of the major construction contract case.

Identifying and locating all the information that is "relevant to the subject matter involved in the pending litigation,"[3] while eliminating that which is irrelevant and immaterial is perhaps the most formidable task awaiting the attorney who agrees to take on a construction contract case. A balance must be achieved in construction litigation discovery. Since the adoption of the Federal Rules of Civil Procedure in 1937, federal courts have allowed, and even encouraged, a liberal discovery policy "to obtain the fullest possible knowledge of the issues and facts before trial."[4] State courts and rules of civil procedure have also adopted a full disclosure policy.[5] Further, a policy of liberal disclosure in civil cases has been found to be "particularly suited" to construction contract cases "where the path to the truth is paved with complex technical issues."[6]

---

[1] Devaney, *Construction Cases: Tools for Discovery,* Nat'l L.J., Mar. 14, 1988, at 15, col. 4.

[2] *See, e.g.,* Mars Assoc., Inc. v. Facilities Dev. Corp., 111 A.D.2d 581, 489 N.Y.S.2d 646 (1985).

[3] Fed. R. Civ. P. 26(b)(1).

[4] Hickman v. Taylor, 329 U.S. 495, 501 (1947) (citations omitted).

[5] *E.g.,* Rios v. Donovan, 21 A.D.2d 409, 411, 250 N.Y.S.2d 818, 820 (1964); N.Y. Civ. Prac. L. & R. § 3101(a) (McKinney 1988).

[6] Crow-Crimmins-Wolff & Munier v. County of Westchester, 123 A.D.2d 813, 507 N.Y.S.2d 428, 429 (1986).

§ 3.2 PURPOSE

On the other hand, if the discovery process is abused, either intentionally or, in the case of a complex construction case, by the floundering and fishing of an inexperienced attorney, time and money will be wasted by all parties:

> Proper and reasonable discovery under the Federal Rules *can* promote a full and fair examination of the relevant facts before trial. However, misdirected and unbridled discovery can become an engine of harassment, impeding the administration of justice and inflating tremendously and unfairly the costs of litigation. It tends to delay adjudication unduly, to coerce unfair and uncalled for involuntary settlements and to make of the legal tools a cynical mockery of justice.[7]

Because of the volume of documents, the number of witnesses, and the extensive technical information generated by a construction project, such abuse or mishandling of discovery in construction litigation is not uncommon. However, with careful planning and focus, the attorney can formulate and implement a successful discovery program even in the most complex construction case.

§ 3.2 Purpose

Discovery is an opportunity to get what you can from the other side and to see what they have on you. This is especially true when representing owners. Owners rarely have the type of documentation in their files that is crucial to the analysis of delay claims. Contractors generally have as-planned schedules that can establish the benchmarks to measure delay, and they usually keep daily reports or diaries reflecting not only the actual progress, but also documenting delays which may occur in the field. Thus, it is imperative for the defendant owner in a construction delay case to obtain these and other records from the contractor.

In addition, the other side, or even a nonparty, may have information that can be useful in supporting the case. For example, it may be that the contractor did not keep scrupulous records of job progress. However, the owner's construction manager or clerk of the works on a project may have detailed daily reports showing personnel and equipment on the job, items of work, weather, and other information that may be lacking in the contractor's records. The attorney representing the contractor may need these records to prove the contractor's case against the owner. Another example involves a subcontractor delay claim against a prime contractor. The prime contractor's records may indicate delays on other parts of the project or in other precedent work which delayed the subcontractor.

---

[7] Pollack, *Discovery—Its Abuse and Correction,* 80 F.R.D. 219, 222 (1979).

Because the subcontractor kept records only pertaining to its specific work items, it may not have the information relating to delays on other aspects of the work. The courts have even recognized that plaintiffs may not be able to fully and finally calculate their actual damages until completing discovery of the defendant.[8]

In general, the path of discovery should be guided by the type of case and the legal theories involved. In a simple claim against the owner for extra work not covered by the contract and not paid by change order, a request for progress schedules or test results may be time-consuming, costly, and probably unnecessary. On the other hand, in a major delay claim, even shop drawing submittal schedules showing when the contractor submitted its detailed plans for the work and when the owner or architect responded may be relevant to the question of responsibility for delay.

Even in the smallest of cases, the attorney should plan the course of discovery in much the same way as he or she plans the course of a trial. Discovery should be planned around the issues in dispute. We discuss the identification of issues in § **1.4**. Proper planning will eliminate red herrings and wild-goose chases and enable the attorney to focus on the true issues of the case and the testimony, admissions, and documents needed to prove them.

§ 3.3 The Discovery Plan

The first thing an attorney presented with a case should do is outline the claims and the defenses. Most contractor claims against owners center around four main issues: contract balance or retainage, extra work performed but not paid for, delay and interference, and inefficiency, which may or may not be part of the delay claim. Most owner claims concern backcharges for liquidated damages or delays in completion, costs to repair defective work, claims for failure to honor warranties and guarantees, and possibly, costs to complete unfinished work. After each issue is identified, the attorney should list the types of documents that will be useful in preparing or defending each item of the claim or defense; other information, individuals, and parties that relate to the issues identified should also be listed. The source and location of the information can then be ascertained.

In claims involving extra work, for example, the contractor will want to establish what the original contract called for, what work was actually performed, whether the contract requirements concerning notice of changed conditions and requests for additional compensation were followed (and if not, why not), any previous rulings or opinions by the architect or owner

---

[8] *E.g.,* Marvin Lumber & Cedar Co. v. Norton Co., 113 F.R.D. 588 (D. Minn. 1986).

§ 3.3 DISCOVERY PLAN

concerning the work, and the costs to perform the work. The owner may want to establish that the work was called for under the contract or that the contractor's claimed costs are excessive. The relevant documents could include:

1. Copy of the contract, including general conditions and technical specifications
2. Plans, including bid set, working set, and as-builts
3. Daily, weekly, and/or monthly reports
4. Inspector's reports
5. Minutes of meetings
6. Transmittal memos
7. Correspondence (incoming and outgoing)
8. Personal diaries
9. Requests for change
10. Change orders (approved and pending)
11. Purchase orders
12. Subcontracts
13. Records of payments to subcontractors and suppliers and cancelled checks
14. Payroll records
15. Equipment records
16. Bid estimate and take-off analysis.

Another example is for claims of delay and interference. The contractor will want to establish the owner's acts or omissions which caused the delay, such as failure to address design problems or denial of access to the site. The owner will want to establish that the delays were either the fault of the contractor, for example, failure to properly staff the job, or were noncompensable events such as strikes or bad weather only entitling the contractor to a free extension of time under the terms of the contract. For damages, the contractor may allege extended supervision costs, extended field and home office overhead, wage and material escalation, additional costs for bonds and insurance, idle equipment costs, and loss of profits. The owner may try to defend on the basis that certain escalations were anticipated in the bid or that the contractor's historical overhead and profit margin were much lower. In addition to the documents listed above, the attorney will probably want to examine:

1. Progress photographs
2. Schedules (originals and updates)

3. Test results
4. Payment requisitions
5. Notice of award and notice to proceed
6. Certificates of partial and final acceptance
7. Financial statements
8. Tax returns
9. Job cost ledger
10. Union agreements
11. Insurance policies
12. Performance and payment bonds.

After listing the documents needed, the attorney should determine the location of each document and witness who should be examined concerning the documents. A "marking deposition" may be useful to have a witness testify under oath as to what records exist, their location, the identity of the custodian, the identity and present whereabouts of the maker of the record, and his or her role in the construction project.

After the records are identified and located, a notice to produce can issue. At the outset of document examination, an inventory should be made. The records should then be reviewed and organized as we discuss in **Chapter 2**. The attorney should then review the documents for the purpose of establishing possible theories of claim or defense, identities of witnesses who should be deposed, items which need further exploration or explanation, and items which support the alleged claims or defenses. After review of all documents, including those of the client, conferences with appropriate representatives of the client and experts can be scheduled. Finally, detailed interrogatories can be drafted and substantive depositions can be held.

§ 3.4 Scope

Limitations on the scope of discovery may be self-imposed or may be imposed by statute, case law, or local court rule. In a case where the potential recovery is at best a small amount, extensive depositions of all parties and nonparties, copying of voluminous amounts of records, and purchasing computer software to organize and sort documents will not be cost-effective or even necessary. Simply because the courts broadly define the scope of discovery is no reason for the responsible attorney to demand everything and anything the other side has in its possession to avoid missing something. Realistically, the attorney will not have the time or inclination to read everything, anyway. A little planning prior to launching discovery, even if it only consists of jotting down an outline of the issues and the

§ 3.4 SCOPE

elements of proof, will go a long way toward saving time, money, and aggravation.

As with any case involving many records, issues, and witnesses, the danger of over discovery in a construction case exists. Discovery is expensive, time-consuming, and may unnecessarily complicate the case. Even if the case is being handled at an hourly rate, the client will not appreciate being billed for hours of document examination or hundreds of pages of depositions in a case involving a few thousand dollars. The courts have now recognized that too much discovery is as bad as too little.[9]

Further, the courts have a responsibility to see to it that the discovery process is not utilized in an oppressive or unfair manner simply to harass or intimidate the other side.[10] What attorney has not been served with a one-inch thick document entitled "Defendant's First Set of Interrogatories"? This situation is particularly true in construction litigation. The potential number of interrogatory questions is large because of the complex facts which could be involved in such cases, but in a simple case, there is usually no need to rebuild the building to adequately prepare or defend a construction claim. The federal courts are frequently using Federal Rule of Civil Procedure 26 in combination with the Rule 16 conference to limit the scope, type, and duration of discovery. The district courts are imbued with a "very wide discretion" in the handling of pretrial discovery matters,[11] and the courts do not take kindly to those who attempt to circumvent local rules.[12] The state courts hold similar views.[13]

Although some judges resist getting involved in "minor pretrial skirmishes,"[14] most courts recognize that a complex case requires active judicial management and control to avoid delays.[15] Some commentators have even suggested that a complex construction case calls for the use of the *Manual for Complex Litigation,*[16] formerly reserved for such matters as antitrust actions and class action proceedings.[17]

---

[9] *See* Herbert v. Lando, 441 U.S. 153 (1979).

[10] Fed. R. Civ. P. 26(c); *see also* Nelco Corp. v. Slater Elec., Inc., 80 F.R.D. 411 (E.D.N.Y. 1978).

[11] Kyle Eng'g v. Kleppe, 600 F.2d 226, 231 (9th Cir. 1979).

[12] *See, e.g.,* Misco, Inc. v. United States Steel Corp., 784 F.2d 198 (6th Cir. 1986) (filing of 2,028 "requests for admissions" was an abuse of the discovery process and an attempt to circumvent a local rule limiting parties to 30 interrogatories).

[13] *See, e.g.,* Boutique Fabrice, Inc. v. Bergdorf Goodman, Inc., 129 A.D.2d 529, 514 N.Y.S.2d 380 (1987).

[14] Crown Cork & Seal Co. v. Chemed Corp., 101 F.R.D. 105, 106 (E.D. Pa. 1984).

[15] *E.g.,* United States v. American Tel. & Tel. Co., 83 F.R.D. 323, 327 (D.D.C. 1979).

[16] Manual for Complex Litigation (2d ed. 1982).

[17] Construction Litigation: Representing the Contractor 316 (R. Cushman, J. Carter, & A. Silverman eds. 1986).

Saving time in the discovery process is not only necessary to contain costs, it may also be required by the court and extendible only upon a well-documented motion.[18] Moreover, the court will have discretion to cut off discovery past a certain date and will do so despite the complex facts involved in construction cases.[19] Again, the attorney can save time spent rummaging in files and questioning witnesses who lack knowledge by doing some prediscovery investigation and planning.

The best gauge for the scope of responsible discovery in a construction case is the identification of issues and the dollar amounts involved (see § 1.4). The attorney can then assess the potential effectiveness of the different discovery devices in obtaining the required information (see § 3.5).

The discovery plan and the entire pretrial preparation process must be evaluated in the light of economic reality. Economic considerations include the dollar amount at stake for each issue, the total amount in dispute, the estimated cost of discovery, and the financial situation of the client and other parties.

There are many ways to reduce the discovery costs in a construction case. For example, costs may be reduced by utilizing client personnel to review the inventory of records and then the documents. The use of portable microfilm or copying machines can greatly reduce copying charges and such use has even been court-ordered in construction cases.[20] If the attorney, experienced paralegal, or client employee goes through and marks each document to be copied (paper clips, turning documents sideways in the file, or using removable self-stick notes are all efficient ways of marking), then virtually anyone can make the copies needed. There are other ways to reduce costs, once the discovery plan has been established, but an effective plan is the key to cost control in discovery.

§ 3.5 Devices

Every discovery device has its proponents and opponents, and each may serve a function appropriate to a particular case. Federal Rule of Civil Procedure 26 lists the various methods of discovery as depositions upon oral or written questions, interrogatories, production of documents or things, inspection of land or other property, physical and mental examinations, and requests for admissions.

---

[18] *See* Marvin Lumber v. Norton Co., 113 F.R.D. 588.

[19] Kyle Eng'g v. Kleppe, 600 F.2d 226.

[20] Crow-Crimmins-Wolff & Munier v. County of Westchester, 110 A.D.2d 877, 488 N.Y.S.2d 429 (1985).

All of the discovery devices have their role in the preparation of a construction case for trial. While some are proponents of the theory that too much discovery will alert the other parties to the theory and strategy of the case and allow them ample time to concoct counterarguments, others subscribe to the theory that the other parties will see how well the case is being investigated and prepared and will therefore be more inclined to settle. Certainly an attorney must be ready enough to participate in the Federal Rule of Civil Procedure 16 conference to avoid the sanctions attendant upon showing up "substantially unprepared."[21]

The attorney should also keep in mind that getting something on discovery and getting it admitted into evidence at trial are two entirely different things. In one case, even the testimony of the attorney that he found a document in the files of the defendant was not enough to authenticate the document for admission into evidence.[22]

Not all of these devices are of equal value to the construction attorney. Further, in each case the attorney should weigh the effectiveness of the devices in obtaining the required information. We now discuss several of the devices, highlighting how they can be used most effectively in construction cases.

§ 3.6 —Interrogatories

Some construction experts praise the use of interrogatories in a construction case,[23] while others find them practically useless.[24] Certainly, to be of any use, interrogatories require the utmost care in drafting. Use of canned interrogatories will not only result in a return of a pile of useless information but may also unnecessarily antagonize the other party. Local court rules may limit the number of interrogatories or even the way in which they can be used.[25] New York Courts bar the use of interrogatories altogether in most actions if a demand for a bill of particulars has been served and if the action is one for negligence resulting in personal injury or wrongful death, and interrogatories and depositions of the same party are not permitted without leave of the court.[26]

Interrogatories in construction cases are useful to nail down a party on such items as identity of employees and expert witnesses; existence, type,

---

[21] Fed. R. Civ. P. 16(f).

[22] Coughlin v. Capitol Cement Co., 571 F.2d 290 (5th Cir. 1978).

[23] Construction Litigation: Representing the Contractor 319 (1987).

[24] Construction Litigation: Representing the Owner 335 (R. Cushman & K. Cushman eds. 1984).

[25] *E.g.,* U.S. Dist. Cts. for S.D. and for E.D.N.Y. R. 46.

[26] N.Y. Civ. Prac. L. & R. § 3130(1) (McKinney 1988).

and location of documents; and other background information. The attorney may use interrogatories to obtain specifics concerning the generalized allegations often found in construction litigation pleadings. For example, in breach of contract actions, interrogatories may request a party to list the specific sections of the contract claimed to be breached and to list each of the events and actions constituting the breach. If violations of building codes are claimed, interrogatories may request specific code sections, applicable years, and other details.

Generally, interrogatories are less costly than depositions, which require the presence of a stenographer and may require travel to the location of the witness. On the other hand, interrogatories do not allow opportunity for immediate follow-up questions upon hearing the answers to the questions posed. The value of interrogatories is diminished by the fact that they are generally answered by opposing attorneys. The answering attorney will assemble information from various sources, filter out certain information, and cast an answer from a legal standpoint. Especially in construction litigation, this process diminishes the value of such answers because of the highly technical nature of many factual situations where additional explanation or elaboration will often be necessary.

The Federal Rules of Civil Procedure permit a party responding to an interrogatory to specify records from which an answer can be derived if "the burden of deriving or ascertaining the answer is substantially the same for the party serving the interrogatory as for the party served."[27] However, a party in a construction case responding to an interrogatory concerning the existence of a document may not simply respond with an answer to the effect that "if we have it, it's somewhere in these project records." The courts place the burden on the responding party to ascertain whether a document indeed exists and, if possible, within what records.[28]

Still, such a tactic is not uncommon in a construction case. Because of the volume of documents, even directing the party to a category of construction records may create a difficult burden. For example, in responding to an interrogatory about damages, a contractor may direct the proponent to contractor cost records. The cost records will include daily labor counts, material invoices, subcontractor vouchers, cancelled checks, payroll records, and a host of other such documents which may or may not have figured into the contractor's calculations. This is one area where the opposing attorney should persist, lest he or she be surprised at trial.

Interrogatories can be used to elicit other parties' opinions or contentions as to facts or the application of law to fact, but the court may

---

[27] Fed. R. Civ. P. 33(c).
[28] State of Colo. v. Schmidt-Tiago Constr. Co., 108 F.R.D. 731 (D. Colo. 1985); *In re Master Key*, 53 F.R.D. 87 (D. Conn. 1971); *see generally* Puerto Rico Aqueduct & Sewer Auth. v. Cion Corp., 108 F.R.D. 304 (D.P.R. 1985).

order that the answer need not be given until discovery is complete or until the pretrial conference.[29] Interrogatories can certainly be used to discover the other side's theory of damages, its calculations, and its expert opinions on the subject.[30]

In *Holiday Inns, Inc. v. Robertshaw Controls Co.*,[31] the plaintiff's failure to timely supplement an answer to an interrogatory resulted in a ruling that an alternate theory of recovery could not be considered. Parties are generally not under a continuing duty to supplement responses to discovery requests if the response was complete when made. However, they do have a duty to supplement with respect to newfound knowledge concerning identity and location of witnesses, identity of experts and the subject matter and substance of their testimony, and responses that need correcting because they were either incorrect when made or they have become incorrect over time.[32] In view of this rule, a simple set of "anything new" interrogatories just prior to the trial is usually a good idea. Failure to amend an answer to an interrogatory may be fatal, as in the case in which a later discovery of a document which the defendant denied existed was found to be a "fraud on the court," warranting a new trial.[33]

§ 3.7 —Depositions

Depositions may be more useful in a construction case to explore the other side's theory and calculation of damages. A party cannot resist such exploration on the basis of the work-product exemption.[34] If, for example, the plaintiff has provided a bill of particulars or another document containing a schedule of damages claimed, the defense counsel at a deposition can take each item of damage claimed and work back through each item of supporting documentation with the witness. Labor costs should be traced through daily reports showing hours worked, payroll records, tax returns, insurance and union records, records to support mark-ups, and cancelled checks. Material costs can be traced through purchase orders, invoices, and cancelled checks. Records of equipment charged to the job, equipment depreciation schedules, equipment rental invoices, and cancelled checks can be used to verify or refute claims for equipment costs.

---

[29] Fed. R. Civ. P. 33(b).

[30] Marvin Lumber v. Norton Co., 113 F.R.D. 588.

[31] 560 F.2d 856 (7th Cir. 1977).

[32] Fed. R. Civ. P. 26(e).

[33] Rozier v. Ford Motor Co., 573 F.2d 1332, *reh'g denied,* 578 F.2d 871 (5th Cir. 1978).

[34] Wheeling-Pittsburgh Steel Corp. v. Underwriters Laboratories, Inc., 81 F.R.D. 8 (N.D. Ill. 1978).

Whether through ignorance or for strategy purposes, damages are often inadequately prepared by claimants in construction cases until immediately before trial. A carefully conducted deposition will place the burden of properly calculating and documenting damage upon the claimant. If the witness is unable to produce the necessary records or is unable to answer the questions, additional depositions can be requested or motions can be made to compel or to sanction (§ **3.15**). However, be warned that some cases have allowed a party to recalculate its damage claims as long as recalculation takes place during discovery and not on the eve of the trial.[35]

Corporations are often parties in construction cases. The Federal Rules of Civil Procedure provide that if the notice of deposition and subpoena names as the deponent a public or private corporation and describes with reasonable particularity the matters on which examination is requested, then it is up to the corporation to designate an officer, director, or managing agent with knowledge of the facts.[36] The testimony of the person designated is then the testimony of the corporation and may be used as such at trial.[37] Other employees may be noticed to testify just as any other witnesses.[38] Alternatively, a party may designate a particular individual to be deposed as an officer, director, or managing agent, but that party will have the burden of proving that the person designated is such an official of the corporation.[39]

Corporations and other parties are obligated to produce someone with knowledge of the facts,[40] and the courts do not appreciate evasiveness.[41] On the other hand, the courts will ensure that depositions are not used for harassment purposes, as where top corporate officials with no knowledge of the facts are noticed for deposition.[42] Heads of government agencies are usually similarly protected.[43]

Corporate or collective answers in construction cases are very important. Field managers often have different knowledge and perspectives than home office executives. The differences can be exploited or minimized by astute counsel. In examining the opponent, counsel will want to determine

---

[35] *E.g.,* Pinkerton & Laws Co. v. Roadway Express, Inc., 650 F. Supp. 1138 (N.D. Ga. 1986).

[36] Fed. R. Civ. P. 30(b)(6).

[37] Fed. R. Civ. P. 32(a)(2).

[38] GTE Prod. Corp. v. Gee, 115 F.R.D. 67 (D. Mass. 1987).

[39] Sugarhill Records Ltd. v. Motown Record Corp., 105 F.R.D. 166 (S.D.N.Y. 1985).

[40] JMJ Contract Mgmt., Inc. v. Ingersoll-Rand Co., 100 A.D.2d 291, 475 N.Y.S.2d 528 (1984).

[41] Dowlitt v. City of N.Y., 113 A.D.2d 722, 493 N.Y.S.2d 560 (1985).

[42] Boutique Fabrice v. Bergdorf Goodman, Inc., 129 A.D.2d 529, 514 N.Y.S.2d 380.

[43] Kyle Eng'g v. Kleppe, 600 F.2d 226.

the official corporate answer as well as the extent of the differences between it and answers from the field. Depositions allow the construction attorney to determine both.

Preparation of witnesses for depositions in a construction case is extremely important, especially if the witnesses are unfamiliar with the entire process. Many individuals who are involved in a construction project that has "gone bad" and resulted in a claim feel they must somehow vindicate themselves and either justify or explain away every incident or blame it on someone else. For example, blaming a problem on the architect does no good and may even be detrimental if the witness is testifying on behalf of the owner and the architect is the owner's agent. Witnesses must be instructed to listen to and answer only the question that is being asked and to resist the temptation to speculate, guess, or try to vindicate themselves.

Some attorneys may find it helpful to select certain documents for the witness to review prior to being deposed in order to be fully prepared. In a construction case, it usually looks bad for a witness not to remember much at depositions and then have his or her memory dramatically improve at trial. At a minimum, most witnesses will need to review the plans and specifications, the daily reports, and the job meeting minutes prior to testifying at a deposition.

While the pretrial selection of documents by counsel in order to prepare for discovery is normally considered attorney work-product, that privilege can be waived. Thus, it was held that opposing counsel could question witnesses as to what documents they used to prepare for the depositions.[44] Further, should the witnesses resort to documents to refresh their memories during the deposition, those documents will be discoverable by all other parties.[45] Even expert witnesses may be required to produce the documents on which they relied to form their opinions.[46]

In theory, depositions take place outside the direct supervision of the courts. However, it has been recognized that such a system depends heavily on the good faith of the participating attorneys to refrain from making obstructive objections or directing witnesses not to answer even when the answer could not possibly result in any prejudice.[47] The Federal Rules of Civil Procedure provide that at any time during a deposition, upon a showing of bad faith, annoyance, embarrassment, or oppression, a party may apply to the court for an order limiting or terminating the deposition.[48] Judicial frustration is evident in such cases as the one in which the court, having

---

[44] Omaha Pub. Power Dist. v. Foster Wheeler Corp., 109 F.R.D. 615 (D. Neb. 1986).

[45] Wheeling v. Underwriters, 81 F.R.D. 8 (N.D. Ill. 1978); Merrill Lynch Realty Commercial Servs., Inc. v. Rudin Mgmt. Co., 94 A.D.2d 617, 462 N.Y.S.2d 16 (1983).

[46] American Steel Prod. Corp. v. Penn Central Corp., 110 F.R.D. 151 (S.D.N.Y. 1986).

[47] White v. Martins, 100 A.D.2d 805, 474 N.Y.S.2d 733 (1984).

[48] Fed. R. Civ. P. 30(d).

been asked to rule in the propriety of some 43 objections to questions, directed the witness to answer any and all questions asked in future depositions.[49] Although an appellate court later reversed the ruling and ordered the trial court to rule on the merits of each objection, at least one judge has commented favorably on the same blanket direction to witnesses as a means of cutting down on excessive motions relating to discovery.[50]

Finally, as previously noted, depositions in a construction case can also be used to identify a party's documents for a subsequent notice to produce. Because of the extensive amount of documentation involved in a construction project, such a deposition may be important as a preliminary step in construction cases. The New York courts virtually require this procedure[51] unless a party "clearly and specifically" identifies the documents sought.[52] After the notice to produce and the inspection of the documents, later depositions can be used to question individuals on the particulars of the project and the documents found.

§ 3.8 —Production of Documents

Production and inspection of documents in the possession of others is perhaps one of the most frequently used and most valuable discovery devices in a construction case. As with interrogatories and depositions, the courts will make sure a notice to produce documents is not overly broad and burdensome, as in the case wherein the court held that a request for all correspondence and memos could not possibly be relevant to a contractor's claim.[53] The use of the words "any" and "all" in notices to produce are red flags to courts that the request is overly broad and burdensome,[54] but use of such words may not always be improper.[55]

In construction cases, compliance with notices to produce may require some time and expense when many documents are involved. However, merely because compliance would be costly or time-consuming is no basis for refusal to comply with a reasonable notice if the requested material is

---

[49] White v. Martins, 100 A.D.2d 805, 474 N.Y.S.2d 733.

[50] Pollack, *Discovery—Its Abuse and Correction,* 80 F.R.D. at 226.

[51] Powlak v. General Motors Corp., 112 A.D.2d 725, 492 N.Y.S.2d 216 (1985).

[52] AGH Distribs., Inc. v. Silvertone Fasteners, Inc., 105 A.D.2d 648, 481 N.Y.S.2d 706 (1984).

[53] Raisler Corp. v. 101 Park Ave. Assoc., 102 A.D.2d 794, 477 N.Y.S.2d 153 (1984).

[54] Zambelis v. Nicholas, 92 A.D.2d 936, 460 N.Y.S.2d 360 (1983).

[55] Craig v. New York Tel. Co., 123 A.D.2d 580, 507 N.Y.S.2d 154 (1986).

§ 3.8 PRODUCTION OF DOCUMENTS

relevant or would lead to the discovery of evidence.[56] Moreover, a private corporation cannot avoid producing documents on the grounds of impossibility if it can obtain the information from sources under its control (subsidiary corporations, for example).[57]

A party generally will not be required to create new documents,[58] to translate documents,[59] or to create new computer programs[60] in order to comply with discovery requests. On the other hand, courts have ordered parties to provide computer printouts prepared in the regular course of business[61] and to provide the other party with a list of documents copied.[62] The Federal Rules of Civil Procedure were amended in 1970 to provide a requesting party with compilations of data translated through detection devices (for example, printouts translated from computer disks) into "reasonably usable form."[63]

This may be the case with computer data used in critical path method (CPM) scheduling and job cost accounting. Raw data printouts may be totally meaningless unless formatted into recognizable categories. Even then, scheduling experts and accountants may be required to explain the purpose of the information and how the data was kept. Thus, follow-up depositions may be necessary after discovery and inspection.

If the discovery requests appear to impose "undue burden or expense," then the court can enter protective orders requiring the requesting party to bear the expense.[64] Courts have even ordered sanctions when it appears a party has concocted a system of record-keeping designed to frustrate the discovery process.[65] While parties to the construction process may not develop their record-keeping systems solely to obstruct discovery, it is not unusual for some parties to utilize systems that are less than meaningful to outsiders. This is especially true of estimating records. Because of the fierce competition involved in low-bid contracting, many contractors consider their estimating techniques and documents to be sacrosanct. Even when produced, the documents may be cryptic, requiring a detailed deposition of the estimators involved in the preparation of the bid.

---

[56] Kozlowski v. Sears, Roebuck & Co., 73 F.R.D. 73 (D. Mass. 1976).

[57] *Id.*

[58] Durham Medical Search, Inc. v. Physicians Int'l Search, Inc., 122 A.D.2d 529, 504 N.Y.S.2d 910 (1986).

[59] *In re* Puerto Rico Elec. Power Auth., 687 F.2d 501 (1st Cir. 1982).

[60] Oppenheimer v. Sanders, 437 U.S. 340 (1978).

[61] Colorado v. Schmidt-Tiago, 108 F.R.D. 731.

[62] Crow-Crimmins v. County of Westchester, 110 A.D.2d 877, 488 N.Y.S.2d 429.

[63] Fed. R. Civ. P. 34(a).

[64] Fed. R. Civ. P. 26(c).

[65] *E.g.,* Kozlowski v. Sears, 73 F.R.D. 73.

§ 3.9 —Requests for Inspection

Another useful discovery device in construction cases is the request to enter upon another party's land for inspection or for other purposes such as testing.[66] The property must be within the control of the other party.[67] The courts may require more than a showing of relevance, and they will balance the anticipated benefits of such inspection with the disadvantages and burdens to the other party.[68] In one case, allowing the defendant to take a small soil sample from the plaintiff's property was found not to impose any hardship on plaintiff or cause detriment to his property.[69]

If a party has not been given an opportunity to inspect a building or piece of equipment prior to repair, then most courts tend to allow that party access to factual data and test results concerning the building or equipment, even if they are incorporated into the expert's reports.[70] However, when one party was given ample opportunity to investigate and remedy a collapsed wall, the court found that they "had their chance" and barred them from taking advantage of the other side's work and initiative in performing a detailed technical analysis.[71] Conversely, when one party was refused access at the time an allegedly defective pipe was excavated, the court was inclined to go one step further and allow discovery not only of the material removed and the pictures taken, but also of the reports of the experts, including their opinions and conclusions.[72] If a party is able to conduct its own investigation and testing, generally that will suffice to preclude the party from obtaining the factual data and test results taken by the opposition.[73]

A defendant in a construction case may wish to audit a plaintiff contractor's financial records, especially if damages are sought for home office or field overhead, labor inefficiency, labor escalation, or interest and finance charges. If an audit is conducted after litigation has commenced, the courts tend to find the audit report to be material prepared for litigation

---

[66] *See* Fed. R. Civ. P. 34.

[67] Santa Fe Int'l Corp. v. Potashnick, 83 F.R.D. 299 (E.D. La. 1979).

[68] Belcher v. Bassett Furniture Industr., 588 F.2d 904 (4th Cir. 1978).

[69] Oremland v. Miller Minutemen Constr. Corp., 133 A.D.2d 816, 520 N.Y.S.2d 397 (1987).

[70] Sanford Constr. Co. v. Kaiser Aluminum & Chem. Sales, Inc., 45 F.R.D. 465 (E.D. Ky. 1968); Town of North Hempstead v. Wiedersum, 131 A.D.2d 661, 516 N.Y.S.2d 743 (1987).

[71] Town of North Hempstead v. Wiedersum, 131 A.D.2d 661, 516 N.Y.S.2d 743.

[72] Sanford v. Kaiser Aluminum, 45 F.R.D. 465.

[73] Crow-Crimmins v. County of Westchester, 123 A.D.2d 813, 507 N.Y.S.2d 428.

and exempt from disclosure.[74] On the other hand, if the audit was conducted prior to litigation and for another purpose, such as by a surety to review operations and expenditures of an obligor on a bond, then the audit reports may be found to be prepared in the ordinary course of business and not exempt from disclosure.[75]

The Federal Rules of Civil Procedure also allow application for an order requiring a party to submit to a physical or mental examination.[76] While such a device is of no use in a construction contract case, it can be useful in a case involving personal injury as a result of a claimed construction or design defect. Interestingly, the author was once served with a request to produce the State of New York for a physical examination, illustrating once again the importance of preparing each case individually and not relying upon a "canned" set of standard forms.

§ 3.10 —Requests for Admissions

Although requests for admissions have been found by at least one court not to be a general discovery device,[77] they are listed as such in the Federal Rules of Civil Procedure.[78] Like interrogatories, the number of requests to admit may be limited by local court rule. Unlike interrogatories, if no response is received within the prescribed time limits, the matters requested are deemed admitted.[79] Thus, upon receipt of a request for admissions, the attorney should establish a method to ensure a timely response.

In construction cases, requests for admissions are useful to authenticate documents and to establish facts not in dispute. Because the matters admitted are considered "conclusively established,"[80] agreement by the attorneys on such matters as contracts and other business records, dates work was performed, and quantities of materials supplied will simplify and shorten the trial. Thus used, requests for admission are a means to simplify the trial process rather than to learn or discover unknown facts. Requests for admissions can also be used to determine whether the opposition considers certain matters as issues in dispute. Because of the complex factual and legal

---

[74] *E.g.*, J.R. Stevenson Corp. v. Dormitory Auth. of the State of N.Y., 112 A.D.2d 113, 492 N.Y.S.2d 385 (1985).

[75] *Id.*

[76] Fed. R. Civ. P. 35.

[77] Misco v. United States Steel, 784 F.2d 198.

[78] Fed. R. Civ. P. 36(a).

[79] *Id.*

[80] Fed. R. Civ. P. 36(b).

issues involved in construction contract cases, the number of issues for trial may be overwhelming. The submission of a set of requests for admission may prompt discussions between counsel geared toward limiting the issues for trial. Accordingly, the trial court will likely support or even strongly encourage counsel in such an endeavor.

§ 3.11   Targeting Information

The types of records kept in the course of a construction project and the number of potential witnesses vary with the type of job and the sophistication of the parties involved. A contractor who has suffered through a claim in the past, who has attended a seminar on claims preparation, or who has purchased one of the many books on the subject will have detailed records, whereas another contractor on a small job will be lucky to be able to find an executed copy of the contract and a complete set of plans.

The attorney should realize that the records may have many sources and may be in many locations. For example, in most construction situations, there may be contractor and owner field records, contractor home office records, owner main office and branch office records, architect records, municipal records, and financial records.

Certain office records may be duplications of field records, but others may not be. For example, correspondence between two principals of contracting corporations may never reach the field. Similarly, the contract between the architect and the owner, or correspondence between them, may not be available to those in the field, but may be important to a contractor's claim of delay because of defects in the plans and specifications. The correspondence between the architect and the owner may reveal that the owner has the same claim. The owner's main office records may also include summary reports from the field, correspondence with regulatory agencies, inter-office memoranda, telephone logs, and records of contractor payments.

In addition, financial records kept by the contractor will be especially useful if an audit of the contractor's claim is contemplated. Such records are also useful simply to verify or prove the damages claimed.

On a public construction project, the public owner may have a computerized project management system and also its own correspondence files, inter- and intra-office memoranda, progress reports, and payment records. The owner's field personnel may also be good witnesses. In a recent case, the author represented a subcontractor who was not paid by the prime based on the allegation that the subcontractor had supplied defective equipment. However, a review of the public owner's records revealed that the problem was with the prime contractor's employees, who were inexperienced in assembling and using the equipment. Since the public owner

§ 3.11 TARGETING INFORMATION

was not a party and had no personal stake in the matter, the records carried even more credibility with the court, which strongly encouraged a settlement in the matter.

In the above-mentioned case, since the public owner was not a party, the records were obtained through a freedom of information request. The federal government has such an act,[81] as do most states.[82] A regulatory public agency or board may have records even if it was not a party to the construction project, for example, requests for permits and exemptions, environmental impact statements, records of public hearings, equal opportunity and minority/women business reports, and code inspection reports. In determining whether material is disclosable under freedom of information laws, the courts will examine whether the matter would have been discoverable under the applicable discovery statute.[83] The courts will attempt to protect attorney work-product and trade secrets from disclosure under freedom of information laws in much the same ways as they would limit discovery under the Federal Rules of Civil Procedure.[84] However, New York's highest court has held that the status of the party requesting the materials under a freedom of information request, that is, litigant or not, is of no moment; even records denied to a litigant under the discovery statute might be available under the freedom of information law.[85] But the New York Court of Appeals did not disturb the ability to claim privilege as a basis for refusing to release certain documents.[86]

In cases where contractor or owner records have been lost or destroyed, or have never existed, other sources for records and information include subcontractor's project records, architect's project records, pictures and articles by local newspapers, surety's records, and records kept by the entity providing the financing for the project.

The contractor's attorney will want to examine certain records kept by the owner and the architect which may validate the client's claim for delay. For example, the architect's shop drawing log may show the inordinate amount of time the architect held shop drawings before approval. The owner/architect correspondence files and minutes of design meetings may show design and program disputes and delays in making decisions affecting the progress of the work. Internal owner memoranda may show staff disagreement on issues such as extra work and the assessment of liquidated damages.

---

[81] 5 U.S.C. § 552 (1988).

[82] *E.g.,* New York Pub. Off. Law Art. 6 (McKinney 1988).

[83] Federal Trade Comm'n v. Grolier, 462 U.S. 19 (1983).

[84] *Id.*

[85] M. Farbman & Sons, Inc. v. New York City Health & Hosp. Corp., 62 N.Y.2d 75, 476 N.Y.S.2d 69 (1984).

[86] *Id.*

The architect seeking payment from an owner will be interested in the correspondence files between owner and contractor in which the owner may defend and even praise the design, plans, and specifications.

Documents of interest to an owner are often found in files of correspondence between a contractor and its subs; these might contain letters accusing the subcontractors of the same delays for which the contractor is blaming the owner. In a case where a contractor is claiming a standard rental rate for self-owned equipment, the owner may request equipment depreciation schedules to attempt to show the true cost of ownership.[87]

An item particularly useful to an owner being sued by a contractor is the contractor's bid estimate, which the contractor may be reluctant to produce on the grounds its trade secrets may be revealed. However, where one party brings an action against another and makes its own otherwise privileged matter an issue, the privilege may be deemed waived, and bid records must be produced.[88] Similarly, contractors resist the production of their income tax records. The federal courts usually require a showing of relevancy coupled with demonstration of compelling need to order tax records produced.[89] At the state level, an even stronger showing may be required.[90]

§ 3.12 Privileges

Resisting discovery may be almost as expensive as obtaining it. In the first instance, the burden is on the resisting party to show that the matter is privileged or that the request is unduly burdensome.[91] As far as possible, cooperation among all parties is the better, quicker, and least expensive course of action and may even include the mutual exchange of documents.

The Federal Rules of Civil Procedure encourage a cooperative process to resolve matters such as claimed privileges. Prior to obtaining the intervention of the court in discovery matters, the attorney making a motion must show he or she has made a "reasonable effort" to reach agreement with the other attorneys.[92] Local rules may require proof of even more good faith efforts. One letter and some follow-up calls by a secretary does

---

[87] Penn York Constr. Corp. v. State, 92 A.D.2d 1086, 462 N.Y.S.2d 82 (1983).

[88] Martin Mechanical Corp. v. City of N.Y., 100 Misc. 2d 1107, 420 N.Y.S.2d 537 (Sup. Ct. 1979).

[89] *E.g.,* Securities & Exch. Comm'n v. Cymaticolor Corp., 106 F.R.D. 545 (S.D.N.Y. 1985).

[90] *E.g.,* Penn York v. State of N.Y., 92 A.D.2d 1086, 462 N.Y.S.2d 82.

[91] Schachar v. American Academy of Opthamology, Inc., 106 F.R.D. 187 (N.D. Ill. 1985); Crow-Crimmins-Wolff & Munier v. County of Westchester, 126 A.D.2d 696, 511 N.Y.S.2d 117 (1987).

[92] Fed. R. Civ. P. 26(f).

not constitute reasonable effort.[93] The states are establishing similar rules.[94] Some items, however, will be fiercely defended, and probably none more so in construction cases than attorney work-product and material prepared for litigation. The Federal Rules of Civil Procedure endeavor to protect against the disclosure of anything relating to the "mental impressions, conclusions, opinions or legal theories of an attorney,"[95] and the courts are similarly protective.[96]

Upon a clear showing that the materials sought are work-product, the burden shifts to the requestor to show that the materials, or their substantial equivalent, cannot without undue hardship be obtained elsewhere.[97] While acknowledging some difference of opinion as to the showing that must be made to obtain another attorney's work-product, the United States Supreme Court has held that a strong public policy protecting the attorney's mental processes requires an extremely strong showing on the part of a party seeking such items as notes and memoranda made by attorneys conducting interviews with corporate officers and employees.[98] The Court found that the notes either revealed confidential communication and were protected by the attorney-client privilege, or that they revealed the attorney's mental processes in evaluating the communication and, in either case, were not discoverable.[99] Thus, the attorney in a construction case may feel free to interview officers and employees of the client company and take notes without fear the notes will be discoverable later.

At the federal level, the work-product protection will exempt material and information compiled "in reasonable anticipation" of litigation but not reports prepared in the ordinary course of business.[100]

An attorney cannot make a document which is otherwise not privileged into a privileged document by handwriting notes containing mental impressions and legal conclusions on the document.[101] Nor can ordinarily discoverable items be made into work-product by transmitting them to an expert.[102] On the other hand, transmitting attorney work-product to an expert does not waive the privilege.[103]

---

[93] Rozier v. Ford Motor Co., 573 F.2d 1332.

[94] N.Y. Civ. Prac. L. & R. § 202.6 (McKinney 1988).

[95] Fed. R. Civ. P. 26(b)(3).

[96] Hickman v. Taylor, 329 U.S. 495.

[97] Fed. R. Civ. P. 26(b)(3); Belcher v. Bassett Furniture, 588 F.2d 904 (4th Cir. 1978).

[98] Upjohn v. United States, 449 U.S. 383 (1981).

[99] *Id.* at 401.

[100] Colorado v. Schmidt-Tiago, 108 F.R.D. 731; Soeder v. General Dynamics Corp., 90 F.R.D. 253 (D. Nev. 1980).

[101] Schachar v. American Academy, 106 F.R.D. 187.

[102] Baise v. Alewel's, Inc., 99 F.R.D. 95 (W.D. Mo. 1983).

[103] *Id.*

Closely related, but not identical, to the exemption of attorney work-product are conversations and documents protected by the attorney-client privilege. This privilege is important in construction cases, because the attorney must often interview and discuss the case with a number of employees of a corporation and must be assured that communications are frank, open, and confidential. Because the privilege restricts discovery, the party asserting it must, in the first instance, present facts sufficient to show that the communication is privileged.[104] This burden may be difficult to sustain in the case of government attorneys who wear many different hats.[105] On the other hand, the Supreme Court has held that limiting the application of the privilege to communications between the attorney and top management officials of a corporation would frustrate the very purpose of the privilege, which is to encourage communication of all relevant information by corporate employees to the attorneys who are advising the corporation.[106] Thus, responses of midlevel employees to questionnaires and interviews by counsel are protected from disclosure; however, the privilege protects only the communication and not the facts disclosed, which may be otherwise discoverable.[107]

Another fertile area for dispute in construction litigation is the discoverability of experts and their reports. As we discuss in **Chapter 4**, experts are often indispensable in construction cases. In most cases involving failure of construction or design, outside experts are called in to evaluate the problem and make recommendations for correction. While the primary motive is the replacement or repair of the work, the experts will undoubtedly be used during any subsequent litigation to prove the case against the contractor or design professional. States like New York still retain the rule that, to be exempt from disclosure, the expert's report must be prepared "solely" in anticipation of litigation.[108] One guideline used by the courts to determine the purpose of the report is the date of commencement of litigation; reports prepared prior to that date are generally considered "multi-motivated" and are discoverable. Reports prepared after the start of litigation are discoverable only upon a showing that withholding will result in "injustice or undue hardship."[109]

In a case involving a surety consultant engaged to assist in the completion of certain bonded construction projects, it was held that the consultant was not hired "in anticipation of litigation," and was not listed as an

---

[104] Delco Wire & Cable, Inc. v. Weinberger, 109 F.R.D. 680 (E.D. Pa. 1986).

[105] *Id.*

[106] Upjohn v. United States, 449 U.S. 383.

[107] *Id.*

[108] Crow-Crimmins v. County of Westchester, 123 A.D.2d 813, 507 N.Y.S.2d 428.

[109] N.Y. Civ. Prac. L. & R. § 3101(d)(2) (McKinney 1988); Crow-Crimmins v. County of Westchester, 123 A.D.2d 813, 507 N.Y.S.2d 428.

§ 3.12 PRIVILEGES

expert witness in response to an interrogatory; the expert was, therefore, an "actor" or "viewer" to be treated as an ordinary witness "from whom all facts known and opinions held are freely discoverable."[110]

The Federal Rules of Civil Procedure provide that discovery of other parties' experts is limited to interrogatories requesting the identity of the experts the other party expects to call, the subject matter of the testimony, and the substance of the expert's facts and opinions.[111] Additional discovery is permitted only upon order of the court and may be subject to the court's order that the requesting party pay the expert's fees.[112] To obtain discovery of the experts not expected to be called as witnesses, a showing of "exceptional circumstances" is required.[113] Local court practice or rule or the practicalities of the situation may foster voluntary mutual production of experts for deposition by all sides. The states are following the lead of the federal courts and liberalizing rules concerning discovery of experts.[114]

In cases where an employee of a party is a fact witness but may also be an expert, the courts may apply different standards than when another party seeks depositions. Generally, such a witness can be questioned on his or her factual knowledge but will not be required to disclose opinions or knowledge gained during preparation to testify as an expert.[115] The problem of the fact/expert witness is frequently encountered in construction cases where, for example, the scheduling consultant who prepared and updated the project schedule is called upon to provide analysis and opinions as to the cause and effect of the delay and the responsibility for it. Or, the engineer in charge of the project may be a fact witness for day-to-day events but may also be qualified to testify as an expert in his or her particular field.

If a trial is truly the search for the truth, the reports of an independent expert should be an aid to all parties. In reality, such reports are often prepared in construction cases by "hired guns" or claims experts who routinely testify for plaintiffs or defendants. This type of practice works a tremendous disadvantage to the party who is not well financed and faced with a barrage of experts who are not searching for the truth but only seeking to discredit another party's theories. Courts have shown a more liberal tendency in granting disclosure of experts in order to permit more effective cross-examination and undoubtedly, simplify and shorten the trial.

---

[110] Livingston v. Allis-Chalmers Corp., 109 F.R.D. 546, 550 (S.D. Miss. 1985).

[111] Fed. R. Civ. P. 26(b)(4)(A)(i).

[112] Fed. R. Civ. P. 26(b)(4)(C).

[113] Fed. R. Civ. P. 26(b)(4)(B).

[114] *E.g.*, N.Y. Civ. Prac. L. & R. § 3101(d)(1) (McKinney 1988).

[115] *E.g.*, Nelco Corp. v. Slater Elec., Inc., 80 F.R.D. 411 (E.D.N.Y. 1978).

§ 3.13 Organization and Management

Another way to shorten the trial is to get organized prior to trial. Nothing is more maddening to a judge, a jury, or an opposing attorney than to sit and wait while an attorney fumbles through piles of papers looking for a specific document. Some courts are trying to avoid this problem, which is rampant in construction cases involving many documents, by requiring pre-marking of all potential exhibits prior to the start of trial.[116] The preparation, pre-marking, and trial itself will go a good deal smoother if the documents are properly organized by the attorney prior to trial.

The pretrial organizational system can be as simple as a notebook containing the pleadings and the documents relevant to proof, including key portions of contracts, depositions, correspondence, and reports cross-referenced to a document or file. At the other extreme, a computer program can be derived or purchased that will sort documents by author, recipient, date, issue, or key word. In the middle are systems with folders containing documents relevant to the testimony of each witness or relevant to a particular issue. The type of system selected will depend on the magnitude and complexity of the case. When the number of documents is small, they can usually be directly filed into a notebook or folder and keyed to a witness, issue, or item of proof. If there are many documents, the attorney will probably want to number all documents in a master file and create a series of subfiles, either by simply listing the document number on legal pads or note cards or by making additional document copies for each particular subfile. We discuss the organizational management of documents in more detail in **Chapter 2**.

One step helpful to judge and jury alike in a complex construction case is the creation of documents that summarize the information contained in many pages of documents. For example, a certain item of work at issue may have been accomplished, along with other work, over a period of weeks. Daily reports will have many pages and will contain records of other items of work, weather, and other information which may not be relevant to the issue. A summary of the work in question can be prepared as an aid to the court. Introduction of the summary into evidence will require the prior introduction of all foundation documents. The utmost accuracy in transcribing information is vital, or opposing counsel will destroy the credibility of the witness and the summary document on cross-examination.

---

[116] *E.g.,* Davis-Eckert v. State of N. Y., 118 A.D.2d 375, 504 N.Y.S.2d 874 (1986), *aff'd,* 70 N.Y.2d 632, 518 N.Y.S.2d 957 (1987).

§ 3.14 Targeting Witnesses

Although the discovery process is a useful tool for obtaining information *from* the other parties' witnesses, it is also useful in obtaining information *on* the other parties' witnesses. For example, depositions are a good way to check out the demeanor, knowledge, and appearance of the other side's witnesses. Is the witness nervous? Tentative? Does the witness have a quick temper, or is he or she defensive or easily agitated? Or is the witness authoritative and confident such that shaking the testimony on cross-examination will be difficult? Such information will be as important in determining whether settlement is warranted as in preparing for trial.

An expert can make or break a construction case; thus, preparation of the expert witness is extremely important. If the expert is deposed prior to trial, his or her performance can also influence decisions on settlement and trial preparation. Ideally, the expert will have testified enough to be calm and to be able to handle direct and cross-examination, but not so often as to look like a professional witness.

In addition to a resume which shows background and experience in the subject matter of the testimony, the expert in a construction case should be able to explain complicated and technical matters in a way that the judge or jury will understand. One danger of having a trial conducted by attorneys, experts, and parties experienced in construction matters is their tendency to "speak the language," and to forget that the trier of fact probably knows little or nothing about construction.

This tendency may also be a problem with the fact witness who may feel open to attack if he or she does not demonstrate a knowledge of technical construction terms and theories during testimony. Potential witnesses for depositions or trial should be prepared to answer questions in the simplest form possible and to avoid elaborating, speculating, digressing, or lecturing.

In the rush to prepare his or her own witnesses, the attorney should not overlook the necessity of preparing to examine the other party's witnesses. If able to depose another party's expert, the attorney can simply examine generally on such matters as background, experience, investigations conducted, materials reviewed, the expert's conclusions and opinions, and the basis for them. However, by doing some general background reading in the particular field, or by getting a quick education from the client, the attorney may catch the expert off guard and may force him or her to qualify formerly unqualified opinions. Similarly, pursuant to the discovery plan, the attorney should review documents and prepare prior to deposing a fact witness produced by another party, because a knowledge of dates and names and a familiarity with issues and documents will tend to keep the witness honest.

As mentioned previously, the identity of fact witnesses can usually be determined through examination of records and through depositions. Sometimes an attorney has trouble locating a fact witness who has left the employ of one of the parties, who no longer practices in the area, or who has retired. Most states that license professionals have current addresses on file. Other sources include personnel departments, state motor vehicle departments, public retirement systems, and the post office. A consult with an attorney who specializes in tracing people may be useful.

Again, nonparty witnesses should not be overlooked, especially because they will appear more credible if they are not interested in the outcome of the litigation. Public agencies, the office of the project architect, and employees of other contractors and subcontractors are all possible sources of impartial fact witnesses.

§ 3.15 Motion Practice

Because construction cases involve volumes of documents, numerous witnesses, and multiple parties, they are fertile ground for breeding discovery disputes. However, the courts do not like to be dragged into petty discovery disputes, which is one reason for local rules requiring the attorneys to try to work it out first. The Federal Rules of Civil Procedure also provide for the assessment of costs against the party who unreasonably seeks or unreasonably resists discovery.[117] A cooperative atmosphere is certainly preferable to taking a chance on a series of rulings like those in a construction case involving 15 parties in four consolidated actions that had been pending for over 10 years. Faced with a series of motions on discovery requests, the apparently frustrated court sent forth a barrage of sanctions ranging from default judgments to striking complaints to preclusion orders, measures which were later described by the appellate court as "draconian."[118]

The Federal Rules of Civil Procedure provide that a party may apply for an order compelling discovery[119] or a protective order limiting discovery.[120] The relief requested can include an order requiring a party to answer questions at depositions, an order requiring a corporation to designate an officer, director, or managing agent to testify on its behalf, and an order compelling inspection.[121] The rules also allow for a motion to compel with

---

[117] Fed. R. Civ. P. 37(a)(4).
[118] J.R. Stevenson v. Dormitory Auth. of N.Y., 112 A.D.2d at 115, 492 N.Y.S.2d at 389.
[119] Fed. R. Civ. P. 37.
[120] Fed. R. Civ. P. 26(c).
[121] Fed. R. Civ. P. 37(a)(2).

§ 3.15 MOTION PRACTICE

respect to interrogatories objected to or unanswered.[122] Evasive and incomplete answers are treated as failure to reply.[123]

If a party objects to interrogatories, the proper procedure is to move for a protective order and not to ignore or refuse to answer objectionable questions. However, this is not the common procedure in construction cases. Many attorneys merely list the objections or refuse to answer without initiating a protective motion. Perhaps this is to minimize the court's involvement in the discovery process. However, failure to move for a protective order or to make specific objections may result in a ruling that all objections are waived.[124] New York courts consistently hold that the failure to make a timely motion for a protective order is a waiver of all objections to the discovery sought unless the demand is "palpably improper" or seeks privileged material.[125] If interrogatories are truly improper, the court may vacate the entire demand rather than engage in "judicial pruning."[126]

Upon failure to comply with an order, the court can order sanctions including contempt of court, an order establishing the facts against the recalcitrant party, an order of preclusion, and an order striking pleadings or rendering judgment by default. Some courts are notoriously reluctant to grant sanctions and will often issue orders on a conditional basis, for example, a party will be precluded unless it makes the required disclosure within a certain time period.[127] Usually a court will require some showing of an effort to resolve the dispute outside the courtroom by the party seeking the disclosure.[128]

However, even a reluctant court can be pushed too far, as in the case of an attorney in a construction case who repeatedly ignored discovery orders, failed to meet deadlines, failed to pay monetary sanctions, proffered incredible excuses, and was finally met with an order dismissing his client's case and the court's suggestion that the client had a remedy against the attorney.[129] State courts react with similar displeasure, especially when the implication is that a party has destroyed or discarded project records,[130] or

---

[122] Fed. R. Civ. P. 33(a).

[123] Fed. R. Civ. P. 37(a)(3).

[124] Casson Constr. Co. v. Armco Steel Corp., 91 F.R.D. 376 (D. Kan. 1980).

[125] Cipriano v. Righter, 100 A.D.2d 923, 474 N.Y.S.2d 839, 840 (1984).

[126] Dykowsky v. New York City Transit Auth., 124 A.D.2d 465, 507 N.Y.S.2d 626 (1986).

[127] Statue of Liberty-Ellis Island Found. v. International United Indus., Inc., 110 F.R.D. 395 (S.D.N.Y. 1986).

[128] Pinkerton v. Roadway Express, 650 F. Supp. 1138 (N.D. Ga. 1986).

[129] Urban Elec. Supply & Equip. Corp. v. New York Convention Center Dev. Corp., 105 F.R.D. 92 (E.D.N.Y. 1985).

[130] Anteri v. NRS Constr. Corp., 117 A.D.2d 696, 498 N.Y.S.2d 435 (1986).

appears to be furtively attempting to conduct discovery of nonparties without the requisite notice to all parties.[131]

Usually the next step after the issuance of a preclusion order is a motion for summary judgment based on the fact that, if precluded from proving certain facts, the plaintiff or defendant will not be able to make out a prima facie case or defense. But, in yet another case which illustrates the problems inherent in relying upon stock forms, the court found it impossible to grant summary judgment following an order of preclusion; this situation occurred because the court was not exactly sure *what* had been precluded by the failure to respond to a demand for a bill of particulars that bore only the most incidental relationship to the complaint the defendant was trying to have amplified.[132]

§ 3.16 Conclusion

Discovery in construction cases requires focus, planning, and persistence. To the extent an attorney can cooperate in the discovery process and still preserve client confidences and protect his or her own work-product, the discovery process in a construction case, albeit still difficult, will proceed in the manner envisioned by the Federal Rules of Civil Procedure. Discovery disputes are costly, time-consuming, and risky for all sides. Many of the reported decisions on discovery in construction cases show the frustration of the court at the contumacious behavior of some parties and attorneys. Moreover, discovery disputes take limited energy and resources away from attempts to resolve the dispute prior to trial and divert attention from the true issues of the case. Extensive appeals on discovery issues can rarely be justified in terms of time, cost, or advancement of the issues. The best approach is a practical approach. The question should be "How can I obtain the most useful information to prepare my case or defense, in the most inexpensive way and in the shortest time possible?" This is the approach that will best prepare a construction case for trial or settlement and, therefore, best serve the client and the laudable goal of a "just, speedy and inexpensive determination of every action."[133]

---

[131] *In re* Beiny, 129 A.D.2d 126, 517 N.Y.S.2d 474 (1987).
[132] Lewitinn v. Loventhal Mgmt. Co., 109 A.D.2d 629, 486 N.Y.S.2d 209 (1985).
[133] Fed. R. Civ. P. 1.

CHAPTER 4

USE OF CONSULTANTS AND EXPERTS

Anthony M. Noce, Jr., P.E., Esquire

Anthony M. Noce, Jr., is vice-president/general counsel for Lisbon Contractors, Inc., a general contractor specializing in utility and highway construction. Mr. Noce has distinguished experience in construction litigation and offers a unique perspective on the use of expert witnesses, having been a practicing engineer, a consultant, and an expert witness. He has also employed consultants and experts both as an attorney and as a client. Mr. Noce is a member of the Bar of the Commonwealth of Pennsylvania and is a licensed professional engineer in Pennsylvania. He holds a bachelor of science in civil engineering from Drexel University and a juris doctorate from the Delaware Law School of Widener University.

§ 4.1   Introduction
§ 4.2   Decision to Retain an Expert
§ 4.3   The Selection Process
§ 4.4   Roles of the Expert
§ 4.5   Interrogatories and Depositions of Opposing Experts
§ 4.6   Cross-Examination of Opposing Experts
§ 4.7   —Foundations of Expert's Opinion
§ 4.8   —Prior Opinions
§ 4.9   —Expert versus Staff Time
§ 4.10   —Compensation
§ 4.11   —Learned Treatises
§ 4.12   Conclusion

§ 4.1 Introduction

Construction litigation commands a higher level of expert and consultant participation than perhaps any other category of lawsuit. The consultant/expert plays an important role in almost every aspect of claim presentation, ranging from development of claim strategy to actual presentation of the case. The right to present an opinion as to the merits of the claim on a trial is reserved for the expert.

The ability of the attorney to channel and effectively direct this powerful tool is critical to the successful presentation or defense of a construction claim. When presenting complex schedules and interpretations of plans and specifications, a skilled expert can educate the attorney as well as assist in educating the trier of fact.

In the area of delay claims (as discussed in **Chapter 5**), a detailed analysis is typically required to establish causation and responsibility. The expert is usually the witness who prepares the analysis and presents the results in graphic form and the opinion in testimony. Very often, in complex cases, the winner of the battle of the experts will be the successful litigant.

This chapter discusses the expanding role of experts in construction litigation, the selection process, the level of participation, the work-product, and the testimony of the expert.

§ 4.2 Decision to Retain an Expert

The evolution of a construction claim is typically as follows:

1. Event giving rise to the claim (for example, differing site conditions or design error)
2. Contractor notification to owner's representative
3. Contractor's presentation of claim (usually after work is completed)
4. Owner's rejection of claim
5. Negotiation
6. Hiring of counsel
7. Threatening letters
8. Institution of litigation or arbitration
9. Extensive discovery
10. Preparation for trial
11. Settlement at pretrial conference.

In the above scenario, expert involvement from the first steps of the process maximizes recovery for the contractor and reduces exposure to the owner. This chapter, however, focuses on the more typical example in which the expert is retained pursuant to pending litigation.

It is of utmost importance to determine at the outset of litigation whether expert involvement is required. When retained by the plaintiff, the expert can assist the attorney in formulating the technical issues and calculating damages before filing a complaint. Participation by the expert in developing theories of recovery will ensure consistency between the expert's eventual testimony and the pleadings.

Retaining an expert at an early stage in the litigation process has the added benefit of allowing the expert to visit the project site shortly after the construction has been completed to conduct testing or other inspections that may eventually prove critical during the presentation of the case.

§ 4.3 The Selection Process

While one can appreciate the benefits of retaining an expert early in the proceedings, the economics of litigation, as well as the natural proclivity of lawyers to procrastinate, often results in the selection of the expert on the eve of trial. In such a scenario, it is critical that the potential expert is presented with a concise statement of the issues so that a preview of the expert's eventual opinion is apparent during the interview. Further, at such a late date, it is imperative that certain analytical and organizational tasks already be performed. For example, the careful practitioner will identify the technical issues that would benefit from expert testimony. The issues should be grouped by technical discipline, because it is rare that an expert can offer a truly expert opinion in more than one discipline.

The critical documents describing the issues should be assembled and sorted first by issue, and then chronologically within each issue. This allows the expert to see the issue develop through the paper trail. Unfortunately, many attorneys do not undertake this document organization task in a manner that lends itself to expedited expert analysis; they organize them chronologically or by author, but not by technical issue. Thus, the expert is often called upon to organize the documents as well as provide opinions.

When the expert is retained shortly before trial in a large case involving various issues, the expert's role should be limited to a review of the facts that are central to the issues on which he or she will be questioned. While a general understanding of the case is recommended, experts will not be able to effectively handle cross-examination in areas outside those in which they have studied. Accordingly, their role should be limited to opinions in their specific areas of expertise, and their opinions should be based on specific probable facts.

The attorney should then assemble a list of potential experts for the issues. This list can be compiled either from client contacts, attorney contacts, or by the use of various services that provide lists of experts to attorneys. These services generally advertise in professional publications.

Interview. The potential experts should then be interviewed by the attorney and the client. The client can generally be the judge of the potential expert's technical knowledge. The attorney would naturally evaluate whether the potential expert would make a credible witness, and whether a rapport with the attorney and the trier of fact can be developed.

The attorney should present a brief summary of the issues surrounding the case to the potential expert in the interview. The expert should also be provided with the critical documentation to review in the interview. Based on the limited review of the case presented in the interview, the expert should be able to provide an advance view of possible opinions. In addition, if studies are required to assist the expert in solidifying the opinion, the attorney should solicit the expert's advice on an approach to such studies. The attorney should be careful not to expect a definite opinion based upon such an interview. Nor should the attorney select the expert who provides the answer most biased to the client's position. This can be fatal, because the expert's opinion will surely be tested by the adversary during both the pretrial and trial process.

The interview, when well organized by the attorney, will serve a dual purpose. First, it will allow the attorney to test possible theories on an independent party. Second, the attorney will be able to view how the witness may react under cross-examination.

Although time considerations usually preclude an extensive interview period, at least three experts should be interviewed prior to making a selection. The interviews should be scheduled on the same day, if possible, with the same interview team, so that a fair evaluation can be made.

Proposal. Following the interview process, each potential expert should be requested to prepare a proposal describing the proposed services. The proposal should include:

1. Approach to problem
2. Price
3. Time frame to complete study
4. Resumes of all support staff personnel
5. Prior testimony experience.

The attorney should ask the experts to structure their proposals in this format.

§ 4.3 SELECTION PROCESS

In the approach section, the expert should describe how the expert's resources and expertise will be applied to the client's situation. This should include a description of the proposed services, why the services are necessary, and what result or work-product will be generated. From this approach, the expert should be able to quantify the limits of the professional hours involved. Because expert fees are often computed on an hourly basis, the estimate of professional hours is an essential ingredient of the proposed fee. Further, a breakdown of the proposed professional hours will allow the attorney to assess whether the expert proposes to do the necessary homework. The attorney should also request that the proposal contain a breakdown of service hours by level of support staff. This will allow the attorney to assess whether the proposed expert will be intimately involved in the expert analysis or merely a mouthpiece at trial.

In a process that is so heavily weighted to the perception of expertise, the professional resume is an important ingredient in the expert's proposal. While expertise can be developed from experience, the expert's education, degrees, and registrations are also important objective criteria in determining credibility. Of course, the resume should address the hands-on experience of the expert. Education without application will serve to undermine the perception of expertise. Past testimony experience is also an important criterion for expert selection. The trial-by-fire ordeal of cross-examination is the true test of an effective expert. With so much at stake, the attorney does not want a forensic novice.

The proposal will also give the attorney a unique perspective on the expert. Because a factfinder's perception of the expert depends as much on presentation as on credentials, the proposal will provide a preview of the potential expert's presentation skills. In addition, in presenting the approach, the expert will generally describe an understanding of the underlying issues. This presentation will allow the attorney to judge whether the expert was able to obtain a firm grasp of the issues in the interview. A competent expert may be able to present perspectives and insights into the issues of the case different from those of the attorney after only a brief recitation of the facts.

Each of the proposals should be reviewed by both the attorney and the client; the following factors should be used to evaluate the proposals:

1. Technical expertise
2. Professional registration/credentials
3. Prior experience with similar issues
4. Strength of support staff
5. Presentation skills
6. Cost

7. Time
8. Involvement of expert and support staff.

The weighting of each factor in the evaluation process varies in each situation. In a jury trial, for example, a greater emphasis would be placed on credentials and presentation skills. On the other hand, in arbitration or a bench trial, technical expertise may be more important. As the client may be a sophisticated participant in the design and construction process, he or she may have developed criteria of technical competence that can be used to evaluate the expert. Hence, the attorney should place a greater emphasis on the client's impressions. With certain factors such as presentation skills, the attorney is more qualified to evaluate the proposals.

Scope of services. Once the proposals have been evaluated and a selection is made, the attorney and client should develop a specific scope of services for the expert to perform. In most instances, this scope will be consistent with the proposal submitted by the expert. However, it is important at this stage for the attorney to have a good idea of what the final work-product of the expert will be and what it will cost.

Many experts will tailor their proposals to include a phased approach to the review of the claims. The expert will first want to study the critical documents, interview the key players, and, if appropriate, visit the project site prior to submitting a detailed scope of work and estimate.

Generally, the expert will offer to complete this first review phase quickly and for a relatively modest cost, depending on the size of the claim and the volume of the documentation. The work-product from this phase will be a detailed proposal for additional studies along with a summary of the case and an indication of where the expert's eventual opinion will be centered. The detailed proposal will then be the tool for the attorney to use in focusing the expert's attention, evaluating performance, and monitoring costs.

§ 4.4 Roles of the Expert

As described earlier in this chapter, the expert/consultant plays a varied and pivotal role in the preparation of a case for trial. For the purposes of this section, assume a hypothetical construction claim containing several contested change orders and a delay claim. The magnitude of the case and the economics of litigation largely define the eventual role that the expert will be asked to play. For purposes of this hypothetical case, we will assume that the use of the expert is not severely limited by economic considerations.

After the expert is retained, the first undertaking should be to clearly identify the issues in dispute to confirm that the attorney is on the right

§ 4.4 ROLES OF THE EXPERT

track. This issue identification process continues throughout the document examination and technical evaluation stage. However, as we discuss in **Chapter 1**, it is important to provide an exhaustive list of potential issues early in the evaluation.

Preparing the list of issues is especially important before undertaking detailed document analysis. The expert and staff should identify and catalogue all of the documents in the case. This information can then be loaded into a database system so that sorts can be completed on a variety of parameters. As we discuss in **Chapter 2**, this is an important undertaking.

After the document retrieval system is set up, the expert should analyze and study the major issues in the case. A narrative report should be completed for each major issue, including a technical analysis and the effect of the issue on the schedule.

The expert should then prepare a detailed schedule analysis to determine causation and responsibility for project delays. First, a summary as-planned schedule is completed, identifying the contractor's proposed method of completing the project. Next, a summary as-built schedule is completed, identifying actual dates work was performed on the project.

As we discuss in **Chapter 5**, the as-planned schedule should then be studied at different points in time and compared to the as-built schedule to determine where the delays were on the project. This study is commonly referred to as a time impact analysis. The result of this study is a determination of the periods of delay on a project, the cause of the delay, and the responsibility for the delay.

The results of the time impact analysis can then be used to calculate damages for delay. In **Chapter 7**, we discuss the process of evaluating damages in construction cases, as well as the various types of damages. The attorney must take seriously the need to perform detailed analysis of both the technical issues and the damages. Perhaps separate experts will be required.

The time impact analysis, the issue analysis, and the damage calculations will form the basis of the expert's opinion. The careful practitioner must consider that the expert's report may be discoverable under Federal Rule of Civil Procedure 26(b) and/or many similar state rules modeled after the federal rules (see **Chapter 3**). Accordingly, it may be wise to ask for an informal study with a verbal presentation of findings to the attorney before a formal report is prepared. Under the Federal Rules of Civil Procedure, however, attorneys need not disclose the names of experts or consultants whom they do not intend to call on as witnesses.[1] In this light, the use of consultants that are not expected to testify may prove beneficial to the attorney preparing the case for trial. The attorney will have the benefit of the technical view of the consultant, but will not be required to disclose opinions or conclusions obtained from the consultant.

---

[1] Fed. R. Civ. P. 26(b)(4).

Another pivotal role of the expert is assisting the attorney in discovery. The attorney would be well advised to bring the consultant to document inspections of the opposing party. The expert will be able to quickly locate relevant documents and project records and will assist the attorney in his or her evaluation. Further, the expert will be able to determine whether all of the requested documents are produced. Often attorneys will not be as familiar as the expert with the types of documents kept during construction.

The expert can also provide the attorney with assistance in deposing opposing party witnesses. When the expert is preparing an analysis, many questions routinely arise that are unable to be answered by the client. By incorporating these questions into a carefully prepared deposition outline, the attorney will be able to assist the expert in verifying assumptions, and will avoid having those assumptions rebutted at trial. In certain circumstances, it may be useful to have the expert attend the deposition of the opposing expert. When highly technical issues are involved, the attorney will benefit by having an expert immediately available to interpret answers, highlight the significance of certain responses, and suggest follow-up questions.

Thus, the ability of the attorney to have the expert's analysis completed prior to discovery will assist the attorney in focusing deposition questions and interrogatories on the critical issues of the case. Selecting the expert after discovery is completed prevents the attorney from capitalizing on the full benefit of the expert's assistance.

The last area where the expert will typically assist the attorney is in the preparation of presentation charts and graphics for trial. Often overlooked by inexperienced counsel, a professionally prepared colorful chart will focus the attention of the trier of fact on the statistics or data that most convincingly presents the party's position.

The adage "A picture is worth a thousand words" is probably conservative when used in relation to construction litigation. Abstract engineering theories and expert conclusions that are conclusive to a person knowledgeable in the issues may go completely unnoticed by the lay juror unless attention is specifically focused on the critical point by a well-prepared exhibit.

Typically, the expert will prepare a series of charts summarizing the time impact analysis to identify responsibility and duration of project delays. Without this tool, it would be virtually impossible to describe how the delay in one portion of the project impacts the completion of the entire project. Sample graphics are provided in **Chapter 5**.

Charts are also used to summarize manpower levels and to establish claims for inefficiency. Damages can also be depicted using graphics, as demonstrated in **Chapter 7**. Many consulting firms, especially in the area of claim analysis, employ draftspersons and commercial artists who can tailor the exhibits to illustrate and effectively communicate the key points for juries.

When the case is finally ready for trial, the attorney will reap the benefits of all of the preparation and thought that went into selecting and educating the expert about the facts of the case. Trial preparation consists mainly of reviewing exhibits and preparing the expert for cross-examination. After this preparation, the attorney and the expert will both know what the expert testimony will consist of. Special emphasis, however, must be placed on phrasing both the question and the answer to state the expert's opinion on the issue. For example, if the issue is whether the contractor should have anticipated rock after a reasonable review of boring information provided with the bid documents, the question should be phrased as follows:

Q. Based on the information provided to the contractor with the bid documents, should a reasonable contractor have anticipated rock excavation?
A. No. The boring information provided with the bid documents clearly shows the presence of silt and clay soils. A reasonable contractor would not have anticipated rock.

It is critical that the expert repeat the opinion in his or her own words. A simple "yes" or "no" answer does not demonstrate the expert's conviction to the stated opinion. Further, the repetition of the position in the question and the answer reinforces the jury's perception of the validity of the opinion.

§ 4.5 Interrogatories and Depositions of Opposing Experts

Under Federal Rule of Civil Procedure 26(b)(4)(A)(i),

[A] party may through interrogatories require any other party to identify each person whom the other party expects to call as an expert witness at trial, to state the subject matter on which he is expected to testify, and to state the substance of the facts and opinions to which the expert is expected to testify and a summary of the grounds for each opinion.

At the outset of litigation, the attorney should always propound expert interrogatories upon opposing parties. This is an effective tactic that, in light of the continuing nature of interrogatories, provides continuous information to counsel in the event that other parties retain an expert. However, since the rule limits discovery to experts whom counsel expects to call as witnesses at trial, the determination as to whether a potential witness will testify may not be made until the case is ready for trial.

The attorney may also, upon motion to the court and upon appropriate order, depose opposing experts. Even though Federal Rule of Civil Procedure 26(b)(4)(A)(i) would indicate that only interrogatories are the norm for expert discovery, standard practice in construction cases is to allow for deposition of experts without special motions. Generally, the attorneys for opposing parties will agree voluntarily to such an exchange. This is a de facto recognition that, in many instances, construction litigation is a battle of the experts. Part of the battleground involves the distillation and presentation of facts and opinions by experts. An exchange of expert depositions will allow an opportunity to test the validity of theories of recovery and the effectiveness of your own expert witness.

In one case, for example, the attorney for the plaintiff contractor based the case for delay damages upon dual theories of design deficiencies and differing site conditions. The plaintiff retained two different experts: an architect and a geotechnical engineer. The architect expert survived the pretrial deposition and effectively portrayed the design as substantially lacking. Unfortunately, the geotechnical expert was uncertain of some key facts, and his conclusions were challenged during a deposition. By researching and verifying the missing geotechnical data, the contractor's attorney was able to prevail under both theories of recovery. The grueling ordeal experienced by the soils engineer actually assisted the plaintiff's attorney by exposing weaknesses previously unknown. Had the supporting data not been verified subsequent to the deposition, the case could have had a different outcome, because the plaintiff's attorney was tempted to settle or withdraw the differing site condition claim.

§ 4.6 Cross-Examination of Opposing Experts

Once the identity of an opposing expert is determined, the attorney should do as much research as possible to learn about the expert's background. Background information such as education, relevant experience, and professional registration gives the attorney a profile of the expert that will tailor the approach to cross-examination or deposition.

For example, in one construction delay case, counsel for the defendant owner encountered a previously unknown expert proposed by the plaintiff. Very little information was provided in the interrogatories, despite the defendant's motion to the court to provide a more detailed resume. The owner's attorney invested in a thorough background search and discovered that the plaintiff's expert was formerly the chief executive of a bankrupt contracting firm that left numerous and costly problems to its surety. At trial, the defendant's counsel apparently devastated the jury's perception of the plaintiff's expert by exposing and focusing upon the mismanagement of the expert's previous firm.

Another background matter involves professional registration. Although many valuable construction engineers have not obtained professional registration in their field, it is certainly desirable for an expert witness to have the best credentials. Many experts have offered opinion testimony only to be impeached on the ground of lacking official professional registration.

§ 4.7 —Foundations of Expert's Opinion

Because of the fact that the expert is permitted to give opinion testimony on the ultimate issue or issues in the case, the foundations of the expert in arriving at his or her opinion are critical and should be thoroughly questioned during cross-examination. However, a detailed examination of the basis of the expert's opinion will provide the expert with an opportunity to reiterate key themes and facts to the jury. Thus, the attorney should not wait until trial to commence a fishing expedition as to the premises of the opposing expert's opinion. The better course is to identify certain weak points, questionable facts, and baseless assumptions that underlie the opposing expert's opinion.

For example, in one delay case involving a general contractor and a subcontractor, the subcontractor's expert testified that all of the delays were attributable to the general contractor, and that the subcontractor did not contribute to any project delays. Apparently, the subcontractor's expert was unaware of the fact that a second-tier subcontractor had walked off the project. The general contractor's attorney confronted the subcontractor's expert with this fact during cross-examination, startling the expert. Rather than driving the point home, the general contractor's attorney merely emphasized the startled look on the expert's face. Other experts and fact witnesses were then brought in to document and expound upon the impact of the second-tier subcontractor's default.

There are several other tactics that are generally effective in impeaching the testimony of the expert by eroding the foundation of the expert's opinion. One is to question the qualification of the expert in the particular field. The alleged expert may not always have specific hands-on experience with the subject of the litigation; thus his or her opinions are based on related experience in other areas. Distinctions between the experience and the issue should be developed and stressed on cross-examination. For example, a mechanical engineer may be trained and experienced in waste water treatment facilities. Despite training as a mechanical engineer, this person may have little expertise in evaluating design and delay in the installation of building heating, venting, and air conditioning systems.

The attorney should stress that, although the experience is related, not all of the particular nuances of the case at bar exist in the areas of the expert's experience. This argument should first be made in an attempt to disqualify the expert prior to testimony and then again during cross-examination and closing arguments.

The rules of evidence generally preclude questions during cross-examination that are outside the scope of the direct testimony. However, since experts are testifying on the ultimate issue, questions related to the foundations of the expert's opinion, whether covered in direct testimony or not, should be unobjectionable.[2] First, the attorney should, during depositions, try to ascertain the opinions of the expert on issues that are marginal to the case but, nevertheless, are in the attorney's favor. Also, attorneys often agree to exchange expert reports. Either way will provide the opposing attorney an opportunity to discover such marginal opinions which can be used to "capture" the opponent's expert. During cross-examination, the skillful attorney can make the expert his own by asking the expert an opinion on those issues. This tactic places the opposing attorney in the unenviable position of either impeaching his own witness or accepting the testimony.

Finally, an agreement by opposing attorneys to exchange expert witness reports and depositions will also provide the astute attorney with an opportunity to identify areas where the expert may have changed his or her mind on certain matters. On one such an occasion, the expert admitted in a deposition that he prepared an earlier draft of the expert report, and he even provided copies of the earlier draft from a stack of documents in front of him. A comparison of the draft and final reports provided ample opportunity for opposing counsel to question and impeach the expert at the subsequent trial. Even though the matters involved in the revisions were not fundamental, the opposing attorney was able to detract the jury from an unquestioned reliance upon the expert.

§ 4.8 —Prior Opinions

Prior testimony and publications authored by the expert provide an invaluable tool for cross-examination. Frequently, the expert who has previously testified or authored works has taken a position that is contrary to his present position. The attorney who has records of the prior work has the rare opportunity to ask a trial lawyer's favorite question: "Were you mistaken then or are you mistaken now?"

In one case, an expert was retained to analyze and quantify a contractor's delay damages. This expert had authored an article questioning the validity of the *Eichleay* formula[3] (see **Chapter 7**) to calculate the extent of

---

[2] *See, e.g.,* Fed. R. Civ. P. 703.
[3] Eichleay Corp., ASBCA No. 5183, 60-2 B.C.A. (CCH) ¶ 2688 (1960).

unabsorbed home office overhead costs. The article was written as a commentary on an appellate case where the court rejected the application of the *Eichleay* formula. The expert's commentary appeared to agree with the appellate court, which questioned the propriety of utilizing the *Eichleay* formula. When the expert proposed to apply the formula to the present case, the attorney for the owner challenged this element of damage based upon the expert's own article. Such a dialogue can impeach the expert's credibility completely. Obviously, these tactics should be reserved for cross-examination during trial rather than in depositions.

§ 4.9 —Expert versus Staff Time

Another common tactic is to question the time spent personally by the expert versus the supporting staff. In many cases, the expert witness has a staff of people who review documentation and prepare reports and position papers for the witness. The witness's own time on the case may only represent a fraction of the time spent by the staff. This should be brought out during cross-examination, both in terms of actual hours spent by the witness in arriving at the opinions, and then in terms of the witness testifying on behalf of other people's (supporting staff) opinions. In one case, the opposing attorney discovered errors in the as-built schedule prepared by an expert. The expert passed off the error as being made by technical staff. This opened a Pandora's box by allowing inquiries into the amount of time spent on the case by the expert and by the supporting staff. It turned out that the time spent by the expert was disproportionately small compared to the time spent by the staff.

§ 4.10 —Compensation

The amount of compensation received by the expert for professional services should also be brought out during cross-examination. Even if the attorney using the expert is savvy enough to disclose the compensation during direct testimony and to develop the idea that the compensation would be paid whether the opinion was favorable or not, the point should be made again during cross-examination. Expert fees of $50,000 to $100,000 are not at all unusual in construction litigation, and those fees, when presented to a lay jury, will give the impression that the expert is being paid for an opinion. The hired gun concept can be further reinforced if the expert is paid a higher hourly rate for time spent at trial or deposition or, better yet, if the expert is paid a contingent fee. Surprisingly, there are several experts who will accept contingent fees.

§ 4.11 —Learned Treatises

Learned treatises are another tool that can effectively be used in cross-examination of an expert. When a publication is identified as a recognized standard of the industry, and this admission is obtained from the expert, any inconsistencies between the publication and the testimony will be ammunition to the cross-examiner for impeachment purposes. For example, there are several treatises that are widely recognized as authoritative on the subject of critical path method (CPM) scheduling as applied to the construction industry. A careful reading and familiarity with these treatises may allow the construction litigator an opportunity to cross-examine purported experts in construction scheduling and delay. Because of the frequency with which delay and disruption claims are litigated, construction attorneys should have various scheduling books in their personal library.

§ 4.12 Conclusion

The use of experts can be critical to the attorney's ability to present a case in the most effective and efficient manner. Allowing experts to lead the attorney may result in excessive fees and questionable results. The attorney, when deciding to use the services of an expert, should be prepared to manage the expert throughout the course of the investigation, receiving updates on progress and providing direction with respect to the focus of the study.

PART II
EVIDENTIARY ISSUES

CHAPTER 5

PRESENTATION OF DELAY AND ACCELERATION CLAIMS

Barry B. Bramble, Esquire

Barry B. Bramble is executive counsel of the construction management and consulting firm, MDC Systems Corp. of Philadelphia, the Construction Services Division of Day & Zimmermann, Inc. He is a recognized expert in the area of construction claims and a frequent speaker for professional societies, trade organizations, legal associations, and civic groups. Mr. Bramble has written numerous articles on construction industry topics and is a co-author of *Construction Delay Claims, Deskbook of Construction Contract Law, Discovery in Construction Litigation,* and *Avoiding and Resolving Construction Claims.* Mr. Bramble is a member of the Bar of the Commonwealth of Pennsylvania and the Bar of the State of New Jersey. He is a member of several committees of the American Bar Association, including the Forum Committee on the Construction Industry, Fidelity and Surety Law Committee, and the Public Contract Law Section. He also serves as a member of the American Arbitration Association's panel of construction arbitrators.

§ 5.1   Introduction
§ 5.2   What Is Delay?
§ 5.3   What Is Acceleration?
§ 5.4   Need for Reliable Analysis
§ 5.5   —Scheduling Techniques to Demonstrate Delay
§ 5.6   Approaching the Forum
§ 5.7   Explaining CPM Scheduling
§ 5.8   Explaining Delays
§ 5.9   Explaining Acceleration
§ 5.10 Using Graphics

§ 5.11 Developing Themes for Presentation
§ 5.12 Defenses to Delay Claims
§ 5.13 Conclusion

§ 5.1 Introduction

Disputes arising out of delayed or accelerated construction progress are a widespread phenomenon plaguing the construction industry. The frequency with which such problems arise is compounded by the complexities of evaluating the cause and responsibility for delay. As we discuss in § 5.2, the evaluation of construction schedules involves the application of network scheduling techniques as well as complex construction and engineering procedures. But in order to convince an adversary or factfinder of the merits of your position, the complexities of the analysis must be made understandable. Unfortunately, this is not often achieved by the parties to a construction dispute. This is the challenge when making any presentation concerning the causation and responsibility for construction delay.

Simplification and clarification are important to the effective presentation of a complex delay or acceleration analysis. Simplification is not the same as simplemindedness.[1] Simplification requires the summarization of complex ideas without distorting the rationale of the logic. The essence of the findings must be captured without allowing false premises and conclusions to detract from those findings. The level of detail is reduced without distorting the meaning of the details; exactness and sophistication are brought to the proper level for comprehension by the audience. Clarification involves the use of words, concepts, and ideas to facilitate understanding by the audience. Effective communication involves using the language, experiences, and culture of the audience.

Both the simplification and the clarification processes are subject to distortion when trying to justify a predetermined position. This is anathema to the scientifically minded engineer, but it is the lifeblood of the advocacy oriented attorney. It is in the area of delay and acceleration claims that these two professions will cross paths. The legal profession may presume relativity; the engineering profession may not even appreciate the concept.

In the following sections, the concepts of simplification and clarification will be applied to the presentation of construction delay and acceleration claims. The presentation may be to a client, to another party involved in the dispute, or to a mediator, arbitrator, juror, or judge involved in the formal process of resolving construction disputes.

---

[1] B. Bramble & J. O'Connor, Avoiding and Resolving Construction Claims 6-2 (1987).

§ 5.2 What Is Delay?

In approaching a delay claim, the attorney truly must understand what project delay is. In the context of recovering damages for extended performance or obtaining time extensions, the delays must affect the overall project completion. It is not enough that a troublesome event occurred. That event must be demonstrated to have delayed the overall project completion. This distinction is often lost in the process of advocating a claimant's position, perhaps because of a lack of clear understanding on the advocate's part, or a conscious effort to blur the distinction. Regardless, the claimant's position is untenable if the distinction is lost. The late completion of *the project* must have been caused directly by the events and problems alleged.

Scheduling with the critical path method (CPM) has been utilized to demonstrate the effects of problems and events upon the overall project completion. As we discuss in § 5.5, some of the methods employed to impact a schedule are distortions of CPM. Attorneys must keep this in mind when making presentations or refutations of delay claims.

At first blush, when examining the history of the project, the attorney for the claimant will encounter numerous potential delay-causing events. The attorney may be tempted to advocate every one of these events in presenting the claimant's position. However, the presentation of several hundred events is a complex undertaking, and it may detract from the clarity and simplicity necessary for effective advocacy.

Two suggestions are appropriate. First, the advocate should examine the exhaustive list of potential delays and find the few winning arguments. It may be more convincing to argue that the project was delayed by four drastic events rather than dying the "death of a thousand cuts." The criteria for winning arguments would include: clear responsibility of the opposing party for the delay; delays with long durations; acts of egregious behavior, either willful or negligent; problems for which the claimant gave clear advance warning to the opposition; and delays that are not concurrent with the claimant's own delay-causing problems.

In some instances, the advocate must deal with a project that truly was hampered by numerous short delays, the "death of a thousand cuts." If this is the case, even those many events can be classified into perhaps six or seven categories for simplification. Typical categories of delays would include delays caused by design defects or changes, differing site conditions, negligent contract administration, lack of workers on the project, procurement problems, and trade contractor coordination. The numerous delays may be symptoms of these general problems. Thus, the presentation may be made more convincing by arguing the few fundamental project difficulties that resulted in several hundred delay-causing events.

§ 5.3 What Is Acceleration?

Acceleration is an attempt to speed up the progress of the work in order to have an earlier project completion or to overcome project delays. Contractor claims to recover the costs of acceleration frequently accompany their claims to recover damages from project delay caused by the owner.

There are two bases for acceleration claims: directed and constructive. The owner may specifically instruct the contractor to complete the project earlier than the stipulated completion date. Alternatively, the work may be "constructively" accelerated without a specific directive. Some act or statement by the owner may be reasonably interpreted by the contractor as an order to accelerate the pace of the work. Typically, constructive acceleration claims are asserted when the contractor encounters excusable delays, and the owner fails to provide time extensions and further insists that the contractor meet the originally specified completion date.

In proving a constructive acceleration claim, generally the contractor must demonstrate at least one of five things: (1) excusable delay was experienced and a time extension is justified; (2) a time extension was requested in a timely fashion and in accordance with the contract requirements; (3) the owner failed or refused to grant the time extension; (4) the owner by some action, inaction, or statement required the contractor to complete the work within the originally scheduled period, or without the benefit of a time extension to which it is entitled; and (5) the contractor incurred additional costs in attempting to comply with the owner's demand.[2]

Claimants routinely fail to present convincing proof of one or more of these elements, yet they are undaunted in submitting acceleration claims. Often acceleration claims are submitted as a gambit to raise the ante in negotiating delay claims. Further, as we discuss in § 5.5, the claimant often manipulates the project schedules in an attempt to demonstrate acceleration. For example, when the total duration of the alleged delays plus the as-planned schedule period greatly exceeds the actual project duration, the claimant may find an easy explanation—acceleration. More often, the actual reason is that the claimant overstated the impact and duration of delays, and did not account for concurrency of delays and their actual impact upon the critical path.

Credibility for acceleration claims is bolstered by a sensible schedule analysis. Further credibility is achieved by providing proof of bona fide attempts to increase the work force with a concerted and well-managed plan. Proof of acceleration cost is also difficult. Typical acceleration costs include lost labor productivity caused by such factors as overly crowded conditions or the unavailability of work areas. Unfortunately,

---

[2] *Id.* at 2-21.

labor productivity data is routinely manipulated to inflate actual losses. We discuss productivity in detail in **Chapter 6** and damages in **Chapter 7**.

§ 5.4 Need for Reliable Analysis

In analyzing construction delay, there are two fundamental parameters—the as-planned schedule and the as-built schedule. These two documents establish the bounds of possibilities. The difference between the two is the theoretical range of liability for either party for delay to the project completion. For example, if the contractor was responsible for all of the delays, the owner may assess liquidated damages for the entire period. On the other hand, if the owner caused all of the delays, the contractor may recover delay-related costs for the period of time between the planned completion date and the actual completion date. Yet on most projects, both parties contribute to late completion, and some delay is beyond the control and without the fault of either party. Therefore, rigorous analysis must be made to determine the extent of liability and concurrency.[3] When two or more independent delays occur during the same period of time, an attempt should be made to apportion responsibility.

Further, an analysis of all major delays should be made to determine the cause of delay, the extent of overall project delay resulting from each event, and whether the delays were excusable, compensable, or nonexcusable. An excusable delay will serve to justify an extension of the contract performance time. Excusable delays (typically including strikes, unusually severe weather, and acts of God) are generally defined in the construction contract. A compensable delay will entitle the contractor to recover the costs associated with the delay as well as additional time for performance. Depending upon the terms of the contract, compensable delays may result from change orders, differing site conditions, and owner-directed suspension of the work. A nonexcusable delay is one for which the contractor assumes the risk of the cost and consequences. This generally includes failure to provide an adequate work force, failure to order materials in a timely manner, and failure to coordinate the work of subcontractors.[4]

In looking ahead to the trial presentation, the attorney should make sure that any analysis of construction delay by the scheduler, construction expert, or other technical professional is performed in accordance with valid principles. These principles include the type of scheduling (network or bar chart), construction methods, engineering requirements, and schedule impact techniques.

---

[3] *See* B. Bramble & M. Callahan, Construction Delay Claims 9 (1987).

[4] A more complete discussion of the legal and technical foundation for these classifications is provided in B. Bramble & M. Callahan, Construction Delay Claims 2–6 (1987).

Network schedules rather than bar charts are required by most courts in order to demonstrate the cause, responsibility, and extent of construction delay.[5] This is because network schedules can depict both the interrelationship of project activities and the relationship of activities to the overall completion of the project. However, even if network scheduling techniques are employed, the schedule can be manipulated to justify a predetermined position, rather than to evaluate the source of project delay in an independent manner.[6]

§ 5.5 —Scheduling Techniques to Demonstrate Delay

Various techniques, ranging from simplistic to complex, have been used to demonstrate the impact of project delays. The easiest methods to explain often suffer from simpleminded logic that distorts reality. The most complex are often the most accurate, yet they may be difficult to explain to the factfinder unless techniques of simplification and clarification are employed.

Global Impact Method

One approach to demonstrating impact on construction schedules is called the global impact method.[7] Although simplistic and easy to present, it is often an inaccurate way to depict the impact of delay-causing events.

Using this method, all of the delays, disruptions, and similar occurrences are simply outlined in a narrative text. The start and end dates are determined for each event, and the duration of each delaying event is computed. See **Figure 5–1**.

Sometimes the alleged duration of the delay is merely an arbitrary assignment. Often the delaying event will not have any effect upon the project completion date. For example, the approval of a shop drawing may take two weeks longer than stipulated in the contract, but the procurement of the item will only take four weeks *and* it is not needed on site for at least six months.

The total delay to the project is purported to be the sum total of the durations of all delaying events, even though there was concurrency, or overlap,

---

[5] Natkin & Co. v. George A. Fuller Co. 347 F. Supp. 17 (W.D. Mo. 1972); Minmar Builders, Inc., GSBCA No. 3430, 72-2 B.C.A. (CCH) ¶ 9599 (1972); *see* B. Bramble & M. Callahan, Construction Delay Claims 149–51 (1987).

[6] D'Onofrio, *Evaluating Construction Delay Claims,* MDC Advisor 1 (Spring 1988).

[7] B. Bramble & J. O'Connor, Avoiding and Resolving Construction Claims 4–14 (1987).

§ 5.5 SCHEDULING TECHNIQUES

GLOBAL IMPACT METHOD

| MONTHS | 1 | 2 | 3 | 4 | 5 | 6 | 7 | 8 | 9 | 10 | 11 | 12 | 13 | 14 | 15 | 16 | 17 | 18 | 19 |

PLAN — 365 DAYS

ACTUAL — 485 DAYS

JUSTIFIABLE EXTENSIONS — 515 DAYS

ACCELERATION (30 DAYS)

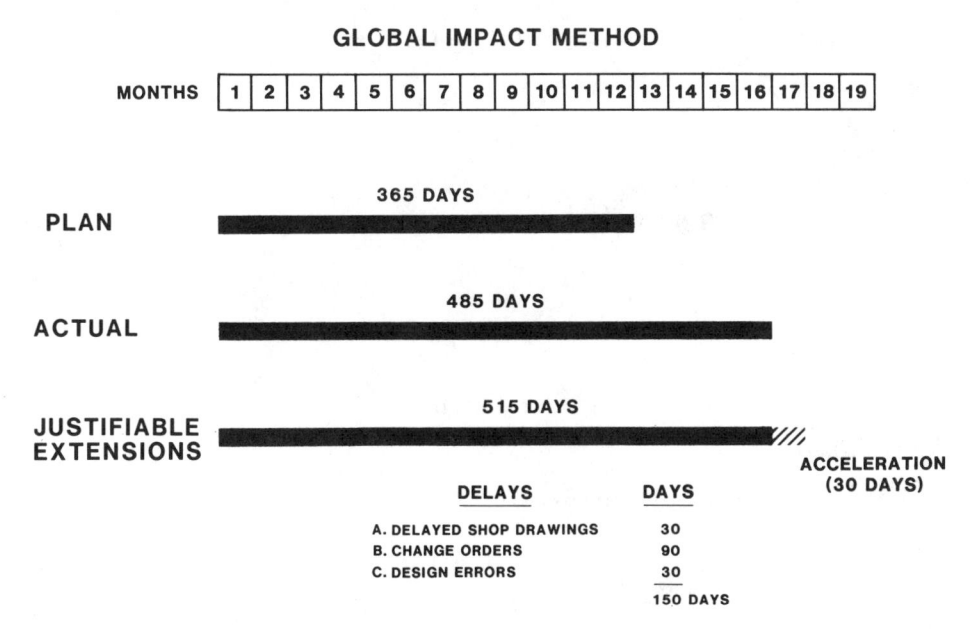

DELAYS	DAYS
A. DELAYED SHOP DRAWINGS	30
B. CHANGE ORDERS	90
C. DESIGN ERRORS	30
	150 DAYS

Figure 5-1. Global impact method.

in the delaying events. Further, claimants often make no attempt to make adjustments for errors in their original schedule or for any of their own delays. This technique does not demonstrate that any particular delay impacted the overall project completion. The analysis presumes that the delay in processing one of the change orders automatically delayed the project completion. All occurrences are assumed to be critical.[8]

There are many problems with this impact technique, but the primary problem is concurrency. Concurrent delays occur when there are two or more independent delays during the same period. When two separate delaying events occur during the same week, the claimant is not entitled to a 14-day time extension. This way of calculating delays frequently results in a claim for time extensions that extend well beyond the actual project completion. The difference between actual completion and the requested time extensions is often claimed to be acceleration. In actuality, it is more likely just exaggeration of the impact of the delaying events or the failure to account for concurrency. For example, in **Figure 5-2**, the actual dates of the alleged delays are shown, and the delay periods overlap. Thus, of the 150 days of delay claimed, 30 of the days overlap or are concurrent.

Attorneys who utilize this technique to present a delay claim in court will likely fail to recover for their clients because of these shortcomings in

---

[8] Leary & Bramble, *Project Delay: Schedule Analysis Models and Techniques,* in Project Management Institute 1988 Symposium Proceedings 65 (1988).

GLOBAL IMPACT METHOD

| MONTHS | 1 | 2 | 3 | 4 | 5 | 6 | 7 | 8 | 9 | 10 | 11 | 12 | 13 | 14 | 15 | 16 | 17 | 18 | 19 |

PLAN — 365 DAYS

ACTUAL — 485 DAYS

JUSTIFIABLE EXTENSIONS — 515 DAYS

DELAYS
- A. 30
- B. 90
- C. 30

ACCELERATION (30 DAYS)

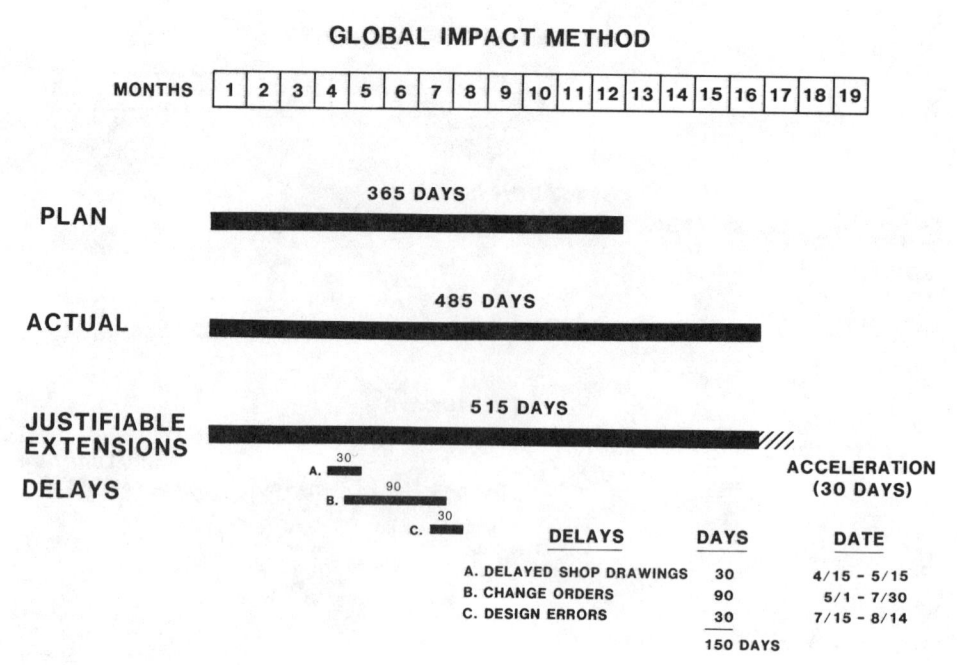

DELAYS	DAYS	DATE
A. DELAYED SHOP DRAWINGS	30	4/15 - 5/15
B. CHANGE ORDERS	90	5/1 - 7/30
C. DESIGN ERRORS	30	7/15 - 8/14
	150 DAYS	

Figure 5-2. Global impact method showing dates of delay.

logic. However, this approach has often been used by claimants and their attorneys in making initial requests for time extensions, long before lawsuits are filed. In some instances, it has been successfully employed to convince an owner to grant time extensions.

Net Impact Technique

In order to address the obvious problem of concurrency, claimants often employ another technique that allegedly depicts only the net effect of all claimed delays on a bar chart. Thus, it has been deemed the net impact technique.[9] Utilizing this method, claimants ask for a time extension for the entire delay period from the planned completion as in the contract to the actual completion of the work.

In presenting this analysis, all delays, disruptions, and suspensions are plotted on an as-built schedule, as depicted in **Figure 5-3**. Numerous delays are frequently identified and depicted. Typically, change orders are also depicted as delays, which assumes that every change had an impact on the overall project completion. With an extensive number of delaying events displayed on the as-built schedule, the claimant argues that the only logical conclusion is that the combined overwhelming effect has delayed

---
[9] *Id.*

§ 5.5 SCHEDULING TECHNIQUES

NET IMPACT TECHNIQUE

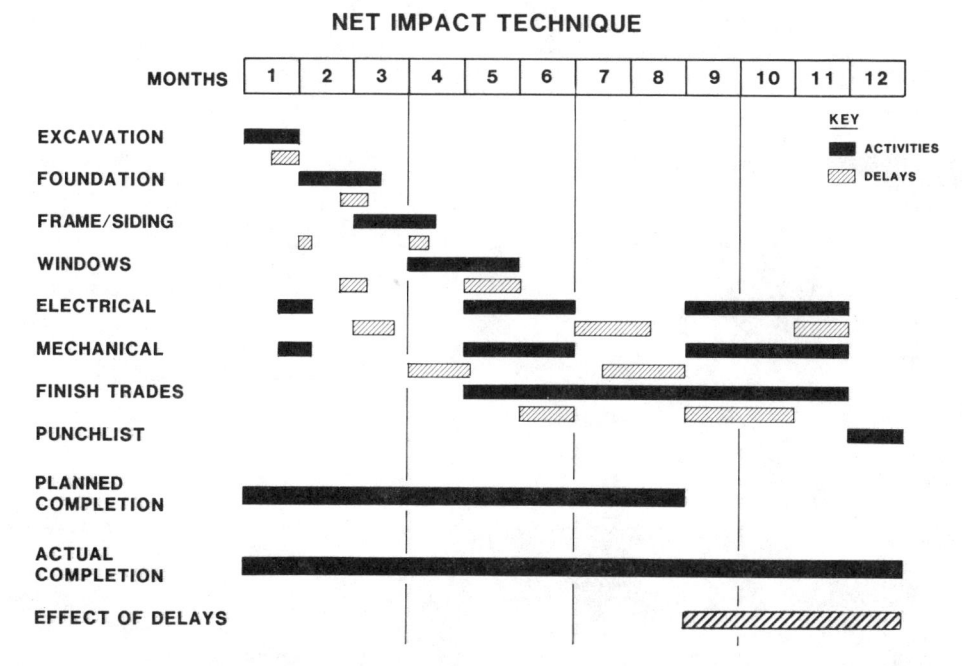

Figure 5–3. Net impact technique.

the project. The duration of each individual delay may be stated, but the cumulative sum of all of the delay durations is not at issue. Rather, the requested time extension is the difference between the as-planned completion and the actual completion, a net impact approach. Unlike the global impact method, the claimant avoids counting parallel or concurrent delays more than once. Indeed, the claimant avoids calculating the effect of *any* individual delay.[10]

As-Planned CPM Technique

Another common, but simplistic, technique of demonstrating the impact of delay is to impact the as-planned CPM schedule (see **Figure 5–4**). The various delays are presented as events with time durations and added to the as-planned network schedule, without considering the status of the schedule when the delays actually occurred. This is often a fatal flaw in logic, because by the time the delaying event occurs, the contractor's actual sequence and progress may be significantly different from the as-planned schedule. The change in sequence may be the result of circumstances unrelated to the claimed delay. Construction schedules are dynamic, and CPM scheduling allows for adjustments in the updating

---

[10] *Id.* at 66.

IMPACTED AS-PLANNED CPM

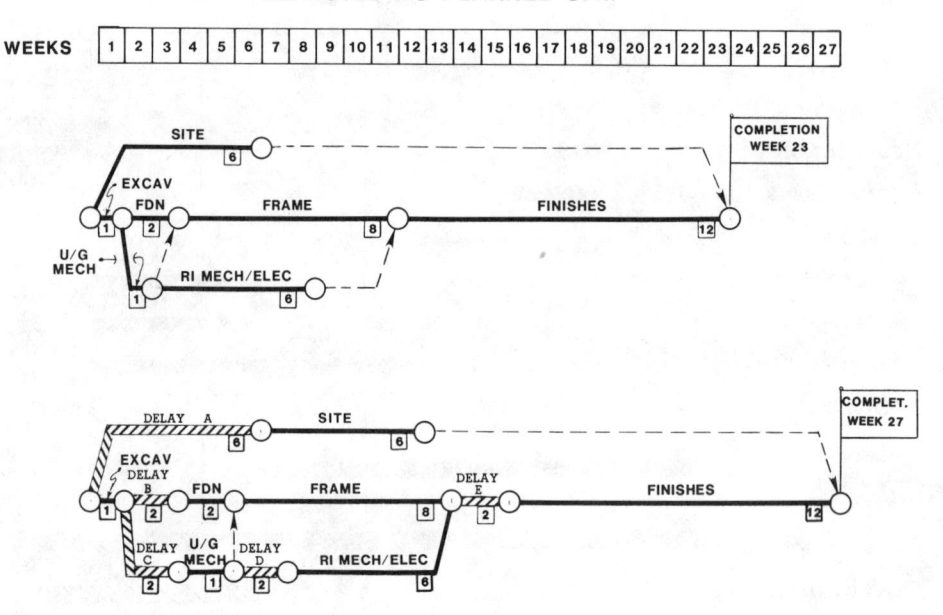

Figure 5-4. Impacted as-planned CPM.

process. Impacting an as-planned schedule that has not been updated is analogous to using last year's bus schedule to catch a bus this year; schedules change.

Further, it is often assumed in applying this technique that the claimant is not responsible for any concurrent or critical delays. Only the delays that are excusable or compensable are inserted into the impacted as-planned schedule. The conclusion is that the claimant is entitled to the difference in duration between the as-planned completion date and the adjusted completion date.

"But-For" Analysis Using As-Planned CPM

In order to address delays that are known to the opposition and are clearly the responsibility of the claimant, a variation of the impacted as-planned schedule technique can be employed. This method uses a "but-for" logic that may be equally as flawed as the impacted as-planned schedule. The basic premise of this approach is that another party can be shown to be liable through a CPM analysis that accounts for the claimant's delays, but places responsibility for the remaining delays on this other party.[11] Again, the as-planned CPM is used as a starting point (**Figure 5–5**). Delaying

---
[11] *Id.*

§ 5.5 SCHEDULING TECHNIQUES

BUT-FOR METHOD USING AS-PLANNED SCHEDULE

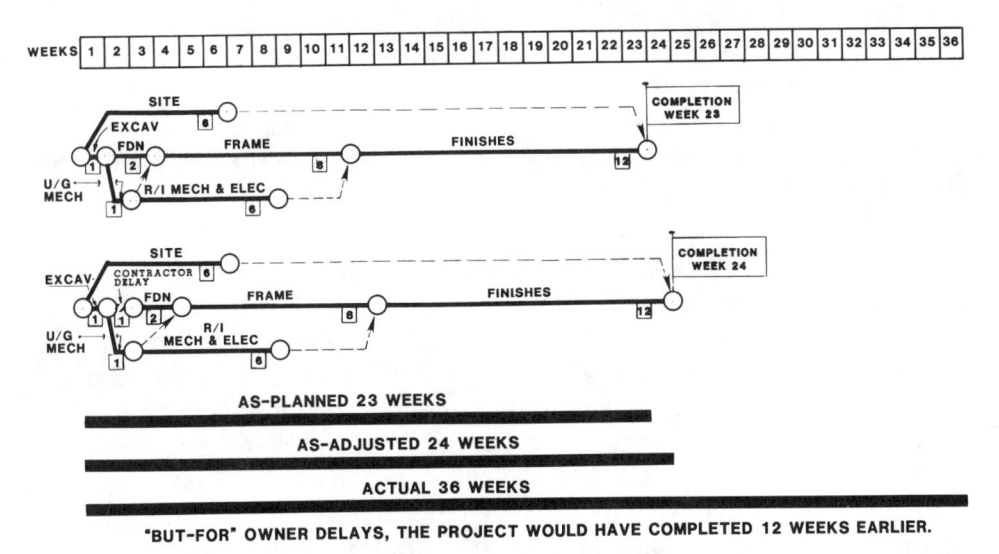

Figure 5–5. "But-For" analysis using as-planned CPM.

events for which the claimant is willing to accept responsibility are inserted into the schedule, and a recalculation of the end date is performed to obtain an as-adjusted schedule. The as-adjusted end date is often not very different from the as-planned end date, but it does account for the fact that the project may have been delayed slightly by the claimant. The actual completion date is generally significantly different from the as-adjusted end date; it is assumed that the difference must be the result of another party's delays or problems beyond the claimant's control. The duration of the claimant's delays are merely subtracted out, leaving the balance to the other party. "But-for" the other party's delays, the project would have been completed in a timely fashion.

Both owners and contractors have used this technique. For example, an owner's "but-for" analysis will identify and remove the effect of owner-caused delays. The logic is that despite the owner delays, the contractor would have been delayed by its own actions. The owner accounts for its delays and assumes that the rest are contractor delays.

Once again, the difficulty with any technique that impacts the as-planned schedule is that the delay-causing events are considered out of context and time. Applying an isolated set of delay causes to the as-planned logic has appeal at first glance. The original as-planned logic is used, and actual delaying events are accounted for. The problem lies in the fact that the adjustments are not made to the status of the schedule at the time the events occurred. The CPM logic that existed at the time of the event was possibly quite different from the as-planned logic. The critical path of a project generally changes during the course of construction. An analysis of the impact of delaying events must take the changes into account.

The "but-for" analysis relies on the presumption of a hypothetical outcome based upon what the analyst says would have happened, had a portion of the historical events not occurred. Too much weight is thrown onto the theoretical, and potentially significant cause and effect relationships are not given proper consideration in a "but-for" analysis.[12]

Collapsed As-Built Method

Another approach is to collapse the as-built schedule by removing the delays of the opposing party. After the delays are subtracted out, the remaining schedule allegedly shows the date the project would have been complete but for the delays of the other party (**Figure 5–6**). Although the starting point is the as-built history, the duration of the delays that are extracted are often arbitrarily established. Further, the schedule extraction process is often manipulated to cover up the effect of the claimant's delays.

Impacted As-Built CPM

Another way of impacting the as-built schedule is to develop it in a network format with restraints. Delaying events are also depicted as distinct

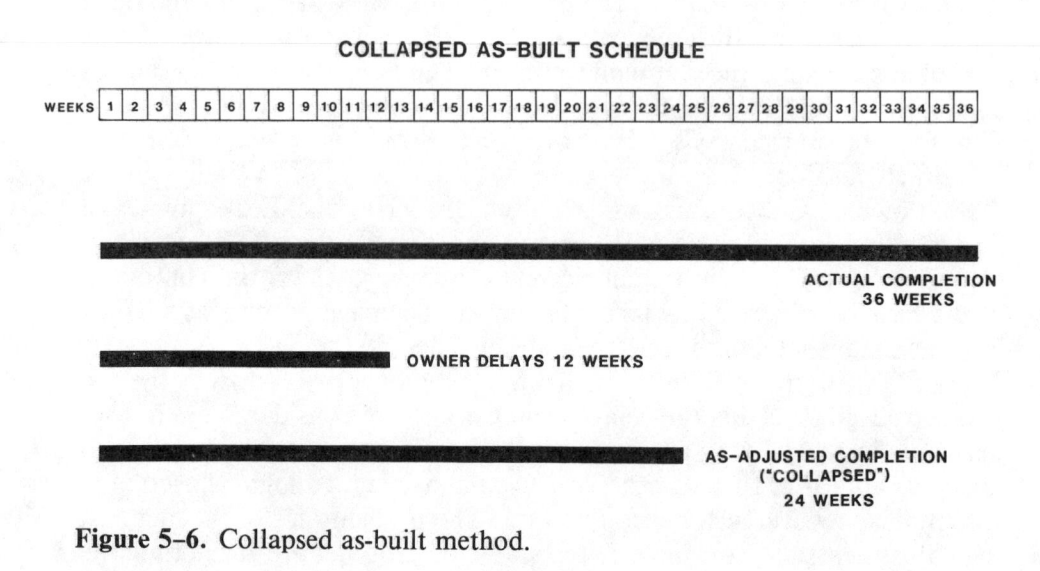

Figure 5–6. Collapsed as-built method.

---

[12] *Id.*

activities and tied to specific work activities by restraints. The critical path is determined only twice—once in the as-planned schedule and again at the end of the project. Claimants invariably tie delaying events that are the responsibility of the other party to the critical path.[13]

This method of analysis is similar to the impacted as-planned analysis, and the graphics appear very similar (**Figure 5-7**). However, the starting point is the as-built schedule rather than the as-planned schedule. Thus, the proponents of this method argue that it is based upon actual progress history.

However, the calculation of the critical path is somewhat contrived for two reasons. First, it is an after-the-fact calculation. CPM scheduling is a forward-looking management tool: it projects the future, not establishes the past. Second, the calculation is made only twice—at the start and the end of the job. It would be more appropriate to calculate the critical path on an incremental basis at the time the delay occurred. The critical path of a schedule will change dynamically throughout the course of construction. Thus, when a claimant uses the as-built schedule technique, one may question the veracity of the alleged critical path. In this sense, the as-built CPM technique is not much better than the net impact technique utilizing a bar chart. The two techniques are similar in that the claimant will acknowledge its own delays by depicting them on the as-built schedule in such a way as to reflect that they were not critical or in a manner to minimize the impact. But no attempt is made to isolate the individual impact of each delay on the project completion.[14]

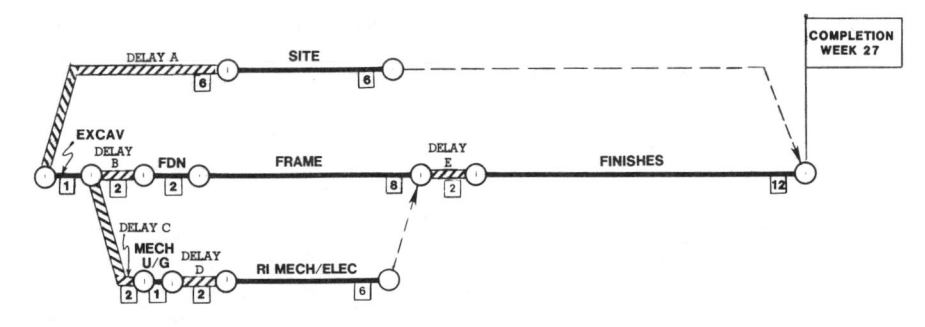

Figure 5-7. Impacted as-built CPM.

---

[13] B. Bramble & J. O'Connor, *Avoiding and Resolving Construction Claims* 4–17 (1987).

[14] Leary & Bramble, *Project Delay: Schedule Analysis Models and Techniques,* in Project Management Institute 1988 Symposium Proceedings 66 (1988).

Time Impact Analysis

Another analytical model strives to isolate and quantify the impact of individual delay-causing events through an examination of the status of the project at certain times during the course of construction. This technique or scheduling model is known as time impact analysis (TIA).[15]

The goal of TIA is to develop a "stop-action" picture of the project each time it experiences a major impact to the schedule. These impact points are known as status dates. The actual project history is determined up to the status date. Then the planned duration and sequences are used to forecast the work remaining to be completed following a status date. If the contractor's plan was revised to deal with problems and delays, the revised plan will be depicted. Thus, the TIA method accounts for both the contractor's dynamic plan and the actual project history. The overall delay to project completion for a particular impact can be determined by comparing the new adjusted completion date to the previous completion date (see **Figures 5-8** and **5-9**).

An independent evaluation is made to determine the effect that each major alleged delay-causing event had on the schedule. Perhaps progress in certain areas did not proceed for reasons unrelated to the alleged delay-causing events. Plotting the actual progress up to the status date may reveal

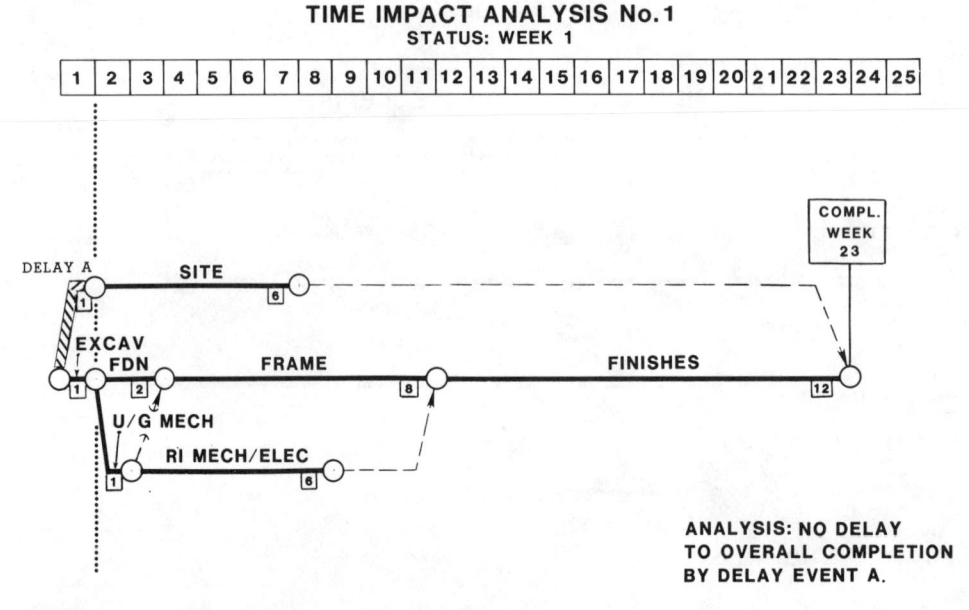

Figure 5-8. Time impact analysis no. 1.

---

[15] D'Onofrio, *Evaluating Construction Delay Claims,* MDC Advisor 1 (Spring 1988).

§ 5.5 SCHEDULING TECHNIQUES

TIME IMPACT ANALYSIS No. 2
STATUS: WEEK 3

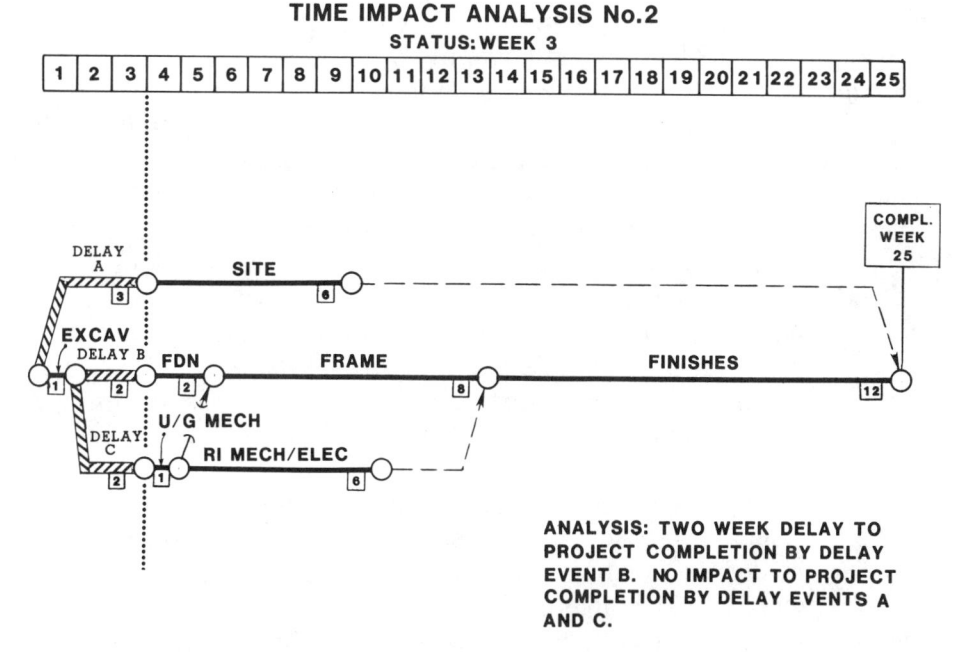

Figure 5-9. Time impact analysis no. 2.

this. A "fragnet" or subnetwork of activities may be developed to indicate the effect of events not anticipated by the original schedule. The project schedule may also have to be adjusted to reflect planning changes instituted after the project began.[16] All of these factors may be considered in impacting the project schedule at the status date.

A thorough time impact analysis will likely demonstrate the actual impact of delaying events on the remaining work. The effect of any given impact may be: (1) a day-for-day increase to the project completion date; (2) consumption of the available float[17] until the fragnet path becomes critical, and then a day-for-day increase to the project completion; (3) consumption only of the available float; (4) concurrency with another delay; or (5) recovery of the time by accelerating the pace of the work or resequencing the activities.[18]

The time impact analysis uses both the as-planned and as-built schedules to develop a model that accurately simulates the history of a project. The goal is to examine the impact of delays at the time they occurred, as well as to monitor the impact of delays throughout the history of the project. With

---

[16] *Id.*

[17] *Float* is the amount of time an activity may be delayed without extending the project completion date.

[18] B. Bramble & J. O'Connor, Avoiding and Resolving Construction Claims 4-22 (1987).

this model, fact can be separated from fiction and the true causes of project delay often can be identified and quantified.[19]

Frequently a TIA involves several updates and revisions of the project schedule. Further, the schedule may have several hundred activities. This will serve to complicate the analysis, making it difficult for lay persons to comprehend and follow. These problems can be overcome by reducing the level of detail in the schedule without distorting the logic or sequence of major work activities. It may be possible to consolidate some of the updated impacts. Theoretically, the schedule could be updated with impacts on a daily or hourly basis. Often this detail is not required to determine the effect of project delays. In **Figures 5–8** and **5–9**, we have depicted the analysis at only two status dates. The analysis for this sample project should continue to update the project history when major impacts occur.

Once the analysis has been performed in sufficient detail, the impacts can be consolidated and details summarized for presentation purposes. However, the detailed analysis may be necessary as a backup for the simplified presentation. It is like explaining a scientific theory based upon complex algebraic and calculus equations: to explain the theory for lay persons, the intricacies of the mathematics need not be detailed in the presentation, but the calculations should be available in order to demonstrate the validity of the theory. We discuss techniques for explaining network (CPM) theory to a lay jury in § 5.7.

§ 5.6 Approaching the Forum

Effective advocacy involves meaningful communication to the audience or finders of fact. The various forums available in the resolution of construction claims involve different categories of factfinders as well as different individuals. The delay claim should be structured to the specific forum as well as to the individuals serving as factfinders.

The forums include jury trials, bench trials, boards of contract appeals, arbitration, mediation, and minitrials. Advocacy in these forums is discussed in **Chapters 8** through **11**. However, delay claims may provide unique challenges that we consider in this section.

As we discuss in § 5.1, construction delay claims involve complex technical and scheduling issues. These matters should be summarized and clarified for presentation. The detail to which they are summarized and the terms of the clarification will depend upon the forum. For example, jury trials often involve great effort to lay the proper legal and factual foundation to satisfy the judge. Strict adherence to evidentiary

---

[19] D'Onofrio, *Evaluating Construction Delay Claims*, MDC Advisor 1 (Spring 1988).

§ 5.6 APPROACHING THE FORUM

and procedural rules is often a prerequisite to the submission of evidence to a jury. This is unfortunate, because it adds a dimension of detail to an already complex factual case. In addition, the factual details concerning daily reports, daily activities, scheduling aspects, individual technical issues, and so forth must be painstakingly entered into the record to lay a factual basis. Alternatively, an expert can override this tedious foundational requirement by testifying that this data is the type of information generally relied upon by experts in the field. However, the expert must explain the concept of construction scheduling, how the events worked to delay the project, the technique used to demonstrate delay, and the conclusions. This may be a very tedious undertaking for the average juror.

To relieve the tedium, many trial attorneys attempt the dramatic, appealing to underlying emotions. Another effective technique is to develop a simple theme concerning the delay. This theme serves to flavor the entire presentation; it is not just a matter of repetition by the lawyer. We discuss this in § **5.11**.

When a bench trial is undertaken for a delay claim, a no-nonsense approach based upon solid schedule analysis is generally successful. Effective advocacy will avoid novel or emotional appeals based upon the severity of the loss. Proceeding under certain legal theories, like total cost damages, is dangerous because of prerequisite conditions that judges may apply.[20] Further, defenses based upon mundane technicalities, like reliance upon the claimant's failure to comply fully with a tedious notice clause, may also be unsuccessful. Further generalizations about presenting delay claims in bench trials may require analysis of the individual judge. We discuss this in **Chapter 11**.

In the same way, generalizations about how to present delay claims before arbitration panels depend upon the composition of the panel—the number of arbitrators and their professional backgrounds and personalities. However, proponents of the arbitration of construction disputes claim that the parties will receive more predictable results from arbitration because the panelists "are themselves experts."[21] In most instances, a more sophisticated analysis of construction delay is both possible and desirable in arbitration. Most arbitrators understand the basics of construction and

---

[20] The prerequisites in resorting to total cost damages may include proof that (1) there is no other way of estimating damages; (2) there are no errors or underbids in the claimant's bid; (3) the claimant's inefficiencies (if any) can be distinguished; and (4) the actual costs incurred by the contractor are reasonable. G.M. Shupe, Inc. v. United States, 5 Ct. Cl. 662 (1984); Pittman Constr. Co. v. United States, 2 Cl. Ct. 211 (1983); Moorehead Constr. Co. v. City of Grand Forks, 508 F.2d 1008 (8th Cir. 1975); *see* B. Bramble & M. Callahan, Construction Delay Claims § 10.6 (1987).

[21] American Arbitration Association, The Lawyer and Arbitration 6.

network scheduling. However, conventional understanding is often inadequate for comprehending a detailed, sophisticated, and accurate analysis of project delays. Any attempt to educate the panelists on construction scheduling may fall on deaf and resisting ears because they may already perceive themselves as experts. Therefore, effective advocacy in arbitrating delay claims may involve a basic presentation of conventional construction scheduling and an appeal to the panel's "expertise," even if it is not truly accurate. The author has observed this phenomenon when expert witnesses used "but-for" and collapsed as-built analyses accompanied by detailed, colorful, and complex charts that were somewhat misleading. It was a difficult undertaking to convince the panel that the appealing graphics were based upon faulty analysis.

The advocate will often find the judges in the federal contract forums to be more sophisticated and more predictable than arbitration panels. Like arbitration hearings, the surroundings may appear informal. However, many of the boards of contract appeals and claims court judges are detail-oriented, having authored numerous findings of facts relating to contract disputes. A complex analysis will often be appreciated and understood, especially if tied to specific facts and project records. Use of network analysis techniques to prove delay is almost mandatory. The attorney should appeal to the technical expertise of the judge in contract scheduling matters. Novel theories may be tested, but they should not be the sole basis for recovery. The concepts of constructive acceleration, cumulative impact, and unabsorbed overhead had their origin and development in such forums. Further, it is possible to predict the disposition of such judges by studying their opinions in other contract disputes. In this author's opinion, many well-reasoned, technically sound, and equitable decisions come out of the federal contract forums.

In attempts to avoid formal disposition of claims by a third party (judge, jury, arbitration), the parties may resort to voluntary methods of resolution such as mediation and minitrials. These forums, often used in construction disputes, are designed to get the disputing parties to resolve the dispute themselves, rather than have a decision imposed upon them. In dealing with such a forum, the attorney should keep in mind that the goal is to convince the opposition of the merit of your case.

In a minitrial, the case is made in the presence of the other parties. Although the presentation is directed at the minitrial panel to obtain a favorable advisory verdict, another level of advocacy should be directed to the opposition, who must decide whether to accept the advisory opinion or to otherwise settle the case.

Because of the summary nature of the minitrial proceedings, it is difficult to present a detailed and complex explanation of construction delay. Thus, many attorneys are tempted to employ an analytical technique such as the net impact method, as we discuss in § **5.5**. The technique is simply explained, the number of delaying events appears overwhelming, and it does not take much time. The minitrial panel may be impressed, but the opposition has examined the same events, and may have a similar chart depicting an overwhelming number of delays that it attributes to your client.

A more sophisticated technique should be employed to convince both the minitrial panel and the opposition of the extent of delays suffered by your client, and to minimize the extent of delays alleged by the opposition. However, the challenge is to do this in a summary fashion. The theory of the case and methodology can be explained, and the complex analysis of one or two delays can be presented as examples of the approach. Then the other delays can be discussed as events, but with the detailed schedule analysis summarized. Thus, the overall theory of the case is presented, but the detailed scheduling analysis is limited to one or two delays; however, the entire detailed analysis should be available for examination by the minitrial panel or the opposition.

When resorting to the mediation process, the attorney must realize that communication to the opposition is made indirectly through the mediator. Presentation of a detailed analysis to the mediator is often unwarranted. From individual discussions with the parties, the mediator will look for weaknesses in their positions. Often details of the scheduling analysis and facts relating to specific delays are not the basis for mediation. Overall and equitable considerations may prove more compelling to the mediator. Thus, the attorney must fashion a delay analysis and presentation with this in mind.

§ 5.7 Explaining CPM Scheduling

Network scheduling techniques have been developed and applied to construction projects for well over two decades. However, these management techniques are not universally understood or applied in the construction industry. There are many who profess a passing knowledge of them, but the level of conventional knowledge within the industry is probably relatively low.

Many attorneys elect to utilize CPM scheduling or other network scheduling methodology to prove or refute project delay. Indeed, this may be mandatory in certain jurisdictions.[22] If this is the case, the attorney may find it necessary to present background and explanatory testimony on how network scheduling works and how it identifies the critical path activities.

---

[22] Natkin & Co. v. George A. Fuller Co., 347 F. Supp. 17 (W.D. Mo. 1972); Minmar Builders, Inc., GSBCA No. 3430, 72-2 B.C.A. (CCH) ¶ 9599 (1972); *see* B. Bramble & M. Callahan, Construction Delay Claims § 9.4 (1987).

This is especially true if the factfinder is a lay jury rather than an arbitration panel. Arbitrators perceiving themselves as experts in the construction industry may be insulted by the presentation of elementary scheduling instructions. In a bench trial, the judge may welcome the explanation, unless the forum is the United States Claims Court or one of the boards of contract appeals. Even in these federal forums, it may be appropriate to suggest to the judge in a pretrial briefing that a brief background explanation of scheduling techniques at trial might be helpful.

When an explanatory overview of CPM scheduling is appropriate, the attorney should proffer expert witness testimony. It may be appropriate for the expert to select an everyday event common to the factfinders, and schedule it using CPM. The author has observed such presentations using the preparation of meals, fixing a flat tire, doing laundry, and cleaning the house. Whatever the project, it should be one requiring the management of several concurrent tasks that are performed by more than one person. Preparation of meals is especially popular; some that have been used are the Thanksgiving meal, a steak dinner, breakfast, and even regional favorites such as hominy grits, Cajun cooking, and barbecue. Whatever the event, it should be geared to establish a rapport between the expert and factfinder. Use of amusing anecdotes depends upon the humor of the factfinder. Often such amusement is a welcome relief to the otherwise tedious nature of hearings in construction disputes.

The illustration should include one activity that is clearly crucial to the timely completion of the project. For example, in preparing a Thanksgiving dinner, the critical activity would be cooking the turkey. If the turkey goes into the oven later than planned, dinner will almost inevitably be late. Thus, the factfinder can understand the concept of the critical path. This analogy can be the point of reference to the critical path of the construction project. For example, an analogy can be made between the timely erection of structural steel and the roasting of the turkey. Appropriate analogies to concurrent delays, noncritical activities, and excusable delays can be derived from the meal examples. Care should be taken to assure that the example illustrates the type of situations encountered by the client, and preferably debunks allegations by the opponents.

§ 5.8 Explaining Delays

The scheduling example used to explain the concept of CPM scheduling can also be used to provide illustrations of project delays. In most instances, delay to one particular activity will not serve as the basis for a delay claim; the overall project completion must be delayed. The delay must affect a critical activity. For example, during the first hour of meal preparation, a 15-minute delay in the preparation of the salad will not likely delay dinner. The salad is a noncritical activity. However, delay in putting the turkey in the oven will delay dinner.

The concept of concurrent delays can also be illustrated by the meal example. The carving of the turkey may be delayed because of a malfunctioning electric knife. In such an instance, the late arrival of one guest could be considered concurrent. These same examples may illustrate the concepts of excusable and nonexcusable delays. For example, the cook generally would not consider it excusable for a next-door neighbor to be late for dinner in an attempt to be "posh." However, the other guests may excuse the host for a brief delay to locate an appropriate carving knife.

When the analogies no longer illustrate the point, the attorney should cease reference to the meal scheduling exercise. The opposition's attorney also will likely object to liberal reference to the analogy, or worse yet, use the illustration to demonstrate its own case. Logical flaws in the sample schedule or analogies may prove equally embarrassing.

§ 5.9 Explaining Acceleration

Resort to the meal schedule can illustrate the concept of acceleration as well as delay. The turkey dinner shows the difficulty of accelerating any project. Increasing the oven temperature from 400° to 450° will not expedite the roasting of the turkey. Perhaps the turkey could be transferred into a microwave oven, but this may be undesirable in terms of browning the turkey and even thorough cooking. Likewise, there may be unsatisfactory side effects of acceleration in construction projects.

The dilemma of constructive acceleration can also be illustrated. A critical activity may be delayed, for example, by a 30-minute power outage to the electric range, but the host will not allow the cook to postpone dinner. The frantic cook may resort to the microwave oven and bring in additional kitchen help to handle the emergency. Similarly, contractors refused a time extension after suffering an excusable delay may undertake desperate attempts to make up for the lost time.

§ 5.10 Using Graphics

Graphic illustrations are very valuable to the advocate in persuading the factfinder to understand and accept the client's position concerning construction delay. Very complex situations can be summarized and depicted in graphic form. Rather than reading from a script or notes, an expert witness can use the graphics as a cue card to discuss the details of project delay. The factfinder will welcome the change in pace offered by a visual presentation, because much of the other evidence in a construction delay case is oral testimony and voluminous documentation. Time concepts are easily depicted and understood by use of a timeline. Thus, a two dimensional graphic can illustrate the flow and disruption of time on a construction project.

Color is routinely used on timeline exhibits to add interest and meaning to the chart and to the opinion concerning the delay. Typically, red is used for delays, yellow for delays to noncritical activities or activities performed with reduced productivity, and green for acceleration. Colors and contrasts may be used to distinguish as-planned durations from as-built durations. But the use of too many colors or noncomplementary colors may have a deleterious impact upon the viewer. The author has observed some delay claim graphics that resemble a color selection chart in a psychedelic paint shop. The first reaction is curiosity, and then the complexity of color scheme leads to tedium.

The problem of graphic complexity must be squarely faced by both the expert and the advocate. Too much detail in color or too many schedule activities may give the appearance of thoroughness, but they result in boredom. Too few graphic elements may give the impression that the expert is glossing over important issues. It is not only the complexity of the individual graphic, but the number of graphics that must be considered. Perhaps the solution is to proffer many graphics, but only in such a way as to demonstrate that a thorough analysis has been performed and is available. One or two detailed graphics are examined in detail, but the summary chart is used as the deus ex machina to culminate the case.

The attorney must also realize that colorful and appealing graphics cannot substitute for sensible and thorough analysis. Effective graphic design will not serve to cover a simpleminded analytical technique. On the other hand, the disposition of many scheduling engineers to pedantic detail must be made presentable, understandable, and appealing to the factfinder.

§ 5.11 Developing Themes for Presentation

When examining construction delay, the attorney often will encounter several hundred individual events that may be the cause of construction delay. The mind as well as the patience of any factfinder would be overwhelmed by such a number of delays. Advocating the merits of such a number of issues is almost an impossible task unless the issues are categorized in some meaningful way that can reduce the complexity of the matter. One way is to eliminate all but the most important delay-causing problems. Another way is to underscore and compare the dilemma of the factfinder to that of the claimant: in the same way that the jury is overwhelmed by the number of problems, so was the claimant.

Perhaps a more effective technique is to categorize the various delays into a few underlying or related problems. There may have been innumerable change orders, requests for design clarification, information requests, and shop drawing problems, all of which delayed the project either individually or cumulatively. Any of these matters may be symptoms of poor design by the architect. The fundamental problem of poor design becomes the advocate's theme, and the numerous events become meaningful as examples of the underlying problem. Another tactic is to allege that the project delay was the result of mismanagement of the contract administration process by the owner and architect: the change orders, clarifications, shop drawings, and so forth were being processed in a tardy fashion. Each late shop drawing will assist in proving both delay and mismanagement.

It is possible for the contractor's attorney to develop a theme that does not blame either the owner or the designer. For example, the project delay was the result of the contractor encountering several problems which were unknown at the time of the bid: rock beneath the surface, asbestos concealed by existing walls, and mislocated utility lines. No one is to blame because these were hidden conditions. A claim like this can be presented to the owner and designer, who may not take personal offense. Such differing site conditions may even be the basis for the owner to receive a grant adjustment by a funding agency.

Themes are important in the presentation of delay claims, and they can also be used to simplify the complex in other types of construction claims, as we discuss in **Chapter 11**.

§ 5.12 Defenses to Delay Claims

Several approaches have been employed by attorneys to defend against delay claims. These attorneys may be representing owners defending against contractor claims or contractors defending against subcontractor claims. The defenses can be classified as legal, factual, strategic, scheduling, and cost.

Legal defenses often rely upon contractual provisions. For example, the contract may contain a no damages for delay clause which would purport to limit the contractor's recovery to a time extension (not costs) for any delays. As with other exculpatory clauses, courts have developed several exceptions to avoid enforcement of the clause when it may lead to a harsh result.[23] Other legal defenses may rely upon what are perceived as boilerplate clauses, such as notice and documentation requirements.[24] These

---

[23] B. Bramble & M. Callahan, Construction Delay Claims §§ 2.42–2.47 (1987).
[24] Id. §§ 2.12–2.17.

defenses are often ineffective, because courts may resort to such legal fictions as constructive notice[25] to overcome the exculpatory effect of procedural contractual requirements.

Other defenses are based upon factual considerations. Typically it is argued that the claimant was not truly delayed because there were several available work areas despite the problems encountered. This argument assumes that it was reasonable for the claimant to resequence its work, and that other available work areas were connected to critical activities. Another factual allegation is that the reason for project delay was that the claimant failed to provide an adequate work force. Often this leads to a "What came first, the chicken or the egg?" dispute. The claimant will allege that the work force was reduced because of the defendant-caused problems or in anticipation of the problems. The defendant will argue that the claimant was understaffed, and the occurrence of the other problems was a mere fortuity, not a cause of project delay. Alleging claimant mismanagement is a more difficult defense to prove. It is very easy to uncover incidents of what appear to be contractor mismanagement—superintendents given to alcohol, arguments with subcontractors, broken equipment, and lazy workers. But such facts do not prove delay unless tied to the schedule analysis.

Often such strategic maneuvers are "spoiler" defenses. The defendant's attorney is attempting to muddy the waters by creating a doubt as to the merit of the contractor's claim. Unfortunately, this is often ineffective advocacy for the defense of delay claims. In a civil case, it is not enough for the defendant to create a reasonable doubt. Rather, the defendant should endeavor to identify specific claimant-caused problems that resulted in project delays. The schedule analysis can be a major line of defense. Perhaps delays attributable to the claimant can be shown to be concurrent with otherwise compensable delays. Unless the delays can be clearly apportioned, courts may not allow the claimant to recover for otherwise compensable delays.[26] Perhaps the defendant's scheduling expert can demonstrate that the events alleged by the claimant had no impact upon the overall project completion, that is, the delays were not critical.

If all else fails, the defendant can resort to challenging the claimed damages. We discuss damages in **Chapter 7**. Perhaps an audit will reveal that the delay had no impact upon the claimant's cost of performance. More realistically, the audit may reveal that despite the delay, the contractor still made a lot of money on the job, perhaps more than anticipated by the bid. The claimant will then have to argue that even more money could have been made but for the delays. The latter argument often elicits little sympathy and small recovery. Finally, the audit may

---

[25] *Id.*

[26] *Id., see* B. Bramble & M. Callahan, Construction Delay Claims § 2.37 (1987).

reveal significant overstatement of damages. Again, this behavior by the claimant may result in an unsympathetic jury.

§ 5.13 Conclusion

Construction delay claims are very complex, and often turn upon the ability of the attorney to marshal an overwhelming number of facts. A crucial aspect of preparation is a thorough and sophisticated schedule analysis. However, in order to persuade the factfinder, it is imperative that the delay claim be simplified for presentation. This can be accomplished by developing a few straightforward themes and by using graphics effectively. The attorney should make analogies to everyday life experiences, because time is an important commodity in the life of most people in the twentieth century. The strategies described in this chapter can be used to make construction delay understood and appreciated by different factfinders in the various forums used to resolve construction claims.

CHAPTER 6

LOST PRODUCTIVITY CLAIMS

Stephen M. Rymal, P.E.

Stephen M. Rymal graduated cum laude from Villanova University in 1978 as a civil engineer, and is a member of Tau Beta Pi and Phi Kappa Phi National Honor Societies. In 1983, he became a licensed professional engineer in the State of Pennsylvania. Mr. Rymal worked with the Naval Facilities Engineering Command as a resident engineer in charge of construction and thereafter was employed with MDC Systems Corp., a subsidiary of Day & Zimmerman, Inc., specializing in engineering and construction litigation. While working as a professional engineer, Mr. Rymal earned a juris doctorate at Temple University School of Law. He is a member of the National Society of Professional Engineers, the American Bar Association, the American Arbitration Association, and the Society of American Military Engineers. He is currently employed with the Philadelphia-based firm of Cozen and O'Connor.

§ 6.1   Introduction
§ 6.2   Definition of Loss of Efficiency
§ 6.3   Obstacles to Recovery for Lost Productivity Claims
§ 6.4   Judicial Recognition of Lost Productivity Claims
§ 6.5   Causes of Loss of Efficiency
§ 6.6   —Increased Labor Forces
§ 6.7   —Trade Stacking
§ 6.8   —Overtime
§ 6.9   —Adverse Weather
§ 6.10 —Out-of-Sequence Work
§ 6.11 —Acceleration
§ 6.12 —Change Orders
§ 6.13 —Constructive Changes

§ 6.14   —Disruption
§ 6.15   Proving Lost Productivity Claims
§ 6.16   Liability
§ 6.17   Causation and Injury
§ 6.18   —Experts
§ 6.19   —Trade Publications
§ 6.20   —Historical Data
§ 6.21   —Job-Specific Data
§ 6.22   Damages
§ 6.23   Conclusion

§ 6.1   Introduction

Despite the most thorough planning efforts and the use of sophisticated computerized scheduling techniques, construction remains a risky business. Some risks such as seasonal weather, material lead time, equipment downtime, trade coordination, and labor strikes are inherent in the nature of construction. Other unanticipated events may impact the planned flow of field operations, causing delays and disruptions. The result can be higher labor and equipment costs and a relentless attack on anticipated profits. Success in the construction industry is often simply defined as survival.

The astute contractor recognizes the potential for additional unexpected costs. One approach is to factor them into the bid as a contingency with the hope that they are sufficiently covered. Another approach is to keep records of these costs and submit them as a change to the contract or as a claim. The second approach may be appropriate when the cause of the disruption can be attributed to the direct actions (or inactions) of a third party—the owner, the architect/engineer, or the construction manager. Such third-party actions or impacts include excessive changes, design errors/conflicts, missing information, delays/holds on all or part of the work, and unexpected or differing site conditions. These problems will likely impact the contractor's original construction plan and drive up the cost of the construction project. The impact of these problems is twofold: delay costs due to extension of the project completion and loss of labor productivity. **Chapter 5** discusses delay claims. In this chapter we examine claims for lost productivity, also called loss of efficiency claims.

§ 6.2   Definition of Loss of Efficiency

Loss of efficiency is a generic phrase that encompasses a wide range of phenomena afflicting complex projects, primarily construction projects. At its core, loss of efficiency relates to an additional expenditure of limited

§ 6.2 LOSS OF EFFICIENCY

resources, that is, labor, material, and equipment, without achieving a commensurate increase in productivity. Loss of efficiency is the additional effort required to complete a work activity above and beyond the estimated resources originally anticipated. Simply put, the issue is the increased level of effort required to complete an activity. For example, that which was estimated to take four labor hours to complete takes eight labor hours due to the occurrence of some external phenomena. In this example, the actual expenditure of eight labor hours less the estimated four labor hours leaves us with four labor hours of inefficiency. This represents a 50 percent productivity loss.

The phenomena causing loss of efficiency usually take the form of disorders in the anticipated planned sequence of events.[1] Some of the causes of inefficiency are:[2]

1. Increased labor/additional crews
2. Trade stacking
3. Overtime
4. Adverse weather
5. Out-of-sequence work
6. Disruption
7. Acceleration
8. Contract changes
9. Constructive changes
10. Restricted access
11. Learning curves.

In fact, it is not uncommon for subcontractors to estimate a bid contingency amount to cover any anticipated minor disruptions.[3] The issue of reasonable foreseeability and trade practice in this area is the primary cause of tension between the owner and the contractor, or between the general contractor and subcontractor. Specifically, the issue is whether the encountered disruption should have been foreseen by the contractor and a contingency included in the bid price.

This tension, however, is a product of the bidding environment. If the contract is negotiated between the parties, then the contractor has an

---

[1] "When the actual progress of the work differs from the schedule provided in the bidding documents, the contractor will experience wasted manpower, lower productivity, excessive costs for familiarizing new employees, and other unanticipated additional cost." National Elect. Contractors Ass'n, Rate of Manpower Consumption in Electrical Construction (May 1983).

[2] *See* U.S. Indus., Inc. v. Blake Constr. Co., 671 F.2d 539, 546 (D.C. Cir. 1982).

[3] "Certain factors affecting productivity of pipefitters should be recognized and allowances made during preparation of job estimates." Mechanical Contractors Ass'n of Am., Management Methods Committee Bulletin No. 21 (Dec. 1968).

opportunity to discuss contingencies and include them in its pricing. On the other hand, if the contract is awarded on the basis of competitive bids, the inclusion of a contingency factor, no matter how minimal, threatens the contractor's chances of being low bidder.

Regardless of the bidding environment, a contractor suffering extreme loss of productivity may seek to recover its losses through the change order or equitable adjustment process, or through litigation. Lost productivity claims are becoming more frequent, though there are some difficult proof problems that claimants often face.

§ 6.3 Obstacles to Recovery for Lost Productivity Claims

The major difficulties in recovering for a lost productivity claim are (1) accurate quantification of damages, and (2) realistic assignment of liability. Despite the myriad of construction cost controls implemented by knowledgeable contractors, these fundamental aspects of a lost productivity claim are difficult to establish.

Proving losses from construction delay is not as difficult as proving losses from reduced productivity. The general acceptance of critical path method (CPM) scheduling as a construction management tool has greatly facilitated analysis of delay impacts and issues. Many projects of even moderate size employ CPM scheduling as a specification requirement or as a standard approach for managing the project. If properly executed, the delays caused by specific impacts to the construction operation can be logically established, either manually or by a computer. The associated time-related damages can then be readily identified as a basis for the claim. These damages generally include such items as extended field management costs, extended field office costs, extended equipment rental costs, and related indirect costs.

The analysis of the lost productivity impacts to construction operations presents a more difficult problem. Not only must the specific disruptions be identified, but a realistic dollar value also must be determined that can be attributed solely to the disruption, as opposed to other ongoing, nonimpacted construction activities. In many instances, this appears to be a virtually impossible task. Alternative approaches that are acceptable to both the opposing parties and the adjudicating entity must be devised to solve this problem.

Quantification is straightforward when labor, equipment, and their respective time frames can all be clearly identified and directly associated with the disruption. Only assignment of responsibility remains to be resolved. However, more often than not, the issue of responsibility is clouded at best, and damages are difficult to quantify except in gross terms.

There is no doubt that lost productivity due to disruption is a very costly matter. Partly due to the increasing cost of labor, a loss of efficiency claim can easily approach thousands of dollars per hour. For example, assuming an average labor cost of $30 per hour (including benefits, federal, state, and local taxes, etc.), a medium-sized construction force of 250 workers costs $7,500 per hour or $60,000 per day. A construction force of 500 workers doubles the cost to $15,000 per hour or $120,000 per day. Thus, any disruption lasting even a few hours can be extremely costly.

Contractors are discovering that labor inefficiencies can easily double projected manpower for a multiplicity of reasons. If the inefficiencies are owner-caused, then contractors may resort to legal remedies to recover damages. However, due to the complex nature of construction and the simplistic tendency to term all construction problems as delays, contractors frequently couch their claims in terms of delay, and fail to establish responsibility and proper proof of damages for lost productivity.

§ 6.4 Judicial Recognition of Lost Productivity Claims

Judicial recognition of loss of efficiency claims in construction has been a painful, evolutionary process due to the complexities of construction, limited analytical yardsticks, and poorly documented case files. Lost productivity claims are problematic because hundreds of sophisticated details must be presented to the trier of fact in a comprehensive and cohesive manner. As a result, they are not easily understood by judges and juries alike. Sometimes, the parties to the litigation themselves do not understand all the intricate details of the case.

> [E]xcept in the middle of a battlefield, nowhere must men coordinate the movement of other men and all materials in the midst of such chaos and with such limited certainty of present facts and future occurrences as in a huge construction project. . . . Even the most painstaking planning frequently turns out to be mere conjecture and accommodation to changes must necessarily be of the rough, quick and ad hoc sort, analogous to ever-changing commands on the battlefield. Further, it is a difficult task for a court to be able to examine testimony and evidence in the quiet of a courtroom several years later concerning such confusion and then extract from them a determination of precisely when the disorder and constant readjustment, which is to be expected by any subcontractor on a job site, became so extreme, so debilitating and so unreasonable as to constitute a breach of contract between a contractor and a subcontractor.[4]

---

[4] Blake Constr. Co. v. C.J. Coakley Co., 431 A.2d 569, 575 (D.C. 1981).

One of the restraints on the development of loss of efficiency claims is the common practice of citing disruption and delay claims as being synonymous. In fact, they are very different, especially in terms of damages. Over the years, courts have generally recognized delay claims filed by contractors as valid and compensable provided they are delays for which the contractor is not responsible.

In *U.S. Industries, Inc. v. Blake Construction Co.,*[5] the court upheld a jury award of $9.2 million in favor of a subcontractor, U.S. Industries, Inc. (USI), against the general contractor, Blake Construction Co. (Blake). Of the total award, $4.8 million was disruption damages due to (1) rework of areas damaged by Blake and (2) Blake's failure to schedule and coordinate the work, which diminished USI's productivity. It is important to note that the $4.8 million award for disruption damages was in addition to $3.3 million awarded for delay damages. Therefore, the court as well as the jury clearly recognized a difference between the two types of claims.

The circuit court reasoned that "[u]nlike the delay claim, the disruption claim is not intended to redress USI's loss from being unable to work, but compensate USI for the damages it suffered from Blake's actions that made its work more difficult and expensive than USI anticipated and than it should have cost."[6]

At trial, the district court clearly instructed the jury that they must eliminate any possibility of a double recovery for the same damages under both theories. In reviewing the jury's verdict and damage award, the circuit court felt that the jury properly distinguished the two claims and properly allocated the damages incurred by USI between disruption and delay.

In *Luria Bros. & Co. v. United States,*[7] the court awarded loss of efficiency damages to a contractor in addition to delay damages where there was a 518-day overrun in contract completion. The court clearly acknowledged the differences between the delay and disruption claims and their respective damages. "That loss of productivity in labor resulting from improper delays caused the defendant is an item of damage for which plaintiff is entitled to recover admits of no doubt . . . nor does the impossibility of proving the amount with exactitude bar recovery for the item."[8]

In fashioning a remedy for the disruption claim, the court allowed a percentage of the total labor cost as the loss of efficiency damages based on the unrebutted testimony of the contractor's expert witness. These loss of efficiency damages were in addition to the standard delay damages, which included idle equipment, field supervision, winter protection,

---

[5] 671 F.2d 539 (D.C. Cir. 1982).
[6] *Id.* at 546.
[7] 369 F.2d 701 (Ct. Cl. 1966).
[8] *Id.* at 712.

rehandling materials, maintaining excavations, wage and material price increases, insurance premiums, and home office overhead. Therefore, by awarding damages based on a percentage of the total labor cost incurred, the court recognized that loss of efficiency damages relate strictly to the actual growth in labor without a commensurate increase in productivity. Although arbitrary, the percentage allowed reflects that part of the total labor cost incurred that could not be reasonably anticipated and that resulted from the differing site conditions and subsequent government interference (disruption) in the planned sequence of work.

Both of these cases clearly demonstrate that the courts recognize the validity of loss of efficiency claims. In addition, the cases distinguish loss of efficiency claims from delay claims in fact patterns dealing with both. Thus, loss of efficiency claims have emerged from the shadow of delay claims.

Other cases in this chapter indicate that courts recognize lost productivity claims as a theory for recovery separate and apart from delay. However, proof of liability, causation, and damages for lost productivity present difficult factual and legal issues that are often misunderstood.

§ 6.5 Causes of Loss of Efficiency

As discussed in § 6.2, there are many causes of lost productivity. Many of them may appear to overlap or even be associated with the same phenomena. However, courts have recognized the following factors as potential causes of recovery:

1. Increased labor/additional crews
2. Trade stacking
3. Overtime
4. Adverse weather
5. Out-of-sequence work
6. Acceleration
7. Contract changes
8. Constructive changes
9. Disruption.

This list is far from exhaustive and only represents those factors that are more common to the majority of construction projects generally and that courts have recognized specifically. The cases that follow demonstrate the acceptance or rejection by the courts of the phenomena causing lost productivity, and at the same time offer some insight into the obstacles facing the attorneys involved in construction litigation.

§ 6.6 —Increased Labor Forces

The loss of efficiency associated with increased labor and additional crews resembles what economists have termed the law of diminishing returns. Applied to construction, the theory propounds that once an optimum level of labor is achieved, subsequent infusion of labor will only impair productivity and result in a net loss of efficiency. Construction managers would agree that, theoretically, there is a limit to the number of workers that can be optimally productive in any defined work space, such as a floor of a building. Unfortunately, they may not necessarily agree on the analytical method of computing the optimum work force.

The optimum crew size and number of crews depend upon the trade involved, the specific work activity being performed, the quantity of work, the physical location of the work, the available equipment and tools, and the specified quality of work. Despite this, the prevalent mindset of most people is still that the more workers you have on a project, the more productive the workers will be. This pitfall is particularly appealing to owners and general contractors who prefer to mask any interferences they created with allegations that the subcontractors do not have sufficient labor forces on site.

In *S. Leo Harmonay, Inc. v. Binks Manufacturing Co.*,[9] a mechanical piping contractor, S. Leo Harmonay (Harmonay), sued a general contractor, Binks Manufacturing Co. (Binks), as a result of a project involving the expansion of an automotive assembly plant. Despite the existence of excusable delays, Harmonay was directed to meet the original completion date. Harmonay increased its crew size from 26 workers to a peak of 98 workers. In addition, it introduced two additional shifts, thereby conducting 24-hour per day operations.

Harmonay claimed that the increased labor and additional crews resulted in a net loss of efficiency. The additional labor force exceeded the anticipated, optimum labor levels as well as the work available. The court awarded Harmonay damages for loss of efficiency based on the personal observations of their expert witness who compared the situation to "a zoo, fiasco, a nightmare."[10]

§ 6.7 —Trade Stacking

Trade stacking involves the pyramid effect of having more than one trade working in the same area simultaneously. Optimum efficiency within a particular trade is generally achieved by allowing each trade exclusive access to an area. The introduction of other trades into the same area reduces

---

[9] 597 F. Supp. 1014 (S.D.N.Y. 1984).
[10] *Id.* at 1029.

efficiency as different workers attempt to maneuver around and over each other's work, material, tools, and equipment.

Trade stacking can aptly be described by the adage "Too many cooks spoil the broth." The effect in the kitchen is similar to that on a construction project—confusion and congestion. Forcing two or more contractors to work within the same defined space only results in congestion of personnel, inability to stock materials and equipment, increased safety hazards, and limited mobility to move equipment or scaffolding.

In *McCarty Corp. v. Pullman-Kellogg*,[11] a thermal insulating subcontractor, McCarty, sued the prime contractor, Pullman-Kellogg, for breach of contract. McCarty claimed that Pullman-Kellogg obstructed McCarty's performance in several ways, including overmanning the jobsite. Pullman-Kellogg awarded subcontracts to three local welding and pipefitting companies and removed its own welders and pipefitters from the jobsite, resulting in many more workers on the site.

The court specifically recognized the theoretical proposition proffered by McCarty's expert witness that it is possible to introduce only so many workers on the same jobsite at the same time before they interfere with each other's job performance.

§ 6.8 —Overtime

Overtime reduces work output and efficiency through physical fatigue and depressed mental attitude.[12] Studies conducted by the Business Roundtable's Construction Industry Cost Effectiveness Task Force indicate that overtime impairs productivity because of physical fatigue, increased absenteeism, increased likelihood of accidents, and overall reduced quality of work installed.[13] For instance, the Task Force reported that, as a general rule, when overtime exceeds eight hours per day and 48 hours per week, three hours of overtime are equivalent to only two hours of productive work for light activity. For heavier activity, two hours of overtime are equivalent to only one hour of productive work.

As a general rule, courts have accepted the proposition that overtime results in loss of efficiency.[14] In *Havens Steel Co. v. Randolph Engineering Co.*,[15] the exhaust stack erection and insulation subcontractor,

---

[11] 571 F. Supp. 1341 (M.D. La. 1983).

[12] *See* Mechanical Contractors Ass'n of Am., Management Methods Bulletin No. 58 (Jan. 1978).

[13] Business Roundtable Constr. Indus. Cost Effectiveness Task Force, Scheduled Overtime Effect on Construction Projects (Nov. 1980).

[14] *See* Maryland Sanitary Mfg. Corp. v. United States, 119 Ct. Cl. 100 (1951); Appeal of Casson Constr. Co., GSBCA No. 4884, 83-1 B.C.A. (CCH) ¶ 16,523 (1983); Appeal of Metro Eng'g, AGBCA No. 6069, 1962 B.C.A. (CCH) ¶ 16,143 (1962).

[15] 613 F. Supp. 514 (W.D. Mo. 1985).

Randolph Engineering (Randolph), sued the prime contractor, Havens Steel (Havens), for large amounts of overtime work resulting in a loss of labor efficiency and increased costs. Under the terms of the contract, Havens fabricated and delivered a 180-foot stack to the construction site. Randolph erected and insulated the stack for Havens. Due to Havens's delay in fabrication and delivery, the owner directed Randolph to work overtime in an effort to recover some of the lost time. The court accepted the testimony proffered that "generally . . . the working of overtime hours does adversely affect labor efficiency."[16]

However, the court considered it essential that the plaintiff offer some method of quantifying what the efficiency loss might have been. Plaintiff developed a chart which purported to incorporate statistics from the Department of Labor, the National Electrical Contractors Association, and the Mechanical Contractors Association. But the court refused to accept the proponent as an expert witness under Rule 702, Federal Rules of Evidence, because he apparently lacked training and experience in the calculations of inefficiency due to overtime. Therefore, the court denied recovery on the basis that without expert testimony, it could not quantify the loss of efficiency that resulted from overtime work.

§ 6.9 —Adverse Weather

Weather has a significant impact on construction,[17] provided the work is exposed to the elements. The types of weather impacting productivity include rain, abnormal humidity, frozen ground, subfreezing temperatures, extreme heat, and excessive wind. Weather is explicitly acknowledged as an excusable cause of delay in just about every construction contract. Relief is typically provided only if the weather was unusually severe, and thus, unforeseeable. Such relief usually consists of an extension of contract time for completion without any monetary compensation. However, if a compensable delay forces the contractor to perform work during a period of inclement weather, then the contractor may be entitled to additional time for the delay as well as compensation for loss of efficiency for its labor force.[18]

In *Luria Bros. & Co., Inc. v. United States,*[19] the plaintiff contractor, Luria Bros., claimed that the government breached the contract through defective and faulty plans, dilatory corrective action, and implementation of a trial and error remedy. In addition, Luria claimed that the nature of

---

[16] *Id.* at 535.

[17] Nat'l Elec. Contractors Ass'n, The Effect of Temperature on Productivity (Feb. 1987).

[18] *See* F.H. McGraw & Co. v. United States, 82 F. Supp. 338 (Ct. Cl. 1949); Abbett Elec. Corp. v. United States, 162 F. Supp. 772 (Ct. Cl. 1958).

[19] 369 F.2d 701 (Ct. Cl. 1966).

the changes and their increased magnitude and frequency exceeded the scope of the contract. As a result, these breaches increased the cost of construction and protracted contract performance 518 days into two periods of severe winter weather.

The court stated that:

> winter weather and adverse weather conditions reduce the efficiency of a labor force in the performance of construction work only stands to reason. It has been held by this court that when loss of productivity brought about by these conditions results from defendant's breach of contract, the plaintiff is entitled to recover its additional costs occasioned thereby as damages.[20]

The expert witness estimated that the labor productivity was reduced by one-third during the first winter weather period. The workers had to work outside on frozen trench excavations and foundation construction wearing gloves and heavy clothing. The expert also estimated the loss of efficiency during the second winter period was 20 percent as a result of working in only a partially completed structure. These estimates were based on the expert's observation and experience.

The court reduced the estimates on the loss of productivity offered by the plaintiff's expert witness because he was the plaintiff's former employee for 10 years, even though he was not in the plaintiff's employment at the time he testified. Also, the court indicated that no comparative data, no standards, and no corroborating testimony were offered to support his estimates. However, since the defendant failed to rebut these estimates, the court employed its own knowledge and experience and reduced the estimates to 20 percent for the first winter period and to 10 percent for the second winter period.

§ 6.10 —Out-of-Sequence Work

As its title implies, out-of-sequence work involves a change in the ordinary and anticipated sequence of construction based upon industry standards and practices. Typically, the order of construction starts with site excavation, followed by building foundations and erecting the superstructure to the top of the building. Next, the building enclosure activities such as masonry, precast panels, metal siding, curtain walls, windows, and roofing are completed, lagging behind the progress of the superstructure, usually by a few floors. Then the interior rough-in trades, including electrical wiring, mechanical piping and ductwork, and studs and drywall, commence from the basement and continue their way up the building, floor by floor. Finally, the finish work, such as finish carpentry/millwork, electrical/mechanical fixtures, wall coverings, painting, and carpets, similarly begin on

---

[20] *Id.* at 714.

a floor-by-floor basis, starting at the basement and following the completion of the rough-in activities. Although this may sound logical and straightforward, the subtle relationships, both independent and dependent, of these trades upon one another require a high degree of coordination to maintain an orderly sequence of construction. Coordination of trades is essential to the effective utilization of the labor forces.

Out-of-sequence work costs have been recovered under a variety of legal theories, including breach of contract, delay, and constructive changes. However, disruption caused by out-of-sequence work would also likely impact labor productivity. In *Bagwell Coatings, Inc. v. Middle South Energy, Inc.,*[21] a structural steel fireproofing subcontractor, Bagwell, sued the owner through the owner's construction management agent, Bechtel, for breach of contract. The contract between the owner, Middle South Energy (Middle South), and Bagwell incorporated the instructions of the specified insulation manufacturer, Carboline Co. (Carboline). Carboline's published instructions stated that the fireproofing was to be applied to the structural steel before ducts, pipework, equipment, and other similar obstructions were installed. Bagwell's witnesses testified that they intended to perform its work in one continuous flow using rolling scaffolding.

Bagwell began applying fireproofing in July, 1977. Work was suspended by Bechtel in March, 1978, due to a lack of available work areas. Bagwell demobilized. In August, 1979, Bagwell was remobilized to complete its work. By this time, Bagwell's efforts to fireproof the structural steel were seriously hindered by the presence of HVAC (heating, ventilation, and air conditioning) ducts, electrical conduit, mechanical piping, and other obstructions installed between the first and second mobilizations. In order to apply the fireproofing, Bagwell's employees had to climb over and around the various obstructions. Installation of the mechanical, electrical, and ventilation systems usually follows, not precedes, fireproofing of the structural steel. In this case, the application of fireproofing was at variance with the standard construction practice of applying fireproofing to the structural steel before installing any material or equipment that would obstruct the complete coating of the steel with fireproofing material.

The district court awarded Bagwell damages for the second mobilization because Middle South breached a contractual provision that it would provide Bagwell with unobstructed access to the structural steel. Thus, Middle South's breach of the contract provision prohibiting obstruction of access increased Bagwell's cost of performance. This award was upheld by the Fifth Circuit.

In *Blake Construction Co. v. C.J. Coakley Co.,*[22] another structural steel fireproofing subcontractor, C.J. Coakley (Coakley), sued the general

---

[21] 797 F.2d 1298 (5th Cir. 1986).
[22] 431 A.2d 569 (D.C. 1981).

§ 6.10 OUT-OF-SEQUENCE WORK   117

contractor, a joint venture of Blake Construction Co. (Blake) and U.S. Industries, Inc. (USI), on the construction of the Walter Reed Hospital in Washington, D.C. Coakley sued Blake for breach of an express contract provision that provided that "Ducts, piping or conduit or other suspended equipment that could interfere with the uniform application of the fireproofing material are to be positioned after the application of the sprayed fireproofing."[23]

Delays in ordering and delivering structural steel resulted in late completion of the entire superstructure, including roof and interstitial floors. Early starts by other trade contractors resulted in the installation of pipes, ducts, and electrical conduits and fittings on an accelerated basis. Coakley notified Blake that it was incurring costs of performance in excess of those anticipated as a result of out-of-sequence construction, that is, the ducts and piping were being installed before the fireproofing. Blake failed to take effective steps to prevent the continuation of these interferences with Coakley's fireproofing.

The court held that Blake breached the contract provision as to the reasonable sequencing of work to permit Coakley to perform under its subcontract. In fact, the court stated that the "delays were not contemplated by the parties and resulted from conduct amounting to active interference, largely due to Blake's improper work sequencing."[24] Therefore, the no damage for delay clause did not bar recovery.

In *Electronics & Missile Facilities, Inc. v. United States,*[25] the plaintiff contractor, Electronics, was entitled to recover loss of efficiency damages from the government caused by rescheduling the work and performing it out of sequence, which was the result of a grading change directed by the contracting officer for the government.

Electronics constructed a 300-unit housing project at Hill Air Force Base, Utah. Because of the existing terrain, the plaintiff estimated that 24,000 cubic yards of fill would be needed over and above the fill available from the work site. During construction, the contracting officer directed Electronics to strip six inches of dirt from all lawn areas in the project and to replace this surface material with topsoil.

Electronics claimed that the trades experienced a loss of efficiency due to the disjointed operation required because of the constructive change to remove six inches of dirt and replace it with topsoil. The plaintiff computed the claim by applying a 30 percent loss of efficiency factor to the total payroll. The court recognized that the change "must adversely have affected the rest of the work."[26] The court held that the plaintiff is entitled

---

[23] *Id.* at 572.
[24] *Id.* at 579.
[25] 416 F.2d 1345 (Ct. Cl. 1969).
[26] *Id.* at 1360.

to an equitable adjustment for the increased costs, which were the direct and necessary result of the change when such change directly led to disruption of the labor force.

§ 6.11 —Acceleration

We explain acceleration claims in **Chapter 5**. In this section we give some case examples of acceleration as a cause of lost productivity.

Courts have recognized acceleration as the cause of lost labor productivity. In *S. Leo Harmonay, Inc. v. Binks Manufacturing Co.*,[27] a mechanical piping subcontractor, Harmonay, sued one of a number of general contractors (Binks) for breach of contract on the construction of two additions to a General Motors automobile assembly plant.

The contract between General Motors and Binks specified that the project site was to be available to Binks and its subcontractors by February 1, 1981. The scheduled date for substantial completion was between August 15 and September 20, 1981.

After award of the contract, several project delays occurred, including delayed site availability, late production of contract layout drawings from the general contractor, and late installation of various tanks, decks, and platforms which were essential steps to the plaintiff's piping installation. The delays associated with contract layout drawings and lack of equipment ready for piping installation continued through July. As of late July and August, the defendant had modified the contract layout drawings and required the removal of up to 50 percent of the work already installed.

Instead of extending the time to complete the contract for excusable delays beyond Harmonay's control, Binks directed Harmonay to increase its crew sizes, put on a second shift, and work both crews overtime on the weekends and holidays during an acceleration period from July 1 through September 30, 1981.

Harmonay claimed that it suffered a 30 percent loss of labor efficiency during the acceleration period due to excessive overtime. "[O]verly crowded conditions, the unavailability of tools, materials and storage, defendant's delay in supplying drawings and equipment, and the constant revisions in the contract drawings—all of which resulted in confusion and interruption of the orderly progress of work."[28]

The district court held that the record fully supported Harmonay's claim that the loss of efficiency experienced during the acceleration period was 30 percent of the actual costs in wages and fringe benefits incurred by Harmonay.

---

[27] 597 F. Supp. 1014 (S.D.N.Y. 1984).
[28] *Id.* at 1029.

In *Baltimore Contractors, Inc. v. Albro Metal Products Corp.*,[29] the court upheld a jury award of $450,000 to E.C. Ernst, the electrical subcontractor, against Baltimore Contractors (BCI) on a claim for acceleration and resequencing of work on Hahnemann Hospital in Philadelphia. Apparently BCI responded to various project delays by denying all requests for extensions of time and resequencing and accelerating the pace of Ernst's work. The court carefully distinguished the claim as one for acceleration, not delay, that forced Ernst to perform its work in an inefficient manner beyond that which could have been reasonably anticipated at the time of bidding.

§ 6.12 —Change Orders

The owner's right to make changes to a contract is usually reserved by explicit language contained in the general contract provisions. This right, however, is limited to the original scope of work. The definition of the scope of work is unfortunately elusive, lingering in the realm of that which is reasonable under the circumstances.

As a cause of loss of efficiency, the impact of changes depends upon the size of the change, the timing of the change, the nature of the change, and the volume of changes. If the floor layouts are changed after installation of stud walls, electrical wiring, and mechanical piping, then the rip-out and reinstallation of work has a severe impact upon productivity. The impact takes shape in the loss of the rhythm and flow of construction, reassignment of manpower to mitigate damages, reduced worker morale and attitudes, and ripple effect upon the follow-on trades.

When negotiating a change order, the contractor may be unaware of the indirect effect of the work in the change order on the otherwise unchanged work. These impact costs often include labor inefficiency on the otherwise unchanged work. The change order procedure usually requires the contractor to delineate specific costs of the change order. The contractor may be precluded from recovering for any costs not specifically included in the change order because of release language that is incorporated into many change orders.[30] If a contractor has accepted a formal change order that does not include impact costs, the contractor must devise a theory of recovery. These theories have included breach of contract, defective specifications, cardinal change, and "cumulative impact" equitable adjustment.

---

[29] Nos. 79-4231 & 81-3887 (E.D. Pa., filed Sept. 13, 1984) (unreported case).

[30] *See* B. Bramble & M. Callahan, Construction Delay Claims, § 7.6 (Supp. 1988) (citing John Price Assocs. v. Davis, 588 P.2d 713 (Utah 1978); United States v. Centex Constr. Co., 638 F. Supp. 411 (W.D. Va. 1985); Appeal of Central Mechanical Constr., ASBCA No. 29434, 86-3 B.C.A. (CCH) ¶ 19,240 (1986)).

In *Luria Bros. & Co. v. United States*,[31] the plaintiff contractor sued the government for breach of contract. The contract required the plaintiff to construct a large airplane hanger with a reinforced concrete arched roof spanning 150 feet. The arches were supported by concrete columns that in turn were supported by underground footings. These footings carry the entire weight of the structure, which is essentially a concrete roof supported by nine arches. These arch-column footings were designed to bear upon rock.

During construction, layers of clay were discovered at the elevations where the footings were designed to bear. As a result, the government stopped all work. A subsurface investigation was initiated and revised design elevations for the footings were developed. When construction resumed, however, the plaintiff was not permitted to excavate down to the revised elevations. The government required the plaintiff to excavate one or two feet at a point starting from the original design elevation and then level off and trim the excavation into finished form for inspection and load-bearing capacity testing. If the defendant's representatives were not satisfied that the exposed rock possessed sufficient strength to support the foundation, the plaintiff was required to excavate another foot or two and then level off and trim the excavation for reinspection and load-bearing capacity testing. "This trial and error procedure which prolonged significantly the construction of the footings was contrary to good engineering practice and a substantial change in the construction procedure from the original drawings as well as a distortion of the revised design."[32] The court held the trial and error method of excavation to be unreasonable. Combined with the extremely slow recognition and correction of the defective plans, the defendant breached "the implied obligation contained in every contract that neither party will do anything that will hinder or delay the other party in performance of the contract."[33]

On the other hand, in *Wunderlich Contracting Co. v. United States*,[34] the court adopted a conservative position on change orders:

> There is no exact formula for determining the point at which a single change or a series of changes must be considered to be beyond the scope of the contract and necessarily in breach of it. Each case must be analyzed on its own facts and in light of its own circumstances, giving just consideration to the magnitude and quality of the changes ordered and their cumulative effect upon the project as a whole.[35]

---

[31] 369 F.2d 701 (Ct. Cl. 1966).
[32] *Id.* at 707.
[33] *Id.* at 708.
[34] 351 F.2d 956 (Ct. Cl. 1965).
[35] *Id.* at 966.

The *Wunderlich* court held that 35 change orders amounting to six percent of the contract value did not prove that the defendant was responsible for all losses on the contract. The court reasoned that even though the plaintiff's performance had been lengthier and costlier than anticipated at the time the bid was submitted, they ultimately constructed essentially the same project as agreed upon in the contract. Therefore, the changes did not materially alter the nature of the bargain; nor were they beyond the contract scope as to constitute a breach of contract, that is, cardinal change.

In *Pitman Construction Co. v. United States*,[36] the court denied the contractor's claim for inefficiencies and disruptions allegedly due to change orders. Pitman's contract price was increased by $3.0 million to a total of $25.6 million (12 percent increase), and the time for performance was increased 102 calendar days to a total of 1102 calendar days (10 percent increase) because of the issuance of 206 change orders by the government. The court held that these changes did not amount to a fundamental change in the character of the work and that the additional costs were foreseeable.

The *Pitman* court cited *Appeal of Ingalls Shipbuilding Division, Litton Systems, Inc.*,[37] for the proposition that several thousand change orders increasing the contract value 58 percent reach the level of a fundamental change to the character of the work. The court also cited *Appeal of Dyson & Co.*,[38] for the proposition that a 19 percent increase in contract value due to 39 changes is not enough to deem them sufficient to secure a claim for indirect or cumulative impact costs.[39] Cumulative impact costs include the inefficiencies and disruptions associated with change orders that are so overwhelming in number and magnitude as to give rise to a separate compensable impact claim. Therefore, although it may not be a bright-line test, the percentage of change orders above the base contract amount offers the court an analytical tool to gauge the case at hand against prior decisions.

§ 6.13 —Constructive Changes

Constructive changes are a legal fiction allowing the contractor to be paid for changes to the manner, method, or scope of work, even when there is no formal change order. Recovery may be allowed under some contract

---

[36] 2 Cl. Ct. 211 (1983).

[37] ASBCA No. 17579, 78-1 B.C.A. (CCH) ¶ 13,038 (1978).

[38] ASBCA No. 21673, 78-2 B.C.A. (CCH) ¶ 13,482 (1978), *aff'd on reconsideration*, 79-1 B.C.A. (CCH) ¶ 13,661 (1979).

[39] *Id.*

adjustment clauses when there is some action or inaction by the owner or the owner's agent that is tantamount to an order or directive to the contractor.[40] The theory has been well established in federal contract forums, and it is gaining acceptance in other jurisdictions under other construction industry contracts.[41]

Constructive changes typically result from directions issued at the construction site by the owner or general contractor to the subcontractor. If the direction modifies the terms of the contract and the subcontractor reasonably relies on the apparent authority of the individual, then the contractor may collect the additional costs associated with the direction as a change to the contract. Frequently, lost labor productivity is a cost claimed as part of a constructive change.

For example, in *Electronics & Missile Facilities, Inc. v. United States*,[42] the contractor was entitled to recover loss of efficiency damages from the government caused by rescheduling the work and performing it out of sequence, which resulted from a grading change directed by the contracting officer for the government.

The change was deemed a constructive change and the contractor was allowed to recover its claimed loss of efficiency due to a disjointed operation. The claimant computed its loss of efficiency by use of a 30 percent loss factor. The court allowed an equitable adjustment for the labor losses that were the direct and necessary result of the constructive change involving labor disruption.

The other examples of constructive changes involve design flaws,[43] differing site conditions,[44] and failure to coordinate separate prime contractors.[45] All of these types of constructive changes may result in labor productivity losses.

§ 6.14 —Disruption

As a cause of loss of efficiency, disruption operates as a catchall category encompassing a wide range of elements. These elements include, but are not limited to, poor job site conditions (lighting, ventilation, and interior environmental control), safety considerations, the learning curve of new

---

[40] McLeod & Grove, *Suing the Private Owner* in Construction Litigation: Representing the Contractor 55 (R. Cushman, J. Carter, & A. Silverman eds. 1986).

[41] *Id.*

[42] 416 F.2d 1345 (Ct. Cl. 1969).

[43] John McShain, Inc. v. United States, 412 F.2d 1281 (Ct. Cl. 1969); Appeal of Miles Constr., VABCA No. 1674, 84-1 B.C.A. (CCH) ¶ 16,967 (1983).

[44] Merritt-Chapman & Scott Corp. v. United States, 429 F.2d 431 (Ct. Cl. 1970).

[45] Pittman Constr. Co. v. United States, 2 Cl. Ct. 211 (1983).

§ 6.14 DISRUPTION

labor (necessitated by attrition or increased scope of work),[46] strikes, damaged work, and ripple effects of prior events on the trades following them. The extent to which any one of these elements is foreseeable by the contractors and included in its bid price depends upon the nature of the work involved, the disruption encountered, and the reasonable conduct and expectations of all the parties.

In *U.S. Industries, Inc. v. Blake Construction Co.*,[47] U.S. Industries, Inc. (USI) and Blake Construction Co. (Blake) had entered into a joint venture agreement to perform as the prime contractor on the Walter Reed General Hospital in Washington, D.C. Blake was the managing partner and represented the joint venture in its dealings with the government. As part of the joint venture, Blake awarded the mechanical subcontract for the project to Federal Sheet Metal, one of USI's unincorporated subsidiaries. The original price of this subcontract was $20 million, which increased to $35 million by contract completion.

USI sued Blake for breach of the joint venture agreement and the mechanical subcontract in delaying the project completion and in disruption of USI's work. USI in fact claimed two kinds of disruption. First, USI claimed that Blake ripped out and damaged portions of its work and forced it to reinstall the work. Second, USI claimed that Blake failed to schedule and coordinate the work, resulting in a loss of productivity. As part of the latter claim, USI asserted that Blake failed "(1) to schedule USI's and other subcontractor's work so that the work could be done smoothly and quickly, (2) to give USI notice of work to be done, (3) to provide USI with work space and storage space, and (4) to give USI use of a hoist."[48]

The district court instructed the jury, with respect to the disruption claim, that Blake as a general contractor had a duty

> not to interfere with the work of a subcontractor like Federal Sheet Metal, if at the time Blake could have foreseen that such interference would unreasonably hinder or unreasonably disrupt the contractor's completion of its work by requiring Federal Sheet Metal to perform its work in an unnecessary, disorderly, or inefficient manner.[49]

The district court submitted the issue of disruption damages to the jury separately from the issue of delay damages, with explicit instructions to eliminate any double recovery or duplication of damages under both theories. The court of appeals upheld the $4.8 million jury verdict for disruption damages as supported by the evidence.

---

[46] Appeal of Groves-Black, ENGBCA No. 4557, 85-3 B.C.A. (CCH) ¶ 18,398 (1985).
[47] 671 F.2d 539 (D.C. Cir. 1982).
[48] *Id.* at 546.
[49] *Id.*

§ 6.15 Proving Lost Productivity Claims

In order to recover damages under a contract, the plaintiff bears "the basic and fundamental burden of establishing the fundamental facts of liability, causation and resultant damage."[50] The plaintiff does not have to prove its damages with absolute certainty or mathematical exactitude, but with a reasonable basis for computation even though the result is only approximate.[51] However, the courts continually emphasize that this leniency as to the actual mechanics of computation does not relieve the contractor of its essential burden of proof.[52]

Too often the intricate complexities of construction distract the focus of the litigation from proving the essential elements of liability, causation, and damages. Depending upon the case, a series of details or facts must often be proven just to establish one of the required elements. Broad generalizations used in presenting the case should be saved for opening and closing arguments. Although a broad brush puts the litigation into perspective for the trier of fact, the brush must be assembled bristle by bristle with sufficient facts to establish each of the required elements. If the brush is too thin, the trier of fact will be presented with an argument lacking evidentiary weight. "Broad generalities and inferences to the effect that defendant must have caused some delay and damage because the contract took . . . longer to complete than anticipated are not sufficient."[53] The contractor must offer proof: (1) that the owner owed the contractor a duty, either contractual or implied; (2) that the owner failed to perform that duty; (3) that the owner's failure to perform injured the contractor; and (4) that the contractor suffered monetary damages as a result of the injury. In proving lost productivity claims, it is necessary to expound upon the nature of the injury because productivity losses may be perceived as somewhat nebulous. This involves focused and straightforward evidence of how the owner's actions caused the productivity losses, the extent of these losses, and the monetary damages associated with the labor productivity losses. The proof usually consists of job cost records, fact witnesses, and expert testimony.

§ 6.16 Liability

Liability simply refers to proof that the defendant owed the plaintiff a duty and that the defendant failed to perform the duty. The source of

---

[50] G.M. Shupe, Inc. v. United States, 5 Cl. Ct. 662, 737 (1984).
[51] Wunderlich Contracting Co. v. United States, 351 F.2d 956, 968 (Ct. Cl. 1965).
[52] *Id.*
[53] *Id.* at 969.

the duty usually is contractual, expressed or implied. The failure to perform the duty manifests itself as a breach of contract.

In *Bagwell Coatings v. Middle South Energy*,[54] the contract between the owner and Bagwell specified the adoption of the manufacturer's guidelines for use of its cementitious fireproofing material. These guidelines required the fireproofing work to proceed before installation of fixtures or equipment obstructing access to the steel members. The court held that the owner's construction management agent violated a specific contractual duty to provide Bagwell unobstructed access to the structural steel for fireproofing. Therefore, proof of the construction manager's failure to perform its duty established the liability of the owner to the contractor.

It is unusual to find explicit contract language relating to labor productivity. Therefore, courts often look to implied contractual duties. In *S. Leo Harmonay v. Binks Manufacturing Co.*,[55] the plaintiff, a mechanical piping subcontractor, alleged that Binks broke the "well established rule that a contractor is entitled to a reasonable opportunity to perform his contract without obstruction or interference, and that neither party will do anything that will hinder or delay the other party in performance of the contract."[56] This duty is an implied obligation.[57] In addition, there were applicable contractual provisions contained in the Harmonay-Binks subcontract and the Binks-Owner prime contract that related to the defendant's liability for production of layout drawings. Liability was proven by an implied obligation not to obstruct the subcontractor's work, as well as by an explicit contractual duty.

In *Luria Bros. & Co. v. United States*,[58] the court stated that it is well settled that when the government implicitly warrants that if its specifications (prescribing the character, dimension, and location of the construction work) are complied with, satisfactory performance will result. The court held that a contractor is entitled to recover damages for defendant's breach of this implied warranty against defective specifications.

§ 6.17 Causation and Injury

Causation simply asks the question whether or not the defendant's liability (the failure to perform the duty owed to the plaintiff manifested by a

---

[54] 797 F.2d 1298 (5th Cir. 1986).

[55] 597 F. Supp. 1014 (S.D.N.Y. 1984).

[56] *Id.* at 1027.

[57] *See* Ginsburg & Eshelman, *Implied Duty of Cooperation—Basic Principles and Guidelines,* Construction Briefings (Nov. 1987). *See also* Goldberg, *The Owner's Duty to Coordinate Multi-Prime Construction Contractors, A Condition of Cooperation,* 28 Emory L.J. 377 (1979).

[58] 369 F.2d 701 (Ct. Cl. 1966).

breach of the contract) had adversely impacted or injured the plaintiff. The analysis is similar to the chain reaction analogy used to connect the failure to perform a duty and the plaintiff's injury in tort litigation. "It is incumbent upon plaintiffs to show the nature and extent of the various delays for which damages are claimed and to connect them to some act of commission or omission on defendant's part."[59]

In *Wunderlich Contracting Co. v. United States*,[60] the court held that there was a critical lack of proof of causation. The court also adopted the trial commissioner's findings that the evidence did not establish the extent to which the plaintiff's 20 percent increase in project costs were incurred as a result of a 6 percent increase in the contract price. The plaintiff failed to present details to support its allegations that the higher contract price was caused by revisions and corrections to the specifications necessitated by errors, omissions, and discrepancies. Thus, marshalling the testimony of the fact witnesses and supporting documentation is critical in establishing the cause and effect relationship in construction.

On the other hand, the court in *Luria Bros. & Co. v. United States*,[61] held that the trial and error method of excavation was a result of differing site conditions of such magnitude that it exceeded the scope of the contract and constituted a breach. The court further held that the defendant's breach of contract caused considerable delay in the foundation work, forcing the contractor to work during the winter. The loss of efficiency experienced by working during the winter was directly linked to the government's breach of contract.

In the *Luria* case, the magnitude of the problem apparently was sufficient to convince the court of causation. However, causation should be the subject of attention and proof even in cases of extreme conditions. Causation should not be left to implication as to whether the actions of the defendant are egregious or merely substantial. Regardless of the severity, the defendant's actions that caused labor productivity losses must be proven.

Assuming the plaintiff has met its burden of proof as to liability and causation, then it must also prove injury. Injury is simply proof of some loss caused by the defendant's liability. Conversely, if there is no proof of a loss in productivity, then there is no injury, even though an expert hypothesizes and theorizes that productivity losses could have occurred under these conditions. Having agonized through liability and causation, injury should be a relatively simple element to prove. However, failure to establish injury is fatal to a lost productivity claim.

---

[59] Wunderlich Contracting Co. v. United States, 351 F.2d 956, 969 (Ct. Cl. 1965).

[60] 351 F.2d 956 (Ct. Cl. 1965).

[61] 369 F.2d 701 (Ct. Cl. 1966).

In *Northbridge Electronics, Inc. v. United States*,[62] the plaintiff contractor claimed to have experienced a 25 percent loss of efficiency during shutdown of the final assembly line. The court held that there was no loss of efficiency, because the plaintiff's labor dollars were steadily decreasing during the shutdown period and the plaintiff failed to produce any specific factual testimony. The court also indicated that the plaintiff's work on other projects was increasing and its workers were assigned to other contracts, thereby mitigating any damages.

In *Assurance Co. v. United States*,[63] the plaintiff contractor claimed damages for extra excavation under existing houses to install ductwork and piping where the vertical crawlspace clearances shown on the drawings were insufficient. The court held that the contractor and its subcontractors failed to demonstrate that they in fact suffered any injury. First, there was a complete absence of proof from books, records, or documentation, as well as a failure to adequately explain the absence of proof. Second, the workers were paid on a piecework basis, that is, x dollars per house completed, rather than on a dollars per hour basis. Therefore, even if additional labor hours were expended, there would be no increase in price. Thus it is possible to prove injury (additional labor expended) but no damages (price increase). Lastly, the plaintiff never provided testimony or other proof that it or its subcontractors actually incurred additional or increased monetary expenses.

In the cases above, the damages claimed were not proven to be the certain result of the injury. The *Northbridge Electronics* court felt that the fact that the plaintiff's labor costs were decreasing during the shutdown period clearly evidenced the plaintiff's successful efforts to mitigate damages. The *Assurance* court determined that payments made by the subcontractor on a piecework basis failed to prove damages since the payments did not reflect any labor increase due to loss of efficiency.

There are four types of proof that can help in demonstrating causation and injury in lost productivity cases: (1) expert testimony; (2) trade publications; (3) historical data; and (4) job-specific data. We now examine these.

§ 6.18 —Experts

In construction litigation, the courts have developed an expectancy to hear and to rely upon the testimony of an expert witness.[64] This is due to the

---

[62] 444 F.2d 1124 (Ct. Cl. 1971).

[63] 813 F.2d 1202 (Fed. Cir. 1987).

[64] *See* Lunch, *Expert Witnesses Play Key Role in Construction Cases,* Bldg. Design & Constr. (Aug. 1988); *The Role of Expert Witnesses in Construction Disputes,* Constr. Claims Monthly (Dec. 1988).

technical nature of construction, the subtleties of managing construction, and the specialized insights an expert offers into a world often misunderstood by its participants, let alone the spectators.

Construction claim analysis is a study in cause and effect. In a construction delay claim, the focus is on a quantifiable element—time. There is very little dispute over the fact that a project was scheduled to be completed on a particular date. Similarly, the actual date on which the project is substantially complete can be established with reasonable accuracy through contemporaneous project records. Thus, the number of days of delay is the difference between the planned and the actual project completion dates. The analysis focuses on who caused the delay and demonstrating its impact or effect on the project schedule.

In a loss of efficiency claim, the cause and effect relationship may be more qualitative and less capable of exact scientific measurement. This does not mean that a loss of efficiency claim is fiction. The effect of a disruption upon a construction project can be devastating in terms of labor dollars expended. In addition, due to the intricate and subtle dependencies between the various trades and activities, a disruption in one trade or activity inevitably affects other trades and activities (the ripple effect). The qualitative nature of loss of efficiency claims greatly emphasizes the need for an expert to offer an opinion as to the cause of a disruption and its effect on the project.

In *Luria Bros. & Co. v. United States,*[65] the court stated: "It is a rare case where loss of productivity can be proven by books and records; almost always it has to be proven by the opinion of expert witnesses."[66] Thus, the opinion of an expert witness may be required to quantify the nature, cause, and amount of inefficiency experienced on the project.

However, the testimony of the expert witness must be corroborated by other testimony. In *McCarty Corp. v. Pullman-Kellogg,*[67] the "plaintiff called an expert witness who plotted efficiency curves for both plaintiff and Pullman-Kellogg . . . He opined that this 'overmanning' together with Pullman-Kellogg's own lower than anticipated efficiency on the job caused a reduction in plaintiff's job efficiency which resulted in great expense and damage to plaintiff."[68] Although the court accepted the expert's theoretical proposition "that it is possible to introduce so many workmen upon the same jobsite at the same time that they interfere with each other's job performance, there is no reliable evidence in this record that that is what happened here."[69] In fact, the plaintiff failed to introduce any

---

[65] 369 F.2d 701 (Ct. Cl. 1966).
[66] *Id.* at 713.
[67] 571 F. Supp. 1341 (M.D. La. 1983).
[68] *Id.* at 1357.
[69] *Id.*

evidence of actual job interference other than the expert's opinion. Therefore the court ruled that the expert's opinions were not reliable as they were based upon arbitrary and assumed efficiency ratings. "The productivity or efficiency rating is only as good as the estimates upon which it is based and the estimates here are not shown to have been reliable."[70]

Similarly, the *Luria* court stated that the testimony on loss of productivity was far from satisfactory. The court felt that the plaintiff's expert was well qualified and competent to offer an opinion on the loss of productivity of the labor. "However, the mere expression of an estimate as to the amount of productivity loss by an expert witness with nothing to support it will not establish the fundamental fact of resultant injury nor provide a sufficient basis for making a reasonably correct approximation of damages."[71] Therefore, the testimony of an expert is only as efficacious as the factual foundation and background established by the testimony of corroborating witnesses and other evidence.

On the other hand, expert witnesses have the unique ability to summarize the testimony of all the other fact witnesses and present the trier of fact with an authoritative opinion. In *Nebraska Public Power District v. Austin Power, Inc.*,[72] the court cited the power of expert witnesses for both parties in a jury trial that lasted over seven months and involved thousands of exhibits and 99 witnesses: "[T]he testimony of each was crucial to the resolution of the case, both to the establishment of causation and nature of the damage and the understanding by the jury of the significance of weeks of testimony by nonexpert witnesses."[73]

Therefore, an expert witness is required to provide expertise in a particular technical field and to put the case into perspective for the trier of fact.

§ 6.19 —Trade Publications

Little is published on loss of efficiency claims because of the perceived qualitative nature of the subject. Three publications have given it some attention. The Mechanical Contractors Association of America[74] and the National Electrical Contractors Association[75] have published assorted

---

[70] *Id.*

[71] Luria Bros. & Co. v. United States, 369 F.2d 701, 712 (Ct. Cl. 1966).

[72] 773 F.2d 960 (8th Cir. 1985).

[73] *Id.* at 975.

[74] Mechanical Contractors Ass'n of Am., Management Methods Bulletin No. 58 (Jan. 1978).

[75] *See* Nat'l Elec. Contractors Ass'n, The Effect of Multi-Story Buildings on Productivity (1975), Project Peak Work Force Report (1980), and Rate of Manpower Consumption in Electrical Construction (1983).

reports and pamphlets on loss of efficiency and its causes. In addition, the Business Roundtable[76] offers several publications regarding construction productivity.

The effects of overtime on productivity have received particular attention. This is logical since overtime is easily quantified. Also, the premise that overtime creates a loss of efficiency appeals to both our common sense and our own life experiences. However, little is written on other causes of loss of efficiency such as trade stacking and design defects. This is largely because of the difficulty in quantifying the effects of these admittedly detrimental occurrences on construction productivity.

One of the Business Roundtable's findings was that "no satisfactory measures of aggregate construction industry productivity data are currently available."[77] The report points out that the Bureau of Labor Statistics, which publishes productivity data for other industries, does not publish construction productivity data because they question its reliability. The Business Roundtable clearly recommends collection of site productivity data to develop histories and baselines with which to monitor productivity.[78]

§ 6.20 —Historical Data

One of the ways to prove loss of efficiency is to maintain project records for several similar projects from which productivity per unit output can be developed. This is particularly applicable to specialty trade contractors as opposed to general or prime contractors who subcontract the specialized work functions.

For example, a specialty trade contractor who exclusively performs stud and drywall work could develop project productivity rates such as square feet of drywall per labor hour. This is calculated simply by dividing the total volume of drywall installed by the total labor hours expended. By doing this for each completed project, the specialty contractor can develop a productivity track record against which current project productivity performance can be compared.

Some contractors choose not to develop this type of self-generated productivity data for fear of publication to its competition or of the potential for the information to be used against itself in a particular case. However, this is short-sighted for two reasons. First, in any litigation or claim to recover damages, the plaintiff bears the burden of proof. A contractor

---

[76] Business Roundtable, Measuring Productivity in Construction, Report A-1 (Sept. 1982).

[77] Id.

[78] Id.

should hesitate to request leniency in proving its damages for loss of efficiency when it decided (actively or passively) not to collect historical data useful in meeting that same burden of proof.

Second, lost efficiency cannot be addressed unless its cause is properly identified. If the lost efficiency is self-induced, then it must be recognized and corrected. Left untreated, it infects project after project like a virus. If the cause for the lost efficiency is externally generated and attributable to a third party, then the historical data should support that allegation.

It is interesting that one of the findings of the Business Roundtable was that "most large contractors have a formal program for measuring labor productivity on job sites."[79] Unfortunately, this data has not often been used to prove labor productivity losses, or to benefit the construction industry in general.

Another productivity yardstick is dollar value of construction in place per labor hour. This method has the advantage of easy record development and universal applicability across a wide range of differing project types, for example, hospitals, hotels, commercial offices, apartments, and industrial complexes. However, its application is inversely proportional to the value of capital equipment involved in that trade. For example, the labor/material ratio for HVAC contractors would be lower than that for studs and drywall contractors. Therefore, for equipment-intensive trades, a dollars per unit labor yardstick would not necessarily be an accurate reflection of labor productivity. In addition, this method incorporates any bid or pricing errors which may have caused the subsequent labor overrun in the first place.

§ 6.21 —Job-Specific Data

One of the best ways to demonstrate productivity losses is through the use of data specific to the project. However, such records are generally not maintained on the majority of construction projects. There are many ways to collect productivity data for a particular project at the job site. The important points to keep in mind are that (1) the plaintiff bears the burden of proof, and (2) courts accept no excuses for failure to maintain accurate cost records.

The Business Roundtable[80] has developed a manual that describes a basic site productivity measuring system. As stated by the Business Roundtable, contractors should not lose sight of the primary purposes for measuring productivity:

---

[79] *Id.*

[80] Business Roundtable, Manual on Construction Site Productivity Measurement app. B-2 (Sept. 1982).

1. To understand productivity
2. To evaluate alternative systems
3. To ultimately improve the effectiveness of the existing system.

Although it can be used to substantiate losses incurred on a project, a productivity measuring system should be a contractor's good faith attempt to monitor and improve internal as well as external productivity factors.

According to the Business Roundtable, there are eight basic steps to develop and maintain a useful productivity measuring system.

The first step is to establish cost accounts of manageable blocks of work or work packages. The cost accounts could be structured on a variety of bases such as schedules of values/prices, trade or subcontractor, company standards, industry standards (American Institute of Architects cost coding system), building systems, and building floors or areas. In addition, the cost codes could be subcoded, that is, coded by trade first and then within each trade code by floor or by area.

The next step is to record the quantity take-off that measures the amount of work to be completed for each cost account. This defines the scope of work included and the amount of labor and materials required to accomplish each task and includes the basis for determining both.

In planning the productivity system, it is important to estimate the costs for each account in sufficient detail to identify measurable work increments for better accuracy. Contractors should think the process through and develop the method by which actual data will be collected and associated with the appropriate cost account.

The most crucial aspect is to measure progress regularly using the parameters developed above. By comparing the actual amount of material installed with the amount estimated, performance is monitored and tracked to determine which cost accounts will exceed budget. Some of the errors commonly made are estimating the amount installed by means of a subjective percentage instead of using hard evidence like cubic yards of concrete, linear feet of pipe, or square feet of drywall. These objective units offer a better yardstick than pure "guesstimation." In addition, overly optimistic estimates of completed work too early into the construction process hide rather than expose the impact of design problems in layout and dimensions. Finally, billings reported by payment applications or progress invoices can be used to demonstrate performance trends, but they may be inaccurate to the extent that they include early capital expenses for material, shop drawing preparation, and equipment fabrication.

It is equally important to record the actual labor hours expended. This requires proper allocation of field hours to the respective cost account. Both the project foremen and the company payroll department should check to make sure the field personnel are segregating their time properly and that these cost accounts are being charged as accurately as possible.

To assure proper monitoring, the labor status report should be prepared regularly, for example, weekly, biweekly, or monthly. In addition, the labor report should track the information previously developed, recorded, and updated. The shorter the reporting interval, the quicker management recognizes and reacts to events.

Management should review the labor status report regularly to identify problems and their causes as soon as possible. If the lack of productivity is externally caused, documentation is well underway to substantiate a request for compensation. If the low level of productivity is internally caused, then prompt corrective action should be taken.

It may be necessary to refine and revise the original job cost estimate upon identification and implementation of alternative construction techniques and methods that are designed to avoid, or at least mitigate, the extent of the loss of productivity.

The net benefit of employing a productivity measuring system is careful project planning and monitoring. The following considerations should be kept in mind when using such a system:

1. Site access and layout
2. Construction methodology and sequencing
3. Material laydown and storage
4. Material lifting requirements and crane locations
5. Adequate site facilities such as heat, electrical power, lighting, and temporary elevators
6. Adequate manpower
7. Timing and coordination of trades.

In this way, the contractor will learn more about the project early into the construction process. The knowledge gained and data collected by using a productivity measuring system should make the proof of causation and damages more palatable to the courts.

In addition, owners may be more willing to settle productivity claims and to minimize interference with contractor's performance if such detailed productivity data are available to them.

§ 6.22 Damages

In *Story Parchment Co. v. Paterson Parchment Paper Co.*,[81] Justice Sutherland established the general rule and policy in awarding damages:

> It is true that there was uncertainty as to the extent of the damage, but there was none as to the fact of damage; and there is a clear distinction

---
[81] 282 U.S. 555 (1931).

between the measure of proof necessary to establish the fact that petitioner had sustained some damage and the measure of proof necessary to enable the jury to fix the amount. . . .

Where the tort itself is of such a nature as to preclude the ascertainment of the amount of damages with certainty, it would be a perversion of fundamental principles of justice to deny all relief to the injured person, and thereby relieve the wrongdoer from making any amend for his acts. In such a case, while the damages may not be determined by mere speculation or guess, it will be enough if the evidence shows the extent of the damages as a matter of just and reasonable inference, although the result be only approximate. The wrong-doer is not entitled to complain that they cannot be measured with the exactness and precision that would be possible if the case, which he alone is responsible for making, were otherwise . . . .[82]

Justice Sutherland made a distinction between the plaintiff's fundamental burden of proof necessary to establish that it has been injured and the burden of proof required to fix the amount of damages. Once the plaintiff has established that an injury resulted from the defendant's breach, then the proof of the amount of damage is more flexible. Uncertainty in the amount of damage is not fatal to the claim.

Although the *Story* case was one of tort rather than contract actions,[83] the general policy of courts on damages would seem to apply to loss of productivity claims. Such leniency regarding the proof of damages once injury has been established is custom-made for loss of efficiency claims because of the qualitative nature these types of claims often have.[84] With the use of expert testimony based on project performance and cost data, the cause and effect relationship between a loss of efficiency disruption and resulting injury may be demonstrated and understood. However, proving the amount of damages is problematic since the inefficiencies are

---

[82] *Id.* at 562.

[83] Koehring Co. v. Hyde Constr. Co., 254 Miss. 214, 178 So. 2d 838 (1965) (court ruled that where a breach of contract has been proven and causation of some substantial damage has been established, then the proof needed to award damages is much more flexible):

Although the method used in obtaining the measure of damages is not entirely without fault, it may be said, as a general rule, that a party who has broken his contract will not be permitted to escape liability because of the lack of a perfect measure of damages caused by his breach. Therefore, a reasonable basis for computation and the best evidence which is obtainable under the circumstances of the case, and which will enable the trier to arrive at a fair approximate estimate of loss is sufficient proof.

[84] *See* Bagwell Coatings, Inc. v. Middle S. Energy, Inc., 797 F.2d 1298 (5th Cir. 1986); Luria Bros. & Co. v. United States, 369 F.2d 701 (Ct. Cl. 1966); Assurance Co. v. United States, 813 F.2d 1202 (Fed. Cir. 1987); S. Leo Harmonay, Inc. v. Binks Mfg. Co., 597 F. Supp. 1014 (S.D.N.Y. 1984).

§ 6.22 DAMAGES

necessarily commingled within broad project cost categories such as labor power and equipment.

In applying the *Story* policy on damages to loss of efficiency cases, the courts have indicated that the general rule barring uncertain damages applies only where the damages claimed have not been causally connected to the breach. However, where the damages are directly attributable to the breach, then they are recoverable even though they are uncertain in amount. "Thus, courts have recognized that a plaintiff may recover even where it is apparent that the quantum of damage is unavoidably uncertain, beset by complexity, or difficult to ascertain, if the damage is caused by the wrong."[85]

The courts have recognized that the ascertainment of damages is not an exact science.[86] When the responsibility for damages is proven, it is not essential that the amount of damages be "ascertainable with absolute exactness or mathematical precision."[87] Thus, the courts have recognized that loss of efficiency damages are not easily quantified nor segregated from other construction costs. However, this lack of scientific certainty will not bar the claim.

Basically, there are two approaches to damages—segregated and unsegregated damages.[88] Segregated damages simply refer to actual itemized costs directly incurred by the plaintiff as a result of the defendant's breach. Obviously, the most reliable and effective way to prove damages is to maintain separate cost codes and records of additional work, sometimes referred to as the actual cost method.[89]

Unfortunately, "[c]ontractors rarely keep their books in such fashion . . . such failure, however, normally does not prevent the submission of reasonably satisfactory proof of increased costs incurred during certain contract periods or flowing from certain events based, for instance, on acceptable cost allocation principles or on expert testimony."[90]

Where the nature of the injury is such that it is impossible to segregate the damages incurred due to the defendant's breach, the courts have awarded damages using unsegregated approaches including total cost, modified total cost, and jury verdict.

The total cost method of computing damages subtracts the contractor's bid estimate from the total of all project costs incurred, producing a total

---

[85] S. Leo Harmonay, Inc. v. Binks Mfg. Co., 597 F. Supp. 1014, 1030 (S.D.N.Y. 1984).

[86] Nebraska Pub. Power Dist. v. Austin Power, Inc., 773 F.2d 960, 968 (8th Cir. 1985).

[87] Electronic & Missile Facilities, Inc. v. United States, 416 F.2d 1345, 1358 (Ct. Cl. 1969).

[88] Bruner, *Construction Claim Recovery Measures: Untying the Gordian Knot,* 20 Forum 278 (1985).

[89] *See* Bruce Constr. Corp. v. United States, 324 F.2d 516 (Ct. Cl. 1963).

[90] Boyajian v. United States, 423 F.2d 1231, 1242 (Ct. Cl. 1970).

cost attributable to the owner's breach.[91] The reluctance to completely embrace this method of computing damages stems from the assumption that the defendant is liable for all of plaintiff's injuries.[92] Thus, the total cost method has been applied by the courts only under exceptional circumstances and then only as a last resort.[93]

In one case, the total cost method was used only when the record demonstrated that no other method of computing damages was available and there was no other alternative.[94] The court of claims dismissed a plaintiff's total cost damage calculations because there was an "insufficient showing" that a direct cost damage calculation could not have been made.[95] In fact, the court went so far as to admonish the plaintiff by saying that "the mere fact that plaintiff's books and records do not, in segregated form, show the amounts of the increased costs attributable to the breaches give it automatic license to use the 'total cost' method."[96]

Although the courts are sympathetic to the contractor where the increased costs of performance are inextricably intertwined with the original contract, they have developed the following tests before the total cost method will be accepted:[97]

1. The defendant's liability has been clearly proven
2. The nature of the injury makes it impossible or highly impracticable to determine damages on a segregated basis with a reasonable degree of accuracy
3. The contractor's original bid was realistic and reasonable
4. The contractor's original bid was complete, accurate, and free from bid errors
5. The contractor's actual costs incurred were reasonable
6. The contractor's increased costs were caused by the defendant and were not self-inflicted in any way.

Construction is as much art as science. Accommodation in problem-solving must, therefore, be the rule rather than the exception. More often

---

[91] Rubin, *The Total Cost Method of Computing an Equitable Adjustment—An Analysis*, 26 Fed. Bar J. 303 (1966).

[92] Wunderlich Contracting Co. v. United States, 351 F.2d 956, 965 (Ct. Cl. 1965).

[93] New Pueblo Constructors, Inc. v. State, 144 Ariz. 95, 696 P.2d 203 (1985).

[94] Boyajian v. United States, 423 F.2d 1231 (Ct. Cl. 1970); Baltimore Contractors, Inc. v. Albro Metal Prods. Corp., Nos. 79-4231 & 81-3887 (E.D. Pa., filed Sept. 13, 1984).

[95] *Boyajian,* 423 F.2d at 1242.

[96] *Id.*

[97] *See* Nebraska Pub. Power Dist. v. Austin Power, Inc., 773 F.2d 960 (8th Cir. 1985); Boyajian v. United States, 423 F.2d 1231 (Ct. Cl. 1970); New Pueblo Constructors, Inc. v. State, 144 Ariz. 95, 696 P.2d 203 (1985).

§ 6.22 DAMAGES

than not, boundaries are fluid, although precisely defined. As a result, reasonable compromise struck during the stress of bidding or realistic attempts to minimize contractor inefficiencies may not appear reasonable or realistic to the trier of fact exposed to the job several years later. Therefore, few projects are able to meet the six tests imposed on the use of the total cost method without some adjustment.[98] In fact, the total cost computation can be viewed as a "starting point" that must be "refined by appropriate adjustments."[99]

The modified total cost approach has been accepted by the courts as being a more reasonable approach because it refines the defects contained in a pure total cost claim.[100] In *Bagwell Coatings v. Middle South Energy, Inc.*,[101] the district court's award on a modified total cost basis was upheld on appeal. The district court subtracted 10 percent of Bagwell's total cost claim for Bagwell's admitted internal inefficiencies,[102] despite the fact that Bagwell had made normal allowances for reduced labor efficiency in its bid.[103]

In *Boyajian v. United States*,[104] the court analyzed the damages awarded in four different cases[105] normally cited for the total cost method and decided that the total cost computation is only a beginning.[106] Appropriate adjustments must be made for any bid errors or other costs incurred not caused by the defendant. The *Boyajian* court felt that there were production interruptions and delays not caused by the defendant and for which the plaintiff failed to adjust its total cash approach.

Finally, a jury verdict approach is used where the plaintiff cannot prove actual costs. In this situation, any evidence relating to the approximate cost of the additional work may be presented to the trier of fact. This evidence may consist of actual cost data, accounting records, estimates by expert witnesses, and calculations from similar projects.[107] A jury verdict

---

[98] *See* Boyajian v. United States, 423 F.2d 1231 (Ct. Cl. 1970).

[99] *Id.* at 1242.

[100] *See* E.C. Ernst, Inc. v. Koppers Co., 520 F. Supp. 830 (W.D. Pa. 1981), *on remand from* 626 F.2d 324 (3d Cir. 1980); Lichter v. Mellon-Stuart Co., 305 F.2d 216 (3d Cir. 1982).

[101] 797 F.2d 1298, 1307 (5th Cir. 1986).

[102] *Id.* at 1242.

[103] *Id.* at 1300.

[104] 423 F.2d 1231 (Ct. Cl. 1970).

[105] J. D. Hedin Constr. Co. v. United States, 347 F.2d 235 (Ct. Cl. 1965); Oliver-Finnie Co. v. United States, 279 F.2d 498 (Ct. Cl. 1960); MacDougald Constr. Co. v. United States, 122 Ct. Cl. 210 (1952); Great Lakes Dredge & Dock Co. v. United States, 96 F. Supp. 923 (Ct. Cl. 1951), *cert. denied,* 342 U.S. 953 (1952).

[106] Boyajian v. United States, 423 F.2d 1231, 1242 (Ct. Cl. 1970).

[107] *See* New Pueblo Constructors, Inc. v. State, 144 Ariz. 95, 104, 696 P.2d 203 (1985).

is only an appropriate approach if liability has been clearly established but proof of actual damages is impossible or inordinately difficult.[108]

In *Nebraska Public Power District v. Austin Power, Inc.*,[109] the court upheld the jury verdict method of awarding damages where the defendant contractor, Austin, doubled its planned manpower from 4.5 million labor hours to 9 million labor hours on a $67 million coal-fired electric generating plant. Austin claimed that Nebraska Public Power breached its contract primarily in failing to deliver owner-furnished equipment in a timely manner, to administer change orders properly, and to generally coordinate the work. The district court required the jury to specify the amount of damages it awarded on two breach claims for which there was specific evidence but allowed the jury to make a lump sum award on the remaining eleven breaches cumulatively. The appellate court held that it was settled law that once the injury has been established, the courts have considerable leeway in computing the amount of damage. The court rejected the argument that the jury was impermissibly influenced by evidence from a total cost computation. Instead it ruled that the total cost evidence is probative and supplies some evidence regarding the reasonableness of the damages.

The jury verdict is probably a last resort method of calculating damages for an injured contractor. The plaintiff may be thwarted by the trial judge's failure to submit the case to the jury or the jury's rejection of the evidence. The defendant will also face the prospect of defending against an uncertain amount of potential damages. "In estimating damages, . . . all that the litigants have any right to expect is the exercise of the [jury's] best judgment upon the basis of the evidence provided by the parties."[110]

§ 6.23 Conclusion

Loss of efficiency claims have emerged from the shadow of the typical construction delay claim. Unfortunately, some courts still blend loss of efficiency and delay together. However, it is our observation that they are becoming more and more receptive to the qualitative merits of loss of efficiency claims. At the same time, the plaintiff must prove the essential elements of liability, causation, and damages. In order to meet this burden of proof, the plaintiff must carefully and methodically marshall the

---

[108] U.S. Indus., Inc. v. Blake Constr. Co., 671 F.2d 539 (D.C. Cir. 1982); Electronic & Missile Facilities, Inc. v. United States, 416 F.2d 1345 (1969).

[109] 773 F.2d 960 (8th Cir. 1985).

[110] Specialty Assembling & Packing Co. v. United States, 355 F.2d 554, 573 (Ct. Cl. 1960).

fact witnesses and contemporaneous project documentation. The broad brush perspective must be painstakingly constructed, bristle by bristle, to gain evidentiary weight. The most powerful weapon available in lost productivity litigation is the expert witness. The expert witness provides the unique capability to summarize for the trier of fact the corroborating fact testimony and documentary evidence into a cohesive, authoritative opinion as to the extent of productivity losses.

CHAPTER 7

ESTABLISHING DAMAGES

Frederic R. Miller, C.P.A.
Paul W. Pocalyko, C.P.A.

Frederic R. Miller is the director-in-charge of the Business Investigation Services Group of the Washington, D.C., office of Coopers & Lybrand. He is also a leader of the firm's nationwide Task Force on Construction Claims. He has 11 years of experience in assisting clients and counsel in the economic, financial, and accounting aspects of commercial and government litigation. His extensive experience in construction includes work for owners, contractors, sureties, and architect/engineers. Among the projects he has been involved in are commercial and public buildings, water and waste plants, nuclear power plants, and hazardous waste sites. Mr. Miller has served as an expert witness in federal court, state court, and before arbitration panels and boards of contract appeals. He has also taught a number of professional education courses in Litigation Consulting and Construction Claims Analysis, including a session for the Public Contracts Section of the American Bar Association. He is a member of the District of Columbia and American Institutes of Certified Public Accountants and the Association of Insolvency Accountants. Mr. Miller obtained his undergraduate degree from Rutgers University and his M.B.A. degree from the Johnson Graduate School of Management of Cornell University.

Paul W. Pocalyko is a manager in the Litigation and Claims Practice of the Philadelphia Business Investigation Services Group of Coopers & Lybrand. He has an extensive background in financial and analytical analysis in construction disputes. Mr. Pocalyko has worked on several multimillion dollar construction matters, including nuclear and electric power plants, commercial buildings, hospitals, and others. He has provided investigative and accounting expertise addressing issues of entitlement and damages. Mr. Pocalyko is a member of the American and Pennsylvania Institutes of Certified Public Accountants. He holds a B.S. degree in accounting and an M.B.A. from Lehigh University.

§ 7.1   Introduction
§ 7.2   Basic Elements of Damages Presentations
§ 7.3   —Quantifying Incremental Impacts
§ 7.4   —Linking the Liability and Damage Aspects of Claims
§ 7.5   —Importance of Well-Supported Documentation
§ 7.6   —Simplicity and Clarity of Damages Presentation
§ 7.7   General Damage Theories
§ 7.8   —Total Cost Claims
§ 7.9   —Specific Identification Claims (Cause and Effect Method)
§ 7.10 —Modified Total Cost Claims
§ 7.11 —Quantum Meruit Claims
§ 7.12 Presentation of Specific Types of Damages
§ 7.13 —Change Orders and Extra Work
§ 7.14 —Defective Work
§ 7.15 —Delay and Disruptions
§ 7.16 —Overhead
§ 7.17 —Cost Overruns and Related Documentation
§ 7.18 —Interest
§ 7.19 —Labor, Material, and Equipment Escalation during Construction
§ 7.20 Conclusion

§ 7.1   Introduction

In construction litigation, the damages aspect typically requires more of the trial attorney's attention than in other types of litigation. Damages are often the central focus of a construction litigator's case because they are integrally linked with liability issues. The damages "tell the story" in many cases; they show both how and why the plaintiff or defendant was or was not injured. Therefore, the presentation of damages in a construction litigation case is critically important to the overall success or failure of the case.

This chapter is devoted to a discussion of some effective methods used by experienced construction claims experts to present damages in a trial or arbitration panel setting. Not all approaches to establishing damages are described herein, but rather the focus is on some methods of presenting damages that have proven, in practice, to work.

§ 7.2 Basic Elements of Damages Presentations

There are no definitive cut-and-dried requirements for effective presentation of damages. In fact, in our experience, a wide variety of methods and approaches have proven successful in establishing and proving damages. Specific aspects of damages presentations are often dictated by the construction contract, federal or local laws, or industry practice. However, great latitude can also be given to claimants by judges or arbitrators, despite agreed upon contractual or local laws.

Regardless of the lack of standard "cookie cutter" approaches to effective damages presentations, three overall guiding principles are generally present in any such presentation: equity, reasonableness, and economic sense.

Equity. Every damages presentation should be based on a careful examination of the specific facts and circumstances of the case, which provide the expert with a basis for the decision regarding equity, that is, what is the true harm (or lack thereof) suffered by the parties in dispute. Despite a very well supported damage presentation, the claim may not be accepted by a judge, jury, or arbitration panel because it does not address basic equity. The objective of any claim presentation should be to "make the injured party whole," no more, or no less. Only the actual economic harm incurred by the plaintiff should be presented. Puffery for the sake of increasing a claim's dollar value has no place in an equitable claim presentation. Also, the costs of mitigation efforts should not be disregarded since they speak to equity from the standpoint of the defendant.

Reasonableness. The damages also should be able to pass certain tests of basic reasonableness. For example, in a construction delay dispute, if a contractor's claim includes equipment rental costs for concrete forms that greatly exceeds the current replacement cost of these forms, this cost may not be reasonable despite its accuracy. It would be unreasonable for the contractor to rent the forms when they could be purchased at a much lower cost. Each damage theory or specific aspect of damages being claimed or critiqued should be reviewed for reasonableness, because the presence of even one unreasonable aspect in a claim could strain the credibility of other aspects, and thus taint the perceived objectivity of the presentation.

Economic sense. The various aspects of the damage claim should also make economic sense. Blind adherence to theoretical approaches, contractual or statutory requirements, or seemingly relevant professional principles (for example, generally accepted accounting principles) that fly in the face of economic sense should be abandoned in a damages presentation. Once again, it is the specific case facts and circumstances that should be controlling in a damages presentation.

We have found that etching a small number of the most important points very clearly in the minds of the deciders of fact is far more effective than attempting to make a vast number of points, none of which is clearly grasped by the audience. **Tables 7–1** and **7–2** compare a simple damage presentation with one that is too complex. In presenting damages, one should remember to avoid information overload.

Additionally, all well-prepared claims for damages typically have the following characteristics, whatever the specific calculation or format:

1. They isolate and quantify the incremental effects of the alleged impacts of the parties. That is, they focus on what the situation would have been but for the alleged acts or omissions of the parties in dispute;
2. They link the damage amounts to the liability or entitlement issues being argued, indicating the cause and effect relationship;
3. They are well supported, to the extent possible, by books and records of the pertinent companies prepared during the course of the project, or accurate re-creations of these records; and
4. They are clear and concise. Presentations of damages are best when they follow the K.I.S.S. ("Keep It Simple, Stupid") approach.

In §§ **7.3** through **7.6**, we describe each of these characteristics in more detail.

§ 7.3 —Quantifying Incremental Impacts

To maintain credibility when presenting a damage calculation in a construction matter, the presentation should typically be focused only on incremental damages, that is, the additional costs incurred as a result of the liability issues. Costs that would have been incurred regardless of the liability issues are irrelevant. A damage calculation (or critique of a damage

| | ABC Construction Claimed Costs | | |
| | Claimed Costs | | |
	General Contractor	Subcontractors	Total
Materials cost	$1,200,000	$1,800,000	$3,000,000
Labor cost	600,000	900,000	1,500,000
Overhead cost	200,000	300,000	500,000
Total	$2,000,000	$3,000,000	$5,000,000

ABC Construction Claimed Cost

	General Contractor	Masonry	Finishing	Plumbing	Electrical	Sewerage	Total
Material costs							
Phase 1 construction	$ 600,000	$ 375,000	$150,000	$225,000	$120,000	$ 30,000	$1,500,000
Phase 2 construction	276,000	172,500	69,000	103,500	55,200	13,800	690,000
Additional material requirements	144,000	90,000	36,000	54,000	28,800	7,200	360,000
Increased price adjustments	120,000	75,000	30,000	45,000	24,000	6,000	300,000
Modification allowance	60,000	37,500	15,000	22,500	12,000	3,000	150,000
Subtotal	$1,200,000	$ 750,000	$300,000	$450,000	$240,000	$ 60,000	$3,000,000
Labor costs							
Base labor	$ 342,000	$ 213,750	$ 85,500	$128,250	$ 68,400	$ 17,100	$ 855,000
Direct labor	180,000	112,500	45,000	67,500	36,000	9,000	450,000
Indirect labor	60,000	37,500	15,000	22,500	12,000	3,000	150,000
Casual labor	12,000	7,500	3,000	4,500	2,400	600	30,000
Part-time labor	6,000	3,750	1,500	2,250	1,200	300	15,000
Subtotal	$ 600,000	$ 375,000	$150,000	$225,000	$120,000	$ 30,000	$1,500,000
Overhead costs							
Home office overhead	$ 90,000	$ 56,250	$ 22,500	$ 33,750	$ 18,000	$ 4,500	$ 225,000
Site overhead	70,000	43,750	17,500	26,250	14,000	3,500	175,000
Extended duration overhead	30,000	18,750	7,500	11,250	6,000	1,500	75,000
Fixed overhead allowance	10,000	6,250	2,500	3,750	2,000	500	25,000
Subtotal	$ 200,000	$ 125,000	$ 50,000	$ 75,000	$ 40,000	$ 10,000	$ 500,000
Total cost	$2,000,000	$1,250,000	$500,000	$750,000	$400,000	$100,000	$5,000,000

Table 7-2. Complex presentation of claimed costs.

calculation) should include any costs that may have been avoided or are unrelated to liability issues. An example of this is one-time costs in a dispute involving delay/disruption damages. One-time costs (for example, site cleanup) should not be included in the delay/disruption damages, because the site cleanup costs were anticipated to be incurred once, regardless of the project's delays or disruptions. However, if site cleanup activities and costs were to expand because of the actions of the owner, then the additional or incremental portions of these costs might be reasonable to include in a damages presentation.

§ 7.4 —Linking the Liability and Damage Aspects of Claims

In a typical construction claim, a contractor or subcontractor is seeking compensation for the reasonable additional cost and profit due as a result of an act or omission by the project's owner or manager. This act might be a constructive change order, a compensable delay, or other such item. The basic theory of damages in most of these cases is that one person or party (typically the owner) caused the second party (typically the contractor) to incur additional costs, and that these costs should be reimbursed. Thus, the damages sought would make the claimant whole.

The liability or entitlement portions of the construction case focus on the causation issue, that is, did, in fact, the first party cause the second party to incur the additional costs? To make the most effective damages presentation, it is critical to link the damages presentation to the liability aspects. That is, the damages presentation should demonstrate quite clearly that:

1. Additional costs were incurred by the injured party; and
2. These additional costs flowed from the act or omission alleged to be the fault of the other party.

Many very detailed, voluminous, and quite expensively prepared damages presentations have failed to result in damage awards because there was no link made between the liability/entitlement issues and the damages issues. For example, in a classic construction case, *Kansas City Bridge Co. v. Kansas City Structural Steel Co.,*[1] the court rejected the plaintiff's claim for delay damages because it failed to offer proof that the delays had caused additional overhead costs.

It is incumbent upon the litigator and the cost expert to insure that the damages presented flow directly or indirectly from the liability/

---

[1] 317 S.W.2d 370 (Mo. 1958).

§ 7.5 IMPORTANCE OF DOCUMENTATION

entitlement issues presented. Without making this link, even the most thoroughly prepared and well-documented construction claim will not be able to withstand competent cross-examination.

One reliable method of establishing this link between liability and damages is to prepare an analysis showing the differences between construction costs, as bid, compared to costs, as incurred (see example in **Figure 7-1**). The focus of this type of analysis would be a demonstration that the overruns being claimed did in fact occur in the areas of work where the liability exists, and that the costs were incurred because of specific acts of the owner.

§ 7.5 —Importance of Well-Supported Documentation

In general, the better supported a litigator's damage claim is, the higher the likelihood of success. This does not imply that massive efforts need to be undertaken to support every dollar claimed. However, if strong support is presented for the critical features and assumptions of the claim, such support can be the linchpin to successful results.

The best possible scenario for damages presentation is where the additional costs of changed work or disputed issues have been segregated or separately identified in a contractor's records. In this situation, much of the damages presentation could be provided from the contractor's own

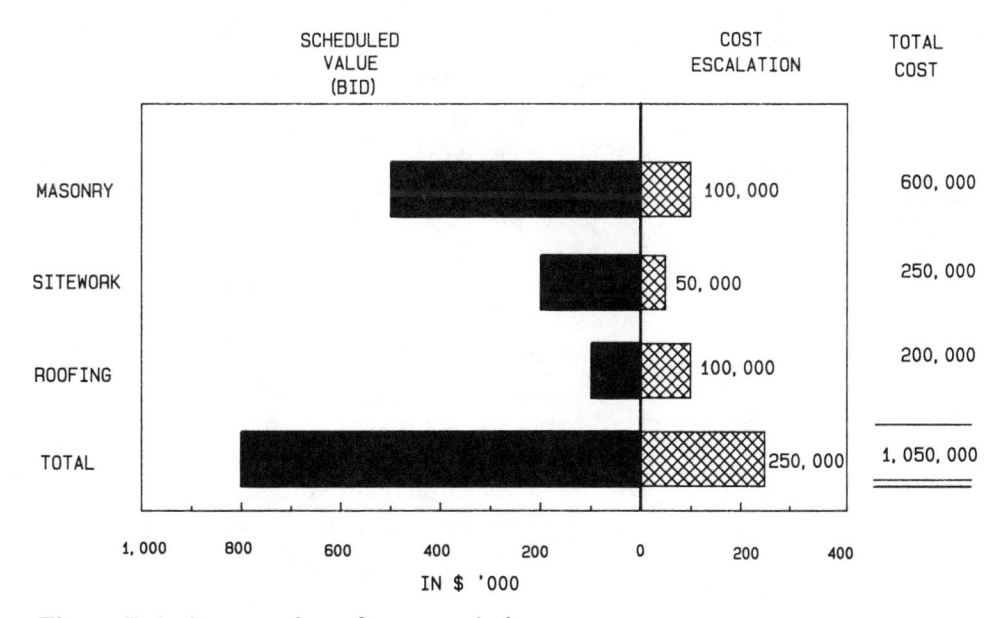

	SCHEDULED VALUE (BID)	COST ESCALATION	TOTAL COST
MASONRY		100,000	600,000
SITEWORK		50,000	250,000
ROOFING		100,000	200,000
TOTAL		250,000	1,050,000

IN $ '000

Figure 7-1. Presentation of cost escalation.

cost records. However, more often than not, the costs of changed work or disputed issues have not been segregated in a contractor's cost records, since their cost systems are organized to be useful in their normal course of business rather than in claims litigation. Therefore, re-creations of cost impacts and analyses within the records are typically required. In these analyses, the individual preparing and presenting the damages will, by necessity, have to make assumptions (for example, unit costs and productivity). These assumptions are often quite important and are also typically the focus of an opponent's cross-examination effort. Therefore, the better supported these assumptions are, the higher the probability of success.

In supporting these assumptions, reliance should be placed on:

1. The contractor's own records and performance on the project
2. The contractor's performance on similar projects elsewhere
3. Industry averages for performance (in that specific location, if possible)
4. Standard industry reference guides (for example, the R.S. Means Guide for construction cost estimating)
5. Expert witness testimony.

§ 7.6 —Simplicity and Clarity of Damages Presentation

Simplicity is a key element in presenting damages. The individual presenting the damages must always remember the audience to whom the damages presentation is being given. That audience may be the standard jury of six or twelve ordinary citizens, a judge, or an arbitration panel of experienced construction attorneys or engineers. There may be striking differences in the audience's understanding of construction accounting and cost concepts; therefore, the damage presentation must be tailored to the specific audience.

The use of graphics to increase clarity and comprehension is also very important. **Table 7-3** and **Figure 7-2** present the same information, demonstrating how the graphic form can drive a litigator's point home much more clearly and permanently.

In a jury trial involving an owner's damages for nonperformance by the HVAC, electrical and plumbing subcontractor, the use of a simple bar graph brought to life the extreme overbilling by the subcontractor for work performed on the project (**Figure 7-3**). The expert witness presenting damages was able to identify costs incurred from the subcontractor's cost accounting records; these were compared to the subcontractor's billings to the owner ("excess payments"). Additionally, the expert established the

§ 7.6 CLARITY OF PRESENTATION 149

	Allowable Costs	Unallowable Costs	Questionable Costs	Total Claimed Costs
Materials	$2,000,000	$200,000	$500,000	$2,700,000
Labor	1,000,000	100,000	250,000	1,350,000
Overhead	500,000	200,000	0	700,000
Total	$3,500,000	$500,000	$750,000	$4,750,000

Table 7-3. Tabular presentation of claimed costs analysis.

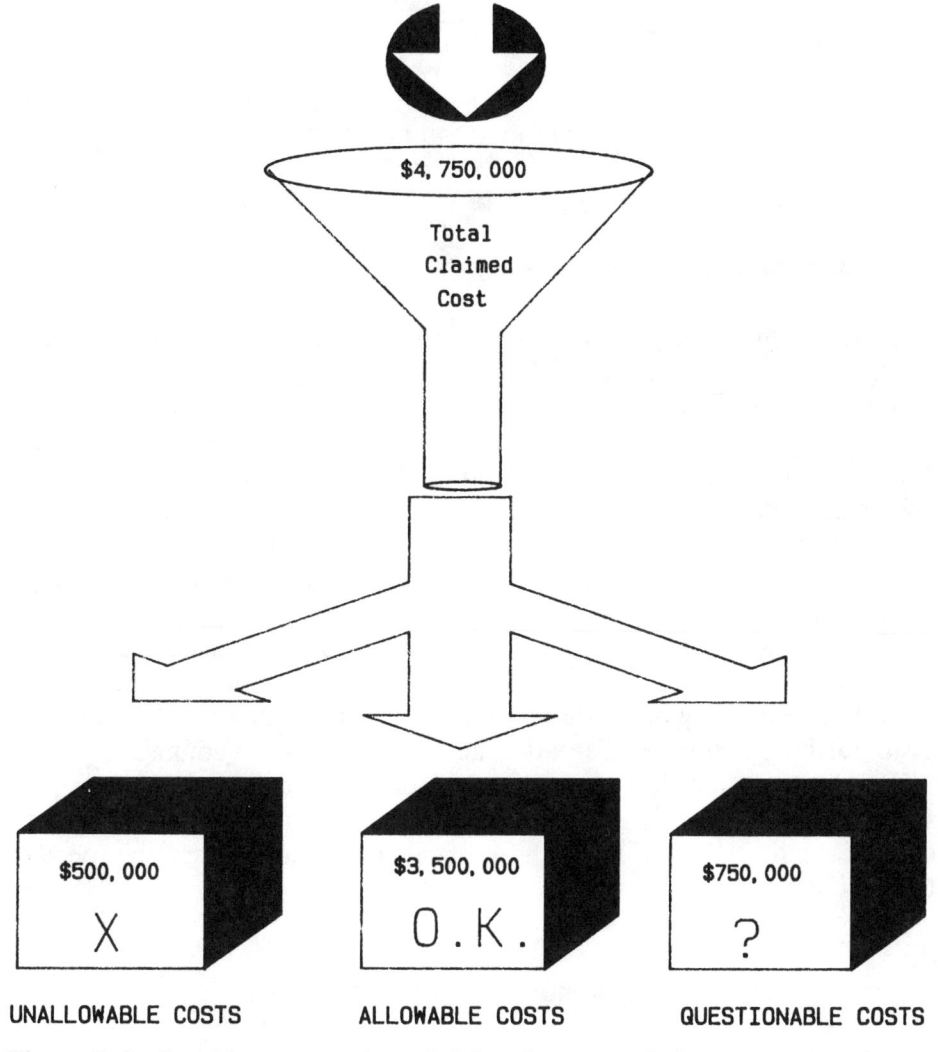

Figure 7-2. Graphic presentation of claimed costs analysis.

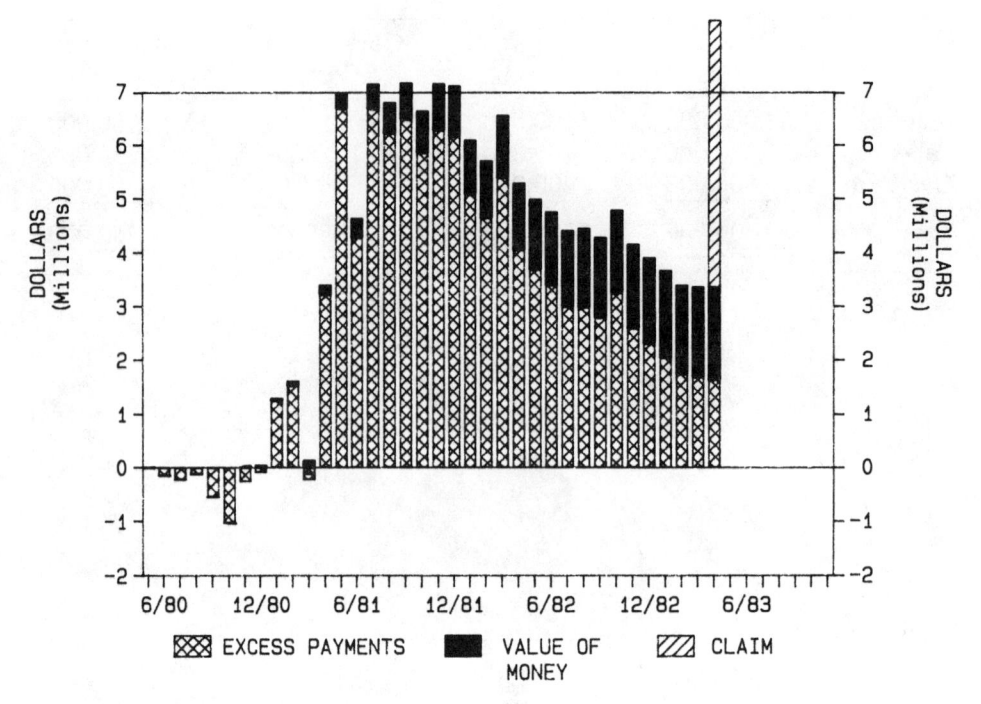

Figure 7-3. Total payments in excess of costs.

interest earning ("value of money") accruing to the benefit of the subcontractor as a result of these overbillings. The expert also identified the financial impact of the extra overhead claim offered by the subcontractor. This claim presented by the subcontractor was in excess of the bills already submitted for payment and paid by the owner. The jury awarded the owner the reimbursement of approximately $30 million, including $1 million in punitive damages to be paid by the subcontractor. The jury relied primarily on the egregious nature of the subcontractor as demonstrated in the expert's use of graphic presentation.

As is clear to most litigators in the construction arena, these cases, if not brought alive to their audiences, can become too technical and boring. Therefore, especially in the damages area, a more lively approach can help distinguish an expert's presentation and make it more memorable.

We now turn to a discussion of some additional points on damage presentations: (1) reviewing the general theoretical methods of presenting damages, and (2) discussing methods of calculating and presenting specific types of damages.

§ 7.7 General Damage Theories

In calculating and presenting damages, there are a few well-recognized and accepted general theoretical frameworks. These basic frameworks are

§ 7.8 TOTAL COST CLAIMS

total cost claims, specific identification claims, modified total cost claims, and quantum meruit claims. The first three types of claims are variations of cost-based claims. The quantum meruit claim uses a different measurement basis, that is, the value accruing to the owner from additional work or cost. In the following sections, we discuss basic approaches to presenting damages using these general frameworks, as well as their strengths and limitations.

§ 7.8 —Total Cost Claims

The total cost claim approach is the least complex and most easily applied methodology used in calculating and presenting construction damages. It also tends to be the most frequently used general theory. In its basic form, damages are calculated by comparing the original bid to the actual costs incurred on the project. The relative simplicity of the methodology is in its ease of understanding (see **Figure 7-4**). Additionally, the data needed to present this type of claim can typically be easily extracted directly from the contractor's records.

However, despite its high score in clearness and conciseness, this method suffers in the areas of equity and reasonableness. There are several disadvantages to the use of a total cost claim, including an extremely strict, legal standard of proof and the necessity to prove the following underlying assumptions:

1. Other methods of calculating damages are impossible or impractical
2. Recorded costs are reasonable
3. The contractors bid or estimate was accurate (that is, contained no underbidding)
4. The actions of the plaintiff in no way caused any of the cost overruns.[2]

The standard of proof for a total cost claim is based on the validity of these four assumptions. Determining that other methods are impossible or impractical is a function of the nature of the case's facts and circumstances. For example, in a situation in which the contractor does not have detailed cost records, it may be relatively simple to demonstrate that this method is the only one practical.

The reasonableness of recorded costs is also not typically a difficult assumption to prove. The expert or other presenter must demonstrate the

---

[2] G.M. Shupe, Inc. v. United States, 5 Cl. Ct. 662 (1984); Chicago College of Osteopathic Medicine v. Fuller, 719 F.2d 1335 (7th Cir. 1983); John F. Harkins Co. v. School Dist. of Philadelphia, 313 Pa. Super. 425, 460 A.2d 260 (1983).

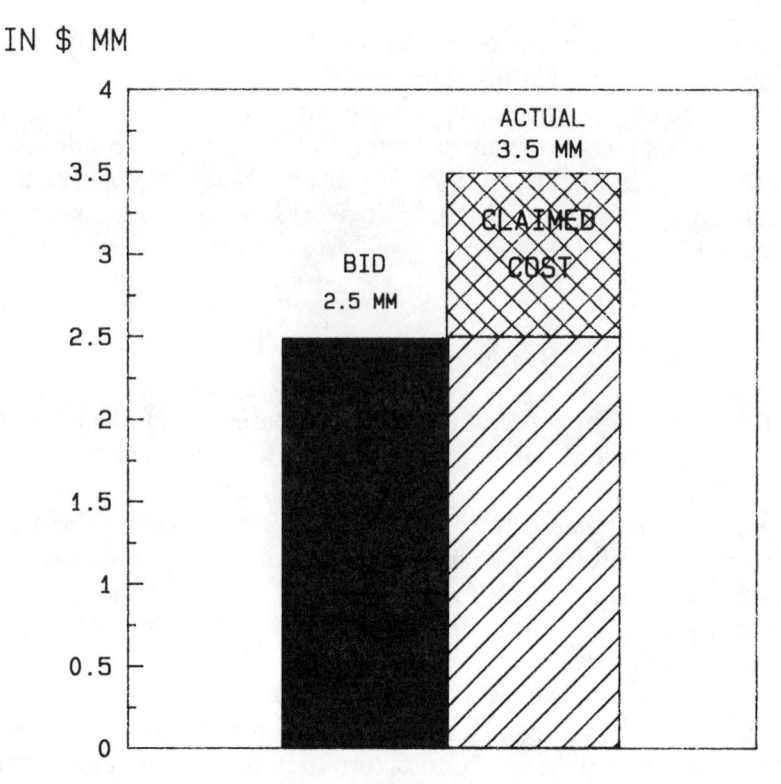

Figure 7-4. Comparison of actual cost to original bid.

appropriateness of costs, the reliability of the contractor's accounting methods and systems, and a relationship to industry practices and standards.

However, proving that the contractor's bid was strictly accurate can be extremely difficult. For example, it might require a comparison of supplier and subcontractor quotes to bid amounts, as well as the comparison of material quantity estimates to contract drawings. Presenting such an analysis is expensive, often difficult to follow, and easily refutable, because most bids rely heavily on assumptions. Many of these assumptions, due to the nature of the bidding process, are accumulated in the absence of accurate information.

The most difficult assumption to prove in the total cost approach is that the plaintiff was blameless for cost escalation or overrun. The premise is easily attacked by demonstrating only a single area of potential blame attributable to the contractor. This could erode the credibility of the entire total cost claim. That is why this method has often been defeated in practice, and why parties may seek to make the modifications discussed in § 7.10.

Additionally, the total cost method as typically presented, does not specifically link the claimed costs to any specific liability issues. Rather, it is commonly argued that the calculated damages resulted from the overall impact of all liability issues. This may create a situation where no true link between causation and effect has been demonstrated.

§ 7.9 —Specific Identification Claims (Cause and Effect Method)

The true linkage between damages and the liability issues that allegedly caused them is much more evident in a specific identification claim. The use of this cause and effect methodology most often yields an accurate, well-defined, and defensible presentation of damages.

In this approach, the importance of each event is tied directly to the cost impact of that event, such as late material delivery and the impact of idle labor time, or the disruptive impact on productivity caused by over-inspection. Many courts now require that plaintiffs establish a cause/effect scenario in proving claimed damages. Therefore, the specific identification method suits these cases perfectly. However, this methodology also requires that the events or transactions in question can be individually identified and isolated, and that the impact of each event can be assessed. This may be extremely difficult in the absence of detailed record-keeping and sophisticated cost control systems that segregate changed work or the impact of disputed issues.

Most often, the specific identification methodology requires some re-creation of records, based on expert analyses, testing assumptions, discussions with project personnel, and so forth. As previously noted, such analyses and re-creation will be subject to scrutiny based on the validity of the assumptions used, and the accuracy and reasonableness of the analyses. However, in presenting such a damage methodology, if the appropriate level of support and testing of the assumptions can also be presented, it can prove to be devastatingly effective. **Figure 7–5** gives an example of this method.

This method tends to have added credibility when the individual presenting the damage shows that the sum of all specifically identified damages does not equal the total difference between the bid cost and total cost (that is, the total cost method); this remaining difference is the costs related to contractor-caused events that have been excluded from the claim.

§ 7.10 —Modified Total Cost Claims

Another general approach to calculating and presenting damages borrows from the concepts of both the specific identification and total cost methods. The modified total cost method quantifies damages by using the inherent simplicity of the total cost approach. Modifications are offered to

154   ESTABLISHING DAMAGES

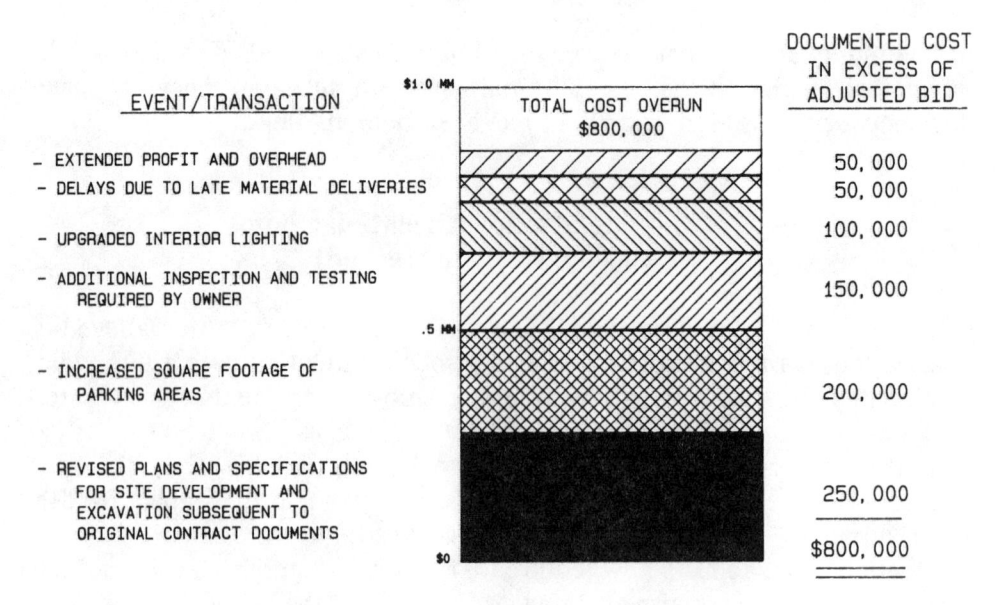

EVENT/TRANSACTION	TOTAL COST OVERRUN $800,000	DOCUMENTED COST IN EXCESS OF ADJUSTED BID
– EXTENDED PROFIT AND OVERHEAD		50,000
– DELAYS DUE TO LATE MATERIAL DELIVERIES		50,000
– UPGRADED INTERIOR LIGHTING		100,000
– ADDITIONAL INSPECTION AND TESTING REQUIRED BY OWNER		150,000
– INCREASED SQUARE FOOTAGE OF PARKING AREAS		200,000
– REVISED PLANS AND SPECIFICATIONS FOR SITE DEVELOPMENT AND EXCAVATION SUBSEQUENT TO ORIGINAL CONTRACT DOCUMENTS		250,000
		$800,000

Figure 7–5. Causes of claimed cost overrun.

demonstrate the cause and effect relationships that exist between the costs and the events or transactions presented in the specific cost approach. The success of the approach often depends upon the extent of the modifications which demonstrate the cause and effect dynamics.

The initial step in calculating damages under this method involves an analysis of the contractor's bid to adjust for any weaknesses uncovered during job performance, including items such as amounts "left on the table" or misbid. A reasonable bid (an as-adjusted bid) is thus established. The recorded project costs are then examined for reasonableness. Unreasonable items such as excessive equipment rental costs should be excluded. These calculations would then yield the "should-have-been" level of project costs, which can then be compared to the as-adjusted "bid."

Rather than performing an aggregate comparison of the as-adjusted bid to "should have been" costs, such comparisons are made for specific component costs related to individual events or transactions linked or related to liability issues. This type of comparison will provide the cost overrun attributable to each liability event or transaction. Then further adjustments can be calculated for those remaining portions of cost overruns that were contractor-caused and as such, represent an improper element of damages. These costs might include the cost of contractor inefficiency due to labor shortage or scheduling problems with subcontractors and suppliers.

This methodology is typically less expensive than using the specific cost method, it can be performed faster, and it holds up reasonably well under cross-examination. However, it is somewhat difficult to present on the stand and is subject to some of the limitations of the total cost method.

§ 7.11 —Quantum Meruit Claims

A final type of damage theory involves an analysis of the "reasonable value" of the work performed. Contractors and subcontractors are afforded protection under mechanic's liens to recover the value of labor and materials used in improving property. The theory of quantum meruit is often used in damage claims when a subcontractor does not have a direct contractual relationship with an owner but the owner has been "unjustly enriched" by work performed by the subcontractor.

The theory of quantum meruit entitles the subcontractor recovery for its contract price plus the cost of extras if:

1. The costs incurred are reasonable and value has accrued to the owner from the work
2. Adjustments (reductions to claims) have been made for any defects in performance
3. Substantial performance of the work is completed.[3]

Various state statutes will determine the amount and methods for recovery under a mechanic's lien action based on quantum meruit. Presentation of this type of claim can also be made using some of the methods described above for cost-based claims. However, these claims are infrequently seen because they can usually only be used in very specific factual circumstances.

§ 7.12 Presentation of Specific Types of Damages

In the previous section, we discuss general damage theories premised on the development of the cost elements and the relationship of these costs to the issues of liability in the litigation or arbitration matter. We now discuss the establishment of these costs as damages with the aid of graphics. The cost elements discussed are not intended to be an inclusive listing, but are examples that highlight the most common areas of construction disputes. Each example demonstrates different techniques and applications of fact to emphasize the cause and effect relationship identified previously.

---

[3] B. Bramble & M. Callahan, Construction Delay Claims, § 10.7 (1987).

§ 7.13 —Change Orders and Extra Work

The most hotly disputed area of construction damages centers around the area of change orders and extra work claims. A distinction between the two is the degree of formality attached to the increased scope of work during the construction process. Change orders are usually formalized in writing, and extra work claims often are developed by contractors after the project's completion. In either case, damages are sought based on the alleged increased scope of work which was not contemplated in the original interpretation of the contract, and the associated dollar cost of the work. Examples of such items are the addition of a higher quality material than originally specified, or the removal and replacement of unsuitable fill materials encountered during excavation. **Figure 7–6** presents a breakdown of an extra work claim including inefficiency.

§ 7.14 —Defective Work

Defective work claims are an effort to recover damages for the correction of improperly performed construction techniques or the use of inferior materials. These damages take the form of either a direct cost of repairs or replacement or the diminished value of the project when corrective

EXTRA COST RELATED TO:

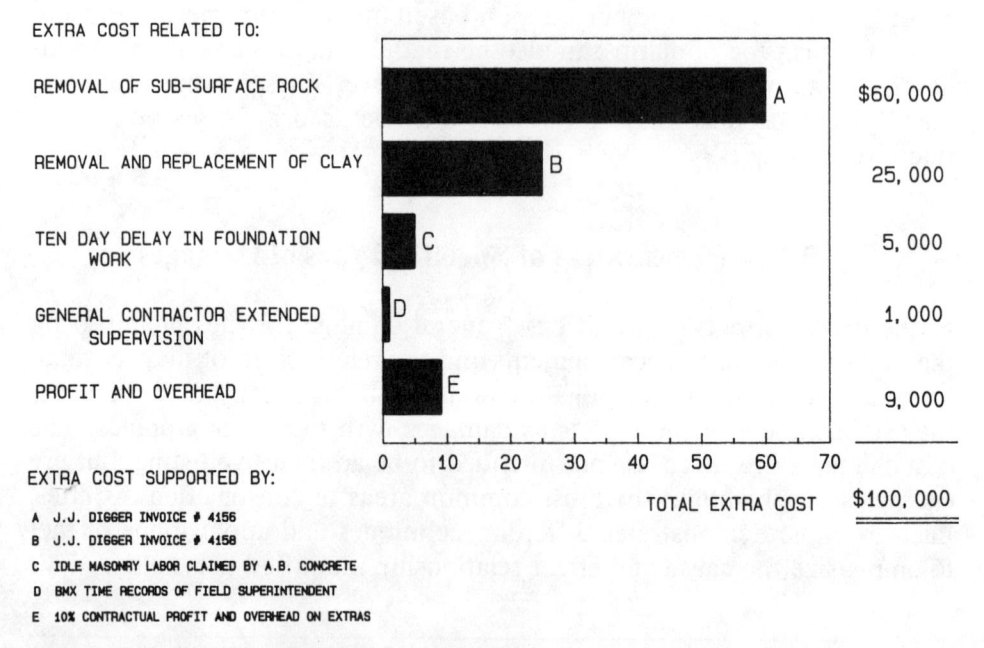

REMOVAL OF SUB-SURFACE ROCK (A)	$60,000
REMOVAL AND REPLACEMENT OF CLAY (B)	25,000
TEN DAY DELAY IN FOUNDATION WORK (C)	5,000
GENERAL CONTRACTOR EXTENDED SUPERVISION (D)	1,000
PROFIT AND OVERHEAD (E)	9,000
TOTAL EXTRA COST	**$100,000**

EXTRA COST SUPPORTED BY:
A J.J. DIGGER INVOICE # 4156
B J.J. DIGGER INVOICE # 4158
C IDLE MASONRY LABOR CLAIMED BY A.B. CONCRETE
D BMX TIME RECORDS OF FIELD SUPERINTENDENT
E 10% CONTRACTUAL PROFIT AND OVERHEAD ON EXTRAS

Figure 7–6. Extra work claim for excavation.

§ 7.16 OVERHEAD

actions are not provided. The underlying concept is to make the owner of a project whole for the cost of correcting the defective work.

The determination of the cost of corrective action can be based on the actual costs incurred by the owner if these are reasonable, or the estimated (bid) costs to perform the work.

§ 7.15 —Delay and Disruptions

The occurrence of a delay or disruption is extremely expensive to both the contractor or the owner. Virtually all construction projects experience some type of delay or disruption as a result of the interdependent nature of construction sequencing. These scheduling variations lead to a highly disputed area of construction costs between owner and contractor.

Delays take many forms, but they are most practically presented as a comparison of actual events to those that were scheduled at the onset of the construction process. **Figure 7–7** reflects a comparison of this type. The matter of construction delay is discussed more fully in **Chapter 5**.

§ 7.16 —Overhead

The increase of a contractor's construction activities through increased scope of work, delays, or other factors can cause an increase in overhead

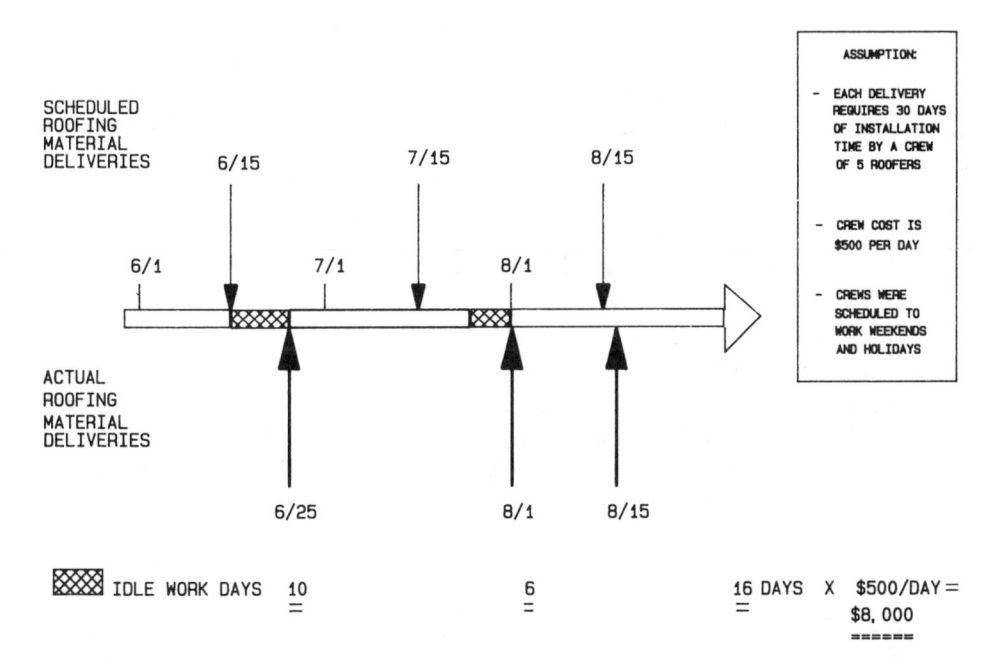

Figure 7–7. Comparison of scheduled deliveries to actual deliveries.

costs related to the project. Overhead includes items such as home office costs associated with a project. These expenses can be either fixed or variable. The ability of the contractor to recover is based upon providing accurate records supporting the increased nature of the costs. Field overhead costs such as trailers, office equipment, security, and trash removal are frequently documented by invoices. But home office overhead is not so easily proved.

A reasonable basis for determining the allowable level of home office overhead costs is difficult to estimate with any level of certainty. As a result, the use of formulas, including the *Eichleay* method,[4] have been developed as a basis. The example below demonstrates the calculation of overhead in a delay situation.

$$\frac{\text{Contract Billings}}{\text{Total Billings during Contract Period}} \times \frac{\text{Total Overhead Incurred during Contract Period}} = \frac{\text{Contract Overhead Cost}}$$

$$\frac{\text{Contract Overhead Cost}}{\text{Number of Days of Contract Performance}} = \text{Daily Overhead Cost}$$

$$\text{Daily Overhead Cost} \times \text{Number of Days of Compensable Delay} = \text{Extended Overhead Cost}$$

The calculation by itself is not adequate to establish a claim for increased overhead costs. In addition, evidence should be provided describing the logical relationship between the extended overhead and the contractor's actual costs incurred on the project. This is demonstrated in **Figure 7–8**.

§ 7.17 —Cost Overruns and Related Documentation

The calculation of cost overruns is normally performed after the responsibility for such costs (owner, contractor, subcontractor, or architect) has been determined. The elements of these costs are derived from a series of records related to the general contractor and its subcontractors. **Figure 7–9** outlines the types of records and the issues to which they may relate in determining a cost overrun. This type of an analysis is useful in

---

[4] Eichleay Corp., ASBCA No. 5183, 60-2 B.C.A. (CCH) ¶ 2688 (1960); *see also* Southern New England Contracting Co. v. State, 165 Conn. 644, 345 A.2d 550 (1974); *but see* Novak & Co. v. Facilities Dev. Corp., 116 A.D.2d 891, 498 N.Y.S.2d 492 (1986).

§ 7.17 COST OVERRUNS 159

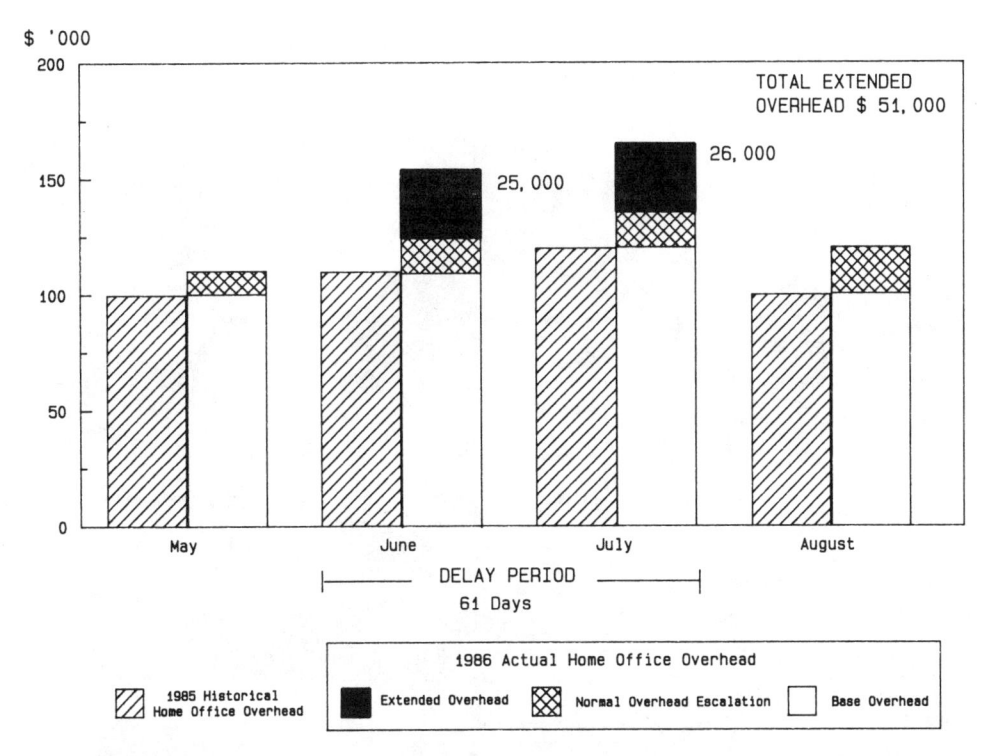

Figure 7-8. Extended overhead costs comparison.

establishing the link between liability and damages and the appropriate evidence.

In effect, a systematic analysis of the records outlined in **Figure 7-9** will allow a determination of the reasonable cost of construction. The contract formation records can serve as a basis for comparing what was estimated versus what actually happened. Deriving explanations for these differences is done through the records related to costs; these establish the underlying accounting support for the components of construction, including labor, materials, equipment, and overhead.

Records related to cash flow help to determine if the costs accumulated were in fact paid to suppliers and subcontractors. Records related to other projects with subcontractors afford a comparison of the reasonable nature of costs claimed by a contractor. An analysis of other projects and related costs can be compared to the project in dispute to determine if the components of the total cost are the same as the components on other projects. If for instance, the labor rate for a subcontractor on another similar project is $25 per hour and on this particular project it rose to $50 an hour, the difference can be disputed as an unfair element of the cost overrun.

160 ESTABLISHING DAMAGES

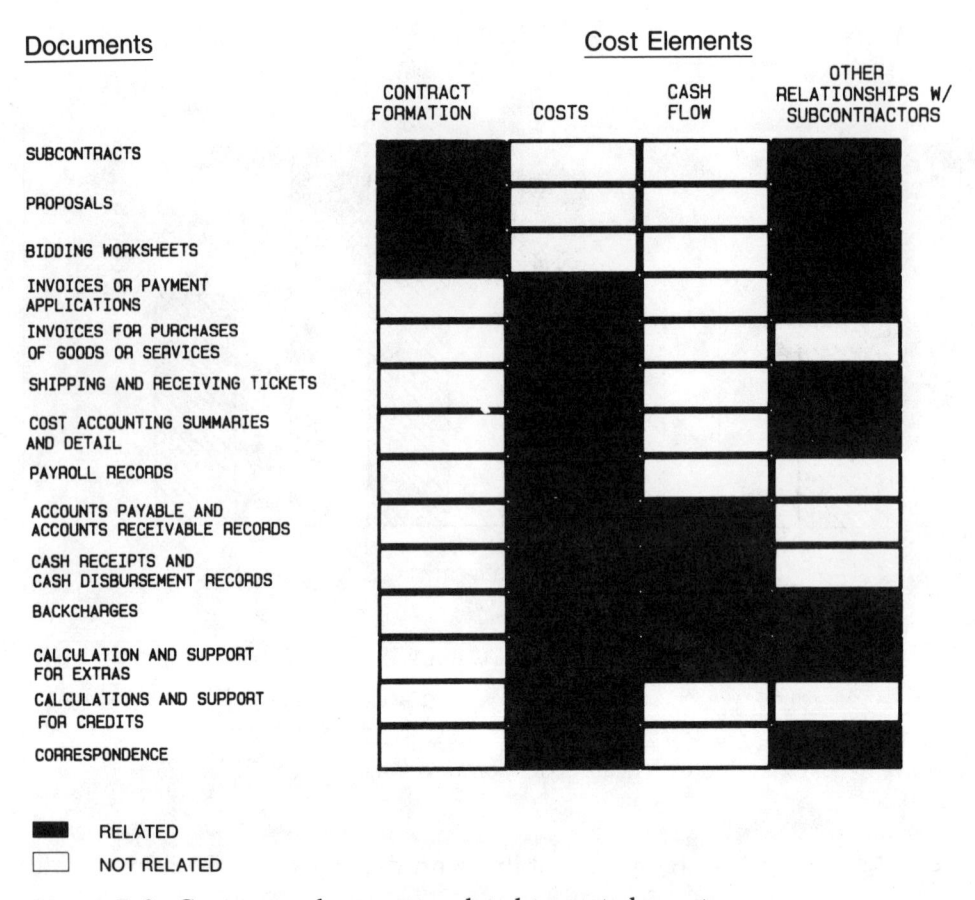

Figure 7-9. Contractor documents related to cost elements.

§ 7.18 —Interest

Interest is one of the less obvious elements of construction cost overruns. Interest in its simplest form relates to the cost of financing the project. This financing cost escalates as project costs increase over time. The expense is developed through an analysis of the time period, an appropriate rate, and the increased project costs. **Figure 7-10** depicts a typical claim for interest related to construction delay.

Many jurisdictions permit the recovery of prejudgement interest, or interest accruing prior to the award of damages.[5] The standards of proof for the recovery are very stringent and are primarily based on the damage calculation being reasonable and based on accurate and reliable cost

---

[5] *E.g.*, Nebraska Pub. Power Dist. v. Austin Power, Inc., 773 F.2d 960 (8th Cir. 1985); Tempo, Inc. v. Rapid Elec. Sales & Servs., 132 Mich. App. 93, 347 N.W.2d 728 (1984).

§ 7.19 LABOR & MATERIAL ESCALATION 161

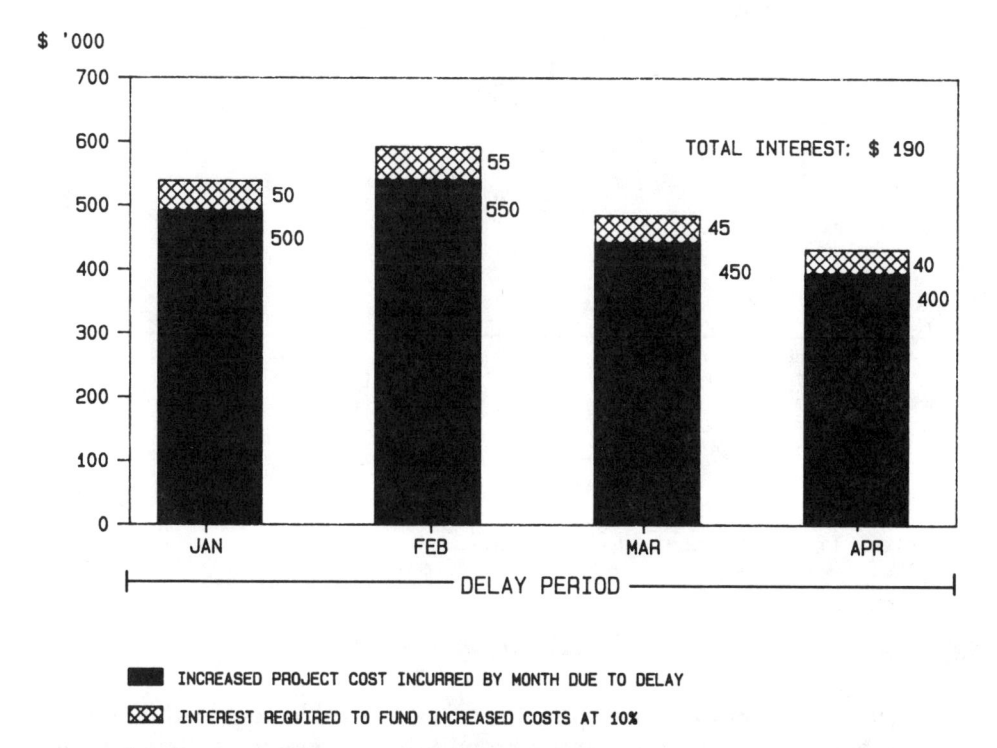

Figure 7-10. Interest costs related to project cost.

information. Interest rates are generally prescribed by statute.[6] Interest may be denied for speculative or poorly substantiated costs. This element of damage should also include consideration of the contractor's expected and actual project cash flows.

§ 7.19 —Labor, Material, and Equipment Escalation during Construction

The escalation of construction costs during the construction period often form the basis for a damage claim in both delay and increased scope of work situations. The components of the damages must be measured against a reasonable and identifiable benchmark. The original bid or the estimated scheduled value are often used as a benchmark from which to measure escalated costs (see **Figure 7-1**).

In addition to presenting an overall quantification, it may be necessary to itemize the cost escalation in terms of events that caused the increased cost (**Figure 7-11**).

---

[6] *E.g.*, 28 U.S.C.A. § 2516(a) (West 1988).

COMPONENT OF DELAY	INCREASED SCOPE OF WORK
LABOR RATE ADJUSTMENT	MATERIAL COST ADJUSTMENT
$60,000	$40,000

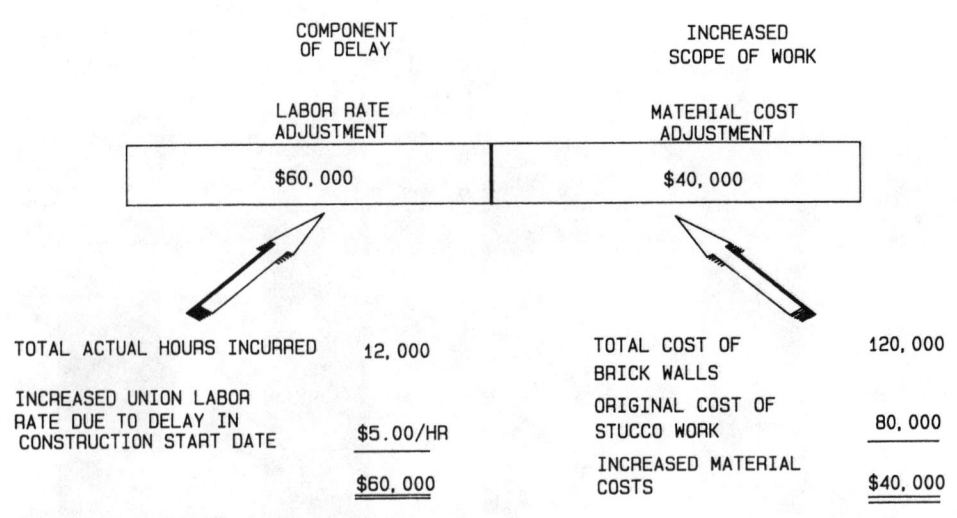

TOTAL ACTUAL HOURS INCURRED	12,000	TOTAL COST OF BRICK WALLS	120,000
INCREASED UNION LABOR RATE DUE TO DELAY IN CONSTRUCTION START DATE	$5.00/HR	ORIGINAL COST OF STUCCO WORK	80,000
	$60,000	INCREASED MATERIAL COSTS	$40,000

Figure 7-11. Cost escalation for masonry.

§ 7.20 Conclusion

The successful construction litigator should be able to tell the story of damages in a construction dispute by building the elements discussed and presented within this chapter. It is critical to emphasize simplicity, clarity, and readability in the preparation of trial exhibits utilized in establishing damages.

The qualified cost expert is essential in today's construction disputes. The complex nature of construction documents and related records require careful and thorough evaluation to establish evidential links between liability issues and the recovery of damages. The use of an expert witness in the damage area can help to consolidate a vast amount of detail into concise explanations, depicting the scenarios relevant to proving damages.

Effective damages presentations should be based on common sense, should be given in a lively presentation, and should demonstrate a solid, well-documented understanding of the facts and details. A combination of these elements with the testimony of a qualified cost expert can be the foundation for successful recoveries in the trial or arbitration of construction disputes.

PART III
FORUM ISSUES

CHAPTER 8

ADVOCACY IN CONSTRUCTION ARBITRATION*

Peter Goetz, Esquire

Peter Goetz is a founder and senior partner of the New York City law firm of Goetz, Fitzpatrick & Flynn, which concentrates on construction and engineering matters throughout the United States and abroad. Mr. Goetz graduated from Rensselaer Polytechnic Institute with a Bachelor's degree in civil engineering and practiced for a number of years with the consulting engineering firm of Ammann & Whitney. After graduation from Brooklyn Law School and admission to the New York Bar, he concentrated his attention on the practice of construction contract law. Mr. Goetz has been a member of the Arbitration Committee of the Bar Association of the City of New York, the Forum Committee on the Construction Industry, the Construction Committee of the Litigation Section, and the Public Contracts Law Section, all of the American Bar Association. He is on the national panel of the American Arbitration Association and serves as a member of the Practice Committee for the Commercial Rules of the AAA. He is also a member of the Construction and Surety Division of the New York State Bar Association, the American Society of Civil Engineers, and the Pilot-Lawyers Bar Association. Mr. Goetz writes monthly articles for two construction trade publications, and he has been a guest speaker at numerous construction seminars.

§ 8.1   Introduction
§ 8.2   Agreement to Arbitrate
§ 8.3   Types of Arbitration
§ 8.4   Arbitration under the American Arbitration Association
§ 8.5   —Selection of Arbitrators from AAA Panel Lists

*The AAA Rules included in this chapter are copyrighted © 1988 by the American Arbitration Association and are reproduced with permission.

§ 8.6	—Arbitrator Categories
§ 8.7	—Sole Arbitrator Selection
§ 8.8	—Selecting the Right Arbitrators
§ 8.9	—Arbitrator Disclosure and Disqualification
§ 8.10	—Special Arbitrator Selection Procedures
§ 8.11	Tripartite Arbitration
§ 8.12	Consolidation of Arbitrations
§ 8.13	—Elements Necessary for Consolidation
§ 8.14	Alternatives to Consolidation
§ 8.15	Advocacy Style
§ 8.16	Conduct at Hearings
§ 8.17	Opening Statements
§ 8.18	The Evidence
§ 8.19	Closing Statements
§ 8.20	Hearing Format
§ 8.21	Hearing Transcript
§ 8.22	Post-Hearing Briefs
§ 8.23	Site Visits
§ 8.24	Adjournments
§ 8.25	Demonstrative Evidence
§ 8.26	The Award
§ 8.27	Punitive Damages
§ 8.28	Other Elements of an Award
§ 8.29	Vacating the Award
§ 8.30	Conclusion

§ 8.1 Introduction

Surprisingly, even today, neither clients nor their attorneys are very knowledgeable or experienced in arbitrating construction disputes. Everyone knows about court litigation, or at least think they do, thanks to television serials like "Perry Mason" or "L.A. Law." As different as a real courtroom trial is from a Hollywood depiction, there is at least a slight resemblance to the real thing. When discussing arbitration with a typical contractor, developer, or anyone else in the construction business, their concept of what an arbitration is does not even slightly resemble the real thing.

Many years ago, when I first started practicing construction law, I redrafted a construction contract for a client that was a sophisticated building construction contractor/developer. Since this contractor did work in

§ 8.1 INTRODUCTION

many different geographical areas, I suggested that it would be advisable to insert an arbitration clause in their standard contract so that any disputes arising with local subcontractors could be resolved in home territory by a panel of experienced construction people instead of an out-of-state jury consisting of people who may not know a backhoe from a garden hoe. We decided to insert a standard American Arbitration Association (AAA) arbitration clause into the contract with applicable Construction Industry Rules. AAA arbitration is a nationally accepted forum for arbitration in the construction industry and the AAA arbitration clause is routinely enforced by the courts throughout this country.

As luck would have it, the client encountered a serious dispute with one of his subcontractors with whom he had a long-standing relationship. The dispute involved substantial dollars and the parties seemed to be unable to work out any mutually satisfactory solution. I suggested to the client that we could invoke the arbitration clause by demanding arbitration, to which my client responded: "Yeah, yeah, that's good, we'll have a friendly arbitration and find out who's right." I immediately cautioned my client that having "a friendly arbitration" is the same as being "a little pregnant." It became obvious to me after only a few minutes of discussion with my client that he had no concept of what arbitration was all about. He thought binding arbitration was something like a mixture of mediation and negotiation, where both sides sat around the conference table before a panel of arbitrators. He envisioned each party giving their side of the story in a business conference atmosphere, and at the conclusion the arbitrators would give their decision. The procedure appeared to him tantamount to two pals who had an argument and chose a mutual friend to decide the issue. I advised him diplomatically that he had a misconception of the arbitration process.

I mention this story because, although this happened almost 25 years ago, I still find today experienced people in the construction industry who are very sophisticated in their business dealings but who do not have the foggiest concept of how arbitration works in real life.

More astonishing, I find experienced trial attorneys undertaking complex construction arbitration cases, although they are unfamiliar with rules and procedures of the AAA. They proceed to handle the arbitration hearings in the same manner as if they were trying a court case, and usually with ruinous results. The fact that an arbitration matter resembles a court case does not make it the same beast any more than a zebra that resembles a horse could be considered to be one.

The techniques used in successful arbitration advocacy may resemble the advocacy used in a court trial, but the approach is definitely not the same. In a court case, there are statutory rules of procedure enforced by the judges. The trial is held where the attorneys are required to comply with the rules of evidence and civil procedure, which are strictly construed by the court. In arbitration, there may or may not be rules that apply to the arbitral procedure. The AAA Commercial or Construction Industry Rules may apply, but, if it is a private arbitration, no specific rules may be applicable and the arbitrators apply their own procedural regulations. In a court of law there are substantive laws and principles of law that apply to the case by which the judge and/or jury are required to decide the case.

The case law decisions of prior cases in a state or federal jurisdiction, known as *stare decisis,* will determine how the court applies the facts and law in a case. In arbitration, the arbitrators are not bound by stare decisis. Arbitration proceeds on the rationale that the best persons to determine an industry dispute are industry peers. What exactly does this mean? Does a party need an attorney for representation in the arbitration? No, individuals, partnerships, or corporations do not need to use an attorney in an arbitration, as contrasted to a lawsuit, in which a corporation cannot appear pro se and must be represented by an attorney. Must the arbitrators be attorneys, retired judges, or have legal training? No, the concept is to have arbitrators who are peers in the industry from which the dispute arose. In a dispute as to the cause of a roof failure, was it because of faulty workmanship, defective materials, an act of God, or owner abuse? The parties should have arbitrators knowledgeable in the roofing industry. Contrary to court cases in which the jury will almost assuredly have no knowledge of construction industry practices or technology, the arbitrators, if they are selected properly, will have this knowledge.

The concept of arbitration is to have a dispute between parties resolved by people knowledgeable in the area of the dispute. But the term "construction industry" has many different meanings because of the many different categories of people within this industry. For example, in a dispute involving the sufficiency of toilet fixtures installed in a new highrise condominium, a soils engineer would not be a very suitable arbitrator. Yet a soils engineer is surely a participating member of the construction industry. Likewise, in the case of a subsurface soil settlement problem, a soils engineer would be a good choice as an arbitrator but not the plumber who was ideal for the toilet fixture case.

§ 8.2 Agreement to Arbitrate

It is important to understand how an arbitration is commenced and when arbitration is attainable. Arbitration is a creature of agreement and stands or falls on the agreement creating the right of arbitration. The first rule is that if the parties do not have a valid arbitration agreement, then unless there is mutual consent, there will be no arbitration. A party, lacking an agreement to arbitrate, cannot capriciously decide to send the dispute to arbitration. There must be an enforceable arbitration agreement in

§ 8.2 AGREEMENT TO ARBITRATE

existence. The courts will not compel a party to arbitrate without such agreement.[1]

Agreeing to arbitrate can be through a clause in the construction contract or it can be pursuant to an agreement arrived at after the dispute has arisen. Agreements to arbitrate future controversies are the most common form of agreements. Such agreements are contained in the construction contract. The AIA standard contract forms are commonly used for prime contracts, subcontracts, and professional design services. They all contain arbitration clauses designating the AAA as the administrator. The arbitration clause can be broad, covering all disputes under the contract, or it can be restrictive, limiting arbitration to specific issues, for example, the cost of additional rock removal in the foundation area. If there is a limited arbitration clause, it will be interpreted as such by the courts and will not be expanded to include other disputes. On the other hand, a broad arbitration clause will be construed by the courts as such, and will include all conceivable disputes arising out of, or related to, the underlying contract. An example of a broad arbitration clause would read:

> Any controversy, dispute or disagreement arising out of this Agreement or the breach thereof shall be settled by arbitration in accordance with provisions set forth in paragraph twenty seventh of this Agreement, and any award rendered by the arbitrators shall be enforceable in any court having jurisdiction of the parties.

Of course, the reference to another paragraph in this broad arbitration clause relates to a paragraph which sets out the arbitration forum to be used or how the arbitrators are to be selected.

Arbitration agreements must be in writing. Even if the contract itself does not contain an arbitration clause, if it refers to another contract or document and incorporates by reference the terms of those documents in the body of the contract, then an agreement to arbitrate which is incorporated by reference may be enforceable. The subcontract agreement usually incorporates by reference all terms and conditions of the prime contract, including the general conditions. If the prime contract happens to have an arbitration clause in it, then a dispute arising out of a subcontract between the prime contractor and subcontractor may be subject to arbitration. In certain jurisdictions the agreement to arbitrate must clearly manifest the intent of the parties, and if it is referred to by reference, it must be clear and convincing.

Where incorporation by reference has been held to be insufficient to compel arbitration, the courts generally find that one of the parties did not intend to resolve the dispute through arbitration. As an example,

---

[1] M. Domke, The Law and Practice of Commercial Arbitration, § 5.01 (1968).

suppose the subcontract states specifically that the prime contract arbitration clause is incorporated by reference into the subcontract. This is sufficiently specific for the courts to find that both parties intended to arbitrate their dispute. If the subcontract provides merely that the terms and conditions of the prime contract are incorporated by reference, and the prime contract happens to have general conditions including an arbitration clause, many courts would find that this incorporation by reference is too obscure to enforce arbitration.

An interesting example of incorporation by reference is found in *P.R. Post Corp. v. Maryland Casualty Co.*[2] In this case the surety under a contractor's performance and payment bond was held to be bound to an arbitration clause contained in the construction contract because the bond included the construction contract by reference. A similar position is expressed in *First Baptist Church of Timmonsville v. George A. Creed & Sons, Inc.*[3]

§ 8.3 Types of Arbitration

There are basically two types of construction arbitration that parties can agree upon in advance to resolve disputes that may arise in the future. The most common forum is the American Arbitration Association (AAA), a national nonprofit administrative agency. Less popular, but often equally effective, is the preselection of two of the three arbitrators by the disputing parties, followed by selection of the third arbitrator by the first two. This is known as tripartite arbitration.

§ 8.4 Arbitration under the American Arbitration Association

AAA arbitration probably accounts for a substantial portion of construction industry arbitrations. The standard arbitration clause recommended by the AAA for a broad construction arbitration provision reads:

Standard Arbitration Clause

Any controversy or claim arising out of or relating to this contract, or the breach thereof, shall be settled by arbitration in accordance with the Construction Industry Arbitration Rules of the American Arbitration Association, and judgment upon the award rendered by the arbitrator(s) may be entered in any court having jurisdiction thereof.

---

[2] 68 Mich. App. 182, 242 N.W.2d 62 (1976).
[3] 276 S.C. 597, 281 S.E.2d 121 (1987).

§ 8.5 SELECTION OF ARBITRATORS

The AAA has two sets of rules governing the administration of arbitrations, the Commercial Rules and Construction Industry Rules. Always make sure that the arbitration agreements provide for Construction Industry Rules because they are, naturally, more applicable for disputes in the construction field, and the arbitrator panel lists from which arbitrators are selected contain people experienced in the construction industry.

After a demand for arbitration is mailed by the claimant to the adversary and is filed with the AAA with the appropriate filing fee, the arbitral process begins. The AAA acknowledges the filing of the arbitration demand, mails notices to the parties, and gives the respondent the opportunity to file an answer. After these preliminary procedures are completed, the selection of arbitrators gets underway.

If the other party (respondent) feels that the arbitration demand is improper, that the dispute is beyond the scope of the arbitration, or that there is no arbitration agreement, it is at this stage that the respondent must start a court action to stop the arbitration. In most jurisdictions, if a court action is not promptly commenced, the objection to arbitration will be deemed as a matter of law to have been waived.

Assuming there is no objection to arbitration and the respondent eagerly awaits the opportunity to challenge the claimant's position, and perhaps even files a counterclaim against the claimant, then the stage is set for the arbitration process.

§ 8.5 —Selection of Arbitrators from AAA Panel Lists

The next event in an AAA arbitration is the selection of arbitrators. If jury selection in a court case is considered important, then arbitrator selection in an arbitration must be considered critical. The arbitrators selected will determine the manner, style, and pace by which the arbitration proceeds. Suppose the claimant is seeking to prove a breach of contract based on a broad view of industry practice as a major ingredient of the case; if the selected arbitrators are all experts in highly specialized facets of technology in the industry, the outcome may be a panel of nitpickers who miss the forest for the trees. On the other hand, if the breach of contract revolves around a highly technical issue pertaining to the structural design of a unique structure, then the nitpicker approach may be ideal for the claimant's case.

The AAA sends to both parties, or their attorneys if they are represented by counsel, an initial list of arbitrators and a hearing calendar for selection of dates. Depending on the amount claimed in the arbitration demand, one or three arbitrators will preside over the case. The present policy of the AAA is to designate one arbitrator for cases involving less than $100,000 and three arbitrators for matters involving greater amounts. Of course, the parties can mutually agree on any number of arbitrators they wish to have for their case, although the standard practice is one or three.

With the three-arbitrator panel, a very abbreviated biography of each arbitrator is included with the arbitrator list. In my experience, these biographies are generally inadequate to get a true picture of the person. The biography gives current employment, prior companies and years worked for them, college and professional degrees, year of graduation, and university. They do not give an adequate job description and at best provide only a sketchy picture of prospective arbitrators.

The first thing to do upon receiving the list of panelists is distribute it and the biographical information to the client and to all members of the law firm. The list should be reviewed internally by the attorney for conflict and prior experience with any panelist. As everyone knows, the construction industry is a small world when it comes to everyone knowing each other. Of course, selecting arbitrators who may have a "good old boy" relationship with your adversary should be avoided. If there is any chance of partiality, the name should be scratched immediately.

§ 8.6 —Arbitrator Categories

What type of arbitrators do we look for? This depends on the case. If the dispute is between a contractor and owner concerning alleged extra work and delays resulting from design changes and deficiencies in the plans, the ideal arbitrators from the contractor's viewpoint will undoubtedly differ from those of the owner. Therefore, the attorney should attempt to categorize the arbitrators into interest groups or professional disciplines, such as contractors, owner-developers, and engineers. I have found that few attorneys, except those experienced in arbitration, take this all important step to attempt to ensure a balanced panel. As an example, say 15 potential arbitrators are on the list submitted to the parties. If an owner and the owner's attorney select from the list without placing them into any category, they are in for a big surprise if a letter comes from the AAA designating three contractors as the three arbitrators for the case. To avoid the possibility of having an unbalanced panel, the parties should request the AAA to designate the arbitrators from a specific category of panelists.

It has been my experience that when serious issues of law are involved in an arbitration, an attorney should be on the panel. Usually, the other two arbitrators suggest that the attorney-arbitrator act as the chairman. This can be good and bad, depending upon the nature of the case and more importantly, the personality of the attorney-arbitrator. I have been involved in arbitrations where the touchstone issues were nonlegal matters such as complex engineering evaluations. I was successful in persuading the arbitrators that the appropriate chair for the case was the engineer and not the attorney. I believe it is the policy of the AAA to suggest that the attorney member chair the panel. This issue can be discussed at a pre-hearing conference with the AAA, which can easily be arranged.

It should be noted that many of the attorneys listed in the Construction Industry Panel are not really experienced construction attorneys. It would seem that attorneys who have constructed a fence around their house or have poured a replacement patch of sidewalk sometimes submit themselves to the AAA as experienced construction attorneys. The point is that when seeking a legal person with a construction background, you may be disappointed when it comes to the latter.

§ 8.7 —Sole Arbitrator Selection

The selection process for a one-arbitrator proceeding involves different considerations than for a three-arbitrator panel. With three arbitrators to be selected, the aim for each party is to get the most people sympathetic to its cause on the panel. In an owner-contractor dispute representing the contractor, of course one wants as many contractors on the panel as possible, and vice versa when representing the owner.

If the arbitration will only involve the appointment of one arbitrator, then try to obtain an arbitrator most familiar with the relevant trade practices of the industry. It is inadvisable to have an attorney as the sole arbitrator unless it is an attorney who specializes in the construction law field.

§ 8.8 —Selecting the Right Arbitrators

What qualities should you look for in selecting an arbitrator for an AAA arbitration using Construction Industry Rules? The names furnished by the AAA are from the National Panel of Arbitrators, who were designated by the National Construction Industry Arbitration Committee. This panel comprises members of 13 different construction and professional associations, running the gamut from the American Construction Owners Association to the National Utility Contractors Association. All facets of the construction industry are represented on the national panel. The trick is to get the AAA to furnish arbitrators who are most suitable for your case. Getting the appropriate list requires the initiative of the attorneys.

When the demand for arbitration is filed with the AAA by the claimant or the answer is filed by the respondent, it is appropriate to advise the AAA of the desired number and category of arbitrators. The tribunal administrator of the AAA does not know anything about your case except for a brief description contained in the demand or answer. If the attorney does not advise the administrator of the desired kind and category of arbitrators, the AAA will prepare the list of panelists for the case, without any appreciation as to the issues in dispute. If this is allowed to occur, the chances are that the panelists selected will be unsuitable for the case. For example, you certainly do not want a geologist deciding a case involving a structural steel dispute, nor a structural engineer sitting on a case involving a malfunctioning heating, ventilation, and air conditioning (HVAC) system.

If you have given the tribunal administrator an adequate description of the dispute and received an inappropriate list of proposed arbitrators, you should not compromise and try to make your selections from an inappropriate list. Either return the list and indicate why it is being returned, or strike out all the undesirable panelists and return it with the scant selections you were able to make. I have often seen attorneys furnished a panel list of a dozen arbitrators who were hesitant to strike out ten of them. If the list is returned with most of the names stricken, then an explanation should be given with your transmittal back to the AAA as to the reasons for this drastic action. Without a request for a new list, there is a good chance that the AAA will not issue a second list but will instead administratively appoint the arbitrators.

Having the AAA designate the arbitrators for your case deprives you of your right to selection, and more importantly, you become boxed in if you happen to be dissatisfied with the appointment made by the AAA. Unless you have a factual basis upon which to challenge the appointed arbitrators, your objection will be rejected.

When selecting arbitrators always try to find somebody who is knowledgeable in your specific facet of the industry and who will best represent your interest as a participating member in your trade, profession, or industry.

§ 8.9 —Arbitrator Disclosure and Disqualification

Section 19 of the Construction Industry Arbitration Rules provides as follows:

19. Disclosure and Challenge Procedure

Any person appointed as neutral arbitrator shall disclose to the AAA any circumstance likely to affect impartiality, including any bias or any financial or personal interest in the result of the arbitration or any past or present relationship with the parties or their representatives. Upon receipt of such information from the arbitrator or another source, the AAA shall communicate the information to the parties and, if it deems it appropriate to do so, to the arbitrator and others. Upon objection of a party to the continued service of a neutral arbitrator, the AAA shall determine whether the arbitrator should be disqualified and shall inform the parties of its decision, which shall be conclusive.

As can be seen, only circumstances which would affect impartiality, such as bias or financial or personal interest in the results of the arbitration, or any past or present relationship with the parties or their counsel, are grounds for arbitrator disqualification. What exactly does this mean? Is a contractor-arbitrator naturally biased against an owner so as to permit an owner to disqualify him? The answer is a resounding No! under ordinary circumstances. However, in one case where a subcontractor-arbitrator had written a scathing article in a trade publication condemning the entire general contracting industry, the attorney handling the case for the general contractor made an objection, sending a copy of this article to the AAA, and was ultimately successful in having the arbitrator withdrawn.

Certainly if an arbitrator is a personal friend of one of the parties, it would be grounds for disqualification. Is it unwise for a party to select a friend who may appear on the list? This would be courting disaster because the arbitrator, if selected, would probably make the disclosure about the relationship and thus be disqualified by the other party. If the arbitrator failed to make this disclosure (which would be improper conduct) and the case proceeded, then the entire hearing and any award would be in jeopardy if this relationship was subsequently discovered. Any attorney who was advised of such a relationship by the client would be obligated to counsel the client to strike the name from the list.

What about trade relationships where one of the proposed arbitrators knows one of the parties, but only in a business relationship, being members of the same trade association? This is not grounds ipso facto for disqualification, although it can evolve into a knotty issue. What about the situation where the proposed arbitrator is in the same business as one of the parties, and has on occasion played golf or tennis with a principal of the party at various trade outings? No one knows the answer, but a disclosure in advance can avoid the embarrassment and wasted expense of an award which is later set aside.

§ 8.10 —Special Arbitrator Selection Procedures

If embarking on a complex arbitration that involves substantial monies and many weeks of hearings, special measures are necessary in order to assure the proper selection of arbitrators. In a recent case I was handling that involved 50 hearings and millions of dollars of claims and counterclaims, I worked out an arrangement with my opposing counsel to preselect the list of arbitrators from which the AAA would make their final appointment.

The attorneys for both sides met at the AAA office and were furnished the biography cards for all the arbitrators in the regional offices that were within reasonable traveling distance to the arbitration locale. We developed a two-step system leading to the final selection of the arbitrators. First, each side (attorney and client) reviewed all the biographies and preselected the largest possible group of acceptable arbitrators under each of three pre-agreed upon categories. In this particular case we were looking for a contractor, an architect, and an attorney familiar with construction. Then, after each side preselected people from each of these categories, the attorneys had a second session to correlate the names each side had selected. Our objective was to obtain by mutual agreement approximately 15 arbitrators in each category. We were able to accomplish this, although in one category we were required to go back to our clients to expand our selections. From this mutually selected list, the AAA regional office made its final selections.

Although this process was very time-consuming, the results were rewarding in terms of ultimate satisfaction with the arbitrators. We avoided objections by either party, a time-consuming administrative process that can drag on for many weeks, if not months. In this case we were able to appoint an excellent panel of arbitrators well suited to hear the case in approximately three weeks.

§ 8.11 Tripartite Arbitration

A common form of arbitration agreement is to have each party designate its own arbitrator, and have the third arbitrator designated by these two arbitrators. In such a situation, the arbitrator selected by each party is not really impartial or unbiased. In one New York case, *Astoria Medical Group v. Health Insurance Plan,*[4] the court stated: "Arising out of the repeated use of the tripartite arbitral board, there has grown a common acceptance of the fact that the party-designated arbitrators are not and cannot be 'neutral' at least in the sense that the third arbitrator or judge is."

In *Stef Shipping Corp. v. Norris Greenco,*[5] the court citing *Astoria Medical Group* confirmed that the party-designated arbitrators need not be impartial. It is common in tripartite arbitration agreements to designate the means by which the two arbitrators are to agree upon a third impartial arbitrator. Often either the courts or the AAA are designated to appoint the third arbitrator if the party-appointed arbitrators are unable to agree in their selection. In this type of arbitration, the parties are really having

---

[4] 11 N.Y.2d 128, 182 N.E.2d 85, 227 N.Y.S.2d 401 (1962).
[5] 209 F. Supp. 249 (S.D.N.Y. 1962).

the case decided by one arbitrator because the two other arbitrators are not impartial per se.

The party-appointed arbitrator should be selected as carefully as one selects an attorney. The more impartial the party-appointed arbitrator acts, the more effective he or she will be in influencing the thinking of the neutral arbitrator. However, even if party-appointed arbitrators are not impartial, they must always act without prejudice toward the interests of the other party. They may be partisan, but they must accept convincing testimony, and must act honestly in their capacity as arbitrators.[6]

§ 8.12 Consolidation of Arbitrations

Construction industry disputes usually involve multiple issues relating to many different trades, and consequently to many different parties. Typical players in a construction dispute will be the owner, the design professional, the construction manager, the general contractor, and the subcontractors.

Arbitration is a creature of contract. Even though there is an arbitration agreement between owner and contractor, between contractor and subcontractor, and between owner and architect, it may be difficult to get all of the parties together in the same arbitration forum should a dispute arise involving all or some of the parties.

What happens when the arbitration clause in the contract provides that any arbitration arising out of the contract cannot be consolidated with any other arbitration? Is such language binding? The standard AIA (American Institute of Architects) contract between owner and architect contains a restrictive arbitration clause.[7] It provides that disputes between the owner and the architect must be settled by arbitration but that such arbitration cannot be consolidated with any other arbitration. From the owner's point of view this is a very unfair limitation because most of the disputes involved in a construction project between a general contractor and an owner involve some facet of the design. If an owner is brought into an arbitration with a contractor based on allegations of extra work arising from design deficiencies, how does this owner make a claim against the architect if it turns out that the architect is the source of the problem? According to the standard AIA contract, no arbitration between the architect and the owner can be consolidated without the consent of the architect. Undoubtedly the architect will not give consent.

Observe the plight of the owner, who seems to be left to twist in the wind by this restrictive arbitration clause. Assume that separate arbitrations are

---

[6] Domke on Commercial Arbitration § 20.03 (1984).

[7] American Institute of Architects, Document B141, Article 7 (1987).

held. First the arbitration between the owner and the contractor goes to award and the arbitrators decide that the owner was liable to the contractor on its claims, because the extra work was the result of design deficiencies and the owner stands in the shoes of the architect, who is the owner's agent. After being throttled in the contractor arbitration, the owner demands arbitration against the architect, contending that the owner had to pay the contractor because of design deficiencies and should thereby recover from the architect the award obtained by the contractor. Not surprisingly, the architect will probably defend on the grounds that it was not responsible for improper design and that the arbitrators in the owner-contractor case were all wet. Assume that the arbitrators in the architect-owner case agree with the architect and dismiss the owner's claim. This is not an unusual set of circumstances. As can be seen, the owner is left without a remedy and is seriously prejudiced.

This scenario highlights the necessity for the owner to be able to have disputes with its contractors and with its architect heard in the same forum and by the same arbitrators. The appropriate means to accomplish this is by consolidating the arbitrations before the same tribunal.

Not only does the owner need consolidation in a situation such as this, the prime contractor is often in the same position vis-à-vis claims by subcontractors against it, which become pass-along claims by the contractor against the owner. If the prime contractor cannot consolidate arbitrations between its subcontractors and the owner, it will be no better off than the owner was when it was unable to consolidate the architect's arbitration. The same situation exists with the contractor who has a dispute between two of its subcontractors, each of whom claims that the work falls within the other's trade.

It should be apparent at this point that consolidation is often a necessity to assure consistent and equitable results.[8] Why does the standard AIA owner-architect agreement have a prohibition against consolidation? The best answer probably lies in the fact that the document was drafted by architects.

§ 8.13 —Elements Necessary for Consolidation

If there are common issues of fact and law existing between both arbitrations; if substantial prejudice will occur to one party if the arbitrations are not consolidated; and if the consolidation will not cause one party prejudice, then a party may wish to consolidate separate arbitration proceedings unless the arbitration agreement prohibits it.

---

[8] Episcopal Hous. Corp. v. Federal Ins. Co., 273 S.C. 181, 255 S.E.2d 451 (1979).

Ordinarily, the party seeking consolidation will seek to consolidate arbitrations through a court application. In order for the court to order consolidation it must have jurisdiction over all the parties. In situations in which the Federal Arbitration Act is applicable, the courts will enforce consolidation under the authority of federal law. In some recent decisions of the United States Supreme Court, it would appear that the Federal Arbitration Act is a preemptive body of law and is controlling even in state courts when the performance of the construction contract involves interstate commerce. Two recent United States Supreme Court decisions hold that the Federal Arbitration Act "creates a body of Federal Substantive Law" that supplants whatever arbitration act exists in a particular state.[9] Since consolidation is liberally construed under the Federal Arbitration Act, it would behoove the applicant to apply for consolidation under this preemptive statute.

§ 8.14 Alternatives to Consolidation

If the arbitration clause in a contract prohibits consolidation, and it is important that some form of consolidation be implemented in order to avoid inconsistent results, other approaches may be available. In a case in which I was involved, the subcontractor demanded arbitration against the general contractor, alleging extra work caused by deficient plans and specifications in the prime contract. The contractor in turn demanded arbitration against the owner, alleging that if the subcontractor recovered against the contractor, then the contractor was entitled to recover against the owner. By stipulation all three parties agreed to consolidated hearings. The owner predictably demanded arbitration against the architect, alleging that if the owner had to pay an award to the contractor, then it should recover a like amount from the architect. The owner concurrently started a court action to consolidate the arbitrations. The architect predictably objected to consolidation based on the language of the AIA contract, which clearly prohibited consolidation.

The court came up with a rather novel but satisfactory approach. It held that as a matter of law it was compelled to uphold the prohibition against consolidation contained in the architect's arbitration clause, so it denied consolidation. However, the court directed that the same arbitrators who were to decide the owner-contractor-subcontractor case also be appointed to hear the owner-architect arbitration.[10] This is known as a

---

[9] Southland Corp. v. Keating, 465 U.S. 1 (1984); Moses H. Cone Hosp. v. Mercury Constr. Corp., 460 U.S. 1 (1982).

[10] Joseph L. Muscarelle, Inc. v. Two Univ. Plaza Corp., No. A-3658-78 (N.J. Super. Ct. App. Div. June 17, 1980) (unreported decision).

seriatum arbitration. The seriatum arbitration in this instance accomplishes the same results as consolidation except it is a more costly procedure because the pivotal party (in this instance, the owner) is exposed to the cost and expense of two arbitration proceedings. It is noteworthy that the new 1987 AIA architect-owner contract form contains an expanded arbitration clause ostensibly to deal with the situation described in the *Muscarelle* case. The new clause (7.3) reads: "No arbitration arising out of or relating to this Agreement shall include, by consolidation, joinder or in any other manner, any additional person or entity not a party to the Agreement. . . ." As far as the author is concerned, this still does not cover a prohibition against seriatum arbitration.

In certain states, the courts have taken the position that without specific legislation allowing for consolidation, the courts are without power to direct the parties to have consolidated hearings.[11] Massachusetts and California have enacted legislation that empowers the state courts to order consolidation or joinder of arbitration proceedings.[12]

The courts in this country are not in harmony when it concerns consolidation. In *Consolidated Pacific Engineering Inc. v. Greater Anchorage Area Borough School District,*[13] the court was held to be without authority to direct consolidation, despite common questions of fact and law, when the agreement was silent on consolidation and when one party objected to consolidation. This principle was followed by Connecticut courts.[14]

Can the arbitrators themselves determine whether cases should be consolidated? Ordinarily consolidation is the province of the court, but in *Kalman Floor Co. v. Joseph L. Muscarelle, Inc.,*[15] the New Jersey courts once again took a novel approach to the issue of consolidation. In this matter there was a dispute between the owner and general contractor concerning the sufficiency of a slab-on-grade floor for a gigantic food warehouse comprising some 14 acres. The contractor started arbitration against the owner for monies due under its contract because the owner was withholding substantial sums due to rejection of the entire concrete floor. The contractor simultaneously demanded arbitration against the flooring subcontractor, alleging that if the owner was entitled to an award against the contractor for a faulty floor installation, then the subcontractor should likewise be responsible to the contractor for the amount of this award. Neither the owner nor the subcontractor wanted to arbitrate the dispute. It

---

[11] *See* Annotation, *State Courts' Power to Consolidate Arbitration Proceedings,* 64 A.L.R.3d 528 (1975).

[12] Mass. Gen. Laws Ann. ch. 251, § 2f (West 1977); Cal. Civ. Proc. Code, § 1281.3 (West 1986).

[13] 563 P.2d 252 (Alaska 1977).

[14] Megin v. State, 187 Conn. 47, 434 A.2d 306 (1980).

[15] 196 N.J. Super. 16, 481 A.2d 553 (1984), *aff'd,* 98 N.J. 266, 486 A.2d 334 (1985).

was imperative that the contractor have both the owner and the subcontractor in the same arbitration in order to avoid inconsistent results.

The subcontractor and the owner each started separate lawsuits, albeit in different states, to stay the arbitrations. The owner's objections were the easiest to overcome. The New York lower court confirmed the arbitrability of the dispute and the appellate division affirmed the lower court decision. The next step was to have the court direct the subcontractor to go to arbitration and then order that the two arbitrations be consolidated. The subcontractor commenced a court action in New Jersey against the general contractor, the AAA, and individual members of the AAA to stay the arbitration. The New Jersey lower court rendered a unique decision in that it directed the arbitrators to decide the issue of consolidation.

The court's rationale was simple: if the parties agreed to resolve their disputes through arbitration, then why not also have the arbitrators decide the issue of consolidation? Up to this time it had always been the province of the court to pass on the issue of consolidation. This pioneering decision was upheld by the New Jersey Supreme Court.[16] To the author's knowledge, this was only the second reported decision in the United States permitting arbitrators to decide the issue of consolidation, the other case being an obscure decision from Alaska.

The arbitrators held hearings on the issue of consolidation, which the subcontractor chose to boycott, and thereafter issued an interim award directing arbitration. Ultimately, all parties participated in the arbitration proceeding, and after a long and hard-fought arbitration, an award was rendered by the arbitrators in favor of the contractor and subcontractor against the owner.

In conclusion, if there are more than two parties to a dispute, if all the parties have arbitration agreements, if there are common questions of fact or law, if consolidation of the arbitrations will not be prejudicial to any party, if substantial prejudice will occur if the matters are not consolidated, and if there is no prohibition against consolidation in either of the arbitration agreements, then consolidation will under most circumstances be enforced.

§ 8.15 Advocacy Style

As previously stated, arbitration is not litigation, and although the two may be similar in many respects, they are very different overall. In a litigation case, the attorney must convince a judge and often a jury. A judge

---

[16] Kalman Floor Co. v. Joseph L. Muscarelle, 98 N.J. 266, 486 A.2d 334 (1985). A full description of the case can be found in *Construction Law Report,* Builder and Contractor, Nov. 1986, at 14, 15.

(and especially a jury) often will have little or no knowledge of any of the technical complexities inherent in a construction contract dispute.

As an example, take a situation where there is a crack in the masonry wall of a highrise apartment building that is causing water to enter the living space of the dwelling units. The masonry contractor contends it followed the plans and specifications and that the causes of the water leaks are improperly designed masonry joints and building settlement. The contractor contends that anything wrong with the masonry was caused by deficient plans and specifications. The architect contends that the water penetration into the interior space comes from bad workmanship, defective masonry materials, and insufficient interior "through-the-wall" waterproofing.

If these issues are to be decided by a jury, the attorney must reduce the facts of the dispute to their simplest elements. It would be more important for the attorney representing the owner to show clearly in a few instances where the subcontractor deviated from the plans and specifications, and to leave the impression that this was the conduct of performance throughout the work, rather than to hit each and every deficiency in the building. The attorney for the subcontractor would likewise want to show some clear examples of unworkable design and not burden the jury with an entire litany of design deficiencies allowed by the design professional. It would be inadvisable to risk confusing the jury with the detailed technical complexities of the matter. Moreover, the attorney would not want his or her client to appear to the jury as a nitpicker. If representing the masonry subcontractor, the attorney could suggest that the principal of the firm come to court in his work clothes so that the jury can relate to him as just another working man.

How does this approach work with arbitrators? Not well! Arbitrators will be reasonably knowledgeable about the issues in the case. There will probably be a design professional on the panel who will understand the nuances of the problem. Avoid talking down to the arbitrators; although simplicity may be appreciated by the jury, it will probably be thought inappropriate by the arbitrators, who may consider the simplification to be patronizing.

When technical issues are involved, it is acceptable to present the evidence in an unabridged form. If the panel of arbitrators is properly constituted, they should be sufficiently sophisticated to comprehend the direction and substance of the testimony.

§ 8.16 Conduct at Hearings

It is important that the parties and attorneys behave in a dignified manner at the hearings. There is nothing more repugnant to a panel of arbitrators than to witness two attorneys continuously bickering back and forth. One of the most common complaints that I receive from nonattorney arbitrators is the abrasive manner of attorneys at the hearings. In a court case, the jury never gets to hear the bickering between attorneys because anything of this nature takes place before the judge, out of the jury's sight or at least hearing.

It seems that trial attorneys who are unfamiliar with arbitration take advantage of the freedom of the arbitral forum to unleash invectives against their adversaries, which they know would never be permitted in a courtroom setting. This demeanor does not serve the clients' interests because it affects the arbitrators unfavorably. Arbitrators appreciate consideration and good manners. In one of my arbitration cases, the opposing counsel habitually came late to the hearings, letting everyone wait 10 to 15 minutes for him. Although the panel did not complain, it was obvious that this attorney was not endearing himself to the panel members. Another example of good manners during the hearing is the issue of smoking. The issue of smoking may seem very unimportant or irrelevant to successful advocacy (and it may well be), but bad manners in this area can have a negative reflection on the person or even on the case.

Arbitrator's Behavior

There may be some instances in which an overly polite arbitrator may be a drawback. In one case, the chairman of the panel was an attorney, and he made all the rulings on objections raised and set out all the procedural rules we were to comply with during the hearings. It is not unusual for the chairman to undertake these duties, but in this instance, he was making his decisions without conferring with his two co-panelists. After it became evident that the chairman was intent on running the arbitration as a one-man show, I diplomatically made it clear to the other arbitrators that the panel was intended to function as a group of three, and that each member of the panel had equal say on everything occurring during the arbitration. The two arbitrators, who previously relegated the administration to the chairman, soon became active and vocal participants in the hearing.

§ 8.17 Opening Statements

Opening statements are as important in arbitration as they are in court cases, and maybe even more so. In a court case, an opening statement is intended to educate the judge and jury about the case so that they can follow the evidence as it is presented during the trial. The opening statement is intended to sort out for the jury why certain evidence is being presented.

In arbitration I feel that opening statements serve a substantially different function. The need to educate the arbitrator about what will happen in the case is not as important because the panel, as opposed to a jury, can ask questions whenever they want if they get confused.

A significant function of the opening statement is to set forth statements that can be referred back to at the conclusion of the hearings, during the closing statement, and in the post-hearing briefs. Because discovery is generally not available in arbitration, the attorneys often are not very familiar with their adversary's case; in arbitration, the opponent's case generally unravels during the course of the hearings. The trial attorney who is inexperienced in arbitration and feels compelled to give a detailed, punchy opening statement to get the attention of the arbitrators may find that it was a self-defeating exercise by the time the case concludes. Too many promises in the opening statement predictions may not be fulfilled. I generally study my adversary's opening statement carefully at the conclusion of the hearings and find astonishing representations that prove quite embarrassing after all the evidence is presented. Suffice it to say that it is better to be conservative in predictions at the beginning of the case.

§ 8.18 The Evidence

In a court of law there are rules of evidence that must be complied with in order to introduce either testimony or documents. There are rules against hearsay, there are rules governing admissions against interest, and there are a multitude of other rules, all of which must be scrupulously complied with by an attorney wishing to submit evidence at trial. Are rules of evidence followed in arbitration? There is no simple answer. If there are three lawyers on the panel, they will probably require the attorneys to adhere reasonably close to the conventional rules of evidence. That is not by reason of any requirement of law or the AAA, but by nature of the type of arbitrators presiding over the case. Engineers who sit as arbitrators always become more attentive when engineering issues are presented, and attorneys as arbitrators seem to have the common fault of wanting to be "judge for the day."

Every arbitrator is legally bound to hear relevant and material testimony. Further, the arbitrators have discretion to curtail cumulative and repetitive testimony.[17] How remote must the evidence be before the arbitrators have a legal right to preclude evidence? It depends on the particular case; if the precluded evidence prevents one side from obtaining a fair hearing, then the arbitrators acted improperly.

The AAA Construction Industry Arbitration Rules provide:

---

[17] Gallagher v. Schernecher, 60 Wis. 2d 143, 208 N.W.2d 437 (1973).

31. Evidence

The parties may offer such evidence as is relevant and material to the dispute and shall produce such evidence as the arbitrator may deem necessary to an understanding and determination of the dispute. An arbitrator or other person authorized by law to subpoena witnesses or documents may do so upon the request of any party or independently.

The arbitrator shall be the judge of the relevance and materiality of the evidence offered, and conformity to legal rules of evidence shall not be necessary. All evidence shall be taken in the presence of all of the arbitrators and all of the parties, except where any of the parties is absent in default or has waived the right to be present.

As can be seen from the above, "conformity to legal rules of evidence shall not be necessary." What about the situation where the arbitrators decide to require strict compliance with the legal rules of evidence? Although I have come across no case in point, if the arbitrators apply strict rules of evidence, the chances are that they will misapply some rules; if the misapplication turns out to have a material impact on the case and prevents one of the parties from introducing relevant and material evidence, the wronged party will likely have good grounds for an appeal.

Although it is not necessary in every jurisdiction, witnesses should all be required to testify under oath. Under Construction Industry Arbitration Rules (§ 27), the arbitrator has discretion to require sworn testimony, but must require it when it is required by law or requested by either party.

§ 8.19 Closing Statements

In cases in which a jury might be taken in by the silver tongue of an eloquent attorney who mixes fact with wishful thinking, a panel of professional arbitrators is less easily swayed. In one case, my adversary gave an impassioned closing statement that was profoundly articulate, eloquent, and persuasive to the point that he was getting unconscious nods of agreement from the panel of arbitrators as he orated. It was one of the best closing statements I had ever heard, albeit it was not remotely consistent with the proven facts of the case. I decided there and then that I could not compete with my adversary's oratory excellence, but I could compete on the facts established during the hearings, which were clearly in my favor.

I started my closing statement by telling the panel that if I were on trial for murder there would be nobody I would rather have as my lawyer than my adversary. I told them I would want my adversary because he would undoubtedly be able to convince a jury of postal clerks, secretaries, and tollkeepers that black was white and that I was the best guy in town regardless of the evidence in the case. Everyone laughed, I broke the spell, and then I went on to tell them that my adversary seriously misjudged the panel's ability to be romanced into believing his fairy tale version of the facts. The panel members, who were industry professionals, were not deceived by the oratory of my adversary and rendered my client a very substantial award.

§ 8.20   Hearing Format

As far as trial strategy is concerned, there is no substitute for a witness to give testimony. If a witness is not available, the next best thing is an affidavit from that witness. With respect to affidavits the AAA Construction Industry Arbitration Rules provide:

> **32. Evidence by Affidavit and Post-hearing Filing of Documents or Other Evidence**
>
> The arbitrator may receive and consider the evidence of witnesses by affidavit, but shall give it only such weight as the arbitrator deems it entitled to after consideration of any objection made to its admission.

Since the above rule provides that the arbitrator "shall" receive and consider a witness's affidavit, the attorney has a right to insist on the submission of an affidavit. However, my experience has been that arbitrators give little or no weight to affidavits since the other side is at a serious disadvantage in that one cannot cross examine a piece of paper. It would be a mistake to expect to try a case in arbitration through the submission of numerous affidavits. What about the situation where the arbitrators state they will not accept an affidavit and reject its introduction into evidence? Is this a ground for reversal of the award? If this is an AAA arbitration, it certainly is a violation of the rules. However, it must be considered whether the violation prevented a fair hearing. If it did, the award will be overturned.

Must a conventional trial format be followed during the hearings? There is no requirement that an arbitration follow the same evidentiary procedures as a court of law. For example, a single arbitrator who happens to be an engineer, or a panel of three construction-oriented arbitrators would probably not find a courtroom format to their liking if they are not attorneys. It is not unusual for arbitrators to shed the traditional question and answer format on some confusing point and allow the witness to simply tell his or her story in a narrative form, subject only to interruption by the arbitrators or the opposing side for clarifying questions. This is not the best way to proceed, but it certainly would be upheld by a court of law if it were challenged.

§ 8.21 Hearing Transcript

If a case is going to have more than a few hearings, it is recommended that a transcript of the proceedings be kept to record the testimony. It is not unusual, in fact it is quite common, for complex construction arbitration hearings to be heard over a period of many months. It is almost unheard of to find a panel of arbitrators who are willing to sit on a case for several consecutive days until it is completed. Ordinarily, the hearings are spaced out one or two days a week, every other week, over many months. Unless a transcript is kept by a court stenographer, the arbitrators will not likely have a clear recollection of what was said by the various witnesses six months after the fact. Moreover the transcript is an invaluable tool to the attorney in preparing and documenting the post-hearing brief.

Having a court stenographer at the hearings also promotes an orderly hearing. I have been at hearings acting as an arbitrator where the adversary attorneys seemed to end up every half hour in a vitriolic shouting match. Although such behavior is frowned upon by the legal profession and certainly is upsetting to arbitrators presiding over a case, such behavior occurs all too often. With a court stenographer present, this type of altercation is generally nipped in the bud because the court stenographer will protest in utter frustration that it is impossible to take down the dialogue of two persons who are speaking at the same time. This always has a calming effect on the hearings.

§ 8.22 Post-Hearing Briefs

The arbitrators usually do not close the hearings officially until after the post-hearing briefs are submitted, a period of usually two weeks to 30 days after the last hearing. Does that mean that either side can submit new evidence not submitted during the hearings as attachments to their post-hearing brief? Absolutely not! It is not fair play to submit new evidence after the hearings have been concluded. If some new evidence comes into an attorney's possession after the conclusion of the hearings, and the nature of the evidence is of such dire importance that the attorney feels it must come to the attention of the arbitrators, it would then be appropriate to make an application to reconvene the hearings so as to introduce this new evidence. On the other hand, it is improper for one side to simply submit new documents with their post-hearing brief, and it could prejudice the validity of any award rendered. Even if the arbitrators rejected the evidence as untimely, they are the judges in the case and in order to rule they must look at the documents in question. An argument could be made that even the review of this document by the arbitrators, although it was ultimately rejected as evidence, would be so prejudicial as to have unfairly influenced the arbitrators.

This issue was discussed in *R.E. Bean Construction Co. v. Middlebury Association*,[18] where the court held that evidence submitted by a party to an arbitration after the hearing was concluded is per se the basis for setting aside the arbitration award. However, the complaining party must establish that the evidence affected the award and also that he would have been able to rebut, challenge, or modify the evidence in issue. Depending on the nature of the evidence, this could be an easy task for the objecting party. An improper attempt by one party to get that extra bite of the apple may just prove fatal to its case; the best advice is not to submit unauthorized evidence without the approval of the arbitrators.

§ 8.23 Site Visits

In some situations an arbitrator goes to the site and makes an independent investigation without approval of the parties. This is an unauthorized act by the arbitrator and if objected to by one party, it can give rise to the basis to disqualify the arbitrator and vacate the award. However, a party cannot keep quiet about it during the hearing and then if an unfavorable award comes down, become indignant and make an application to dismiss the award. If no objection is made at the time the unauthorized site visit is discovered, then the courts are likely to consider that the party has waived his objection.[19] On the other hand, there is nothing wrong with both parties stipulating that the arbitrator go out alone and visit the site.[20]

From my experience, it is wiser for both sides to attend all site visits made by the arbitrators. To ensure that no one takes advantage, there should be an agenda for the site visit and a procedure for answering questions the arbitrators may have when they make the visit. All of the rules for the site visit should be agreed upon in advance before the arbitrators set foot on the site.

§ 8.24 Adjournments

When the hearing is underway, the issue of adjourning scheduled hearings always comes up if the opposing sides are not in agreement. The claimant generally wants to forge ahead with the case and the respondent always seems to need adjournments to obtain new witnesses and experts. The

---

[18] 139 Vt. 200, 428 A.2d 306 (1981).

[19] *In re* Lebow-Bogner-Seitel Realty, Inc., 55 A.D.2d 695, 389 N.Y.S.2d 51 (1976).

[20] University of Alaska v. Modern Constr. Co., 522 P.2d 1132 (Alaska 1974).

arbitrator has discretion to decide the issue of adjournments. However if the arbitrator denies an adjournment without good cause, it may give rise to the basis for overturning the award on the grounds that the party did not get a fair hearing. If a party is precluded from presenting material and relevant evidence, then the arbitrator's decision not to allow an adjournment may be considered judicial misconduct sufficient to invalidate the award.[21]

With respect to postponements, the AAA Construction Industry Arbitration Rules provide as follows:

26. Postponements

The arbitrator for good cause shown may postpone any hearing upon the request of a party or upon the arbitrator's own initiative, and shall also grant such postponement when all of the parties agree thereto.

The above rule means that the arbitrator has no discretion when both sides agree on the adjournment. It is better to keep a cordial relationship with your adversary and accommodate each other reasonably when it comes to adjournments than to relegate this issue to the arbitrators.

In my experience, the arbitrators themselves are worse offenders than the parties in adjourning scheduled hearings. Frequently the arbitrators will cancel the hearings at the last minute because of some other business commitment. This is very frustrating to the parties, who have probably spent many days preparing their case. As a matter of practicality, there is little that can be done about an arbitrator who chronically cancels scheduled hearings. It would not be very diplomatic for the attorney to tell the arbitrator that he or she is upset with such cancellations because no one wants to alienate the person deciding the case. If it is an AAA arbitration, the attorney can independently or jointly with the opposing attorney render a complaint to the tribunal administrator of the AAA, but I have found that this accomplishes little. Of course if both parties consider it a hardship, they could jointly request removal of the arbitrator. This would remedy the problem, but in reality, there is always one party who thinks the arbitrator favors his or her side and would be unwilling to terminate such an advantage.

§ 8.25 Demonstrative Evidence

Evidence by way of illustrations, special photographs, charts, progress schedules, and models are all evidentiary techniques particularly well

---

[21] A&R Constr. Co. v. Gorlun-Okum, Inc., 41 A.D.2d 876, 342 N.Y.S.2d 950 (1973); Lighting Unlimited, Inc. v. Unger Constr. Co., 217 Pa. Super. 252, 269 A.2d 368 (1970).

suited for construction cases. If the monetary value of the case is substantial, it will almost always warrant the investment in some sort of demonstrative evidence. There are consultants to the construction industry who are adept in preparing striking and elaborate graphic displays that depict in living color such things as design changes, monthly cash flow analyses, CPM and progress bar charts, and subsurface condition details. It is far easier during testimony of a witness to refer to a well-designed graphic display than the scribblings on some blackboard.

Making models for the hearing is very expensive and can run into thousands of dollars. But if the case and the situation warrant it, a model can be invaluable in getting a point across and having the arbitrators comprehend the problem. I have been involved in cases where models were made for only a few hundred dollars and also for many thousands of dollars. In each case the model clarified an essential part of the case and undoubtedly aided the arbitrators in understanding the facts. In one instance we had a millwork contractor who was required to make changes to built-in wardrobes because they could not be brought into a college dormitory building in one piece. With his own facilities, our client constructed scale models of the wardrobe as it was originally designed and as it was ultimately constructed in order to accommodate the building. It was an easy task to show the differences and why the redesign resulted in more costly construction. This model was very inexpensive and proved to be very effective.

In another case, a serious unforeseen subsurface rock condition delayed the construction of a highrise commercial building. The method of rock removal was limited to machine equipment because it was situated over a railroad tunnel. The claimant prepared an elaborate model with movable parts to reflect the various stages of the excavation. This proved to be a very valuable aid to clarify the witnesses' testimony. That model, although it cost many thousands of dollars, paid for itself many times over.

§ 8.26 The Award

After the hearing is closed, the arbitrators are legally bound to render an award. This award, which must be in writing, must be rendered within a certain time period based on the agreement of the parties, by a court order, or by state or federal law. If the award is not rendered within the specified time frame, it may be considered invalid, or there may be legal means to compel the rendering of the award.

The form of the award decision is universally required to be in writing and also to be signed by the arbitrators. If it is a panel of three arbitrators, it does not have to be unanimous, but it must be signed by two of the three arbitrators.

§ 8.27 PUNITIVE DAMAGES

The scope of the arbitration award will depend upon principally two factors: the agreement to arbitrate and the state or federal law controlling the arbitration. If the arbitration agreement is broad, the arbitrators will also have equitable powers. For example, arbitrators are permitted to reform a contract.[22]

§ 8.27 Punitive Damages

Certain states allow arbitrators to award punitive damages[23] and some do not.[24] The ability to award punitive damages is an awesome power because arbitration awards are generally not appealable unless for some serious breach of fair play. The amount of punitive damages that can be awarded in certain respects is limitless. Whereas a breach of contract can only give rise to a limited or quantified amount of damages, punitive damages are in effect punishments meted out by the arbitrators to the party who they feel has acted improperly. Even if the punitive part of the award is excessive, it would be hard to have it overturned by the court if the arbitrators had the power in the first instance to award punitive damages. In recent cases in which arbitrators have awarded punitive damages, the amount of these damages has run as high as two or more times the amount allowed by the basic breach of contract award. Many attorneys feel that the province of punitive damages should only be in the courts, where there are the checks and balances of the court rules and appellate relief.

The Construction Industry Arbitration Rules of the AAA provide:

43. Scope of Award

The arbitrator may grant any remedy or relief that the arbitrator deems just and equitable and within the scope of the agreement of the parties, including, but not limited to, specific performance of a contract.

I have seen arbitration agreements in which the parties have specifically excluded the ability to render punitive damages in the otherwise broad arbitration clause. There are two legal concepts at play in deciding the suitability of arbitrators to award punitive damages. One faction contends that if the arbitrators are deciding all issues of dispute between the parties, why

---

[22] SCM Corp. v. Fisher Park Lane Co., 40 N.Y.2d 788, 358 N.E.2d 1024, 390 N.Y.S.2d 398 (1976).

[23] *E.g.,* Willoughby Roofing & Supply Co. v. Kajima Int'l, Inc., 598 F. Supp. 353 (D. Ala. 1984), *aff'd,* 776 F.2d 269 (11th Cir. 1985); Rodgers Builders, Inc. v. McQueen, 76 N.C. App. 16, 331 S.E.2d 726 (1985).

[24] *E.g.,* Garrity v. Lyle Stuart, 40 N.Y.2d 354, 353 N.E.2d 793, 386 N.Y.S.2d 831 (1976); Shaw v. Kuhnel Assocs., Inc., 102 N.M. 607, 698 P.2d 880 (1985).

not allow them the right to grant punitive damages? The other camp feels that certain types of relief, such as punitive damages and equitable remedies, are beyond the concept of arbitration by industry peers and that damages beyond contractual remedies should remain in the province of the courts.

§ 8.28 Other Elements of an Award

The arbitration award can include both pre-award and post-award interest, provided the interest rates do not exceed that which is allowable by law.[25]

Do arbitrators have to give reasoning for their award? Under most circumstances they do not; the AAA has a policy of having its arbitrators absolutely refrain from rendering opinion types of awards. The rationale is that the more that is stated in an award, the more likelihood that it will be grist for an appeal. Lacking descriptive language as to why or how the monetary award was arrived at, an unsuccessful party has little to use as the basis for an appeal.

Although the arbitrators are not legally bound to give their findings of fact, the court under certain circumstances can make the arbitrators clarify the award.[26] If the court feels that the arbitrators have improperly included an element of damage in their award which would constitute legal error, the court can compel the arbitrators to reconsider their award.

Once an award has been rendered by the arbitrators, there is no authority for them to modify the award except in accordance with the arbitration statute of the state or federal law.[27]

§ 8.29 Vacating the Award

The grounds for vacating an award rendered by arbitrators will be dependent upon the arbitration law of the state in which it was rendered or the Federal Arbitration Act. The basic grounds for vacating an award are corruption, fraud, undue means, bias, irrationality, and noncompliance with the arbitration agreement.[28]

In order to set aside an award for corruption, fraud, or undue means there must be clear and convincing proof that the arbitrator was guilty of such acts. Obviously, if an arbitrator had an interest in the outcome of the award, such would be an act of corruption which would vitiate the award. Partiality or bias is another ground which would give rise to the vacating

---

[25] Brandeis Intsel Ltd. v. Calabrian Chem. Corp., 656 F. Supp. 160 (S.D.N.Y. 1987).
[26] Ferris Constr. Co. v. Lasker, 51 A.D.2d 1081, 381 N.Y.S.2d 352 (1976).
[27] Wolff & Munier, Inc. v. Diesel Constr. Co., 41 A.D.2d 618, 340 N.Y.S.2d 455 (1974).
[28] 9 U.S.C. § 10 (1947).

of an award; this usually occurs when an arbitrator fails to disclose facts that could be interpreted as showing partiality to one of the parties.[29]

An irrational award must be shown to be exactly that. The mere fact that arbitrators have misinterpreted the facts or made errors in the law is insufficient to have the court categorize the award as being irrational.[30] However, arbitrators will be considered to have exceeded their powers and the award can be considered irrational if they decide matters which were not submitted to them.[31]

Misconduct of an arbitrator depends on the circumstances of the particular matter. If an arbitrator has undisclosed meetings with a party during the course of the hearings, such may be construed as misconduct. If an arbitrator refuses to admit clear and relevant evidence to the prejudice of one party, or refuses to postpone a hearing in order to allow an essential witness to testify, such acts will be construed as misconduct and an abuse of discretion.[32]

As to an arbitrator exceeding the scope of the arbitration agreement, that also will be a basis for vacating the award because the arbitration decision goes beyond the scope of the arbitration agreement. If an arbitration agreement only refers to a specific type of claim that can be arbitrated, and over the protest of the other party the arbitrator entertains claims beyond the scope of the arbitration agreement, then the arbitration award will ultimately be vacated by the court.

Once an arbitration award is obtained, it can be reduced into the form of a judicial judgment, which has the same effect as if the case were tried in court and a judge rendered a decision.

§ 8.30 Conclusion

It should be evident at this point that arbitration is not a panacea for the resolution of construction disputes. Depending on circumstances, arbitration has certain distinct advantages over litigation. However, there are a myriad of situations where litigation of a construction dispute is far more desirable. If you do end up in a construction dispute and your contract provides for arbitration, be sure to satisfy yourself that your attorney is experienced in arbitrating construction disputes. I am convinced that if a complex construction claim is properly presented to a well-constituted panel of arbitrators, the likelihood of obtaining a fair award is better than with a jury verdict or judge's decision.

---

[29] Commonwealth Coatings Corp. v. Continental Casualty, 393 U.S. 145 (1968).

[30] Garver v. Ferguson, 76 Ill. 2d 1, 389 N.E.2d 1181 (1979).

[31] T&M Properties v. ZVFK Architects, 661 P.2d 1040 (Wyo. 1983).

[32] Gallagher v. Schernecker, 60 Wis. 2d 143, 208 N.W.2d 437 (1973); Allstate Ins. Co. v. Fioravanti, 451 Pa. 108, 299 A.2d 585 (1973).

CHAPTER 9

FEDERAL CONTRACT DISPUTES AND FORUMS

Alvin A. Schall, Esquire

Alvin A. Schall has had extensive experience in the area of government contracts. Currently, he is an assistant to the attorney general of the United States, a position he has held since September of 1988. Prior to that, he was in private practice in Washington, D.C., specializing in commercial litigation and procurement law. From 1978 to 1987, he was a member of the Commercial Litigation Branch of the Civil Division of the U.S. Department of Justice, first as a trial attorney and then as senior trial counsel. In that capacity, he represented the United States in all aspects of government contract litigation. From 1973 to 1978, Mr. Schall was an assistant United States attorney in the Eastern District of New York. He served first in the Criminal Division of the U.S. Attorney's Office and then in the Appeals Division, where he was chief. As an assistant United States attorney, he tried criminal cases and argued numerous appeals. From 1969 to 1973, he was an associate with a New York City law firm, where he specialized in corporate and banking law. Mr. Schall holds a J.D. degree from the Tulane University School of Law (1969) and a B.A. degree from Princeton University (1966).

§ 9.1   Introduction
§ 9.2   Scope of the Contract Disputes Act
§ 9.3   Contractor Claims
§ 9.4   —Who May Submit a Claim
§ 9.5   —What Constitutes a Claim
§ 9.6   —Certification Requirement
§ 9.7   —Contracting Officer's Decision
§ 9.8   Government Claims
§ 9.9   Appealing the Contracting Officer's Decision
§ 9.10 —Necessity of a Decision

§ 9.11 —Time for Appealing the Decision
§ 9.12 —Election Doctrine
§ 9.13 —Decisions Not Involving Money Claims
§ 9.14 Review of Decisions of Boards of Contract Appeals and the Claims Court
§ 9.15 Small Claims
§ 9.16 Interest
§ 9.17 Payment of Claims
§ 9.18 Fraudulent Claims
§ 9.19 Agency Boards of Contract Appeals
§ 9.20 —Practice before the Boards
§ 9.21 —Bringing an Appeal
§ 9.22 —Discovery, Prehearing Procedures, and Motions
§ 9.23 —Hearings and Post-Hearing Matters
§ 9.24 —Small Claims Procedures
§ 9.25 United States Claims Court
§ 9.26 —Bringing Suit in the Claims Court
§ 9.27 —Discovery, Pretrial Procedures, and Motions
§ 9.28 —Trials and Post-Trial Matters
§ 9.29 Transfer and Consolidation of Cases
§ 9.30 Attorneys' Fees
§ 9.31 Selecting a Forum
§ 9.32 The Miller Act

§ 9.1 Introduction

Disputes arising under construction contracts involving the federal government are governed by the Contract Disputes Act of 1978 [hereinafter CDA or Act].[1] The CDA sets forth a comprehensive scheme for resolving claims by contractors and the government. It applies to contracts executed on and after March 1, 1979; contractors who had claims pending on that date, however, were allowed to elect to proceed under the CDA with respect to those claims.[2]

The first part of this chapter (through **§ 9.18**) covers the CDA requirements with respect to assertion and resolution of contractor and

---

[1] 41 U.S.C. §§ 601–613 (1982) (unless otherwise indicated, all references are to the 1982 version of the United States Code).

[2] Pub. L. No. 95-563, § 16, 92 Stat. 2391 (1978).

§ 9.1 INTRODUCTION

government claims. The second part (§ **9.19** through § **9.32**) discusses the forums—agency boards of contract appeals and the United States Claims Court—where government contract disputes are heard if they are not resolved at the contracting level. It also discusses claims by subcontractors and suppliers against prime contractors under government construction contracts (the Miller Act).

Citations in this chapter are to the appropriate provisions of the CDA, other relevant statutes, and the Federal Acquisition Regulations (FAR), as well as to cases. The CDA and the other cited statutes are in West Publishing Company's United States Code Annotated. FAR citations are from title 48 of the Code of Federal Regulations (CFR) and volume 4 of the Government Contracts Reporter published by Commerce Clearing House (CCH).

The case law relating to the CDA and government contract claims is composed chiefly of decisions of the various agency boards of contract appeals, the United States Court of Claims, the United States Claims Court, and the United States Court of Appeals for the Federal Circuit.

The Court of Claims, which was abolished in 1982, had jurisdiction to entertain suits involving government contract claims, including claims under the CDA. When Congress abolished the Court of Claims, it created the Claims Court,[3] and granted to it all the original jurisdiction of the Court of Claims.[4] At the same time, Congress also created a new United States Court of Appeals for the Federal Circuit.[5] The Federal Circuit reviews decisions of boards of contract appeals and the Claims Court.[6] The Claims Court and the Federal Circuit view decisions of the Court of Claims as binding precedent.[7]

Decisions of the boards of contract appeals are reported in the Board of Contract Appeals Reporter (BCA) published by CCH. Court of Claims decisions are found in both West's Federal Reporter and in the official reports of the Court of Claims (Ct. Cl.).[8] Orders of the Court of Claims are found only in the official reports. Claims Court decisions are reported in West's United States Claims Court Reporter (Cl. Ct.), and decisions of the Federal Circuit are found in both the Federal Reporter and the Claims Court Reporter.

---

[3] 28 U.S.C. § 171.

[4] 28 U.S.C. § 1491.

[5] 28 U.S.C. § 41.

[6] 41 U.S.C. § 607(g)(1); 28 U.S.C. § 1295(a)(10), (a)(3).

[7] South Corp. v. United States, 690 F.2d 1368, 1369 (Fed. Cir. 1982) (en banc); U. S. Cl. Ct. Gen. Order No. 1 (preceding the Rules of the United States Claims Court).

[8] Some decisions of the Court of Claims are reported in West's Federal Supplement rather than the Federal Reporter.

§ 9.2 Scope of the Contract Disputes Act

The CDA applies to any express or implied contract that is entered into by an "executive agency" of the federal government for "the procurement of [the] construction, alteration, repair, or maintenance of real property."[9] The Act also applies to "executive agency" contracts for the procurement of property, other than real property, for the procurement of services, and for the disposal of personal property.[10]

The term *executive agency* is defined in 41 U.S.C. § 601(2). It encompasses entities that commonly are thought of as government agencies, such as the General Services Administration, the Department of Health and Human Services, and the Department of Veterans Affairs (formerly the Veterans Administration). It also encompasses the military departments, the Postal Service, the Postal Rate Commission, and various independent bodies and government corporations.[11]

At the heart of the CDA are the provisions addressing contractor and government claims. The Act describes the way in which such claims are asserted, and it provides for decisions on such claims by agency contracting officers.[12] The Act also gives a contractor the right to appeal a contracting officer's decision, and it affords a choice of forums for such an appeal, either an agency board of contract appeals, or the United States Claims Court.[13]

The first part of **Chapter 9** examines each of the above topics. Using a chronological approach, it begins with the assertion of contractor and government claims and continues through the issuing of contracting officers' final decisions and appeals of those decisions to boards of contract appeals and the Claims Court. It also discusses appeals of board and Claims Court decisions to the Federal Circuit, as well as provisions of the CDA for fraudulent claims,[14] small claims,[15] interest on amounts found due on contractor claims,[16] and payment of claims.[17]

---

[9] 41 U.S.C. § 602(a)(3).

[10] 41 U.S.C. § 602(a)(1), (a)(2), (a)(4).

[11] The "executive agencies" with contracts covered by the CDA are set forth in the statutes listed in 41 U.S.C. § 601(2). The Act contains a provision that deals exclusively with the Tennessee Valley Authority. That provision is at 41 U.S.C. § 602(b).

[12] 41 U.S.C. § 605.

[13] 41 U.S.C. §§ 606, 609(a).

[14] 41 U.S.C. § 604.

[15] 41 U.S.C. § 608.

[16] 41 U.S.C. § 611.

[17] 41 U.S.C. § 612.

§ 9.3 Contractor Claims

The CDA provides that "[a]ll claims by a contractor against the government relating to a contract shall be in writing and shall be submitted to the contracting officer for a decision."[18] The Act further provides that claims by a contractor in excess of $50,000 must be certified.[19] The existence of a claim and the proper submission of that claim to a contracting officer are prerequisites to a contractor's invoking the dispute resolution procedures of the CDA.[20] Until a proper claim is submitted, a contracting officer cannot issue a valid final decision, and a contractor has no right of access to either a board of contract appeals or the Claims Court.[21] If a contractor proceeds to either a board or the court with an improper claim, its suit will be dismissed.[22] Although the dismissal will be without prejudice to the right of the contractor to bring the action again,[23] it will be necessary for the contractor to go through the process of resubmitting its claim to the contracting officer.[24] This will consume additional time and most likely will result in added costs. In addition, interest does not begin to accrue on a CDA claim until the claim is properly submitted.[25] In short, although a defective submission can be remedied, it is very much in the contractor's interest "to get it right the first time."

§ 9.4 —Who May Submit a Claim

Under the CDA, only a person or entity in a direct contractual relationship with the government, for example, a prime contractor, may assert claims against the government. The Act refers to "Contractor claims"[26] and states that the term "contractor" means "a party to a Government contract other

---

[18] 41 U.S.C. § 605(a).

[19] 41 U.S.C. § 605(c).

[20] W.M. Schlosser Co. v. United States, 705 F.2d 1336, 1338 (Fed. Cir. 1983); W.H. Moseley Co. v. United States, 230 Ct. Cl. 405, 677 F.2d 850, *cert. denied,* 459 U.S. 836 (1982).

[21] Skelly & Loy v. United States, 231 Ct. Cl. 370, 376–77, 685 F.2d 414, 419 (1982); Lerma Co. & Assocs., ASBCA No. 34012, 87-3 B.C.A. (CCH) ¶ 19,958, at 101,035 (1987).

[22] *See* Swager Tower Corp. v. United States, 12 Cl. Ct. 499 (1987); G.S. & L. Mechanical & Constr., Inc., DOT BCA No. 1856, 87-2 B.C.A. (CCH) ¶ 19,882, at 100, 582–83 (1987).

[23] Thoen v. United States, 765 F.2d 1110, 1116 (Fed. Cir. 1985).

[24] Skelly & Loy, Inc. v. United States, 231 Ct. Cl. at 377, 685 F.2d at 419; Technassociates, Inc. v. United States, 14 Cl. Ct. 200, 212 (1988); T.J.D. Servs., Inc. v. United States, 6 Cl. Ct. 257, 260 (1984).

[25] Fidelity Constr. Co. v. United States, 700 F.2d 1379, 1383–85 (Fed. Cir. 1985).

[26] 41 U.S.C. § 605(a).

than the Government. . . ."[27] Likewise, § 33.201 of the FAR describes a claim as a demand or assertion "by one of the contracting parties."[28] Generally, subcontractors are not parties to government contracts and are not in privity with the government; accordingly, they may not assert claims against the government under the Act.[29] By the same token, a non-completing surety also is not a contractor for purposes of the CDA.[30] However, a surety who expressly or implicitly assumes contract performance is in privity with the government and thus may assert claims under the Act.[31] Finally, unless the government is a party to the assignment transaction, the assignee of a contractor's rights under a contract with the government does not attain the status of a contractor, and thus is not in a position to assert a claim under the CDA.[32]

Although a subcontractor may not assert a claim directly under the CDA, it is not without a remedy in a situation where it believes that the government, not the prime contractor, is responsible for increased costs that it has incurred. With the prime contractor's consent and cooperation, a subcontractor's claim may be brought against the government in the prime contractor's name and right but on behalf of the subcontractor. In such a situation, the prime contractor is said to be "sponsoring" the subcontractor's claim.[33]

§ 9.5 —What Constitutes a Claim

The CDA states that all claims "shall be in writing and shall be submitted to the contracting officer for a decision."[34] Beyond that, however, the Act

---

[27] 41 U.S.C. § 601(4).

[28] 48 C.F.R. § 33.201 (all references are to the 1987 version of the Code of Federal Regulations).

[29] Erickson Air Crane Co. of Washington, Inc. v. United States, 731 F.2d 810, 813 (Fed. Cir. 1984); United States v. Johnson Controls, Inc., 713 F.2d 1541 (Fed. Cir. 1983); G. Schneider, ASBCA No. 333021, 87-2 B.C.A. (CCH) ¶ 19,865 (1987). However, in the unusual situation where the facts are such that the necessary degree of privity is found, a party that nominally is a subcontractor may be able to assert claims under the CDA. See Acousti Eng'g Co. of Fla. v. United States, 15 Cl. Ct. 698, 700–01 (1988); McMillin Bros. Constructors, Inc., EBCA No. 328-10-84, 86-3 B.C.A. (CCH) ¶ 19,179 (1986).

[30] See Universal Surety Co. v. United States, 10 Cl. Ct. 794, 799–800 (1986).

[31] See Fireman's Fund/Underwater Constr., Inc., ASBCA No. 33018, 87-3 B.C.A. (CCH) ¶ 20,007 (1987).

[32] Thomas Funding Corp. v. United States, 15 Cl. Ct. 495, 499–501 (1988).

[33] Erickson Air Crane Co. of Washington, Inc. v. United States, 731 F.2d at 813–14; Color Dynamics, Inc., ASBCA No. 33686, 87-3 B.C.A. (CCH) ¶ 19,996 (1987); Door Pro Sys., Inc., ASBCA No. 34114, 87-3 B.C.A. (CCH) ¶ 19,997 (1987). See Haehn Management Co. v. United States, 15 Cl. Ct. 50, 51 (1988).

[34] 41 U.S.C. § 605(a).

does not define "claim." Regulations and decisions of courts and boards of contract appeals, though, have given meaning to the term. In *Mingus Constructors, Inc. v. United States*,[35] the court stated that a claim is defined by the terms of the contract at issue.[36] The court in *Mingus* looked to the disputes clause in the contract before it for the definition of a claim.

FAR § 33.214 states that, unless certain conditions apply, each government contract must contain the disputes clause set forth at FAR § 52.233-1.[37] That clause provides, in pertinent part, as follows:

> (c) "Claim," as used in this clause, means a written demand or written assertion by one of the contracting parties seeking, as a matter of right, the payment of money in a sum certain, the adjustment or interpretation of contract terms, or other relief arising under or relating to this contract. . . . [A] written demand or written assertion by the Contractor seeking the payment of money in excess of $50,000 is not a claim under the Act until certified as required by subparagraph (d)(2) below. . . .
>
> (d)(1) A claim by the Contractor shall be made in writing and submitted to the Contracting Officer for a written decision.[38]

Thus, in order for a contractor's claim to be properly filed under the CDA, there must be submitted to the contracting officer in writing: (1) a demand or assertion; (2) which seeks, as a matter of right, the payment of money in a sum certain, the adjustment or other interpretation of contract terms, or other relief arising under or related to the contract; (3) with respect to which a contracting officer's written decision is requested; (4) and which is certified if the amount involved exceeds $50,000.

Written Submittals to the Contracting Officer

The CDA and the regulations provide that claims must be in writing and must be submitted to the contracting officer; an oral demand or assertion is not a claim for purposes of the CDA. Neither is a written demand or assertion that is submitted to a person who is not a contracting officer.[39] The CDA defines a contracting officer as: "[A]ny person who, by appointment in accordance with applicable regulations, has the authority to enter into and administer contracts and make determinations and findings with respect thereto. The term also includes the authorized representative of the contracting officer, acting within the limits of his authority."[40]

---

[35] 812 F.2d 1387 (Fed. Cir. 1987).
[36] *Id.* at 1395.
[37] 48 C.F.R. § 33.214.
[38] 48 C.F.R. § 52.233-1.
[39] Rider v. United States, 7 Cl. Ct. 770, 775–76 (1985).
[40] 41 U.S.C. § 601(3).

A contractor should be able to avoid the problem of misdirected claims simply by ascertaining at the outset of the contract the individuals who, in addition to the contracting officer, are authorized to receive claims.

Elements of a Claim

In submitting a claim, a contractor need not use any particular wording.[41] What the contractor is required to do, though, is present to the contracting officer a clear and unequivocal statement that gives the contracting officer adequate notice of the basis for, and the amount of, the claim.[42] Put another way, a contractor must provide the contracting officer with sufficient information to form a reasoned position with respect to the claim.[43]

Generally, a fairly liberal view has been taken of what constitutes a claim. For example, the following submissions have been found to be claims: (1) a letter in which a contractor specified various items that a government audit had disallowed but to which the contractor claimed entitlement. (The letter was viewed together with a prior letter from the contractor giving a detailed breakdown of the additional amounts to which the contractor believed it was entitled, and referring to the contractor's previous request for "funding of [a] back-wage demand");[44] (2) a letter sent by a company having a contract for transportation services at an air force base stating that the company viewed certain newly demanded bus service as beyond the contract's requirements, and specifically seeking "compensation of $11,000.04 per year, to be billed at $916.67 per month";[45] (3) a letter from the contractor's attorney to the contracting officer that "expressed interest" in a final decision with respect to the contractor's request for contract reformation and that indicated that the contractor was seeking a decision so that it could pursue its appeal routes under the CDA, if necessary;[46] (4) letters which, when taken together, showed the contractor protesting the payment of additional sums

---

[41] Contract Cleaning Maintenance, Inc. v. United States, 811 F.2d 586, 592 (Fed. Cir. 1986).

[42] *See, e.g.,* Tecom, Inc. v. United States, 732 F.2d 935, 936–37 (Fed. Cir. 1984); Metric Constr. Co. v. United States, 1 Cl. Ct. 383, 392 (1983).

[43] *See* Gauntt Constr. Co., ASBCA No. 33323, 87-3 B.C.A. (CCH) ¶ 20,221 (1987). In *Gauntt,* the Armed Services Board of Contract Appeals found the contractor's delay claim submission defective because the submission did not provide any specific instances or dates for the government actions that allegedly caused the delay. In addition, the claim submission contained no references to any contract provisions upon which the contractor relied, and there was no indication as to how the contract work was delayed by the alleged government actions.

[44] Contract Cleaning Maintenance, Inc. v. United States, 811 F.2d at 592.

[45] Tecom, Inc. v. United States, 732 F.2d at 937.

[46] Paragon Energy Corp. v. United States, 227 Ct. Cl. 176, 192, 645 F.2d 966, 976 (1981).

§ 9.5 WHAT CONSTITUTES A CLAIM

under a contract to purchase crude oil from the government and demanding that certain identified wire transfer payments comprising those sums be returned to the contractor.[47]

However, when a contractor fails to demand payment or does not request a contracting officer's decision, it has not made a claim. Thus, in order for there to be a proper claim under the CDA, a contractor must do more than merely state in its release of claims and subsequent correspondence that it intends to present a claim, even if the basis for the claim, which the contractor states that it intends to submit, is known by the government.[48]

A dispute has been recognized as an essential element of a claim.[49] In addition, a contractor must make it clear that it wishes the contracting officer to render a decision which, if unfavorable, may be pursued in the forums set forth in the CDA. For this reason, correspondence from a contractor that contains information detailing costs, but that fails to demand that the contracting officer issue a final decision, and instead merely expresses a willingness to reach an agreement, does not constitute a claim.[50] A letter sent to the contracting officer during negotiations requesting that the contracting officer refer the matter to an auditor does not qualify as a claim either, because the contracting officer has not been asked to issue a decision.[51] Finally, a proper claim exists when the amount sought either is set forth in "a sum-certain,"[52] or is determinable by a simple mathematical calculation or from information given by the contractor.[53] However, a contractor may not submit a claim in an unspecified amount or in an amount which is open-ended.[54]

---

[47] Alliance Oil & Refining Co. v. United States, 13 Cl. Ct. 496, 499–500 (1987).

[48] *See* Mingus Constructors, Inc. v. United States, 812 F.2d 1387.

[49] Esprit Corp. v. United States, 6 Cl. Ct. 546, 549 (1984) ("The plaintiff's requests for contract modifications were never in dispute; they are therefore not claims"), *aff'd mem.*, 776 F.2d 1062 (Fed. Cir. 1985).

[50] Hoffman Constr. Co. v. United States, 7 Cl. Ct. 518, 525 (1985). *See also* Technassociates, Inc. v. United States, 14 Cl. Ct. at 209–10 (letters the contractor sent in order to get the contracting officer to negotiate with it "on the future direction of the contract" did not constitute claims).

[51] G.S.& L. Mechanical & Constr., Inc., DOT BCA No. 1856, 87-2 B.C.A. (CCH) ¶ 19,882 (1987); *see also* Huntington Builders, ASBCA No. 33945, 87-2 B.C.A. (CCH) ¶ 19,898, at 100,654–655 (1987) (letters to contracting officer which, when taken together, alleged defective specifications and requested a 30-day time extension to contract and the release of monies withheld for liquidated damages did not constitute a claim because no specific monetary relief was requested for costs incurred as a result of the contractor's having to comply with the allegedly defective specifications).

[52] Disputes clause ¶ (c), FAR § 52.233-1, 48 C.F.R. § 52.233-1.

[53] Metric Constr. Co. v. United States, 1 Cl. Ct. at 392.

[54] Metric Constr. Co. v. United States, 14 Cl. Ct. 177, 179–80 (1988) (contractor's submissions made it clear that contractor was seeking to recover extended home office overhead and third-party indemnification fees, but the submissions did not constitute a

§ 9.6 —Certification Requirement

The CDA requires that claims in excess of $50,000 be certified.[55] The purpose of the certification requirement is to discourage unwarranted contractor claims and to encourage settlements.[56]

Compliance with the certification requirement is a prerequisite to invoking the dispute resolution procedures of the CDA. Until a claim in excess of $50,000 has been properly certified, interest does not begin to accrue,[57] a contracting officer cannot issue a valid decision,[58] and a contractor has no right of access to either a board of contract appeals or the Claims Court.[59] Because a contracting officer cannot issue a valid decision on a claim that has not been properly certified, a decision mistakenly issued on an uncertified claim or an improperly certified claim is a nullity, and any suit in either a board or the court appealing the decision will be dismissed.[60]

Finally, a failure to certify or a defective certification cannot be cured retroactively before the Claims Court or a board of contract appeals. Certification must take place at the proper time (that is, when a claim is submitted to a contracting officer for a final decision).[61] Thus, the contractor who initially fails to certify but nevertheless proceeds to the court or a board will be required, once the defect is discovered, to start the CDA process over again. The contractor will be required to certify its claim, resubmit it to the contracting officer, obtain a decision from the contracting officer (or wait until the time for the issuance of a decision has passed), and then proceed to the court or the appropriate board.[62]

---

proper claim under CDA because amounts being sought could only be determined by referring to, and making calculations on the basis of, "confusing" and "voluminous" exhibits).

[55] 41 U.S.C. § 605(c)(1), (c)(2).

[56] Paul E. Lehman, Inc. v. United States, 230 Ct. Cl. 11, 14, 673 F.2d 352, 354 (1982).

[57] Fidelity Constr. Co. v. United States, 700 F.2d at 1382–85.

[58] 41 U.S.C. § 605(c)(2); Paul E. Lehman, Inc. v. United States, 230 Ct. Cl. at 16, 673 F.2d at 355; Paragon Energy Corp. v. United States, 227 Ct. Cl. at 183–84, 645 F.2d at 971; Conoc Constr. Corp. v. United States, 3 Cl. Ct. 146, 147–48 (1983).

[59] W.M. Schlosser Co. v. United States, 705 F.2d 1336, 1338–39 (Fed. Cir. 1983); Romala Corp. v. United States, 12 Cl. Ct. 411, 412–13 (1987).

[60] Paul E. Lehman, Inc. v. United States, 230 Ct. Cl. 11, 673 F.2d 352.

[61] W.M. Schlosser Co. v. United States, 705 F.2d at 1338; Aeronautics Div., AAR Brooks & Perkins Corp. v. United States, 12 Cl. Ct. 132, 138 (1987); Sarbo, Inc., ASBCA No. 34292, 88-2 B.C.A. (CCH) ¶ 20,550 (1988).

[62] W.M. Schlosser Co. v. United States, 705 F.2d at 1340. Because of the jurisdictional nature of the certification requirement, it will be necessary for the contractor to go through this process even if it appears to be a foregone conclusion that the claim will be denied (Thoen v. United States, 765 F.2d at 1116).

In connection with the certification requirement, it is important to understand when a claim must be certified, how it must be certified, and who must certify it.

When a Claim Must Be Certified

Certification is required when a contractor asserts a claim exceeding $50,000.[63] In this regard, a contractor cannot bypass the certification requirement by fragmenting a single claim, which is in excess of $50,000, into a series of separate claims, each of which is less than $50,000.[64] The test is whether there exists "a single, unitary claim based on a common and related set of operative facts" that the contractor, unintentionally or otherwise, is seeking to break up into separate and distinct claims.[65] Put another way, do the damages that the contractor is seeking to recover in a series of separate claims arise from the same or from different causative events?[66]

It was alleged in one case that one differing site condition had given rise to three separate claims—one for additional paving costs, one for additional insurance, supervision, and maintenance costs, and one for loss of interest on funds spent to perform additional work—the court concluded that, in fact, there was just one claim.[67] Likewise, when a contract was terminated for the convenience of the government, the court concluded that a contractor's demand for "pre-termination and post-termination items" constituted one claim because both items were directly related to the government's termination of the contract and the resolution of both items depended upon what, if any, liability the government incurred as a result of its action.[68] Similarly, in a case where the contract at issue was for security guard services at five different locations in Boston, the court held that the contractor could not fragment its total dollar claim into separate claims based upon each of the different locations. The rationale was that the amounts claimed from the various locations were based upon the same operative facts (a total number of hours of services performed, for which a total number of dollars allegedly was due).[69] In another case, however, the

---

[63] Certification also is required when the amount in dispute is less than $50,000 but the total amount claimed is over $50,000. Clark Mechanical Contractors, Inc. v. United States, 12 Cl. Ct. 411, 412–13 (1987).

[64] Fidelity & Deposit Co. of Maryland v. United States, 2 Cl. Ct. 137, 143–45 (1983).

[65] Warchol Constr. Co. v. United States, 2 Cl. Ct. 384, 389 (1983). *See also* LDG Timber Enters., Inc. v. United States, 8 Cl. Ct. 445, 452 (1985).

[66] *See* Zinger Constr. Co., ASBCA No. 28788, 86-2 B.C.A. (CCH) ¶ 18,920 (1986).

[67] Warchol Constr. Co. v. United States, 2 Cl. Ct. 384.

[68] Palmer & Sicard, Inc. v. United States, 4 Cl. Ct. 420, 422–23 (1984).

[69] Black Star Security, Inc. v. United States, 5 Cl. Ct. 110 (1984).

Armed Services Board of Contract Appeals determined that where 18 different claims arose from different causative events and were brought under different legal theories, such as differing site conditions and defective specifications, it was proper to separate the claims.[70]

Sometimes, a claim that initially does not exceed $50,000 (and therefore is not certified) increases in amount after a contracting officer's decision is issued. In these circumstances, the question arises whether the contractor can proceed on the basis of the increased amount of the claim before the Claims Court or the appropriate board of contract appeals, or whether it is necessary for the contractor to certify the claim in the increased amount and resubmit it to the contracting officer for a decision.

The question was addressed in *Tecom, Inc. v. United States*.[71] There, the contractor's claim was in an amount less than $50,000 when it was submitted to the contracting officer. However, by the time the company filed its complaint before the Armed Services Board of Contract Appeals, the amount of the claim exceeded $50,000. This increase was the result of two events that occurred after the contracting officer's decision: an improved reevaluation of the claim by the contractor and the government's exercise of an option to extend the contract for an additional year. Under these circumstances, the court held that it was not necessary for the contractor to certify and resubmit its claim.

Tecom stands for the proposition that a monetary claim properly considered by a contracting officer "need not be certified or recertified if that very same claim (but in an increased amount reasonably based on further information) comes before a board of contract appeals or a court."[72] The court stated that it would be disruptive of normal litigation procedures "if any increase in the amount of a claim based on matters developed in litigation before the court [or board] had to be submitted to the contracting officer before the court [or board] could continue to final resolution on the claim."[73] In a footnote, however, the *Tecom* court pointed out that its decision should not be taken as an invitation to seek to evade the certification

---

[70] Zinger Constr. Co., ASBCA No. 28788, 86-2 B.C.A. (CCH) ¶ 18,920 (1986).

[71] 732 F.2d 935 (Fed. Cir. 1984).

[72] *Id.* at 938.

[73] *Id.* at 937–38 (*quoting* J.F. Shea Co. v. United States, 4 Cl. Ct. 46, 54 (parentheticals in *Tecom*)).

Kunz Constr. Co. v. United States, 12 Cl. Ct. 74, 79 (1987) (the court stated a contractor can enlarge dollar amount of its claim in court over what was presented to the contracting officer under two conditions: (1) if the increase is based on the same set of operative facts previously submitted to the contracting officer and (2) if the court finds that the contractor neither knew, nor reasonably should have known, at the time when the claim was presented to the contracting officer of the factors justifying the increase). *See also* E.C. Schleyer Pump Co., ASBCA No. 33900, 87-3 B.C.A. (CCH) ¶ 19,986 (1987) (costs that were merely an additional area of damages from the

requirement.[74] Thus, a contractor who deliberately understates the amount of its original claim (with the intention of raising the amount on appeal on the basis of information that was readily available at the time the claim first was submitted) will find its subsequent suit in the Claims Court or a board of contract appeals dismissed.[75]

How a Claim Must Be Certified

The certification language is set forth in the Act. The contractor must certify "that the claim is made in good faith, that the supporting data are accurate and complete to the best of [the contractor's] knowledge and belief, and that the amount requested accurately reflects the contract adjustment for which the contractor believes the government is liable."[76] Identical language is contained in the procurement regulations[77] and in the disputes clause that is in each contract covered by the CDA.[78]

In certifying its claim, a contractor need not parrot the words of the statute.[79] However, it must simultaneously state all three elements of the certification requirement.[80] It cannot certify in piecemeal fashion.[81]

The following submissions were found not to meet the requirements of the CDA: (1) a certification that varied from the language of the statute and the regulations by referring to "all data used" instead of the

---

same facts which were alleged in the claim could be brought before board even though not presented to the contracting officer).

Glenn v. United States, 858 F.2d 1577, 1580 (Fed. Cir. 1988) (the contractor submitted a claim to the contracting officer in the amount of $31,500. Because the claim was less than $50,000, the contractor did not certify it. The contracting officer issued a final decision denying the claim, which the contractor appealed to the Armed Services Board of Contract Appeals. Thereafter, the contracting officer issued a second final decision. In that decision, the contracting officer stated that he was withholding $66,570.32 from the contractor (consisting of the $31,500 which the contractor previously had sought to recover and an additional $35,070.32). Relying on its prior decision in *Tecom*, the Federal Circuit held that it was not necessary for the contractor to certify its $66,570.32 claim before bringing suit in the Claims Court. "Because Glenn was not required to certify his $31,500 claim before the C.O., he need not have certified the $66,570.32 resulting from the denial of his initial claim . . . and [the] additional setoffs").

[74] 732 F.2d at 938, n.2.

[75] *Id.*

[76] 41 U.S.C. § 605(c)(1).

[77] FAR § 33.207(a), 48 C.F.R. § 33.207(a).

[78] FAR § 52.233-1, 48 C.F.R. § 52.233-1.

[79] United States v. General Elec. Corp., 727 F.2d 1567, 1569 (Fed. Cir. 1984).

[80] W.H. Moseley Co. v. United States, 230 Ct. Cl. at 407, 677 F.2d at 852; Parrino Enters. v. United States, 230 Ct. Cl. 1052 (1982).

[81] *See* Black Star Security, Inc. v. United States, 5 Cl. Ct. at 117.

"supporting data" for the claim (thereby restricting the certification to "unidentified data [which the contractor] chose to use while the statute requires certification of all data that support the claim");[82] (2) a certification that omitted the assertion that supporting data was accurate and complete;[83] (3) a letter in which a contractor demanded money damages that "probably exceeded $150,000" and in which the contractor's president stated that the claim was being made in good faith and wrote, "the supporting data is accurate and complete to the best of my knowledge and belief, and . . . the amounts, unknown at this time, accurately reflect the contract adjustment for which the government is liable";[84] (4) a certification in which the contractor stated that it would not assume any legal obligations that it would not have without the certification, that the data submitted was "as accurate and complete as practicable," and that the contractor was not demanding a "particular amount."[85]

Nevertheless, a contractor whose certification did not contain the amount of the claim involved and did not have the words "the amount requested accurately reflects the contract adjustment for which the contractor believes the government is liable" still was found to be in substantial compliance with the certification requirement. The statement in which the certification was contained did have the remainder of the elements required by the Act, and, when the statement was read in its entirety and together with documents that accompanied it, all of the information and statements required by the statute were found to be present.[86]

Notwithstanding the degree of flexibility that may be allowed, the prudent course is to track the language of the Act when a contractor is certifying a claim.

Supporting Data

A contractor who certifies its claim by tracking the language of the statute still may find itself confronted with the argument that the data supporting its claim is inadequate for purposes of the certification requirement. For the most part, though, neither the courts nor the boards have taken an overly stringent attitude with respect to supporting data.

In *Metric Construction Co. v. United States*,[87] the government argued that the contractor's certification was defective because the contractor had

---

[82] Gauntt Constr. Co., 87-3 B.C.A. (CCH) ¶ 20,221, at 102,412 (1987).

[83] Raymond Kaiser Eng'rs, Inc./Kaiser Steel Corp., a Joint Venture, ASBCA No. 34133, 87-3 B.C.A. (CCH) ¶ 20,140, at 101,940–41 (1987).

[84] T.J.D. Servs., Inc. v. United States, 6 Cl. Ct. 257, 259 (1984).

[85] Cochran Constr. Co., ASBCA No. 34378, 87-3 B.C.A. (CCH) ¶ 19,993, at 101,280–81, *aff'd on reconsideration*, 87-3 B.C.A. ¶ 20,114 (1987).

[86] United States v. General Elec. Corp., 727 F.2d at 1569.

[87] 1 Cl. Ct. 383 (1983).

§ 9.6 CERTIFICATION REQUIREMENT 209

failed to attach copies of the pertinent change order modifications to its claim. In rejecting the government's argument, the court observed that the certification requirement "was not intended, nor should it be so construed, to require a full evidentiary presentation before the contracting officer."[88] The court noted that the contracting officer had not denied the contractor's claim for lack of supporting data and that the data that had been presented had assisted the contracting officer "in making a meaningful determination on the dispute before him."[89]

The Engineering Board of Contract Appeals took a similar position and cited *Metric* with approval in *Newhall Refining Co.*[90] There, in response to the government's argument that the contractors involved had not submitted accurate and complete supporting data when they certified their claims, the board noted that, on their face, the certifications met the requirements of the Act, that the claims were "articulated in a clear and concise fashion," that the contractors had notified the contracting officer of the basis for their claims prior to submitting them, and that the contracting officer already was in possession of information relating to the claims.[91] The board also noted the fact that the claims before it involved a legal issue of contract interpretation, and it found "highly persuasive" the fact that the contracting officer had not requested additional information from the contractors.[92] Under these circumstances, the board determined that the data submitted with the claims was "adequate."[93]

The above cases suggest that when the language of the contractor's certification meets the requirements of the Act and the contracting officer is provided with the needed information to render a decision, the contractor probably does not have to worry about having its case derailed by the contention that it failed to submit adequate supporting data.

Who Must Sign the Certification

The CDA itself is silent on the question of who must sign the certification on behalf of a contractor. The regulations and the disputes clause, however, both address the point. They provide as follows:

---

[88] *Id.* at 391.

[89] *Id.*

[90] EBCA Nos. 363-7-86, 364-7-86, 365-7-86, 366-7-86, 367-7-86, 368-7-86, 87-1 B.C.A. (CCH) ¶ 19,340 (1987).

[91] 87-1 B.C.A. (CCH) ¶ 19,340 at 97,583.

[92] *Id.*

[93] *Id.* When a contractor sponsors the claim of a subcontractor (see § 9.4), it is enough for the contractor, when it certifies the subcontractor's claim, to believe that there is a good faith ground for the claim. The contractor need not believe that the subcontractor's claim is certain. United States v. Turner Constr. Co., 827 F.2d 1554, 1561–62 (Fed. Cir. 1987).

(c)(1) If the contractor is an individual, the certification shall be executed by that individual.

    (2) If the contractor is not an individual, the certification shall be executed by
- (i) A senior company official in charge at the contractor's plant or location involved; or
- (ii) An officer or general partner of the contractor having overall responsibility for the conduct of the contractor's affairs.[94]

From time to time, questions arise concerning the signing of a certification. In this regard, it has been held that a claim is not properly certified when it is signed by a contractor's attorney.[95] In another case, a certification was executed by the contractor's project manager, who was responsible for overall project scheduling, coordinating, and monitoring, but who was not a senior company official or an officer or general partner of the contractor. Someone other than the project manager had been given responsibility to act on the contractor's behalf. Under these circumstances, the court found the certification to be defective.[96]

§ 9.7 —Contracting Officer's Decision

Once a claim meeting all the requirements of the CDA has been submitted, the next step in the dispute resolution process is the issuance of a contracting officer's decision. The issuance of a valid contracting officer's decision, or the failure to issue such a decision within the time allowed by the Act, is a prerequisite to bringing suit on the claim in either the Claims Court or an agency board of contract appeals.[97]

Time Allowed for Issuing the Decision

The CDA provides that in the case of claims of $50,000 or less, the contracting officer will issue a decision within 60 days of receipt of a written request from the contractor that a decision be issued within that period.[98] For claims over $50,000, the Act provides that, within 60 days of receipt

---

[94] FAR § 33.207(c), 48 C.F.R. § 33.207(c); FAR § 52.233-1, 48 C.F.R. § 52.233-1.

[95] Romala Corp. v. United States, 12 Cl. Ct. at 412–13 (1987); T.J.D. Servs., Inc. v. United States, 6 Cl. Ct. at 261–62.

[96] Donald M. Drake Co. v. United States, 12 Cl. Ct. 518 (1987).

[97] Milmark Servs., Inc. v. United States, 231 Ct. Cl. 954, 956 (1982); River v. United States, 7 Cl. Ct. at 775.

[98] 41 U.S.C. § 605(c)(1).

§ 9.7 CONTRACTING OFFICER'S DECISION

of a certified claim, the contracting officer will issue a decision or notify the contractor of the time within which a decision will be issued.[99]

The Act states that contracting officers' decisions are to be issued "within a reasonable time" in accordance with agency regulations, taking into account such factors as the size and complexity of the claim and the adequacy of the information in support of the claim.[100] Thus, although the CDA does not require a full evidentiary submission in order to recognize a claim,[101] it is in a contractor's interest to make its claim submission clear and understandable (see § 9.5). It also is in a contractor's interest to either provide appropriate supporting documentation or to refer to material that is in the government's possession, such as pertinent construction and progress reports and correspondence. In this way, the contractor will have done all it can to minimize the time required for the issuance of a contracting officer's decision.

The CDA also provides that, in the event of undue delay on the part of the contracting officer in issuing a decision, a contractor may request the appropriate agency board of contract appeals to direct that a decision be issued in a specified period of time, as determined by the board.[102] In making such a request of the board, the contractor should be sure that it has provided the contracting officer with all the information reasonably necessary for a proper review of the claim and the issuance of a decision.

Any failure by a contracting officer to issue a decision on a claim within the period required by the Act or directed by a board of contract appeals is deemed to be a decision by the contracting officer denying the claim, and such failure authorizes the commencement of suit in either the Claims Court or the appropriate board.[103] The fact that a contracting officer fails to issue a decision, however, does not mean that the government is barred from contesting the claim in subsequent proceedings. Failure to issue a decision is deemed a denial, not a default.[104]

A contractor should be aware, however, that even when a claim is properly submitted and the contracting officer fails to issue a decision, the Claims Court or a board of contract appeals still has the option of staying proceedings for the purpose of obtaining a decision on the claim.[105] It is reasonable to expect, however, that the court or board will not be inclined to exercise this option in the situation where the contracting officer involved has been directed by a board to issue a decision but has failed to

---

[99] 41 U.S.C. § 605(c)(2).
[100] 41 U.S.C. § 605(c)(3).
[101] Metric Constr. Co. v. United States, 1 Cl. Ct. at 391.
[102] 41 U.S.C. § 605(c)(4).
[103] 41 U.S.C. § 605(c)(5).
[104] Maki v. United States, 13 Cl. Ct. 779, 782 (1987).
[105] 41 U.S.C. § 605(c)(5).

do so, or in the situation where the contracting officer gives no reason for the failure to issue a decision.

Contents of the Decision

The CDA requires that each contracting officer's decision "state the reasons for the decision reached and . . . inform the contractor of his rights as provided in [the Act]. Specific findings of fact are not required, but, if made, shall not be binding in any subsequent proceeding."[106]

FAR also contain provisions for the content of contracting officers' decisions. FAR § 33.211 details the steps that the contracting officer is to follow in issuing a decision and gives guidance as to the matters that should be covered in the decision.[107] The various agencies also have regulations that address the issuing of contracting officers' decisions.[108]

FAR § 33.211 requires that each contracting officer's decision contain a paragraph in substantially the form set forth in the regulation advising the contractor of its appeal rights. A contracting officer's decision is defective if it does not contain such a paragraph.[109] In addition, as more fully discussed in § 9.9, a contracting officer's decision that fails to notify the contractor of its appeal rights does not trigger the running of the period for bringing suit in the Claims Court or for appealing to the appropriate board of contract appeals.[110]

§ 9.8 Government Claims

The CDA also covers government claims. The Act provides that "[a]ll claims by the government against a contractor relating to a contract shall be the subject of a decision by the contracting officer."[111] This means that before the government can pursue a claim against a contractor, the claim must be the subject of a contracting officer's decision.[112] The one

---

[106] 41 U.S.C. § 605(a).

[107] 48 C.F.R. § 33.211.

[108] Agency procurement regulations are found in volume 5 of Commerce Clearing House's Government Contracts Reporter.

[109] Pathman Constr. Co. v. United States, 817 F.2d 1573, 1578 (Fed. Cir. 1987).

[110] Id.

[111] 41 U.S.C. § 605(a).

[112] Joseph Morton Co. v. United States, 757 F.2d 1273, 1279 (Fed. Cir. 1985). It should be noted that at least one tribunal seems to have imposed an additional requirement upon the government before it may assert a claim against a contractor. E.C. Morris & Son, Inc., ASBCA No. 30385, 86-2 B.C.A. (CCH) ¶ 18,785, at 94,652–53 (1986) (Armed Services Board of Contract Appeals addressed a government counterclaim which had been the subject of a contracting officer's decision. After noting that there

exception to this rule is the situation where the government asserts a fraud claim against a contractor. Such a claim need not be the subject of a contracting officer's final decision.[113]

§ 9.9 Appealing the Contracting Officer's Decision

The CDA provides that a contracting officer's decision on a claim (whether a contractor or a government claim) is "final and conclusive and not subject to review by any forum, tribunal, or Governmental agency unless an appeal or suit is timely commenced as provided in the [Act]."[114] Thus, once it receives a contracting officer's decision, a contractor has two alternatives available to it. The contractor can take no action on the appeal, in which event it becomes final, or it can appeal the decision.

Under the CDA, a contractor has two avenues of appeal from a contracting officer's decision. Within 90 days of the date of receipt of the decision, the contractor may appeal the decision to the appropriate agency board of contract appeals.[115] Alternatively, within 12 months of the date of receipt of the decision, the contractor may initiate an action in the Claims Court.[116]

With respect to either an appeal to a board of contract appeals or an action in the Claims Court, it is important to bear four points in mind: first, there can be no appeal or suit unless there has been a valid contracting officer's decision or the failure to issue such a decision within the period required under the Act. Second, once a valid final decision has

---

was nothing in the record to indicate that "the contracting officer discussed the basis for the counterclaim with [the contractor] before issuing the final decision," the board stated that it did not perceive the government's counterclaim "to be embraced by the . . . appeal.") In taking this position, the board relied on Woods Hole Oceanographics Inst. v. United States, 677 F.2d 149 (1st Cir. 1982). *Id.*

The correctness of *Morris* is questionable. In *Woods Hole,* the First Circuit did not hold, as the board states, that failure by a contracting officer to "hear a contractor" before asserting a government claim deprives the contracting officer's decision on the claim of efficacy. 86-2 B.C.A. at 94,653. Rather, the court in *Woods Hole* stated: "We do not find it necessary to consider whether if a government claim is one covered by § 6(a) of the Act, Congress empowered the C.O. to decide such claim *ex parte* without giving the contractor any kind of advance notice or opportunity to be heard." 677 F.2d at 156 n.8. In addition, *Woods Hole* aside, there is no provision in the CDA which imposes the requirement stated in *Morris.* Nevertheless, those involved with government claims before the ASBCA should be aware of the *Morris* decision.

[113] Martin J. Simko Constr., Inc. v. United States, 852 F.2d 540 (Fed. Cir. 1988).
[114] 41 U.S.C. § 605(b).
[115] 41 U.S.C. § 606.
[116] 41 U.S.C. § 609(a)(1), (a)(2). *See* Opalack v. United States, 5 Cl. Ct. 349, 361 (1984).

been issued, it is essential that a board appeal, or a Claims Court suit, whichever the contractor wishes to pursue, be timely commenced. Third, the contractor should realize that, once it has elected either a board or the court as the forum in which to challenge the contracting officer's decision, it may not switch to the other forum. Fourth, different rules apply in the case of contracting officers' decisions which do not involve money claims against a contractor.

§ 9.10 —Necessity of a Decision

As discussed in § 9.7, a contractor can neither appeal to a board of contract appeals nor bring suit in the Claims Court until such time as the contracting officer has issued a decision on its claim or has failed to issue a decision within the time required by the Act or directed by the appropriate board. At the same time, a contracting officer is not authorized, and cannot be directed, to issue a decision until the contractor has submitted a proper claim (see §§ 9.3 and 9.6). In addition, a contracting officer's decision that is issued in the absence of a proper claim is not valid and cannot form the basis for an appeal to a board or a suit in the Claims Court.[117] Thus, to emphasize again, a contractor should always remember that it will have no right of appeal to either a board or the Claims Court unless it begins the CDA process by properly submitting its claim.

§ 9.11 —Time for Appealing the Decision

Another point that a contractor should bear in mind is that there must be strict compliance with the time limits set forth in the CDA for appealing to boards and the Claims Court. Neither a board nor the court can consider an appeal that is not timely presented to it.[118] The periods for challenging contracting officer's decisions set forth in the CDA are jurisdictional and cannot be waived.[119]

Although strict compliance is required with the limitations periods set forth in the CDA, those periods do not begin to run if a contracting officer issues a decision that is defective because it fails to advise the contractor of

---

[117] See Paul E. Lehman, Inc. v. United States, 230 Ct. Cl. at 16, 673 F.2d at 355.

[118] Cosmic Constr. Co. v. United States, 697 F.2d 1389 (Fed. Cir. 1982); Gregory Lumber Co. v. United States, 229 Ct. Cl. 762 (1982); Contract Servs. Co., ASBCA No. 34438, 87-2 B.C.A. (CCH) ¶ 19,850 (1987).

[119] Id.

§ 9.11   TIME FOR APPEALING   215

its appeal rights under the Act.[120] Also, no limitations period is triggered in the situation where the contractor's right to proceed to either a board or the Claims Court arises because the contracting officer has failed to issue a decision on a proper claim within the period of time required by the Act and the claim therefore is deemed denied.[121] In addition, the limitations period may be tolled if a contractor asks the contracting officer in a timely manner to reconsider his or her decision.[122]

Finally, in the case of a contract termination for default, the circumstances may be such that the time the contractor has to challenge the termination does not begin to run when the contracting officer issues the decision terminating the contract, but at a later date. This is because of the *Fulford* doctrine, first articulated by the Armed Services Board of Contract Appeals in *Fulford Manufacturing Co.*[123] The proposition embodied by the *Fulford* doctrine is that when a contractor makes a timely appeal to an assessment of excess reprocurement costs, the propriety of the default termination can be challenged even though the default termination was not appealed.[124] The *Fulford* doctrine has not been repudiated by the CDA.[125] Thus, the limitations periods set forth in the CDA do not "bar a contractor from contesting the propriety of a default termination in an action appealing a contracting officer's decision assessing excess reprocurement costs" if such an action is filed within 90 days (a board appeal) or 12 months (a Claims Court suit) of that decision.[126] Failure to seek review of a default termination within the 90-day or 12-month period, however, bars a contractor from challenging the default termination if excess costs are not assessed.[127]

Thus, a contractor who receives a default termination from the government unaccompanied by any money claim and who wishes to challenge the default termination should give serious consideration to appealing the decision within the period of time applicable to the forum it wishes to use. As discussed in § 9.13, however, a contractor who is confronted with a

---

[120] Pathman Constr. Co. v. United States, 817 F.2d at 1578.

[121] *Id.* at 1573.

[122] Summit Contractors v. United States, 15 Cl. Ct. 806 (1988).

[123] ASBCA Nos. 2143, 2144 (May 20, 1955), 6 Cont. Cas. Fed. (CCH) ¶ 61,815 (May 20, 1955) (digest only).

[124] D. Moody & Co. v. United States, 5 Cl. Ct. 70, 72 (1984).

[125] D. Moody & Co. v. United States, 5 Cl. Ct. 70; Tom Warr, IBCA No. 2360, 88-1 B.C.A. (CCH) ¶ 20,231 (1987).

[126] D. Moody & Co. v. United States, 5 Cl. Ct. at 79; Tom Warr, IBCA No. 2360, 88-1 B.C.A. (CCH) ¶ 20,231 (1987).

[127] *Id.*

default termination standing alone without a money claim may not be able to bring suit in the Claims Court.

§ 9.12 —Election Doctrine

Once a contractor has elected either a board or the Claims Court as the forum in which to challenge a contracting officer's decision, it may not switch to the other forum. In this regard, a contractor who is poised to proceed to either a board or the court should be aware of the Election doctrine. The term *Election doctrine* refers to the body of law that has grown up in light of the fact that under the CDA, a contractor has a choice of forums in which to challenge a contracting officer's decision. However, the Election doctrine recognizes that the Act does not allow the contractor to pursue its claim in both forums.[128] Thus, once a contractor makes a binding election to appeal a contracting officer's decision to the appropriate board of contract appeals, that election stands, and the contractor cannot change course and pursue its claim in the Claims Court.[129]

A binding election takes place when a contractor files an appeal or initiates a suit in a *"forum with jurisdiction over the proceeding."*[130] This means that when a contractor initiates proceedings on its claim before a board of contract appeals in a timely manner, it has made a binding election to proceed before the board and it is barred from initiating suit in the Claims Court; any suit it files in the court will be dismissed.[131] However, the filing of an appeal with the appropriate board of contract appeals is not a binding election if it is determined by the board that the contractor's appeal was untimely, and hence the subsequent filing of a claim in the Claims Court is not barred.[132] The rationale is that a contractor's choice of forums in which to contest the contracting officer's decision is a binding election only if that choice is truly available, which it is not if resort to a board of contract appeals is untimely.[133] An untimely appeal to a board is not a choice that truly is available, the reason being that an untimely appeal to a board is an absolute nullity because the board lacks jurisdiction over the appeal.[134]

---

[128] Tuttle/White Constructors, Inc. v. United States, 228 Ct. Cl. 354, 361, 656 F.2d 644, 649 (1981).

[129] *Id.*

[130] National Neighbors, Inc. v. United States, 839 F.2d 1539, 1542 (Fed. Cir. 1988) (emphasis in decision).

[131] National Neighbors, Inc. v. United States, 839 F.2d at 1541–42.

[132] *Id.*

[133] *Id.*

[134] *Id. See* Cosmic Constr. Co. v. United States, 697 F.2d at 1390.

§ 9.13 —Decisions Not Involving Money Claims

As discussed in § 9.8, a government claim against a contractor generally must be the subject of a contracting officer's decision. In addition, a contracting officer's decision asserting a money claim against a contractor may be challenged in either a board of contract appeals or the Claims Court.[135] A problem may arise, however, when a contracting officer issues a decision that impacts the contractual relationship between the parties but does not involve the assertion of a money claim against the contractor. This is the case, for example, when a contracting officer directs the contractor to take action under the contract (such as perform additional work) or terminates a contract for default but does not assert a claim for money against the contractor.

As seen in § 9.5, claim is defined in the FAR and in the mandatory disputes clause to include "a written demand or written assertion by one of the contracting parties seeking, as a matter of right, . . . the adjustment or interpretation of contract terms, or other relief arising or relating to the contract." On its face, this language seems broad enough to encompass the situation where the contracting officer directs the contractor to perform additional work under the contract or terminates the contract for default but does not assert a claim for money.

Boards of contract appeals have jurisdiction to determine the propriety of a termination for default even when it is not accompanied by a money claim (such as a claim by the government for excess reprocurement costs).[136] The rationale for this is that, in the words of the CDA, a default termination is a claim "by the government against a contractor relating to a contract."[137]

Going beyond default terminations, the Armed Services Board of Contract Appeals has held that the government's determination that a contractor had not complied with cost accounting standards (CAS) was appealable, even though the document setting forth the determination was not designated a final decision and was not in the form required for a final decision.[138] The board based its decision upon the view that final CAS noncompliance determinations are appealable without assertion of a monetary claim "in order to render the statutory regulatory CAS scheme effective."[139] On the other hand, the General Services Board of Contract Appeals has held that a contracting officer's directive that a

---

[135] See § 9.9.

[136] Emily Malone v. United States, 849 F.2d 1441, 1443–45 (Fed. Cir. 1988). *See* Nuclear Research Corp. v. United States, 814 F.2d 647 (Fed. Cir. 1987).

[137] 41 U.S.C. § 605(a). *See* Emily Malone v. United States, 849 F.2d at 1443.

[138] Systron Donner, Inertial Div., ASBCA No. 31148, 87-3 B.C.A. (CCH) ¶ 20,066 (1987).

[139] Systron Donner, Inertial Div., 87-3 B.C.A. (CCH) at 101,608–609.

contractor was liable for replacing a defective compressor was not a final decision, but merely a declaration of rights and obligations (and thus not appealable).[140]

In the Claims Court, there is a split of authority on the question of whether the court has jurisdiction to entertain a challenge to a termination for default that is not joined with a money claim. Some cases have held that a termination for default alone does not create a cognizable claim in the court.[141] These cases rely upon the principle that the Claims Court is not authorized to render declaratory judgments.[142] Under this principle, the court does not have jurisdiction to hear a case that merely presents a challenge to a termination for default without any money claim being present, because such a challenge is seen as seeking a declaratory judgment.[143]

Other cases have taken the position that the Claims Court has jurisdiction over a default termination claim even though the claim is not joined with a specific claim for money by either the contractor or the government.[144] These cases rely upon the holding in *Emily Malone v. United States* that a government decision to terminate a contract for default is the assertion of a government claim against the contractor within the meaning of the CDA.[145] The Federal Circuit has not yet spoken on this issue.[146] However, its holding in *Emily Malone* may foreshadow a determination that the Claims Court has jurisdiction to hear a challenge to a default termination in the absence of a money claim, in view of the fact that jurisdiction of agency boards and the Claims Court is largely coextensive with respect to review of contracting officers' decisions.[147] In any event, once the government has made a money demand upon a contractor in default, a government claim has accrued and the contractor may bring suit under the CDA to determine the propriety of the default termination and the amount of the claimed damages.[148]

---

[140] Griffin Servs. Inc., GSBCA No. 8876, 88-1 B.C.A. (CCH) ¶ 20,305 (1987).

[141] *See* Mega Constr. Co. v. United States, 14 Cl. Ct. 555 (1988); Citizens Assocs., Ltd. v. United States, 12 Cl. Ct. 599, 600–01 (1987); Industrial Coatings, Inc. v. United States, 11 Cl. Ct. 161, 162–64 (1986); Alan J. Haynes Constr. Sys., Inc. v. United States, 10 Cl. Ct. 526 (1986); Gunn-Williams v. United States, 8 Cl. Ct. 531, 535 (1985).

[142] *See, e.g.,* Mega Constr. Co. v. United States, 14 Cl. Ct. at 557.

[143] *Id.*

[144] *See* Russell Corp. v. United States, 15 Cl. Ct. 760, 761–62 (1988); Claude E. Atkins Enters., Inc. v. United States, 15 Cl. Ct. 644 (1988).

[145] Claude E. Atkins Enters., Inc. v. United States, 15 Cl. Ct. at 647. *See* Johnson & Gordon Sec., Inc. v. United States, 857 F.2d 1435, 1437–38 (Fed. Cir. 1988).

[146] *See* Emily Malone v. United States, 849 F.2d at 1444.

[147] *See* Claude E. Atkins Enters., Inc. v. United States, 15 Cl. Ct. at 647.

[148] A downward price adjustment under a contract also is a matter with respect to which the Claims Court can exercise jurisdiction. *See* Shank-Artukovich v. United States, 13

§ 9.14 Review of Decisions of Boards of Contract Appeals and the Claims Court

As noted in § 9.1, decisions of boards of contract appeals and the Claims Court are reviewable in the United States Court of Appeals for the Federal Circuit.

The CDA gives both contractors and the government the right to appeal from board decisions.[149] However, a government appeal from a board decision may be taken only if it is authorized by the agency involved and approved by the Attorney General.[150] Appeals from board decisions, whether by a contractor or the government, must be brought within 120 days of the date of receipt of the decision with respect to which the appeal is taken.[151] This time limit is jurisdictional; failure to comply with it results in dismissal of the appeal.[152] Either a contractor or the government may appeal a Claims Court decision.[153] Appeals from decisions of the Claims Court are brought by filing a notice of appeal in the Claims Court within 60 days of the entry of final judgment.[154]

Decisions of the Federal Circuit are reviewable upon the granting of a writ of certiorari by the United States Supreme Court.[155] The Federal Circuit employs both its own rules and the Federal Rules of Appellate Procedure.[156]

Board decisions are reviewed in the Federal Circuit in accordance with the standards set forth in the CDA.[157] In this regard, the Act provides as follows:

> [T]he decision of the agency board on any question of law shall not be final or conclusive, but the decision on any question of fact shall be final and conclusive and shall not be set aside unless the decision is fraudulent, or arbitrary, or capricious, or so grossly erroneous as to necessarily imply bad faith, or if such decision is not supported by substantial evidence.[158]

Cl. Ct. 346, 349 (1987). However, in Alan J. Haynes Constr. Sys., Inc. v. United States, 10 Cl. Ct. 526, it was held that the court did not have jurisdiction to render a declaration as to a contractor's obligations under a particular provision of the contract at issue.

[149] 41 U.S.C. § 607(g)(1).

[150] 41 U.S.C. § 607(g)(1)(B).

[151] 41 U.S.C. § 607(g)(1).

[152] Placeway Constr. Corp. v. United States, 713 F.2d 726 (Fed. Cir. 1983).

[153] 28 U.S.C. § 1295(a)(3).

[154] *See* Rule 10(a) of the Rules of the Federal Circuit and Rule 4(a) of the Federal Rules of Appellate Procedure.

[155] 28 U.S.C. § 1254.

[156] Introduction, Rules of the United States Court of Appeals for the Federal Circuit.

[157] 28 U.S.C. § 1295(c).

[158] 41 U.S.C. § 609(b).

In light of this mandate, the Federal Circuit reviews board decisions under the substantial evidence standard and to determine whether they are correct as a matter of law.[159] The court's review is limited to issues that were raised before the board.[160]

The Federal Circuit's standard for review of Claims Court decisions is different. A decision of the Claims Court will be set aside only if the court's fact findings are clearly erroneous or its legal conclusions are incorrect.[161]

As discussed in § 9.23, it is not uncommon in board proceedings to have the issues of liability (entitlement) and quantum (damages) bifurcated, or separated. When a board case is bifurcated, a question arises as to whether the bifurcation prevents an appeal from being taken to the Federal Circuit because the board's decision is not final.

In *Dewey Electronics Corp. v. United States*,[162] the contractor brought nine separate claims to the Armed Services Board of Contract Appeals. Considering entitlement only, the board found for the contractor on five of the claims and remanded them to the contracting officer to negotiate the amount due the contractor. The board denied the remaining four claims and the contractor appealed to the Federal Circuit. The court rejected the government's argument that it lacked jurisdiction because the board's decision in the case was not final.[163] The court did this because it concluded that adopting the view urged by the government would reduce the efficiency and flexibility of board administrative proceedings and would be contrary to the routine practice of the boards initially to decide entitlement only.[164]

In *Teller Environmental Services, Inc. v. United States*,[165] however, the Federal Circuit held that a decision of the Armed Services Board of Contract Appeals finding entitlement on a government claim but remanding

---

[159] Afro-Lecon, Inc. v. United States, 820 F.2d 1198, 1200–01 (Fed. Cir. 1987); United States v. Lockheed Corp., 817 F.2d 1565, 1567 (Fed. Cir. 1988); Alvin, Ltd. v. United States, 816 F.2d 1562, 1564 (Fed. Cir. 1987); William F. Klingensmith, Inc. v. United States, 731 F.2d 805, 809 (Fed. Cir. 1984); United States v. General Elec. Corp., 727 F.2d at 1572. Substantial evidence "means such evidence as a reasonable mind might accept as reasonable to support a conclusion." Consolidated Edison Co. v. NLRB, 305 U.S. 197, 229 (1938), *cited in* United States v. General Elec. Corp., 727 F.2d at 1572.

[160] William F. Klingensmith, Inc. v. United States, 731 F.2d at 807.

[161] Milmark Servs. Corp. v. United States, 731 F.2d 855, 857 (Fed. Cir. 1984). A finding is clearly erroneous when, "although there is evidence to support it, the reviewing court on the entire evidence is left with the definite and firm conviction that a mistake has been committed." United States v. United States Gypsum Co., 333 U.S. 364, 395 (1948), *quoted in* Milmark Servs. Corp. v. United States, 731 F.2d at 857.

[162] 803 F.2d 650 (Fed. Cir. 1986).

[163] *Id.* at 653–58.

[164] *Id.*

[165] 802 F.2d 1385 (Fed. Cir. 1986).

to the contracting officer for negotiation of quantum—even though the contracting officer had determined the amount of the government's damages in his decision—was not a final decision.[166] The court reasoned that both liability and quantum had been before the board because they both had been decided in the contracting officer's decision, which was appealed to the board.[167] Hence, the court concluded, by remanding the quantum issue to the contracting officer, the board did not completely decide the case before it. For this reason, its decision was not final.[168]

§ 9.15 Small Claims

The CDA requires that the rules of each agency board of contract appeals include procedures for the accelerated disposition of any appeal from a decision of a contracting officer where the amount in controversy is less than $50,000,[169] and for expedited procedures where the amount in controversy is less than $10,000.[170] Under accelerated procedures, an appeal is to be resolved within 180 days of the date the contractor elects to utilize the procedures.[171] Under expedited procedures, an appeal is to be resolved within 120 days of the date the contractor elects to utilize the procedures.[172] Accelerated and expedited procedures are discussed in § 9.24.

§ 9.16 Interest

The CDA provides that "[i]nterest on amounts found due contractors on claims shall be paid to the contractor from the date the contracting officer receives the claim pursuant to section 605(a) of this title from the contractor until payment thereof."[173] Interest is computed at the rate established from time to time by the Secretary of the Treasury.[174] Interest, however, does not begin to accrue until such time as the contractor properly submits its claim.[175]

---

[166] *Id.* at 1389–90.

[167] *Id.* at 1389.

[168] *Id.* at 1389–90.

[169] 41 U.S.C. § 607(f).

[170] 41 U.S.C. § 608(a).

[171] 41 U.S.C. § 607(f).

[172] 41 U.S.C. § 608(c).

[173] 41 U.S.C. § 611.

[174] *Id.*

[175] Fidelity Constr. Co. v. United States, 700 F.2d at 1382–85; Brookfield Constr. Co. v. United States, 228 Ct. Cl. 551, 661 F.2d 159 (1981).

§ 9.17 Payment of Claims

The CDA provides that judgments by the Claims Court and awards by boards of contract appeals are to be paid in accordance with the procedures of 31 U.S.C. § 1304.[176] That statute provides for payment out of a central judgment fund administered by the Treasury Department, upon direction for payment from the General Accounting Office. The Act requires that payments made pursuant to court judgment or board award are to be reimbursed to the judgment fund by the agencies.[177] The consequence of this is that an agency faced with a judgment or award against it sometimes will choose to pay the contractor directly rather than go through the reimbursement process. This can result in quicker payment for the contractor.

§ 9.18 Fraudulent Claims

The CDA provides that if a contractor is unable to support any part of its claim and it is determined that such inability is attributable to misrepresentation of fact or fraud on the part of the contractor, the contractor is liable to the government "for an amount equal to such unsupported part of the claim in addition to all costs to the Government attributable to the cost of reviewing said part of [the] claim."[178] The government is given six years to determine liability under the section.[179] The government also can assert civil fraud under the False Claims Act.[180] Under the False Claims Act, suit generally must be brought within six years of the date on which the fraud is committed.[181] As discussed in § 9.8, a fraud claim by the government is an exception to the rule that requires a contracting officer's decision before a claim may be asserted.

§ 9.19 Agency Boards of Contract Appeals

The CDA provides that a contractor may appeal a contracting officer's decision to "an agency board of contract appeals, as provided in section 607 of this title."[182] Section 607 of title 41 states that an executive agency may

---

[176] 41 U.S.C. §§ 612(a), (b).

[177] 41 U.S.C. § 612(c).

[178] 41 U.S.C. § 604.

[179] *Id.*

[180] 31 U.S.C. §§ 3729–3731 (1982, Supp. IV, 1986).

[181] 31 U.S.C. § 3731(b) (1982, Supp. IV, 1986).

[182] 41 U.S.C. § 606.

§ 9.20 PRACTICE BEFORE BOARDS 223

establish a board of contract appeals when it is determined that the volume of contract claims involving the agency justifies a full-time board of at least three members.[183] If an agency's volume of contract claims is not sufficient to justify a full-time board, the agency may arrange for appeals from decisions of its contracting officers to be heard and decided by the board of another agency.[184]

Members of agency boards are selected and appointed to serve in the same manner as administrative law judges, with the additional requirement that they must have not fewer than five years experience in public contract law.[185]

The jurisdiction of the boards is spelled out in 41 U.S.C. § 607(d). That section provides that each agency board of contract appeals has jurisdiction to decide any appeal from a decision of a contracting officer relating to a contract made by its agency or to a contract made by another agency, when that other agency or the Administrator for Federal Procurement Policy has designated the board to decide the appeal. The Act states that in exercising their jurisdiction, the boards are authorized to grant any relief "that would be available to a litigant asserting a contract claim in the United States Claims Court."[186]

There are 13 agency boards of contract appeals, each with their own rules of procedure. The boards and their membership are listed in the Commerce Clearing House (CCH) volume *Contract Appeals Decisions* (CAD). That volume also contains the rules of procedure of each of the boards.

§ 9.20 —Practice before the Boards

In discussing practice before the boards, it would be cumbersome and unwieldy to cite to the rules of each board. It also is unnecessary; the rules of the various boards are substantially similar. Accordingly, citations in this chapter are to the rules of two of the boards: the Armed Services Board of Contract Appeals (ASBCA) and the General Services Board of Contract Appeals (GSBCA), the two largest boards.

The discussion of practice before the boards is separated into four parts: (1) bringing an appeal; (2) discovery and prehearing matters; (3) hearings, including post-hearing briefing and decisions; and (4) small

---

[183] 41 U.S.C. § 607(a)(1).

[184] 41 U.S.C. § 607(c). If the agency is unable to enter into such an arrangement with another agency, contract cases arising from the agency are submitted to the Administrator for Federal Procurement Policy for placement with a board of contract appeals.

[185] 41 U.S.C. § 607(b)(1).

[186] 41 U.S.C. § 607(d).

claims procedures. The discussion assumes that all requirements of the CDA, that is, a properly submitted claim and a contracting officer's decision—or the absence of a decision within the required period—have been met. The discussion also assumes that, as required by the Act, the appeal has been brought within 90 days of the receipt by the contractor of the contracting officer's decision. The salient features of board practice are covered here; a contractor or an attorney contemplating a board appeal should, of course, consult the appropriate rules.

§ 9.21 —Bringing an Appeal

A board action is initiated by filing a notice of appeal.[187] The notice of appeal should be signed by the contractor or its attorney and should indicate the following: that an appeal is being taken; the name of the agency (or the component thereof involved); the number of the contract at issue; the name of the contracting officer; the decision of the contracting officer from which an appeal is being taken (this requirement may be satisfied by attaching a copy of the decision); and an estimate of the amount of money involved in the appeal.[188] The contractor is required to furnish a copy of the notice of appeal to the contracting officer whose decision is being appealed.[189]

Generally, the procedure for bringing an appeal from a contracting officer's failure to issue a decision is the same as for appealing a decision. In such a case, the ASBCA rules require that the notice of appeal cite the failure to issue a decision,[190] while the GSBCA rules state that the contractor must either describe "in detail" the claim that the contracting officer has failed to decide, or attach a copy of the claim submission to the notice of appeal.[191]

The rules of the GSBCA provide that a notice of appeal is effective when it is mailed to the board.[192] The rules of the ASBCA do not contain a similar provision. The board has held, however, that when a notice of appeal is mailed, timeliness is determined by the date of mailing.[193] When

---

[187] ASBCA Rule 1(a), CCH Cont. App. Dec. ¶ 185.20; GSBCA Rule 5(a), CCH Cont. App. Dec. 622.

[188] ASBCA Rule 2, CCH Cont. App. Dec. ¶ 185.30; GSBCA Rules 5(a)(1)(i), (a)(1)(ii), CCH Cont. App. Dec. ¶ 622.

[189] ASBCA Rule 1(a), CCH Cont. App. Dec. ¶ 185.20; GSBCA Rule 5(a)(iii), CCH Cont. App. Dec. ¶ 622.

[190] ASBCA Rules 1(b), (c), CCH Cont. App. Dec. ¶ 185.20.

[191] GSBCA Rule 5(a)(1)(i), CCH Cont. App. Dec. ¶ 622.

[192] GSBCA Rule 1(b)(3), CCH Cont. App. Dec. ¶ 618.

[193] American Abrasive Metals Co., ASBCA Nos. 35198, 35410, 88-1 B.C.A. (CCH) ¶ 20,287 (1987).

§ 9.21 BRINGING AN APPEAL

a notice of appeal is received, the appeal is docketed, and a notice of docketing is sent to each of the parties.[194]

The rules also provide for petitions under 41 U.S.C. § 605(c)(4) seeking an order from the board directing a contracting officer to issue a decision.[195]

The docketing of an appeal triggers the commencement of the appeal process. Within 30 days of docketing, the government is required to file the appeal file.[196] This file commonly is known as the Rule 4 file because it is filed pursuant to Rule 4 of the various boards. The requirements for the contents of the file are set forth in the rule. Basically, the file consists of the contracting officer's decision that is being appealed, the contract itself, and relevant correspondence and documents that were generated during the period of the contract, prior to the time the notice of appeal was filed.[197] The file also may contain any additional information deemed relevant to the appeal.[198] Within 30 days of receipt of its copy of the Rule 4 file, the contractor has the right to supplement the file with any additional documents which it feels are relevant to the appeal.[199] Each party has the right to object to the inclusion of documents in the Rule 4 file submitted by the other party, giving the reasons for the objections.[200] Documents in the Rule 4 file, other than those to which an objection is sustained, constitute part of the record upon which the board will base its decision in the appeal.[201]

The docketing of the appeal also starts running the time within which the contractor must file its complaint, if the complaint was not filed with the notice of appeal. The complaint is due within 30 days of the docketing of the appeal.[202] Although no particular form is required for the complaint, the rules state that the complaint should set forth, in simple and direct terms, the factual basis for the contractor's claim.[203] The government's

---

[194] ASBCA Rule 3, CCH Cont. App. Dec. ¶ 185.40; GSBCA Rule 5(c), CCH Cont. App. Dec. ¶ 622.

[195] See ASBCA Rule 1(e), CCH Cont. App. Dec. ¶ 185.20; GSBCA Rules 1(b)(9), 5(b)(ii), CCH Cont. App. Dec. ¶¶ 618, 622.

[196] ASBCA Rule 4(a), CCH Cont. App. Dec. ¶ 185.50; GSBCA Rule 4(a), CCH Cont. App. Dec. ¶ 621.

[197] Id.

[198] Id.

[199] ASBCA Rule 4(b), CCH Cont. App. Dec. ¶ 185.50; GSBCA Rule 4(b), CCH Cont. App. Dec. ¶ 621.

[200] ASBCA Rule 4(e), CCH Cont. App. Dec. ¶ 185.50; GSBCA Rule 4(f), CCH Cont. App. Dec. ¶ 621.

[201] Id.

[202] ASBCA Rule 6(a), CCH Cont. App. Dec. ¶ 185.70; GSBCA Rule 7(b)(1), CCH Cont. App. Dec. ¶ 624.

[203] Id.

answer is due within 30 days of the filing of the complaint.[204] In the appeal, the government will be represented by attorneys of the agency involved.

§ 9.22 —Discovery, Prehearing Procedures, and Motions

Board rules contemplate discovery in the form of interrogatories, requests for the production of documents, depositions, and requests for admissions.[205] Thus, the same sort of discovery available in a court suit is available in a board proceeding. Parties are encouraged to cooperate in discovery on a voluntary basis.[206] In addition, board rules provide for the issuance of subpoenas in connection with depositions and for sanctions for failure to comply with orders of the board.[207]

Board prehearing procedures are flexible. Prehearing conferences can be held, and the boards are empowered to issue orders relating to the conduct of discovery and the prehearing process.[208] Often, in preparation for a hearing, parties will be directed to attempt to narrow the issues involved by stipulation. Generally, they also will be directed to submit exhibit and witness lists and statements as to their respective contentions of fact and law.

After the complaint and the answer are filed, in the course of the prehearing process, the contractor will be required to decide whether it wishes to waive a hearing and have its appeal decided on the record in the case. In addition, if the contractor's claim is $50,000 or less, the contractor has the option of having its appeal processed under the board's small claim procedures. This section of the chapter discusses waiving a hearing. Small claim procedures are discussed in § 9.24.

The CDA requires that boards provide for the "informal, expeditious, and inexpensive resolutions of disputes."[209] Consistent with this mandate, the rules of the ASBCA and the GSBCA both give either party the right to

---

[204] ASBCA Rule 6(b), CCH Cont. App. Dec. ¶ 185.70; GSBCA Rule 7(c)(1), CCH Cont. App. Dec. ¶ 624.

[205] ASBCA Rules 14, 15, CCH Cont. App. Dec. ¶¶ 186.90, 187; GSBCA Rules 15, 16, 17, CCH Cont. App. Dec. ¶¶ 632, 633, 634.

[206] See ASBCA Rule 14(a), CCH Cont. App. Dec. ¶ 186.90.

[207] ASBCA Rules 14(f), CCH Cont. App. Dec. ¶¶ 186.90, 189; GSBCA Rules 15(h), 10(d), CCH Cont. App. Dec. ¶¶ 632, 627.

[208] ASBCA Rule 10, CCH Cont. App. Dec. ¶ 186.10; GSBCA Rule 10, CCH Cont. App. Dec. ¶ 627.

[209] 41 U.S.C. § 607(e).

§ 9.22   DISCOVERY, PREHEARING, & MOTIONS

waive a hearing and to submit its case "on the record" before the board.[210] What composes the record is set forth in the rules.[211] A contractor contemplating waiving a hearing should review the rules of the board hearing its appeal so that the contractor understands exactly what is in the record and, thus, what will be before the board when it decides the case if a hearing is not held. Generally, the record consists of the pleadings in the case, the documents in the Rule 4 file to which no objection has been sustained, and other documents, such as affidavits, which are submitted by the parties and to which no objection has been sustained.

The rules do not specify a time within which a party must elect to proceed on the record without a hearing.[212] In view of the fact that the rules contemplate that the record upon which the appeal will be decided may include material developed in discovery, it would seem that the decision to proceed without a hearing could be made at any time. The board may, however, issue an order directing the parties to notify it at an earlier time as to whether either or both of them wishes to proceed on the record without a hearing.

In deciding whether to waive a hearing and proceed on the record, a contractor should bear several points in mind. First, proceeding without a hearing, particularly when the decision to do so is made at an early stage and there is no discovery, probably will reduce the time it takes the board to decide the appeal and also probably will lessen the cost of the appeal. At the same time, however, there are risks in waiving a hearing. Even if a contractor chooses to have its case decided on the record, it still has the burden of proving its claim.[213] Thus, before deciding to waive a hearing, a contractor and its attorney should carefully assess the strengths and weaknesses of the contractor's case so that they are in a position to decide whether the contractor will be able to make out its case without the benefit of witnesses. The contractor may wish to make its decision to proceed with or without a hearing dependent upon what the government does concerning witnesses, documents, and oral argument.

Board rules provide for both procedural and substantive motions.[214] Often, however, the board will defer ruling on a jurisdictional motion until

---

[210] ASBCA Rule 11, CCH Cont. App. Dec. ¶ 186.20; GSBCA Rule 11, CCH Cont. App. Dec. ¶ 628.

[211] See ASBCA Rule 13, CCH Cont. App. Dec. ¶ 186.80; GSBCA Rule 12, CCH Cont. App. Dec. ¶ 629.

[212] See ASBCA Rule 13, CCH Cont. App. Dec. ¶ 186.80; GSBCA Rule 12, CCH Cont. App. Dec. ¶ 629.

[213] See ASBCA Rule 11, CCH Cont. App. Dec. ¶ 186.20.

[214] See ASBCA Rule 5, CCH Cont. App. Dec. ¶ 185.60; GSBCA Rule 8, CCH Cont. App. Dec. ¶ 625.

there has been a hearing on the merits, or submissions on the record have been received.[215]

§ 9.23 —Hearings and Post-Hearing Matters

Hearings are conducted by board members or hearing examiners[216] and are held at such locations as are most convenient for the parties, giving consideration to the interests of the board.[217]

Generally, board hearings are less formal than court proceedings. ASBCA Rule 20(a) states that "[h]earings shall be as informal as may be reasonable and appropriate under the circumstances," and the parties are allowed to present such evidence "as they deem appropriate and as would be admissible under the Federal Rules of Evidence or in the sound discretion of the presiding administrative judge or examiner."[218] Similarly, although GSBCA Rule 22 states that, "as a general matter," evidentiary rulings will be based upon the Federal Rules of Evidence, the rule also provides that "[a]ny relevant evidence may be received" and that hearsay evidence "is admissible unless the Board finds it unreliable or untrustworthy."[219]

Board rules provide for the issuance of subpoenas to compel the testimony of witnesses.[220] However, parties are expected to cooperate with each other in order to make available witnesses and evidence under their respective control and in order to secure the voluntary appearance of third parties and the voluntary production of evidence by third parties.[221] After the hearing is completed and the record is closed, the parties usually submit post-hearing briefs, which may include proposed findings of fact.[222]

Except when small claims procedures are invoked, board decisions in both hearing and nonhearing appeals are by panels or divisions having at least three members, with a decision of the majority of the panel or

---

[215] *See* ASBCA Rule 5, CCH Cont. App. Dec. ¶ 185.60; GSBCA Rule 8(e), CCH Cont. App. Dec. ¶ 625.

[216] ASBCA Rules, Preface II(c), CCH Cont. App. Dec. ¶ 185.10; GSBCA Rule 18, CCH Cont. App. Dec. ¶ 635.

[217] ASBCA Rule 17, CCH Cont. App. Dec. ¶ 187.20; GSBCA Rule 19(a)(1), CCH Cont. App. Dec. ¶ 636.

[218] CCH Cont. App. Dec. ¶ 187.50.

[219] GSBCA Rules 22(a), (b), CCH Cont. App. Dec. ¶ 639.

[220] ASBCA Rule 21, CCH Cont. App. Dec. ¶ 187.60; GSBCA Rule 20, CCH Cont. App. Dec. ¶ 637.

[221] ASBCA Rule 21(b), CCH Cont. App. Dec. ¶ 187.60; GSBCA Rule 20(a), CCH Cont. App. Dec. ¶ 637.

[222] ASBCA Rule 23, CCH Cont. App. Dec. ¶ 187.80; GSBCA Rule 25(b), CCH Cont. App. Dec. ¶ 642.

division constituting a decision of the board.[223] Frequently, a board appeal will see the issues of entitlement and quantum bifurcated, with entitlement being decided first and quantum being reserved for subsequent proceedings.[224]

Board decisions are in writing.[225] Within 30 days of receipt or issuance of the decision, either party may petition for reconsideration.[226] Board rules also set forth the manner in which payments of awards to contractors are made.[227]

§ 9.24 —Small Claims Procedures

As discussed in § 9.15, the CDA requires that the various boards of contract appeals establish procedures for the resolution of appeals when the amount in controversy is $50,000 or less and also procedures for the resolution of appeals where the amount in controversy is $10,000 or less. These procedures are available at the sole option of the contractor.[228]

Appeals where the amount in controversy is $50,000 or less are subject to an accelerated procedure in which, whenever possible, the appeal is resolved within 180 days from the date on which the contractor elects to utilize the procedure.[229] Appeals where the amount in controversy is $10,000 or less are subject to an expedited disposition, in which, whenever possible, the appeal is resolved within 120 days from the date on which the contractor elects to utilize the procedure.[230]

Certain special provisions of the CDA apply when a contractor elects to have an appeal processed on an expedited basis. The Act provides that such an appeal may be decided by a single member of the agency board involved and that a decision in such an appeal, whether for the government or the contractor, "shall be final and conclusive and shall not be set aside except in cases of fraud" and has no precedential value.[231]

---

[223] ASBCA Rules, Preface II(c), CCH Cont. App. Dec. ¶ 185.10; GSBCA Rule 1(e), CCH Cont. App. Dec. ¶ 618.

[224] *See* GSBCA Rule 26(c), CCH Cont. App. Dec. ¶ 643.

[225] ASBCA Rule 28(a), CCH Cont. App. Dec. ¶ 188.30; GSBCA Rule 29, CCH Cont. App. Dec. ¶ 646.

[226] ASBCA Rule 29, CCH Cont. App. Dec. ¶ 188.40; GSBCA Rule 32, CCH Cont. App. Dec. ¶ 649.

[227] ASBCA Rule 28(b), CCH Cont. App. Dec. ¶ 188.30; GSBCA Rule 36, CCH Cont. App. Dec. ¶ 653.

[228] 41 U.S.C. §§ 607(f), 608(a).

[229] 41 U.S.C. § 607(f).

[230] 41 U.S.C. § 608(a), (b).

[231] 41 U.S.C. § 608(b), (d), (e).

The boards have established procedures for appeals involving small claims. These procedures cover the contractor's election to have the appeal resolved as a small claim and also set forth the way in which the appeal is processed once the contractor makes a small claim election.

Board rules give a contractor a set period of time to elect small claims procedures. Generally, the period of time is tied to the notice of docketing of the appeal. For example, ASBCA rules give a contractor 60 days after receipt of docketing notice to make a small claims election,[232] but in a GSBCA appeal, the contractor has 30 days after the notice of docketing within which to make such an election.[233] The contractor's election must be in writing.[234] A logical time for a contractor to make a small claims election is when it files its notice of appeal or its complaint. ASBCA rules provide that a small claims election may not be withdrawn "except with permission of the Board and for good cause."[235] The rules of the GSBCA do not address the withdrawal of a small claims election by a contractor. They do, however, provide that the board can rescind the contractor's election of accelerated procedures for claims of $50,000 or less if it is determined that the contractor has failed to comply with the schedule established for the appeal, and that the appeal cannot otherwise be resolved within the required 180-day period.[236] Finally, the board rules also set forth discovery and prehearing procedures which are applicable in appeals in which a contractor has made a small claims election.[237]

§ 9.25 United States Claims Court

By statute, the Claims Court has jurisdiction to render judgment "upon any claim by or against, or dispute with, a contractor" arising under the CDA.[238] The court consists of 16 judges who are appointed by the President with the advice and consent of the Senate.[239] Each judge serves for a term

---

[232] ASBCA Rule 12.1(c), CCH Cont. App. Dec. ¶ 186.40.

[233] GSBCA Rule 13(b)(1), CCH Cont. App. Dec. ¶ 630.

[234] ASBCA Rule 12.1(c), CCH Cont. App. Dec. ¶ 186.40; GSBCA Rules 13(b)(1), 14(b)(1), CCH Cont. App. Dec. ¶¶ 630, 631.

[235] ASBCA Rule 12.1(c), CCH Cont. App. Dec. ¶ 186.40.

[236] GSBCA Rule 14(b)(2), CCH Cont. App. Dec. ¶ 631.

[237] *See* ASBCA Rules 12.2, 12.3, CCH Cont. App. Dec. ¶¶ 186.40, 186.50; GSBCA Rules 13, 14, CCH Cont. App. Dec. ¶¶ 630, 631.

[238] 28 U.S.C. § 1491(a)(2).

[239] 28 U.S.C. § 171(a).

§ 9.26 **BRINGING SUIT IN CLAIMS COURT** 231

of 15 years.[240] The court is located in Washington, D.C., but is authorized to hold sessions outside of Washington.[241]

Pursuant to the authority contained in 28 U.S.C. § 2503(b), the Claims Court has adopted rules of procedure. The court's rules are based upon the Federal Rules of Civil Procedure applicable to civil actions tried by a court sitting without a jury.[242] In fact, for ease of reference to comparable rules, chapter titles and numbers of rules of the Claims Court are identical to chapter titles and numbers contained in the Federal Rules of Civil Procedure. Where necessary, additions to the Federal Rules have been made in the Claims Court rules. This is to take into account jurisdictional and structural differences between the district courts and the Claims Court. Local rules applicable only in Claims Court proceedings are set forth in Titles X and XI of the Claims Court rules or in separate appendices. Claims Court judges are given the authority, "[i]n all cases not provided for by rule," to regulate the applicable practice in any manner that is not inconsistent with the rules.[243]

This chapter briefly discusses the Claims Court's rules. However, any attorney who wishes to practice before the court should consult the actual rules.

§ 9.26 —Bringing Suit in the Claims Court

A suit in the Claims Court is initiated by filing a complaint with the clerk of the court.[244] The clerk, in turn, serves the complaint upon the government by delivering a copy of the complaint to the Department of Justice, which represents the government in litigation in the Claims Court.[245] Thereafter, the parties are responsible for serving upon each other all other papers.[246]

The requirements for a complaint are set forth in Rules of the United States Claims Court, RUSCC 8(a). The government has 60 days from the date of service of the complaint to file its answer.[247] The requirements for the government's answer are set forth in RUSCC 12(a). Consistent with

---

[240] 28 U.S.C. § 172(a).
[241] 28 U.S.C. § 173.
[242] Rule 1(b), Rules of the United States Claims Court (RUSCC).
[243] RUSCC 1(a)(3).
[244] RUSCC 3(a).
[245] RUSCC 4(a).
[246] RUSCC 5.
[247] RUSCC 12(a).

the Federal Rules of Civil Procedure, the Claims Court's rules provide for both permissive and mandatory counterclaims.[248]

§ 9.27 —Discovery, Pretrial Procedures, and Motions

The rules of the Claims Court governing discovery and setting forth the various methods of discovery—interrogatories, document requests, requests for admissions, and depositions—are virtually identical to the Federal Rules of Civil Procedure.[249] Discovery in the Claims Court is conducted within the framework of the court's pretrial procedures.

Claims Court pretrial proceedings are governed by Appendix G to the rules of the court,[250] although RUSCC 16 gives the judge discretion to actively manage a case when he or she feels it appropriate. Under Appendix G, within 21 days after the government answers the complaint or the plaintiff replies to a government counterclaim, the attorneys for the parties are required to confer and discuss preparation of a joint preliminary status report.[251] In this context, attorneys are required, among other things, to address each party's factual and legal contentions and their respective discovery needs and proposed discovery schedules.[252] They also are required to discuss settlement of the action.[253]

The next step in the Appendix G process is the submission of the joint preliminary status report. The report is required to be filed no later than 21 days after the attorneys confer in connection with the report.[254] In the report, the parties are required to advise the court on a number of points relevant to the conduct of the case, including whether there are any jurisdictional issues in the case, whether trial of liability and damages should be bifurcated, and whether either party intends to file a dispositive motion.[255] Not infrequently, the attorneys will indicate that, although they presently do not anticipate a dispositive motion, such a motion may be filed upon completion of discovery. In such a situation, it may be appropriate for the parties to agree upon a date by which any dispositive motion shall be filed and to propose that date in the joint preliminary status report. The parties also are required to identify the issues in the

---

[248] RUSCC 13.
[249] *See* RUSCC 26-37.
[250] RUSCC 16(a)(1).
[251] RUSCC, app. G, ¶ 2(a).
[252] RUSCC, app. G, ¶ 2(b).
[253] *Id.*
[254] RUSCC, app. G, ¶ 3.
[255] *Id.*

§ 9.27   DISCOVERY, PRETRIAL, & MOTIONS   233

case, to indicate whether they anticipate a trial, and to set forth a proposed schedule for the conduct of discovery.[256] The attorneys should view the formulation of the joint preliminary status report as an opportunity to work together to fashion a mutually acceptable approach for the resolution of the case.

Following the completion of discovery, there will be a pretrial conference. Appendix G requires that no later than 30 days prior to the pretrial conference, the parties will meet and confer to exchange exhibits and witness lists, to attempt to resolve objections to the admission of oral or documentary evidence, to disclose to each other their respective contentions of fact and law, to engage in good faith efforts to stipulate to facts which the parties know or have reason to know are not in dispute, and to exhaust all possibilities of settlement.[257] Thereafter, following their discussions and prior to the pretrial conference, each party is required to submit a memorandum of contentions of fact and law, a list of witnesses, and a list of exhibits.[258] The parties also are required to submit a joint memorandum regarding stipulations and a joint statement of the issues of fact and law which are to be resolved by the court.[259]

The rules of the Claims Court, like the Federal Rules of Civil Procedure, contemplate both procedural and substantive motions.[260] In connection with motions for summary judgment, in addition to the same provisions in the Federal Rules of Civil Procedure, the rules of the Claims Court require that the parties provide detailed factual submissions.[261]

A contractor contemplating a suit in the Claims Court should be aware of one additional aspect of the court's pretrial procedures: alternative dispute resolution techniques. The court's General Order No. 13, dated April 15, 1987, sets forth two such techniques. The first is having the case referred to a settlement judge for a frank, in-depth discussion of the strengths and weaknesses of each party's position. The second is a minitrial. In this latter procedure, each party presents an abbreviated version of its case before a settlement judge who assists the parties to negotiate a settlement. The minitrial procedure is the more complex of the two techniques and involves limited and expedited discovery. General Order 13 recommends that the court's alternative dispute resolution techniques only be used when the amount in controversy is $100,000 or more, and that the minitrial procedure only be used in cases where there are not novel issues of law or issues of witness credibility.

---

[256] *Id.*
[257] RUSCC, app. G, ¶ 10.
[258] RUSCC, app. G, ¶¶ 11, 12, 13.
[259] RUSCC, app. G, ¶¶ 14, 15.
[260] *See* RUSCC 7, 12, 56.
[261] *See* RUSCC 56.

§ 9.28 —Trials and Post-Trial Matters

Trials are held at locations selected by the court.[262] Generally, the court will accede to the wishes of the parties with respect to the location of a trial, and the trial will be held in a location most convenient for the witnesses involved. Trials are conducted in accordance with the Federal Rules of Evidence,[263] and the issues of entitlement and quantum may be bifurcated.[264]

In all actions that are tried, the court is required to make separate findings of fact and conclusions of law and to enter judgment in the case on that basis.[265] The findings and conclusions may be either in writing or stated orally and recorded in open court following the close of the evidence.[266] The rules state that findings of fact, whether based upon oral or documentary evidence, may not be set aside unless clearly erroneous, giving due regard for the opportunity of the trial court to judge the credibility of the witnesses.[267]

§ 9.29 Transfer and Consolidation of Cases

The CDA provides that, if two or more suits arising from one contract are filed in the Claims Court and one or more boards, "for the convenience of parties or witnesses or in the interest of justice," the court is authorized to order the consolidation of the suits before it or to transfer suits to or among the boards involved.[268] In deciding whether a case should be consolidated or transferred, the court will take into account a number of factors: whether the disputes in the different forums arise out of the same contract; whether the cases present overlapping or the same issues; whether the plaintiff initially elected to initiate proceedings at the board; whether substantial effort in the case already has been expended in one forum but not the other; which proceeding involves the most money; and which proceeding presents the more difficult and complex claims.[269]

---

[262] RUSCC 39(a).

[263] RUSCC 43(a).

[264] RUSCC 42(c).

[265] RUSCC 52(a).

[266] *Id.*

[267] *Id.*

[268] 41 U.S.C. § 609(d).

[269] Glendale Joint Venture v. United States, 13 Cl. Ct. 325, 327 (1987); Multi-Roof Sys. Co. v. United States, 5 Cl. Ct. 245, 248 (1984); E.D.S. Federal Corp. v. United States, 2 Cl. Ct. 735, 739 (1983).

§ 9.30 Attorneys' Fees

Pursuant to the Equal Access to Justice Act (EAJA),[270] boards of contract appeals and the Claims Court are authorized to award attorneys' fees and other expenses. The EAJA amended 5 U.S.C. § 504, Costs and fees of parties (awarded by an agency in agency actions), and 28 U.S.C. § 2412, Costs and fees (awarded by courts in judicial actions).

In order for a contractor to recover attorneys' fees under the EAJA, each of the following requirements must be met:

1. The contractor was the prevailing party before the board or the Claims Court[271]
2. The position of the government in the case was not "substantially justified," and there are no circumstances in the case which would "make an award unjust"[272]
3. If an individual, the contractor must have had a net worth which did not exceed $2 million at the time the case was initiated. If a partnership, corporation, or other similar entity, the contractor must have had a net worth which did not exceed $7 million and must have had not more than 500 employees, both at the time the case was initiated[273]
4. The fees and expenses must be reasonable.[274] The EAJA specifies the types of fees and expenses which may be recovered.[275] In the absence of special circumstances, attorneys' fees may not exceed $75 per hour, and expert witness fees may not exceed the rate of compensation for expert witnesses paid by the agency involved.[276]

Applications for the recovery of attorneys' fees and expenses must be made to a board within 30 days after the final disposition of the case before the board,[277] and to the Claims Court within 30 days after the final judgment of the court.[278]

---

[270] Pub. L. 96-481 (effective Oct. 1, 1981), *amended by* Pub. L. 99-80 (Aug. 5, 1985).
[271] 5 U.S.C. § 504(a)(1); 28 U.S.C. § 2412(d)(2)(B).
[272] *Id.*
[273] 5 U.S.C. § 504(b)(1)(B); 28 U.S.C. § 2412(d)(2)(B).
[274] 5 U.S.C. § 504(b)(1)(A); 28 U.S.C. § 2412(d)(2)(A).
[275] *Id.*
[276] *Id.*
[277] 5 U.S.C. § 504(a)(2).
[278] 28 U.S.C. § 2412(d)(1)(B).

Attorneys' fees also are recoverable for litigation in the Federal Circuit.[279]

§ 9.31 Selecting a Forum

It is reasonable to expect that after a contractor receives an adverse decision from a contracting officer, the first question that it will ask is "Where should I go, to the Board or the Court?" There is no set answer to this question. Each case is different. There are, however, certain points to keep in mind when making the decision.

An important factor to consider is the size of the case. Both the boards of contract appeals and the Claims Court are equipped to handle, and do handle, large, complex matters. However, only the boards have special procedures for small claims. If a contractor simply has one or two claims under $50,000 and it wants to have its claim(s) resolved quickly and with minimal expense, a board appeal is probably the best approach. In the situation where the contractor has multiple small claims, however, the advantage of the boards' expedited and accelerated procedures may be lessened, in view of the fact that it might well be better to have one big case going on rather than a number of little cases.

Another point to bear in mind is the possibility of alternate dispute resolution techniques. They are formally available in the Claims Court, although they are relatively new phenomena and it probably is too early to say how effective they ultimately will be. The boards, however, have not as yet incorporated these procedures into their rules, although there have been instances where they have been used on an ad hoc basis. In any event, a contractor who wants to be sure that these techniques will be available for its case probably will look to the Claims Court.

Ultimately, though, the choice of a forum simply may come down to where the contractor, for whatever reason, feels most comfortable. For example, a contractor may prefer the somewhat less formal atmosphere of a board, as opposed to the procedures of a court.

Finally, there probably are very few, if any, situations in which it makes sense to split forums. Inevitably, a contractor who brings some claims before a board and others before the Claims Court will find itself faced with a motion to consolidate in one or the other of the forums. Even if the contractor ultimately prevails in opposing such a motion, time and money will be spent that otherwise could be devoted to the merits of the case. In addition, solely from a management standpoint, it makes sense for all involved (the contractor, the government, and the boards and the Claims Court) to have all claims arising out of one contract resolved in one forum.

---

[279] 28 U.S.C. § 2412(a); 28 U.S.C. § 451.

§ 9.32 The Miller Act

All government construction contracts in excess of $25,000 are subject to the Miller Act.[280] The Miller Act states that before such contracts can be awarded, two requirements must be met. First, the prime contractor must furnish a performance bond for the protection of the government.[281] Second, the prime contractor must furnish a payment bond which assures payment to persons supplying labor and materials in the course of the performance of the contract work.[282]

The Miller Act further provides that any "person" (which includes corporations as well as individuals[283]) who has furnished labor or materials pursuant to a contractual relationship with a prime contractor or with a subcontractor and who has not been paid within 90 days after the last labor was performed or material was supplied may bring suit on the payment bond for the unpaid balance.[284] However, any person having a direct contractual relationship with a subcontractor, but no contractual relationship with the prime contractor furnishing the payment bond, may only bring such a suit if it first gives written notice of its claim to the prime contractor within 90 days of the date on which it last performed labor or supplied materials to the subcontractor.[285]

Thus, the protection of the Miller Act extends to, but not beyond, the following: (1) suppliers having a direct contractual relationship with the prime contractor; (2) subcontractors having a direct contractual relationship with the prime contractor; and (3) suppliers and subcontractors who have a direct contractual relationship with a subcontractor who, in turn, has a direct contractual relationship with the prime contractor.

Suit under a Miller Act payment bond is brought in the name of the United States for the use of the person suing. The forum for the suit is the United States district court for the district in which the government construction contract was to be performed.[286] Suit must be brought within one year of the day on which the person suing last performed labor or supplied material.[287]

---

[280] 40 U.S.C. § 270a–270f.

[281] 40 U.S.C. § 270a(a)(1).

[282] 40 U.S.C. § 270a(a)(2).

[283] 40 U.S.C. § 270d.

[284] 40 U.S.C. § 270b(a).

[285] *Id.* The requirements for the contents of the notice are set forth in 40 U.S.C. § 270b(a).

[286] 40 U.S.C. § 270b(b).

[287] *Id.*

CHAPTER 10

ALTERNATIVE DISPUTES RESOLUTION

John Anthony Wolf, Esquire

John Anthony Wolf is a partner in the law firm of Ober, Kaler, Grimes, & Shriver (Maryland, Washington, D.C., New York, and New Jersey). Mr. Wolf specializes in construction contract negotiation, arbitration, and litigation in major commercial and industrial construction, and in public project matters. His practice also includes all corporate, general business, and insurance coverage litigation. He is a member of the Litigation Sections of the Maryland State and American Bar Associations, and of the ABA Forum Committee on Construction. Mr. Wolf is a past chairman of the Maryland Bar Association Construction Cases Committee and past vice-chairman of the Construction Cases Committee of the ABA Litigation Section. He serves on the Litigation Section Council of the Maryland State Bar Association and he has lectured on construction law and alternative disputes resolution procedures. Mr. Wolf is an honors graduate of the Washington and Lee University School of Law.

§ 10.1   Introduction
§ 10.2   Benefits of Alternative Disputes Resolution
§ 10.3   Criticisms of Alternative Disputes Resolution

MINITRIAL

§ 10.4   Elements of the Minitrial
§ 10.5   History of the Minitrial
§ 10.6   Types of Disputes Resolved by Minitrial
§ 10.7   The Minitrial Agreement
§ 10.8   —Status of the Pending Dispute
§ 10.9   —Discovery before the Minitrial
§ 10.10 —Procedures to Govern the Information Exchange
§ 10.11 —Logistics at the Information Exchange

§ 10.12 —The Role of the Neutral
§ 10.13 —Confidentiality
§ 10.14 Minitrial Case Study

MEDIATION

§ 10.15 Definition
§ 10.16 Benefits of Mediation
§ 10.17 Mediation Rules
§ 10.18 Role of the Mediator
§ 10.19 Mediation Case Study

SUMMARY JURY TRIAL

§ 10.20 Historical Perspective
§ 10.21 When to Use Summary Jury Trials
§ 10.22 Pretrial Conference
§ 10.23 Jury Selection and Presentation
§ 10.24 Post-Trial Discussion and Negotiation
§ 10.25 Public Access to Summary Jury Trials

§ 10.1 Introduction

The escalating costs of construction litigation and arbitration, the delay in resolving construction disputes, as well as impractical results obtained have sparked creative steps to avoid or lessen these problems. The need to obtain results palatable to the construction industry in an expedited and cost-effective manner has spawned what has come to be known as alternative disputes resolution (ADR). Certainly, ADR is not unique to the construction setting. ADR has, however, proven very effective in resolving construction disputes, and particularly those involving complex issues. The use of ADR in construction is growing in favor, as evidenced by court and agency endorsement and the ever-increasing number of private and public groups offering means to help settle disputes other than by formal litigation or arbitration.

ADR, however, has not had a uniform definition. Some define alternative disputes resolution broadly so as to include anything other than formal litigation. Binding arbitration would fall under this definition. Others define ADR more narrowly, focusing on the nonbinding aspect, and use the term to refer to voluntary, nonbinding techniques, usually incorporating the assistance of a neutral third party to aid in the resolution of disputes between two or more parties. Under such a concept, ADR is a *structured settlement process*. This chapter discusses ADR as such a concept of structured settlement, focusing on the nonbinding techniques generally known as (1) minitrial, (2) mediation, and (3) summary jury trials.

§ 10.2 Benefits of Alternative Disputes Resolution

Cost savings. ADR significantly lowers the expense of resolving disputes by reducing the costs associated with litigation or arbitration, both in terms of conserving out-of-pocket expenditures and human resources. In a properly crafted alternative disputes procedure, significant savings can result from the reduction of expenditures for legal counsel, experts, and support staff. The savings in the second category—the expenditure of human resources in litigation and arbitration—often are not fully appreciated, but they can be just as significant as the savings of out-of-pocket dollars.

Because construction typically generates a large paper exchange, the costs associated with reduced discovery (which usually consume a large portion of litigation expenses) are an immediate benefit. No shortcuts exist in preparation for any worthwhile settlement efforts. Preparation for meaningful settlement negotiations requires a thorough review of a project's documentation. But compared to the paper-intensive formal discovery, which is typical in construction disputes of any size, the savings in employing ADR and avoiding full-scale discovery and trial are real.

Time savings. By limiting discovery, using relaxed rules of procedure in the introduction of evidence, and, probably most significantly, by defusing antagonistic attitudes, ADR assists the parties in resolving disputes promptly. The concept is built on the mutual work of the parties toward an acceptable resolution. By using ADR techniques to settle, parties work together to bypass the courtroom backlog or manipulation of the arbitration process that has become commonplace.

Privacy of disputes resolution. ADR techniques are conducted in private. Information exchanged and results obtained can, by virtue of the parties' agreement, remain totally confidential and off the record.

Revealing core issues. ADR is particularly effective in revealing the true strengths and weaknesses of the parties' positions. Revealing facts reduces (or eliminates if settlement is achieved) the risk and uncertainty of where a court or arbitrator may land. For instance, ADR removes difficult problems of attribution of fault, which generally arise from the complexity of issues in multiparty disputes common to construction. Operative facts in construction cases tend to be technical, which adds to the difficulty in establishing causation. By using an ADR technique that employs a third party with expertise in the area in dispute, focus is brought on core liability issues.

Nonrestricted use. ADR is appropriate at any stage of litigation or arbitration. Indeed, meaningful alternative steps can be undertaken prior to initiating litigation or arbitration. Contract clauses requiring exhaustion of procedures for nonbinding alternative disputes resolution as conditions precedent to the filing of litigation or arbitration are gaining in popularity. However, certain ADR techniques are better suited to different stages of a dispute. For example, a summary jury trial may be considered the last available form of ADR before trial begins. Minitrials lend themselves to situations where the litigation process has already begun. Mediation may be most successful before any formal disputes procedure is initiated. Each ADR technique addressed in this chapter includes a discussion of the circumstances under which to best use it.

Settlement promotion. Simply the process of agreeing to an ADR technique promotes the right frame of mind between the parties. Settlement efforts are effective (and worthwhile) only if there is willingness by each party to attempt in good faith to settle its dispute without going to trial or arbitration. Although this would seem obvious, the parties' desire to settle must be assessed before seriously contemplating any settlement effort. Without a full, frank disclosure of one's case, settlement will not be successful. A participant must be ready to be forthcoming, and comfortable that the other participants will be similarly forthcoming. Otherwise, as in any settlement negotiation, the fear of being "sandbagged" will sour relations and doom any meaningful exchange to failure in the process. ADR adds structure to the settlement process, which encourages a forthcoming approach to settlement.

Business basis for settlements. ADR actively involves the businessmen—and not just the lawyers—in the direct resolution of disputes. Rational business decisions ideally control the process. As such, practical business solutions (and not simply a compulsory dollar result imposed by a binding third-party authority) come out of the process. Oftentimes the parties, although at odds, have an interest in maintaining their business relationship. ADR promotes this end because, unlike adjudication, ADR is not a win/lose process. Rather, by using ADR, the parties can reach an agreement based on business instead of fault considerations. Fault may be recognized and pointed out in the process, but it is not decreed by an authoritative trier of fact. This alone frees the parties to concentrate their efforts on finding a solution to their problem.

§ 10.3 Criticisms of Alternative Disputes Resolution

The ADR movement is, however, not without its detractors. Some commentators have expressed concern that the use of ADR will subvert the purpose of the judicial system. In the words of one commentator, "an oft forgotten virtue of adjudication (not necessarily present in ADR) is that it ensures the proper resolution and application of public values."[1] Another noted critic is University of Southern California law Professor Judith Resnick. In her article "The Declining Faith in the Adversary System," Professor Resnick criticizes the advent of "managerial judges" who are more interested in case management and concluding cases without adjudication than substantive law, the merits of the case, or improvement of techniques for fact finding.[2] Professor Resnick and others do not find ADR techniques any more responsive to meeting the concerns raised by those who criticize the shortcomings of adjudication.

MINITRIAL

§ 10.4 Elements of the Minitrial

A minitrial is a hybrid ADR, consisting of the elements of several other forms of dispute resolution. It is a structured settlement device combining the characteristics of adjudication, arbitration, mediation, and negotiation. The minitrial is a private, trial-like proceeding held out of court with the aid of a neutral third party or panel assisting principals of the parties with settlement authority, followed by settlement negotiations.[3]

An attractive feature of the minitrial format is its flexibility and easy adaptation to many different factual and legal settings. The minitrial is best suited for mixed legal and factual issues. Cases turning solely on legal issues or on credibility factors may be submitted to minitrial efforts, but do not lend themselves to the process.

The typical minitrial contains two essential elements to which the parties can add others to fit their particular needs. The first element is a best-case presentation (by witness presentations or by lawyers) to the principals of the parties, often referred to as an information exchange. It is essential that the principals in attendance have full authority to settle the dispute. This assures that those individuals who will ultimately make the decision hear and see the strengths and weaknesses of the parties' cases, without the results being distilled through the reports of subordinates. Exposing principals to the rigors of the process is also a time-tested means of promoting settlement and is critical to the minitrial process.

---

[1] Edwards, *Alternative Dispute Resolution: Panacea or Anathema?*, 99 Harv. L. Rev. 668, 676 (1986).

[2] Resnick, *The Declining Faith in the Adversary System*, 13 Litigation 3 (Fall 1986). *See also* Resnick, *Managerial Judges*, 96 Harv. L. Rev. 374 (1982).

[3] *See generally* E. Green, *The CPR Legal Program Mini-Trial Handbook* in Corporate Dispute Management 1982.

Oftentimes, the principals immediately enter into settlement negotiations. Experience has shown that even the most complex case can be settled within just a few hours following a minitrial.

The second important element of the minitrial is that there is no binding judgment. The entire proceeding is voluntary and contains no enforcement mechanism.

The parties mutually agree on a neutral advisor, commonly referred to as the *Neutral,* to assist them in reaching a settlement agreement. The selection of the Neutral is a critically important step. The nonbinding nature of the minitrial permits the parties to search out creative and original solutions to their dispute without fear that they will be stuck with a resolution imposed upon them by a judge or arbitration panel.

§ 10.5 History of the Minitrial

Although minitrials are currently growing in popularity in a wide area of commercial disputes, until only recently they were considered radical departures from litigation and used only in an attempt to resolve massive and protracted litigation. The advent of the minitrial concept is most often attributed to its use in 1977 to settle a highly technical and legally complex patent infringement case between TRW and Telecredit, Inc.[4]

Professor Eric Green, then counsel to TRW and now Professor of Law at Boston University and a leading ADR advocate, fashioned the ADR process now known as the minitrial. Professor Green described the case as having languished in federal court for over three years of intense litigation at a cost of several hundred thousand dollars.[5] For various reasons, binding arbitration was unacceptable to the parties and settlement negotiations had proven fruitless. Professor Green and other counsel conceived of the minitrial as a means to get the principals involved. This allowed the business executives to assess the strengths and weaknesses of their claims, which in turn aided them in their efforts to reach a settlement agreement in a businesslike manner. After a two-day information exchange, and with the help of former United States Court of Claims Judge James F. Davis as the Neutral, the principals were able to settle within two hours after the close of the minitrial.[6] Thus, the minitrial was born.

The use of the minitrial has since spread beyond private commercial disputes, and is now part of the adjudicatory process for governmental agencies such as the Corps of Engineers and endorsed by the Rules of the United States Claims Court.

---

[4] Green, *Growth of the Mini-Trial,* 9 Litigation 12 (Fall 1982). *See also* Olson, *An Alternative for Large Case Dispute Resolution,* 6 Litigation 22 (Winter 1980).

[5] Green, *Growth of the Mini-Trial* at 13.

[6] *Id.*

§ 10.6 Types of Disputes Resolved by Minitrial

Experience has shown that minitrials are more complicated and expensive than other types of ADR techniques and are, therefore, more cost-effective for larger disputes. Typically, a minitrial is employed after a case is in litigation (although there is no hard and fast requirement that a case be filed). A minitrial may be too expensive for smaller disputes because of the use of formal discovery and the amount of preparation involved. There is no bright line test in terms of dollars involved; the test of the suitability of employing the process turns on the facts and costs peculiar to the individual case.

For larger disputes, savings can be significant when compared to the expense of preparing and going through a trial or arbitration to conclusion. In smaller or less complicated cases, the assessment of liability and damages exposure can usually be accomplished by the parties sitting down and having a frank discussion. In larger cases involving multiple parties and complex factual patterns, it is more difficult for the parties to gauge liability and damage exposure precisely. This is true despite even the most exacting and probing discovery.

In fact, formal, adversarial discovery has very real limits in getting to the core issues in construction cases. The discovery process many times inhibits information exchange in a rational and coherent manner to assess a case's settlement value. The constraints of court-imposed discovery schedules and the tension within the adversarial system are often the cause of this inhibited exchange of information. Lawyers and clients do not have the time, opportunity, or inclination to engage in meaningful settlement discussions, nor do they have the luxury of viewing all essential facts from the perspective of settlement. A minitrial allows breathing room. Essential facts and issues are presented off the record in a concise and abbreviated manner upon which the principals may base rational decisions either to settle or continue to litigate.

In addition to the size of the dispute, the types of issues raised must also be weighed in deciding whether to engage in a minitrial. A minitrial is best suited to mixed questions of fact and law. Generally, construction disputes have significant questions of fact and law, and are thus well suited to the minitrial format.[7] Although facts may be unsettled and unclear, the questions of law are usually somewhat settled and not novel. A purely legal question, where the facts are not in dispute or where the legal question is new, unique, or in an area of law that is rapidly changing, is in most

---

[7] Killian & Mancini, *Mini-Trials Basic Principles and Guidelines* in Construction Briefings 1 (No. 85-3 Mar. 1985). Messrs. Killian and Mancini report that the following construction issues have been successfully resolved by means of a minitrial: (1) compensability and delay damages, (2) defects in construction, (3) acceleration, (4) differences in site conditions, and (5) constructive changes.

cases best resolved by a court. Experience has also shown that factual determinations based upon the credibility of witnesses are better suited for adjudication where the opportunity for cross-examination exists.

Some advocate that the disputes resolution clause of a contract (negotiated before a dispute arises) include mandatory submission to a minitrial procedure as a precondition to litigation or arbitration. This author advocates a like clause for mediation (see § 10.17), but does not recommend automatic resort to a minitrial until the scope of the dispute is known.

The above considerations are not to be used as a comprehensive checklist, but are recognized factors to be considered and applied to specific disputes. Each case has its own particulars. It is not whether a case is large or small, but whether a particular case is amenable to a minitrial. This applies not only to the minitrial but to all other forms of ADR.

§ 10.7 The Minitrial Agreement

The minitrial is a creature of contract. Every aspect of the minitrial must be governed by a written agreement, painstakingly negotiated and drafted, and entered into by all parties to the dispute. The agreement should be tailored to the dispute. However, the following items should, at a minimum, be addressed in the minitrial agreement:[8]

1. Status of the pending dispute
2. Discovery to be taken before the minitrial
3. Procedures to govern the information exchange
4. Logistics at the information exchange
5. Role of the neutral
6. Confidentiality.

§ 10.8 —Status of the Pending Dispute

To ensure that the status of the pending dispute is maintained, the agreement should provide that the parties will enter into a stipulation regarding necessary further pleadings and/or motions and hearings to bring the case to issue or to a proper legal posture for the minitrial. Of course, court approval and endorsement of the scheduling procedure is required. In the federal courts, this is accomplished by implementation of Rule 16 of

---

[8] *Id.* at 4. *See also* Davis & Omlie, *Mini-Trials: The Courtroom in the Boardroom,* 21 Willamette L. Rev. 531, 538 (Summer 1985).

the Federal Rules of Civil Procedure.[9] Rule 16(c)(7) provides that the district courts may use "extrajudicial procedures" to aid in the resolution of disputes.[10] The Federal Rules Advisory Committee commentary to Rule 16 specifically endorses the minitrial as one such extrajudicial procedure. In state court proceedings, similar rules exist, as does a state court's inherent equity powers to control its own docket; these should be employed to obtain court endorsement of the minitrial as an extrajudicial settlement procedure.

§ 10.9 —Discovery before the Minitrial

Discovery to be taken prior to the minitrial, if any, should be set forth in a written schedule and entered as an order by the court. The order may also stipulate that such discovery will not prejudice any party's right to further discovery on the same or different subject at a later date should the case not settle. If discovery has already taken place before the minitrial, the court order should address the status of discovery to date and what additional discovery is to be undertaken.

§ 10.10 —Procedures to Govern the Information Exchange

One of the true virtues of the minitrial is the flexibility of the information exchange. The parties can agree to a set procedure or be allowed to present their cases as they best see fit, with time limitations being the one real constraint. Presentation of the parties' best case can, for example, range from a lawyers-only presentation (a hybrid between opening statement and closing argument, with recitation of applicable legal principles), to unsworn testimony from witnesses engaged in construction and from expert witnesses. Documentary evidence, videotape, and all types of demonstrative evidence can and should be used. Cross-examination (except, perhaps, by the Neutral or through nonargumentative questions from principals) should be eliminated.

Some control on the type of evidence must be maintained. Lawyers are constrained by ethical considerations not to advance facts or theories that are not supportable, or put on unsworn evidence of questionable credibility. Similarly, in order to minimize the introduction of questionable evidence from the other side, and as a means to expedite the proceedings, guidelines for the introduction of evidence are worthwhile. For instance,

---

[9] Fed. R. Civ. P. 16.
[10] Fed. R. Civ. P. 16(c)(7).

reference to the Federal Rules of Evidence (as a guide only) can assist the Neutral in gauging the "admissibility" of evidence.

Other aspects that need to be considered and addressed in the agreement include the submission of briefs or position papers prior to the information exchange; the use, premarking, and prior exchange of exhibits and written testimony; and the scheduling of post-minitrial negotiation sessions. It is advisable to have the principals available to discuss settlement immediately after the minitrial concludes, as this has proven to be the most opportune time to press for settlement. The agreement should be precise on this requirement.

§ 10.11 —Logistics at the Information Exchange

There are many logistical concerns that need to be addressed at the information exchange. The agreement should name those individuals who are to attend the information exchange for each party. This should include principals with settlement authority, technical experts, and witnesses. Attendance should be restricted to those persons identified.

At some point, either in the initial agreement or at a later date, the time, place, and daily schedule should be agreed upon in writing.

Another important consideration is the apportionment of costs. The fee for the neutral advisor is usually split between the parties. Apparently insignificant items must be addressed and agreed to up front to promote an atmosphere for settlement. Who arranges the room? What audiovisual equipment is necessary? If lunch is to be provided, how is it to be paid for?

§ 10.12 —The Role of the Neutral

The Neutral may function in any manner to which the parties agree. The Neutral is not given authority to bind the parties; nor does the Neutral necessarily serve as a mediator in order to effect a compromise during the information exchange. Instead, the Neutral presides over the exchange to ensure fairness and compliance with the parties' agreement. Following the exchange, the Neutral may then take on the role of mediator to assist the principals in negotiation. The Neutral is usually requested to comment on the information provided during the exchange. In construction and other technical cases, such comments, when based on the Neutral's expertise, lend credibility to the role. Conventional wisdom has it that the Neutral should not, however, produce a written decision or finding. This too often locks the Neutral into a position, alienates one or more participants, and compromises the Neutral's effectiveness in facilitating agreement after the exchange.

§ 10.13 —Confidentiality

There are several groups, such as the Center for Public Resources, located in New York City, and EnDispute, Inc., located in Washington, D.C., that maintain blue ribbon panels who are willing to serve as Neutrals. These panelists are distinguished lawyers, former judges, academicians, and technical experts qualified to assist in this and other ADR formats.

§ 10.13 —Confidentiality

Preserving the confidentiality of the proceedings and all aspects related to the minitrial must be addressed in the minitrial agreement. Without confidentiality, the minitrial exercise (like any settlement discussion) is meaningless. There are two areas that confidentiality must protect against: later admissibility at trial or hearings and susceptibility to discovery.

The starting point for admissibility of evidence connected with the minitrial turns on the common law policy underpinning Rule 408 of the Federal Rules of Evidence, or its state counterparts. Rule 408 provides that "evidence of conduct or statements made in compromise negotiations is . . . not admissible."[11] It must be remembered that the minitrial, as well as all other ADR techniques, are first and foremost structured settlement negotiations and, therefore, must be viewed as off the record and inadmissible. However, it must also be noted that there presently exists no reported case on the inadmissibility of minitrial information.

Compromise offers or statements made during settlement discussions are rendered inadmissible by Rule 408 for the purpose of proving either liability for or invalidity of the claim or its amount. Rule 408 considerations (and the parties' agreement considering admissibility) should prevent the admissibility of anything relating to the minitrial.

Rule 408 (and its common-law roots) is, of course, not an absolute bar to the admissibility of settlement negotiations; it contains two generally recognized exceptions. The first is that the bar does not apply to evidence that is otherwise admissible. The use of a minitrial does not, therefore, render inadmissible otherwise admissible evidence. If evidence is discoverable or otherwise available by independent means, it will not be barred by Rule 408. Second, Rule 408 only applies to evidence that is offered to prove liability for, or invalidity of, the claim or its amount. If offered for other recognized purposes, the evidence may be admissible subject to the court's discretion. Such purposes include those suggested by Rule 408—proving bias or prejudice of a witness, negating a contention of undue delay, or proving an effort to obstruct a criminal investigation or prosecution.

There are, however, measures that can be taken to better ensure that the information conveyed during the proceedings remains off the record and

---

[11] Fed. R. Evid. 408.

inadmissible. The parties must clearly state in the written minitrial agreement their intent to preserve the settlement nature of the proceedings. Reference to Rule 408 (or appropriate state rule or case law) should be incorporated so as to dispel any doubt that the proceedings and all submittals relating to the minitrial remain settlement negotiations.

The second aspect of confidentiality is protecting the evidence offered during the course of a minitrial from discovery. This presents a tougher problem. Rule 408 addresses only admissibility. In the federal courts, the appropriate authority as a starting point is Rule 26 of the Federal Rules of Civil Procedure.[12] Many states have adopted similar rules regarding discovery. Rule 26(b)(1) provides that inadmissible evidence is subject to discovery if it "appears reasonably calculated to lead to the discovery of admissible evidence."[13] This provision sweeps broadly and, therefore, it is not a bar to discovery to assert that the information sought will be inadmissible at trial if the request for discovery meets the "reasonably calculated" test of Rule 26(b)(1).[14]

To protect against unwanted disclosure through discovery, the parties should also expressly recite their agreement that materials specifically created for the minitrial are not discoverable. They should also seek to incorporate a protective order under Rule 26(c) of the Federal Rules of Civil Procedure into the court's endorsement of the minitrial procedure.[15] Rule 26(c) provides that parties may obtain a protective court order such that "a trade secret or other confidential research, development, or commercial information not be disclosed."[16] The proposed order should make reference to Rule 408 that the minitrial is a compromise negotiation and that all offers, promises, conduct, and statements made during the minitrial and materials specially created for the minitrial are confidential and not discoverable. It should provide that any information connected with the minitrial be neither subject to discovery nor admissible for any purpose. One need not be hesitant to use language broader than that found in Rule 408.

Reference in the agreement (and any protective order) should also be made to the conduct and statements of the Neutral, since Rule 408 does not specifically address individuals who are not parties to the dispute. A court will likely be receptive to such an order to promote the strong public policy against disclosure of confidential information presented during a minitrial.

---

[12] Fed. R. Civ. P. 26.
[13] Fed. R. Civ. P. 26(b)(1).
[14] *Id.*
[15] Fed. R. Civ. P. 26(c).
[16] *Id.*

§ 10.14 Minitrial Case Study

There are, however, no guarantees. Not all courts are open minded with regard to contract provisions restricting discovery. For instance, in *Grumman Aerospace Corp. v. Titanium Metals Corp. of America*,[17] the United States District Court for the Eastern District of New York held that private parties engaging in an information exchange incident to a structured settlement negotiation (not a minitrial) would not be allowed "to contract privately for the confidentiality of documents, and foreclose others from obtaining, in the course of litigation, materials that are relevant to their efforts to vindicate a legal position."[18] Care must be taken, particularly if there exist any companion actions not involving parties to the minitrial.

§ 10.14 Minitrial Case Study

A minitrial in which the author participated involved a massively complex and heated construction litigation; the case serves as an example to reveal the effectiveness of the minitrial process.[19]

Five years of construction of a $250 million, 1.6 million square foot hospital degenerated into a maze of claims between owner, designers, multiple prime contractors, and subcontractors. Claims and counterclaims involved delay and acceleration due to incomplete design, defective workmanship, and unauthorized substitutions and deviations from specifications. The hospital also sustained a $1 million fire during construction.

Litigation, which ultimately involved 14 parties in multiple actions in two jurisdictions, was filed 20 months before construction was even completed. In addition, after suits were filed, the construction was abandoned by the contractor for heating, ventilation, and air conditioning (HVAC), plumbing, and fire protection sprinklers. The largest trade contractor on the project, it claimed it was underpaid for extra work. The hospital's completion was delayed almost two years. The project and the litigation ran concurrently and both were emotionally charged. The complex cases were consolidated in one action in federal district court and were to be tried to a jury.

The various prime contracts and subcontracts contained no arbitration clauses. However, in the middle of extensive discovery and pretrial motions practice, and with strong urging from the presiding district judge, the parties agreed to look to an alternative means to resolve the disputes

---

[17] 91 F.R.D. 84 (E.D.N.Y. 1981).

[18] *Id.* at 87–88.

[19] *See* Smith, *Maxi Mini-Trial Partly Solves $200MM Delaware Hospital Case*, 4 Alternatives 1 (Dec. 1986).

outside of court. The parties opted to create a nonbinding minitrial procedure. The cost of discovery and trial, and the multimillion dollar risks in this high stakes jury case were major motivating factors bringing the parties together, at least to explore settlement through minitrial. Simply agreeing to engage in a minitrial was a major accomplishment in view of the strained relations. Without such a structured settlement, and because of the extent of the complexities involved, meaningful settlement negotiations would never have gotten underway.

A detailed minitrial agreement was exhaustively negotiated. It called for discovery, other than depositions, to be conducted prior to the minitrial. The hospital project involved years of planning, design, and construction, and had multiple prime contractors, numerous subcontractors, engineers, architects, and other technical experts. Consequently, the project generated hundreds of thousands of documents. The time-consuming document review process in discovery continued but was not completed before the minitrial. A discovery and litigation moratorium endorsed by court order was entered in the litigation and was begun six weeks before the minitrial so that the parties could prepare for the settlement effort.

The parties agreed to have a noted construction attorney (also a professional engineer) as the Neutral. The Neutral was given the title of referee. The referee was empowered by the agreement to control the minitrial procedure and to engage, at the parties' pro rata expense, whatever technical assistance he needed. Each of the parties further agreed to have principals with full settlement authority sit through all proceedings. The minitrial schedule was explicitly set forth in the agreement created by the parties' counsel and further supplemented by the referee, who took a very active role in formulating the details of the mechanics of the proceedings.

Ten days prior to the minitrial, each of the parties submitted a factual position paper to the referee, and these were also exchanged by the parties. All exhibits to be introduced at the minitrial were premarked and sent to the referee and exchanged by the parties.

The sessions began on a Monday morning and ran continuously through the following Sunday, beginning each day at 8:00 A.M. and running until 9:30 P.M. Each party was allowed an affirmative presentation totaling no more than four hours. Each party was also limited to one hour of rebuttal following the close of all affirmative presentations. Close to 100 people were in daily attendance.

The Federal Rules of Evidence were used, but only as a guide. In actuality, time was the only real constraint on the presentation of evidence. Statements by lawyers and unsworn testimony were presented. No transcription or any other record of the proceedings was allowed.

All matters relating to the minitrial were agreed by the parties to be totally off the record and considered privileged and confidential settlement

§ 10.14 MINITRIAL CASE STUDY

discussions in accordance with Federal Rule of Evidence 408. This was expressly set forth in the formal agreement. Procedural and substantive disputes arising during the proceedings were resolved either by agreement of counsel or by submission to the referee. The court did not become involved in any way in the proceedings, nor was it advised of the substance or results of the minitrial efforts.

There was no cross-examination of witnesses by opposing counsel; however, the referee was empowered to ask questions and did so at the conclusion of each affirmative case. The parties were allowed to submit proposed cross-examination questions. Twenty-five percent of each parties' time for presentation was allotted to cross-examination by the referee.

In addition, two-hour nightly sessions (known as confrontation sessions) were conducted. There the referee (and other witnesses) asked questions of that day's witnesses. During the confrontation sessions the lawyers were banished to the back of the hospital's amphitheater in which the sessions were held and put under strict cloture. The parties were required to bring all witnesses to these evening sessions. With bosses (the parties' principals) present, these "one-on-one, stand up and look your accuser in the eye" sessions were remarkable for their candor. They were also noteworthy for the frank exchanges between the opposing parties' jobsite and managerial personnel.

These sessions were responsible for revealing the personalities involved and motivations for positions taken. In this fashion, the formal presentations were supplemented and, in some instances, refuted; but, most importantly, the parties' minitrial presentations were put into a true perspective. As a result, the minitrial was able to present to the principals virtually all of the critical data needed with which to weigh settlement, and to present it in a fashion that never could be equaled by the formal discovery process.

The parties expressly agreed that following the minitrial they would use the nonbinding written decision of the referee as a basis for attempting to negotiate settlement. The referee was asked to render a decision within one week of the close of the hearings and then hold himself available to act as a mediator should the parties wish. In retrospect, a written decision should not have been required of the referee, for reasons discussed in **§ 10.12**.

The parties engaged in settlement negotiations within days of the minitrial. Settlement was not, however, immediately obtained. Litigation recommenced when settlement could not be reached within a previously agreed time limit (as set forth in the formal agreement). Settlement of all but one of the subcontractors' claims was accomplished, however, in the middle of a crushing three-month deposition schedule in which almost 100 depositions were scheduled to be taken.

The remaining dispute—involving the owner, one of the prime contractors, and the abandoning subcontractor—could not be settled and proceeded to an extraordinary jury trial. Thirty-five witnesses testified and over 900 exhibits were introduced into evidence as the trial consumed 79 days over five and one-half months before a jury. This marathon remains the longest trial in the federal district's history. The jury was remarkable for its devotion to duty and attentiveness throughout. After five days of deliberation, the jury returned a verdict against the abandoning subcontractor and in favor of the owner and prime contractor, and awarded over $21 million by its verdict.

The fact that such a prolonged and expensive trial had to take place, however, by no means shows that the minitrial was unsuccessful. In fact, the referee had estimated at the conclusion of the minitrial that a trial of all issues involving all parties would have taken well over one and one-half years. Moreover, the vast majority of the parties were able to settle their differences in a commercially prudent fashion. The savings in the cost of litigation to all participants is obvious.

The referee and participants at the minitrial expressed the view that it had revealed roughly 95 percent of the pertinent facts and was key in providing the principals the necessary information with which to weigh the risks and benefits of trial or settlement. The principals, thus, had all that was necessary to make the decision either to settle or, in the case of three of the participants, to go forward with the litigation.

MEDIATION

§ 10.15 Definition

Mediation is an informal process by which participants seek to resolve their dispute with the assistance of a neutral third party who helps to isolate disputed issues, develop options, and consider alternatives to promote a negotiated settlement.[20] Generally, the mediator does not impose a settlement, but only guides the parties to achieve their own settlement. Like other ADR techniques, the process is voluntary and nonbinding; the mediator cannot impose a decision (as can an arbitrator), but merely assists the parties to reach agreement. Indeed, mediation supplements arbitration as a procedure endorsed by the American Arbitration Association (AAA) and the National Construction Industry Arbitration Committee (NCIAC).[21]

---

[20] *See* Riskin, *The Special Place of Mediation in Alternative Dispute Processing*, 37 U. Fla. L. Rev. 19 (1985).

[21] *See* American Arbitration Association, Construction Industry Mediation Rules (1985).

Under the AAA rules, a party may submit a dispute to mediation; if the dispute is not resolved by that process, then it continues as arbitration or litigation.[22]

Mediation is, in structure, one step beyond voluntary negotiation between parties by virtue of the addition of a neutral third party to assist in the negotiations. Mediation is useful when the parties have not been able to reach settlement on their own, desire to exhaust settlement efforts before submitting to binding adjudication, and need the assistance of an expert and trained third party to negotiate a settlement.

Unlike a minitrial, mediation contains no adjudicatory element. There is no trial-like setting for an information exchange and formal presentation of arguments. The role of the mediator is more active than the Neutral in a minitrial, and more geared toward proposing settlement options and compromise between the parties.

§ 10.16 Benefits of Mediation

Many of the attributes of, and requirements for, a successful minitrial apply with equal force to mediation. As with the more structured minitrial process, and in contrast to binding forms of dispute resolution, mediation has the following beneficial features.

Nontraditional results. Mediation provides the opportunity for significantly different results from those available with traditional binding litigation or arbitration. Because the parties in dispute must, by definition, cooperate and participate in the resolution, the risk of hostility present in adjudication (the desire to get even and a loss of objectivity) is diminished. Mediation provides the opportunity for catharsis as the parties craft their own, mutually beneficial solution.

Voluntary participation. The proceedings are voluntary. The parties may participate or decline to participate as they choose. The proceedings are private, and no public or private records are kept. Mediation clearly falls within the exclusionary rule of Federal Rule of Evidence 408 as a means of compromise negotiations. The process is noncompulsory and nonbinding and, therefore, the parties retain the option to halt negotiations and continue with binding adjudication.

---

[22] *Id.* at 4.

Nonbinding rules. The parties are not bound by rules of evidence, rules of procedures, or the other sometimes complicated private procedural requirements of a minitrial. For instance, the Construction Industry Mediation Rules published by the AAA and the NCIAC prescribe 17 straightforward, nontechnical rules.[23] This concept allows flexibility for the mediator and the parties to fashion their own workable solution.

Emphasis on solutions. In mediation, the emphasis is not on winning but on finding a creative practical solution to what probably has been regarded as an intractable problem. Because of the great deal of flexibility in fashioning the process and in proposing solutions, the parties are able to create their own remedy and one not limited by legal precedent or limited to only dollar recoveries.

Cost savings. As with other forms of ADR, mediation can result in substantial savings to the parties by avoiding the costs and delay in preparing for adversarial arbitration or court proceedings. Mediation is often used in the early stages of a dispute because it is not necessary to engage in discovery before using the mediation process. It is, therefore, less expensive than other forms of ADR.

§ 10.17 Mediation Rules

The Construction Industry Mediation Rules of the AAA are intended to achieve orderly, economical, and quick dispute resolution by providing maximum flexibility and minimum structure. To implement these rules, the parties may consider inserting the following suggested clause in their contract:

> If a dispute arises out of or relates to this contract, or the breach thereof, and if said dispute cannot be settled through direct discussions, the parties agree to first endeavor to settle the dispute in an amicable manner by mediation under the Construction Industry Mediation Rules of the American Arbitration Association, before having recourse to arbitration or a judicial forum.[24]

To initiate mediation under these rules, a party must file a written request to the AAA and pay the requisite administrative fee. The request

---
[23] *Id.*
[24] *Id.*

must contain a brief summary of the nature of the dispute along with pertinent information about the parties. The AAA will then appoint a mediator or follow the stipulated wishes of the parties as to the choice of a mediator. The mediator fixes the time of each mediation session and agrees with the parties as to the most convenient location.[25]

Each party pays an initial AAA administrative fee, which currently ranges from $250 to $850 per party, depending on the size of the claim. The fee for the mediator is agreed to by the parties and the AAA, and is paid directly to the AAA. Normally, unless otherwise agreed to, this fee is split between the parties.[26]

At least 10 days prior to the first mediation session, each party should provide the mediator with a written document stating its position regarding the issues in dispute. Such documents may be required to be exchanged with the other parties, and the mediator may request supplemental information. The mediator is not vested with settlement authority but may make oral or written recommendations for settlement. The mediator may, if necessary, obtain technical advice, provided the parties agree to cover any resulting costs. The mediator may end the mediation at any time that it is deemed further effort will not result in resolution of the dispute. Mediation may also be terminated by execution of a settlement agreement or by a written statement by any party that it desires an end to the mediation.

The mediation sessions are private and confidential. No stenographic records are kept. Care should be taken by prior written agreement that the mediator should not be compelled to divulge any documents received during the course of mediation or to testify on the mediation effort in any adversary proceeding. There is, however, no "mediator's privilege." Protection of facts obtained by a mediator from compulsory disclosure in a judicial proceeding is not generally recognized, if at all.

§ 10.18 Role of the Mediator

First and foremost, the mediator must be neutral and impartial, and perceived as such by the parties. The mediator must disclose any circumstances likely to create a presumption of bias. Mediators should be chosen on the basis of their skill and training in mediation, and their knowledge and expertise in a particular area. A mediator who is familiar with the subject matter, especially in technical areas, is better able to provide creative and viable solutions.

---

[25] *Id.*
[26] *Id.* at 9.

In general, the role of the mediator is to:

1. Provide procedural structure and see that such structure is adhered to
2. Achieve a rapport with the parties
3.. Determine the facts and isolate the issues
4. Help create alternative solutions from which the parties may choose
5. Guide negotiations and decision-making
6. Provide for legal review and processing of settlement documents
7. Remain available for follow-up review and revision.

In what has been termed classic mediation, the mediator facilitates the process in three phases. The first phase entails separate meetings with the respective parties. Here the mediator helps each party assess its own claims so as to clearly understand issues. From this perspective, the mediator can then help each party formulate goals and objectives while maintaining an open mind as to how to best achieve them.

The next phase is to stimulate communication between the various parties. This is the most well-known aspect of mediation. Here, the mediator shuttles between the various parties, conveying messages with diplomacy. Some mediators not only transmit proposals but offer their own analysis and suggestions. Many times this reveals hidden strengths and weaknesses or erroneous beliefs, and it often prevents faulty or one-sided agreements.

The last phase is to reach some type of agreement. The mediator tries to persuade the parties to adopt a reasonable solution, although it may not always be the best solution for each party. By offering fresh ideas and practical solutions from an objective perspective, a creative mediator can be the most help at this stage.

§ 10.19 Mediation Case Study

The following case study describes a mediation and shows the flexibility available to fit the particular needs of the parties in dispute.

The general contractor on a guaranteed maximum price contract for the construction of a multiunit residential/mixed-use facility claimed entitlement to compensation for extras and delay damages. The claim arose from what it contended to be insufficient design and numerous changes to design provided by the owner's architect. The owner was advised by its architect that his design was sufficient, that changes were not inordinate, and that the general contractor was responsible for its own delays and overruns. The parties were at deadlock on entitlement on every issue.

§ 10.19 MEDIATION CASE STUDY

The parties' standard AIA (American Institute of Architects) contract called for compulsory, binding arbitration. It was anticipated that it would take months to conclude the arbitration process and that the expense of attorneys and consultants would be disproportionate to the amounts at issue. Accordingly, as a first step the owner and general contractor agreed to pursue a rather unusual nonbinding mediation as a means to save time and money in an effort to settle differences.

Particularly unusual was the choice of a mediator. It was an individual knowledgeable in construction, but also an investor in the ownership entity (hence directly related to, but not active as, the "Owner" under the general contract). While mediators should typically be perceived as completely neutral, the parties (and particularly the general contractor) were comfortable with the selection, despite the mediator's identity of interest with the owner.

Unlike the formal minitrial described in § **10.14**, the parties agreed to a nonstructured format consisting of the general contractor presenting its best case through its project manager to the owner and mediator. Rebuttal was contemporaneously provided by the project representative for the architect. Thus, the owner (although financially at risk for the claim) took a passive role and, with the aid of the mediator, listened to the two professionals it hired—an architect and a general contractor—explain whether the general contractor's claims were meritorious. The mediation session and all matters relating to the mediation were private and agreed to be off-the-record settlement discussions.

The general contractor's project manager presented a detailed graphics analysis of the project delays (substantiated by project documentation) comparing the as-planned schedule with the impacted, as-built schedule. He also detailed the claim for extras. The mediator and the owner's representative asked questions of both representatives (the architect's and the general contractor's) during the presentation. The mediation was noteworthy for the exchange of information and presentation of non-antagonistic opposing views during this informal questioning. Lawyers were present, but by previous agreement they played a very limited role. Formal cross-examination would have been distinctly counterproductive, particularly when compared to the frank exchange of information that actually took place.

The presentation and discussion of issues took one session lasting three hours. Unlike most mediations, however, the parties chose not to begin to negotiate a resolution immediately. Instead, the parties asked the mediator to formulate his appraisal of the claims and then separately share his analysis first with the owner, and thereafter with the general contractor. This procedure was followed, and within two weeks the matter settled by a negotiated result and project close-out proceeded without the need for further formal disputes resolution.

SUMMARY JURY TRIAL

§ 10.20 Historical Perspective

A summary jury trial is a settlement device through an abbreviated presentation of a case by the lawyers to an advisory jury.[27] This allows the parties, lawyers, and the court to better know how a formal jury will respond to the case. The summary jury trial procedure was created by United States District Judge Thomas D. Lambros of the United States District Court for the Northern District of Ohio. It was first used in 1980 in personal injury cases.[28] Judge Lambros describes his reason for creating the summary jury trial "as a way to reduce the stresses on the judicial system while safeguarding the time-tested process of trial by jury."[29]

Since 1980, over 65 federal district judges have used the summary jury trial procedure, and nine federal district courts have adopted rules referring specifically to summary jury trials as a disputes resolution technique. The procedures referenced in this chapter have been applied in the federal courts, but state courts, through their inherent powers to prescribe docket control devices, can also employ similar procedures.

Unlike the misnamed minitrial, the summary jury trial simulates a real trial in many respects. This is the central purpose of the summary jury trial—to reveal to the parties how prospective jurors will react to their claims. However, unlike formal adjudication or arbitration, the decision of the jury is nonbinding and is merely advisory. An important distinction between the summary jury trial and other forms of ADR is that the third party is not a skilled neutral advisor, but rather consists of jurors chosen in the same way as jurors for a real trial.

§ 10.21 When to Use Summary Jury Trials

The summary jury trial is best suited for those cases that have failed to settle because the parties hold divergent views about what they believe the jury will find as to liability or damages. One or more of the parties may have an unrealistic view of an essential element of the case, and it takes a mock trial to reveal such misconceptions. Other litigants may feel their

---

[27] *See generally* Lambros, *The Summary Jury Trial and Other Alternative Methods of Dispute Resolution,* A Report to the Judicial Conference of the United States Committee on the Operation of the Jury System, 103 F.R.D. 461 (1984).

[28] Lambros, *Summary Jury Trials,* 13 Litigation 52 (Fall 1986).

[29] *Id.*

§ 10.21 WHEN TO USE SUMMARY JURY TRIALS

case is of marginal value but would be enhanced if put before a jury. Psychologically, it is important for some parties to have their day in court. Perhaps this perceived need to take their case before a jury has impeded settlement. A summary jury trial is a safe and less costly means of meeting these needs and facilitating settlement. The summary jury trial is one last attempt to break a deadlock between the parties by means of a "verdict" from an impartial jury.

Because the summary jury trial is useful only after discovery has been completed, its dollar savings relative to other types of ADR may not be as dramatic. However, savings may very well be substantial when compared to the costs associated with a full trial. Of course, a summary jury trial may not be cost-effective if the actual trial is expected to be short and inexpensive. The savings in attorney fees and fees for expert witnesses, and the opportunity to see how a jury evaluates the case justify the use of the summary jury trial. It must be remembered that a summary jury trial is the last effort to settle the case before surrendering control to the uncertainty of a result obtained from a formal jury.

Unlike the other forms of ADR discussed in this chapter, the summary jury trial is a creature of the court. In federal courts, Rule 16(a) of the Federal Rules of Civil Procedure[30] grants the court power to call a pretrial conference to "expedit[e] the disposition of the action"[31] and to "facilitat[e] the settlement of the case."[32] Similar rules or procedures are found in state court systems.

Among the subjects oftentimes discussed at pretrial conferences is "the possibility of settlement or the use of extrajudicial procedures to resolve the dispute."[33] The summary jury trial is one such extrajudicial means to settle cases without resorting to a full-blown trial. Accordingly, the summary jury trial may be initiated by the parties or by the presiding judge.

In some courts the trial judge may use discretion to mandate the use of a summary jury trial before allowing the case to be tried according to normal procedures. The United States Court of Appeals for the Seventh Circuit has held, however, that litigants may refuse to participate in a summary jury trial. In *Strandell v. Jackson County*,[34] the trial judge found the plaintiff's counsel in criminal contempt for refusing to proceed with a summary jury trial, when the counsel claimed that a summary jury trial would require disclosure of privileged witness statements. The district court held that Rule 16 of the Federal Rules of Civil Procedure granted the

---

[30] Fed. R. Civ. P. 16(a).
[31] Fed. R. Civ. P. 16(a)(1).
[32] Fed. R. Civ. P. 16(a)(5).
[33] Fed. R. Civ. P. 16(c)(7).
[34] 838 F.2d 884 (7th Cir. 1988).

power to order the litigants to engage in a process which will enhance the possibility of "fruitful negotiations."[35]

The Seventh Circuit reversed, ruling that "while the pretrial conference of Rule 16 was intended to foster settlement through the use of extrajudicial procedures, it was not intended to require that an unwilling litigant be sidetracked from the normal course of litigation."[36] The appeals court also concluded that pretrial settlement devices should not detrimentally affect well-established rules concerning discovery and work-product privileges.

The Seventh Circuit acknowledged that courts at times face crushing case loads, but "a crowded docket does not permit the court to avoid trial."[37] This holding may, however, have short application. The Alternative Dispute Resolution Promotion Act of 1987, which has been offered in Congress, would allow district courts to convene mandatory summary jury trials.[38]

In addition, the United States District Court for the Middle District of Florida, in *Arabian American Oil Co. v. Schartone*,[39] ruled that a district court had the authority to order summary jury trials pursuant to Rule 16 of the Federal Rules of Civil Procedure.

§ 10.22 Pretrial Conference

Inasmuch as a summary jury trial is a court-annexed proceeding, most of the procedures will be set forth by rule or established by the judge. According to District Judge Lambros, there are three stages to a summary jury trial: pretrial conference; jury selection and presentation; and post-trial negotiation.[40] The following procedural requirements are often utilized.

All discovery will be required to be completed. This is essential so that what goes before the jury is the same as what a binding jury would hear. All pending motions should be ruled upon on their merits. Just as nothing should be left hanging or undone for a regular trial, the same applies for summary jury trials.

In the final conference before the summary trial, as in a normal trial, the judge (or magistrate) should consider all objections raised by the parties and rule on motions in limine.

---

[35] *Id.* at 886.
[36] *Id.* at 887.
[37] *Id.* at 888.
[38] H.R. 473, 100th Cong. 1st Sess. (1987).
[39] 119 F.R.D. 488 (M.D. Fla. 1988).
[40] Lambros, 13 Litigation at 53.

A few days before the proceeding begins, lawyers for the parties submit trial memoranda, proposed voir dire questions, jury instructions and, if required, exhibit and witness lists.

§ 10.23 Jury Selection and Presentation

On the day of the summary jury trial, principals with full authority to settle are required to be in attendance. The proceedings are closed to the public by order of the court. The court calls prospective jurors from the same pool of jurors used as if it were a normal trial. An expedited form of voir dire is used. Prospective jurors fill out a questionnaire seeking information that counsel would normally look for during voir dire. From this pool, a panel of six, or, as in some instances five (to ensure a majority verdict), jurors are chosen. The court gives the jury a short set of instructions and background information about the proceeding and swears them in.

Parties should expect to have no more than one hour to present their best case to the jury, unless adjustments have been agreed to during the pretrial conference. Fifteen minutes of this time may be reserved for rebuttal. Unlike other ADR formats, the Federal Rules of Evidence are adhered to so as to simulate a real jury trial.

Lawyers present their cases-in-chief in summary form (true to the name of the trial), which usually does not entail the use of witnesses, expert or otherwise. Lawyers may, however, read pertinent parts of depositions, interrogatories, sworn statements, or admissions. They may also relate a conversation held with a witness. Lawyers are obligated by ethical considerations to present such information in a true and accurate manner. This type of presentation is closely monitored by the court, which must hold the attorneys to a good faith representation of the witnesses' statements.

Physical evidence, including documents and demonstrative evidence, may be exhibited as in any other trial. Such evidence is made available to the jury during its deliberation. Because of the abbreviated nature of the proceeding, objections should be kept to a minimum and, as much as possible, be addressed during the pretrial conference. Objections should be limited to those seeking to keep the opposition within the prescribed boundaries of the proceeding.

It should be noted that the summary jury trial does not allow for direct or cross-examination. However, parties should not be hesitant to ask the court to adapt the procedures to their particular case. For instance, if the case turns on the credibility of a witness, the court might allow the witness to testify in an abbreviated form and be subjected to cross-examination.

Lawyers are allowed brief closing arguments. Jury instructions are given and special verdict forms are used to focus the jury on specific aspects of the case in order to obtain its reasoning for arriving at a particular verdict. This is especially useful to provide the parties with insight into the strengths and weaknesses of their cases as perceived by the jury. A unanimous verdict is preferred, but the jurors may return individual verdicts if necessary.

§ 10.24 Post-Trial Discussion and Negotiation

After the jurors deliberate and return a verdict, the case is discussed among all the participants, including the jury. This post-trial discussion is a most important phase of the summary jury trial, because it often provides the necessary inducement for settlement. The jurors are no longer passive observers. The reasons for their findings and observations are solicited. The jurors may be asked which arguments they found most persuasive and which least persuasive. Lawyers (not often given the opportunity) may even want to ask the jury about their personalities and style. The procedure, therefore, offers an opportunity to assess a case and its presentation not otherwise available in conventional litigation.

It is wise for the parties to enter immediately into settlement negotiations following the conclusion of the summary jury trial. This is the reason for the presence of the principals with settlement authority. Since this is a court-annexed proceeding, settlement negotiations will usually include court assistance, but the judge may allow the parties to negotiate privately or call a settlement conference for a later date. One court is known to schedule a regular trial a few days following the summary jury trial as a means to encourage prompt settlement. If a regular trial is necessary, it should usually run more smoothly and efficiently because the parties have already had a dress rehearsal.

One perceived drawback to the summary jury trial is that the exercise reveals trial strategy should it ultimately be necessary to engage in a regular trial. Another drawback is that jurors in a summary jury trial generally are not able to assess live testimony and witness credibility. Depending upon the importance of the testimony (and credibility) of witnesses, this might very well skew the perception and verdict of the jurors in a summary jury trial as compared to those in a regular jury trial. Nevertheless, in those jurisdictions that use the summary jury trial on a consistent basis, the proceeding has proven to be successful in inducing settlement. In one jurisdiction (the Northern District of Ohio), 92 percent of the cases settled after the summary jury trial and before going to full trial.[41]

---

[41] 103 F.R.D. at 472.

§ 10.25 Public Access to Summary Jury Trials

In *Cincinnati Gas & Electric v. General Electric Co.*,[42] the plaintiffs brought an action alleging that the defendant breached its contract for the construction of a nuclear power plant and also alleged fraud and RICO claims. At the outset of the litigation, the parties negotiated, and the court approved, a comprehensive protective order to preserve the confidentiality of documents.

Thereafter, the district court ordered the parties to participate in a summary jury trial. The district court ordered that the proceedings were to be confidential and barred the press and public from attending. The court also imposed a gag order on the jurors participating in the summary jury trial. Transcripts and jury lists were sealed. The district court then denied the right of the press to intervene for the purpose of gaining access to the closed proceedings.

After the conclusion of the summary trial, the action settled. The district court approved the settlement and ordered that the gag orders and all orders sealing documents, including transcripts and jury lists, remain in effect.

The United States Court of Appeals for the Sixth Circuit affirmed the district court's denial of press and public access to the summary proceedings. The Sixth Circuit first noted that summary jury trials were designed to enhance settlement, and that there existed no recognized right of access to such proceedings. The court also noted that access would undermine the settlement function. In rejecting the argument of the press, which was based on the analogy of access to criminal proceedings, the court noted that unlike a preliminary hearing in the criminal process, summary jury trials are nonbinding and do not directly affect the rights of the parties.

---

[42] 854 F.2d 900 (6th Cir. 1988).

CHAPTER 11

COURT TRIALS

Walter T. Wolf, Esquire

Walter T. Wolf is a partner in the New Jersey law firm of Farr, Wolf & Lyons where he specializes in construction litigation. He is a certified civil trial attorney and represents owners, contractors, designers, sureties, and developers. He is a member of the bars of New Jersey and the District of Columbia, as well as an active member in several committees of the national, state, and local bar associations, including the Litigation and National Resources Sections and the Construction Industry Forum of the ABA. Mr. Wolf holds engineering and law degrees from Notre Dame, and is a member of the American Society of Mechanical Engineers and the American Society of Civil Engineers.

§ 11.1 Introduction
§ 11.2 Unique Characteristics of Construction Claims
§ 11.3 Forum Selection
§ 11.4 —Consideration of Site Viewing
§ 11.5 Advocating a Construction Claim to a Jury
§ 11.6 Jury Selection
§ 11.7 —Professional Assistance
§ 11.8 —Voir Dire
§ 11.9 Opening Statement
§ 11.10 Direct Examination
§ 11.11 Fact Witnesses
§ 11.12 Expert Witnesses
§ 11.13 Documents and Demonstrative Evidence
§ 11.14 Closing Arguments and Jury Charges
§ 11.15 Advocating a Construction Claim to a Judge
§ 11.16 Use of Special Masters
§ 11.17 —Sample Order for Appointment of Special Master
§ 11.18 Conclusion

§ 11.1 Introduction

In other chapters, we discuss arbitration, federal contract forums, and alternative forms of dispute resolution. In this chapter we discuss the unique challenge of court trials as applied to construction disputes.

There are certain truisms that are always applicable to the construction dispute in a court situation. For example, as anyone involved in construction disputes will attest, the construction process is deeply embedded in business records created and maintained as the construction process unfolds. These business records include memoranda, schedules, labor records, photographs, plans, drawings, tape recordings, and the like. Such records are often crucial in proving or disproving construction claims.

Judicial history has seen the accumulation of rules relating to authentication and admissibility of evidence because judges need to ensure that witnesses do not lie or fabricate evidence. These evidence guidelines are generally strictly adhered to by judges (especially before juries) and the rules themselves have a long history of guiding judges in their interpretation. These rules provide important safeguards, but, as we discuss, they may be exasperating to parties in construction disputes as they attempt to prove their cases with construction business records.

Compared with alternative disputes resolution mechanisms, court trials of construction cases tend to be more expensive, take a longer time to reach a final hearing stage, consume more time in the hearing process, and are of such a nature that the hearings can extend over a number of days or weeks without a break. The hearing process is relatively inflexible and is more resource-intensive than alternative disputes resolution techniques. The expenses of attorneys' and experts' fees and costs of litigation, when added to the burdens on the client to make available key personnel to assist the attorneys in preparation for and to testify at trial, assist in records management, and support the needs of the experts, make court trials much more costly and demanding.

Many of the alternate disputes resolution mechanisms were formed specifically in response to construction industry disputes. On the other hand, the courts must hear a variety of legal issues and factual disputes that reflect our society. Thus, the specialization needed to address the substantive aspects of construction claims is not readily available in the courts.

Another challenge is that the participants in the judicial process have different backgrounds and perspectives from those involved in the construction industry. The court system is staffed by judges, lawyers, and lay people, none of whom have any particular expertise, except by accident, in the construction process. Additionally, these people are not usually

§ 11.1 INTRODUCTION

business people, even though their role in court is resolving disputes between those who are involved in the economics of the construction process. It is the economic factors, without a doubt, that motivate the actors in the construction process, whether owner, architect, or contractor.

The first opportunity for an attorney to influence the outcome of the client's case in a construction dispute is in drafting the contract. There, the construction attorney has the chance to assist the client in choosing:

1. Which law will apply
2. The venue of any subsequent litigation
3. Whether the matter should be arbitrated
4. The method of service of process
5. Whether trial by jury will apply
6. The standards by which the client's conduct will be judged
7. The types and limits of damages.

Advocacy in court trials should begin with drafting the contract.

After drafting the contract, the second opportunity for the construction trial attorney to influence the outcome of the client's case in court is by recognizing when the construction problems at the jobsite occur. From these problems, legal disputes may arise. The prudent owner, contractor, or supplier will be quick to perceive this. Sometimes an immediate response to a jobsite problem is crucial in determining victory in the courtroom several years away. An attorney should not hesitate to step from behind the desk and visit the construction site with the client to view the problem and speak with personnel, public officials, and others. Early identification, resolution, and mitigation of problems should be accomplished at the site if possible. Alternatively, a plan should be developed to discover and preserve evidence. Early intervention by seasoned counsel may assist the client to identify critical areas in the construction process which, if promptly and properly addressed, will give the client the upper hand in maintaining control of the litigation process.

If appropriate on these occasions, the attorney should take along a photographer, videocamera, court reporter, or tape recorder. The voice-over of a witness on a videotape is a powerful statement and evidence (at a later trial) of events that are occurring but are being covered up as the work progresses. For example, assume that concrete is being delivered to a job; the concrete is defective as demonstrated by slump tests, which are accepted in the industry as evidence of a breach of the material supply contract. Do not hesitate to film the slump tests of the concrete as they are performed if the mixture is so bad as to visually demonstrate its failure.

§ 11.2 Unique Characteristics of Construction Claims

In order to properly apply these general principles to the construction dispute, the unique characteristics of construction claims must be understood.

It is at the problem stage that the attorney will be called upon by one of the participants in the project team (whether owner, designer, contractor, supplier, or equipment renter). It should be evident, even to the novice, that the typical construction project involves an extensive number of parties and relationships. For example, an apparently simple project such as a blacktop parking lot involves surveying (outbound and topographic); clearing; site preparation; soil compaction; provision for drainage and utilities; construction of curbing; delivering and spreading of one or more sizes of aggregate for the base or sub-base; compaction; and delivering and applying the required types and thicknesses of bituminous concrete materials, sealant, and striping.

Thus, the following people and activities would be involved:

Professionals

Engineer—soils tests (wetlands, stability, drainage)
Engineer/architect—design
Engineer/surveyor—field layout
Engineer—testing during construction and after completion (coring)

Contractors

Field clearing, grubbing
Earthwork
Soil compaction
Drainage installation
Utility line installation or protection (sanitary or storm sewers, gas, water, electric, telephone, T.V. lines)
Asphalt
Concrete
Sealing
Striping
Warning devices
Watchmen
Traffic control
Landscaping

§ 11.2 UNIQUE CHARACTERISTICS

Suppliers

Gravel or substitute base
Aggregate for base/sub-base
Pipe
Concrete
Asphalt
Cast iron grates for drainage
Precast concrete items
Nursery supplies
Lumber
Forms for concrete curbing

The engineers and architects can subcontract portions of their work to others (testing laboratories, well drillers, and so forth). Further, the contractors can subcontract portions of their work, and the suppliers may be simply distributors. Add to this those involved in the inspection process on behalf of the owner, architect, tenant, lender, bonding company, utilities, and the city or county, and what appears to the observer as a simple project when completed actually is a complex job if done properly.

Because the project itself is complex, those involved will have specialized knowledge, training, or experience. There are all kinds of design specialists: architects, geotechnical engineers, structural engineers, mechanical engineers, interior designers, electrical engineers, planners, and the like. There are other professionals like surveyors, estimators, schedulers, and inspectors who apply their special training to a project. Contractors also specialize in certain types of work, and various subcontractors and suppliers specialize in a particular trade or type of system.

Extensive management and coordination is required on a construction project. This inevitably involves a great deal of documentation, including drawings, blueprints, specifications, schedules, change orders, and shop drawings. Indeed, the "paper trail" is overwhelming to the participants in the construction process, not to mention the attorneys who may later be involved.

The construction process is resource-intensive because it involves land, equipment, labor, and materials, all of which cost money. Superimposed on this is the urgency of completing the project at the earliest time to minimize the cost of money and put the project to productive use.

On top of all these internal aspects of the process, there are externally imposed conditions on the performance of the construction team. Constructing a major project is a high-risk venture, at best, involving weather conditions; laws and regulations; strikes, injunctions, and other labor problems; material and supply testing and rejections; shipping delays; subsurface or other unknown conditions; equipment maintenance, availability, and breakdowns; and the ever-present problem of financing all of this with the uncertainty of interest rates and prices over a lengthy project.

All of these risk factors may contribute to the cause of disputes. Sorting out responsibility is often difficult. In the construction contract, many of these risks may be allocated between the parties signing the contract or shifted to third parties such as bonding companies and insurance companies.

Whatever the case, the attorney litigating these disputes in a court trial is in a position very similar to someone explaining farming to a person who has never lived outside the city or explaining the strategy and tactics of warfare to a monk.

§ 11.3 Forum Selection

In general, the trial attorney considering litigating the client's case in court should initially determine where the case will be tried. Lawyers call this forum selection. This decision is a function of jurisdiction (where the case can be brought) and a number of other practical considerations; these relate to where the attorney and the client desire to try the case among the options available within jurisdictional parameters.[1] Even assuming jurisdiction, a court can either dismiss a case or transfer it to another court under the doctrine of forum non conveniens.

There are two court systems, federal and state, and there are 50 states. Given jurisdiction in two or more courts, the practical considerations are the convenience of the parties, their attorneys, and the witnesses; the procedural and substantive law applicable to the case (including statutes of limitation and repose) in the particular court; and the costs associated with the choices. Detailed consideration of such an analysis is beyond the scope of this book.

§ 11.4 —Consideration of Site Viewing

A factor unique to construction litigation in court trials is the construction project itself, whether it be a bridge, building, or road. Construction cases, in general, are site-specific and visible from, at least, the outside. Thus, the construction litigator must consider authorized and unauthorized inspections, or views, of the project by either a judge or jury. Such views are more likely if the project is located within the geographic jurisdiction of the court.

---

[1] Casad, *Introduction* to Jurisdiction and Forum Selection 1–21 (1988).

§ 11.4 SITE VIEWING

In a construction case tried to a judge, it is usually discretionary as to whether the judge can view the project in dispute. Usually such a determination is made with the consent of the parties.[2]

Without the consent of the parties, there is the potential of an ethics violation by the judge: "A judge should disqualify himself in a proceeding in which his impartiality might reasonably be questioned, including . . . instances where: (a) he has . . . personal knowledge of disputed evidentiary facts concerning the proceeding."[3]

Even with the consent of the parties, or if the judge's view of the project is otherwise proper, the same case law holds—the judge may not base findings of fact on what is learned by the inspection. Although in certain jurisdictions the judge can use what is learned as evidence, in most jurisdictions the judge's view of the project is only for the purpose of better understanding the evidence heard or seen in the courtroom.[4]

The usual criteria to be considered in deciding whether an inspection will be done is whether the conditions at the site during the trial accurately portray the factual issues in dispute, and whether those facts can be adequately produced in court by testimony or demonstrative evidence.

With respect to a case tried to a jury, the problems are much more complex. Generally, the law is the same as it is with the case tried to a judge. The lapse of time, the changing of conditions at the site, and other factors all are relevant to a determination as to whether a view will be permitted.[5] However, once a view is allowed, suitable instructions (dependent on the jurisdiction) to the jury must be given by the judge.[6]

The possible unauthorized viewing of the project by the jury is a matter that should be considered by the attorney. Without a proper background explanation of the facility or conditions, the juror may get a distorted conception of the project from an unauthorized viewing. The attorney may address the issue of unauthorized visits either in the presentation of the case without raising it as an issue, or confronting it as an actual issue in the trial proceedings.

Quite simply, if viewing the scene or the project will, in all probability, benefit the client's case, the only thing to keep in mind is whether the trial testimony and exhibits will substantially conform to what a juror would see at the project.

---

[2] Peoples Trust Co. v. Board of Adjustment Borough of Hasbrouck Heights, 60 N.J. Super. 569, 576, 160 A.2d 57 (1959).

[3] Code of Judicial Conduct, Canon 3(c)(1)(a).

[4] Morris County Land Imp. Co. v. Parsippany—Troy Hills Township, 40 N.J. 549, 193 A.2d 232 (1962); Ascrone v. City of Union City, 77 N.J. Super. 542, 187 A.2d 193 (1962).

[5] 75 Am. Jur. 2d *Trial* § 72 (1974); Wimberly v. City of Patterson, 75 N.J. Super. 584, 183 A.2d 691 (1962).

[6] 75 Am. Jur. 2d *Trial* § 72 (1974).

If viewing the project is unlikely to benefit the client's case, this point should be brought out in the voir dire under appropriate instructions from the judge. This may prevent the jurors from believing that the trial attorney and the client are presenting testimony and evidence in court contrary to what would be obvious at the site.

In connection with a properly authorized view by a judge or jury in a construction litigation case, the following issues should be considered by the trial attorneys.

Written plan.   A plan should be prepared in writing to answer the questions of where the view is to take place, what is to be viewed, when it will take place, and how the logistics are to be handled. The plan should be placed on the record in court out of the presence of the jury. An appropriate pleading, reciting the legal reasons for the view, should be prepared; this would include the statutory authority, the factual findings addressing the complexity of the matter, and the desire to better assist the factfinders in understanding the evidence.

Timing.   When during the trial should the view take place? The evidence that has thus far been produced, including exhibits and photographs, as well as testimony, should be considered. Weather conditions might also influence the timing of the view. If the essence of the case involves anything other than fair weather, such as cold, wind, rain, or snow, consideration should be given to attempting to view the site under similar conditions.

If the issue in the case relates to reflections, lighting, visibility, and the like, time of day should be taken into consideration in determining the timing of the view.

Transportation.   How can the judge and staff or the jury be transported from the courtroom to the site? Since maintaining control of the view is essential, the attorney certainly does not meet them at the site. Whether the jurors should be transported in a bus or permitted to follow a lead car in their own vehicles should be considered, as well as the possibility of automobile accidents and other mishaps. The cost of transporting and assembling the jurors at the site is another issue, as are an assembly point and transportation within the jobsite itself. (The jury should view the site in a group, not individually.)

Attendance.   The attorneys, of course, should be present, and they should evaluate the presence of clients and their representatives. The judge and individual members of the judicial staff may or may not attend a view by the jury. The presence of the court reporter, especially if the judge desires to dictate impressions or actually, when permitted, make findings of fact at the scene, should also be considered. Sometimes the appointment of "showers" in the case of the jury is appropriate. (These are people agreeable to all parties who are knowledgeable about the site and who "show" relevant aspects of the site to the jury.)

Security. Construction safety, including the availability of hard hats and any other equipment, should be considered, as well as weather conditions at the site, which may require special precautions. The personal safety of those attending may be a factor if the site is in a hazardous part of town, and the presence of bystanders who might improperly communicate with the jurors should be considered. Security clearances may also be necessary.

This author participated in a view by a judge in a nonjury trial that extended over a year and involved an 11,000-acre site. The presence of numerous buildings in various conditions and the varying topography of the site made a view almost a necessity in assisting the court to understand the testimony, maps, plans, and photographs that were produced in court. The length of the trial and the necessity for the court to have an overview of the site made the view helpful. Conditions of the buildings and roads, drainage, irrigation, and natural resource availability (ground pits, well water, and so forth) were almost impossible to duplicate in the courtroom, even with aerial and ground photographs.

In another nonjury case in a northeastern state, the condition of warehouses in a suit by an owner and tenant against the builder arose out of the failure of the builder to address deficient soil conditions. Allegedly this condition caused the floor and foundations of the warehouse to sink. The supporting columns and roof also sank, creating a large "belly" in the floor and on the flat roof. This condition permitted water to accumulate on the roof rather than to run off, and opened spaces at the perimeter of the roof system next to the outside walls. A view was requested by the defense because these problems were hard to conceptualize without a visual inspection. The trial was protracted and extended into the winter. The view, which had been scheduled some days in advance, occurred on a day after it had snowed. The melting snow dripped through the skylights and perimeter spaces onto pallets of product (covered with temporary plastic covers), puddling on the floor. The dramatic testimony as to the fact of damage and its impact on warehousing operations was a significant event in the trial.

§ 11.5 Advocating a Construction Claim to a Jury

The goal of the attorney advocating a construction claim to a jury is to reach a reasonable settlement, and failing that, to achieve a favorable verdict. This is done by developing and implementing a winning theory and theme for the case.

There are five main challenges in a construction claim jury trial:

1. Jury selection
2. Opening statement
3. Direct and cross-examination of fact and expert witnesses
4. Presenting documents and demonstrative evidence
5. Closing arguments (and jury charges).

Each of these is an opportunity to present the case to the jury. However, the attorney must plan and implement the message and theme of the case to be effective in each of these aspects of a jury trial. Effective advocacy requires proper pretrial preparation.

Advocacy in presenting a construction claim to the jury begins, as with all cases, in developing a theory for the case that is susceptible to the jury's acceptance.

Contemporaneous with developing the case theory should be some method of "trying out" the theory on those who will be later called upon to accept that theory, namely, potential jurors. Behavioral scientists believe that those who customarily work in or around law offices (lawyers, paralegals, secretaries, experts, and the like) are usually notoriously poor judges of the thinking of those who are not regularly a part of the judicial process. The jurors' only exposure to the facts of a case is hearing or seeing those facts revealed to them in the artificial setting of a courtroom.[7]

Failure to adopt a case theory at an early stage of trial preparation can be disastrous. As a matter of fact, developing the theory of the case should begin when the construction dispute is first brought to the attention of the attorney. As we discuss in **Chapter 1**, the sooner the attorney can focus on the critical factual area or areas of the client's case, the better.

For example, in proving a delay claim, the owner's finger may be pointing at the contractor. The truth of the matter may be that the delay was due to unforeseeable causes beyond the control of the contractor, and may, in fact, have been because of the acts or omissions of the owner or architect or other external factors. The sooner the attorney can determine the factual basis to support the client's position, the better. Hopefully, this can be done even while the construction process is going on. This will afford both the attorney and the client the opportunity to adopt an investigation plan (interviews, testing, schedule updates, photographs, videotapes) that will later support the theory of the case at a trial. Later, the opposing party will want to do the same thing, but by that time, areas of construction may be closed in or covered up, transient workers may have moved from the area, memories have faded, and documents have been lost. If and when the opposing counsel obtains the test results, photographs, videotapes, and documents in discovery, such information allows

---

[7] Discussions with John Lamberth, Ph.D., a social psychologist, faculty member in the Department of Psychology at Temple University and a recognized jury selection expert from West Chester, Pennsylvania.

a more realistic assessment of the relative positions of the parties at trial, despite any preconceived notions.

The case theory is the thread that connects the jury selection with the opening statement and the examination of witnesses, coupled with the presentation of evidence and the closing arguments. As we discuss in **Chapter 1**, the real challenge to the attorney in construction litigation cases tried to a jury is attempting to make something complex understandable for the jury. Fortunately, however, the subject matter of the dispute usually lends itself to the use of tangible evidence such as writings, flow charts, models, and the like. Thus, one of the main disadvantages of this type of litigation (its complexity) can be turned to an advantage by using tangible evidence, because people generally remember what they see and hear better and longer than what they simply hear. Every prosecutor in a homicide case tries to introduce into evidence (to have the jury see) color photographs of the deceased at the scene, as well as the murder weapon, even when the defense has an alibi. This is advocacy in presentation. So, too, the construction attorney may choose to introduce into evidence photographs of a contractor's crew and equipment performing work on a jobsite in a delay claim to support the concept that the client did, in fact, mobilize the job on the date in question, even though this can normally be proven by volumes of computer records.

§ 11.6 Jury Selection

There are several considerations involved in jury selection for construction cases: identification, humanization, inherent biases, and common frustrating experiences. While experts in jury selection address these factors on any type of jury trial, they have important and unique considerations for construction litigation. It is important to properly apply these factors to the theme of the case, the client, the industry segment involved, and the facts.[8]

When it comes to jury selection, the experts in this field have indicated that the ideal juror is one who will identify with the client. The important issue is the specific area of identification that will benefit the client. However, it does not necessarily follow that if the client is an architect, a group of six or twelve architects would be the best jurors; as a matter of fact, depending on the facts of the case, the reverse may be true. Architects may disagree theoretically or factually with the client and hold the client to different standards than a lay person would.

It is also important to humanize the client to the fullest extent possible. Most of the parties to the design and construction process are companies

---

[8] Herbert & Barrett, *Attorney's Master Guide to Courtroom Psychology* in Executive Reports Corporation 103 (1981).

and organizations rather than individuals. Simply because the client is a large national corporate owner of dozens of warehouses does not mean that the attorney cannot "humanize" the client, and thus permit the jury to identify with the company. Careful selection of both the corporation's representative in court and the witnesses can perform this function.

The trial attorney must select, to the extent possible, a jury that identifies with the client, and especially with the individuals chosen to represent the corporate client. This often involves overcoming inherent biases and common frustrating experiences. For example, statistics have shown a high degree of dissatisfaction with contractors and subcontractors on the part of homeowners. Most homeowners have had home repairs or remodeling done at one time or another, and many have undoubtedly had unsatisfactory experiences. It is amazing how easily these experiences translate into a bias against contractors and in favor of owners. But sometimes the biases are more subtle. Preliminary investigation of the case theory using a sample of jurors will help to identify the demographic characteristics of those who are most and least prejudiced against your client.[9]

Another potential problem in jury selection in construction cases is the technical or scientific knowledge, education, or training of a prospective juror. While this would be desirable in the arbitration context, such a situation should be closely watched in jury selection. On the surface, one might think that such experience would be helpful. However, such a person may have his or her own views concerning a construction issue—views that are not favorable to the trial attorney's position. It would generally be better if such a prospective juror is excluded since that person's opinion will be based on data not produced in the trial. The attorney will have lost control, to some extent, of the trial dynamics. Worse, if that person is adverse to the attorney's case, and happens to be looked up to as an authority in jury deliberations, he or she may sway the entire panel.

§ 11.7 —Professional Assistance

In a major construction case where the stakes are high, the attorney should consider professional assistance in selecting juries.

In one construction case, the issue was the proper application of a coating on the coping of in-the-ground swimming pools in many states on the East Coast. The coating was chipping and the dealer alleged severe economic losses. The dealer's theory was that potential customers commonly swim in a neighbor's pool and become enamored with the idea of having one of their own, thus becoming prospective customers of the

---

[9] Discussions with John Lamberth, Ph.D., a social psychologist, faculty member in the Department of Psychology at Temple University and a recognized jury selection expert from West Chester, Pennsylvania.

pool company that installed it. In this case, the chipping of the coating was unsightly, along with other problems, and was deemed to be an adverse factor causing a loss of future sales. In addition, there were increased expenses in returning to the defective pools for maintenance.

A professional jury expert was engaged who prepared an analysis of the case and surveyed over 150 members of a past jury panel from the same county by phone. The survey was to determine the profile of the ideal juror and the probable response in damages. The attorneys in the matter felt the ideal juror would be a homeowner with a socioeconomic background suitable for purchasing pools of this type, and who would be offended by the manufacturer's failure to insure the quality control necessary for the proper application of the coating.

In fact, the professional reported back that his survey revealed that the ideal juror would be a single woman in her 20's or early 30's, preferably in a lower income group. During his survey, the consensus of those who responded favorably within that group indicated extreme dissatisfaction generally with manufacturers of defective household products (such as toasters, irons, coffee makers, and vacuum cleaners). Women in the category mentioned were least able to get the appliances working because they worked for a living and could not conveniently get back to the store or repair center. Consequently, they had a high degree of frustration and bias. It was this category of juror who apparently would respond best to liability and damages issues.

However, professional assistance has its limitations. I participated in the extensive selection of a jury in a major construction case representing a contractor. Our jury selection expert developed a suitable juror profile, as well as an unsuitable juror profile. A field investigation was conducted and other expensive techniques were used. A particular juror appeared quite suitable and the attorneys were ready to select him when our client told us to get rid of him as soon as possible. It turned out that our client had a contract with the town where the juror lived for the reconstruction of a sanitary sewer line on the very street where this particular juror resided. Our client had been informed by municipal officials of the dissatisfaction on the part of all homeowners on the street with the progress of the construction, traffic, dust, and noise control. The juror had presented himself in such a way as to gain acceptance on the jury with obviously predictable purposes.

§ 11.8 —Voir Dire

The trial begins with the voir dire. Once the theory of the case is adopted and in place through the gathered evidence, the case is advanced in the questions the attorney or the judge addresses to the panel or the prospective jurors. These questions should include key evidence the attorney intends to present. The judge, or in some jurisdictions, the attorney, should make sure that the jurors are well aware of what the attorney intends to prove, so that a commitment can be obtained from them to accept the client's story if they are satisfied with the degree of proof that is offered. If possible, use a tangible exhibit in questioning the jury. If this is not possible, a homey example may be used.

During voir dire, it is imperative that the attorney recognize and use cues from a prospective juror. At this point relationships should be assessed realistically. Do you have a better relationship with the judge than your adversary does? If so, potential jurors who show signs of submissiveness to the judge are, all other things equal, better for you. If your relationship with the judge is weak, or his or her analysis of your theory is unfavorable, then jurors who clash with the judge may be more acceptable to you. The relationship between the judge and jury and between the attorney and judge is often overlooked, but is one more part of the mosaic that must be evaluated. This is probably even more important in jurisdictions where attorney-conducted voir dire is prohibited.

The relationships between jurors can be critical. An evaluation of the jury as a group is often overlooked, even though in some instances this evaluation turns out to be as important as the individual evaluations of the jurors.

The point is, the voir dire should be used to make sure that you do not end up with someone (or, worse, a group) with a bias against you or your client and, on the positive side, to gain a commitment from the prospective juror that they will buy your story if they buy your proofs.

§ 11.9 Opening Statement

The next challenge is the opening statement. In any type of jury trial, the stated purpose of an opening statement to a jury is to inform them in a general way of the nature of the action and the basic facts so they can be better prepared to understand the evidence. The real purpose is to win the jury to your side (or, if the voir dire was successful, to keep them there) and gain a good settlement or winning verdict on behalf of your client.

In pursuing these goals, the advocate must take seriously the often-stated phrase that first impressions count. Important first impressions are mainly the conduct of the trial attorneys, what they have to say, and the appearance of the clients. It is really the performance of the attorney and the client's appearance that counts. Since most cases are won or lost during opening statement, this is the most important challenge of the trial process.[10]

---

[10] Stern, *Basic Techniques and Strategies in Trial Advocacy,* New Jersey Institute for Continuing Legal Education 11 (1983).

There are two levels of conversation a trial attorney must handle during a trial. One is the stated level of conversation with the factfinder, judge, or jury. The other is with the attorney's own client and with opposing counsel and his or her client. On this second level the construction trial attorney must master the technical aspects of the case to a degree sufficient to gain the respect, not only of his or her own client, but the other attorney-client team as well.

The primary goal of the trial is a favorable and early settlement. Settlements are achieved by clients. Thus, the opening statement provides the trial attorney with an opportunity to talk to the other lawyer's client directly. Hopefully, that person will know:

1. More about the subject matter of the case than anyone in the courtroom except your client and, therefore, the real problems in the case;
2. That the process is out of his or her control and in the hands of the lawyers;
3. Through what you say and how you say it in your opening statement, that he or she is in deep trouble. This leads to settlements.

There are four important points to remember in the opening statement of a construction litigation case tried to a jury. First, you must explain the context or history behind the point that you are trying to make factually in the case. In an automobile accident personal injury case, almost everyone knows about cars, brakes, red lights, stop signs, and so forth. As far as damages are concerned, everyone has experienced pain and suffering and at least knows about loss of wages, medical expenses, and the like. In a construction litigation case, on the other hand, you must explain to the jury the trade or profession involved in order for them to understand the evidence produced in the trial. While this is normally and properly done through an expert witness, there may be other witnesses who precede the expert and can provide important foundation evidence, although they may not be as articulate as you are in succinctly explaining the technical issue at stake.

Second, an important and difficult issue in construction cases is the matter of causation. In other types of cases, causation may not be a difficult issue. For example, in an automobile accident, the alleged negligence of the defendant, the accident, and the injury are almost simultaneous so that proximate cause is not really a problem. In a construction litigation dispute, however, it may be much more difficult for a jury to understand the interplay between a contractor's loss of profits and the interference by another contractor. Further, the damages, for example, office overhead, may be foreign to a jury's understanding. The necessity of supervisory personnel, a jobsite trailer, insurance, and other factors contributing to the damage claim may not even come up in the trial for days or even weeks.

The intervening sets of witnesses may not have meaning unless the general scope of the claim is outlined to the jury in the opening statement.

Third, the jury should be told at the outset of certain terms or expressions that will come up during the trial so that they will be able to understand them. The construction and the specialty trades have their own language. For example, stones and dirt in the road construction context may be referred to as drainage windrow aggregate, borrow excavation, or unsuitable material. Not only should the terms be defined, but the reasoning behind the explanation should be given. For example, the cost of different types of dirt, its availability, its transportation, and its ultimate purpose should be explained to the jury if that is the nub of the dispute. "Cutting" and "filling" should be explained as well as the importance of a proper design in the first place to utilize on-site materials wherever possible. If all of this is explained in the opening, it will be much easier for the jury to understand the testimony of the witnesses later, especially the lay witnesses.

Fourth, not only should the context be explained as well as the terminology, but, if at all possible, demonstrative evidence should be used in the opening statement, even if it consists only of printed words on a board or an overhead projector. For example, if the subject of the dispute is dirt, either because of excess or deficient quantities, or the quality of the material, a simple sketch to show the function of dirt in the construction process will help the jury understand the facts and be more sympathetic to your point.

Further, you can define what you mean by soil aggregate. You can tell the jury that it consists of particles or fragments of stone, slag, gravel, or sand with some silt-clay or stone dust in it. Whether the specifications for this material have been met by the supplier could mean the difference between the failure and success of a constructed project. The specifications may call for a percentage of the material to pass through a certain size sieve. Why the material should be made up of different percentages of its component parts is something that should be explained to the jury in the opening statement so they can appreciate the importance of the point and not regard it as nitpicking.

Definitions are especially important in a situation where the damage has not yet occurred. In other words, if a core is taken from a roadway and the base or sub-base is found to be insufficient, it may be necessary for the contractor to tear up the road and replace it. This may give rise to a claim against the supplier of the material. The claim will occur before the road has failed or even been accepted by the construction authority. Thus, it is not only important to explain to the jury the requirements of the base and sub-base for supporting the road and allowing for drainage, but the effects of failing to use the proper materials should also be explained. This is best done by a sketch or an actual core of the material.[11]

---

[11] Julian, *Opening Statements* § 9.0 in Structure and Demolition of Cases.

§ 11.11 FACT WITNESSES

Often, if the matter is given advance thought, pretrial stipulations can lead to agreement on the admissibility of physical evidence. Devices such as requests for admission can be used to insure the admissibility of tangible items. These are powerful tools to use in the opening statement to the jury.

In summary, the opening statement to a jury is often the determining factor in the case. In construction litigation cases, unique possibilities are available for the attorney in effectively conducting the voir dire and producing a winning opening to the jury.

§ 11.10 Direct Examination

After jury selection and the opening statement, the next step in presenting the case is the introduction of evidence through the direct testimony of witnesses, both lay and expert. Witnesses provide the primary source of evidence upon which the jury relies in reaching a decision in the case.

The purpose of producing witnesses is to provide evidence in support of the essential elements of the substantive law you are required to comply with. How well this is done may determine which side will prevail. Thus, there are two reasons for direct examination: one is to make out a prima facie case so that the judge does not throw your case out of court or suppress your defense. The second reason is to win.[12]

Keep in mind that the judge determines whether someone is allowed to be a witness and whether evidence is admissible. The judge will not permit a witness to testify about something unless evidence is introduced that indicates that the witness has personal knowledge concerning the matter of the proposed testimony. The evidence to show that a witness can testify can come from the very same witness.

In a construction litigation matter, direct examination is the heart of the case. The attorney repeats the theme of the client's position in a forceful, yet humane manner, in readily understandable terms, and within a context a jury will understand.

Remember the comments concerning the three unique aspects of an opening statement in a construction case: context, terms, and demonstrative evidence. These principles also apply to direct examination in construction cases.

§ 11.11 Fact Witnesses

In the direct examination of a fact witness, the key to success is preparing the witness and structuring his or her testimony. While the witness may

---

[12] Stern, *Basic Techniques* at 45.

know a lot about the project or job in issue, the construction litigation attorney must know the elements needed to support the case. These elements guide the selection of witnesses and determine their responsibility in proving the case. Once this is decided, the attorney must then structure the questioning. But it is still a good idea to brief the witness in connection with the other issues in the case. Opposing attorneys sometimes have a nasty habit of bringing out other facts within that witness's knowledge that can be harmful to the case.

Preliminary questioning is necessary not only to lay the foundation for the witness's ability to testify on personal knowledge, but in order to give the jury the benefit of that witness's training, education, and experience, and to provide the context of the testimony. Furthermore, oftentimes the weight or credibility the jury gives the witness is determined by the witness's preliminary questioning.

For example, if the critical question is the structural integrity of a brick wall, it will be necessary for you to have the mason testify concerning the mixing of the mortar and the proportions of sand, cement, water, and other additives, as well as exactly how the wall was laid up. More importantly, it will help you persuade the jury that your client did a proper job by having him further testify about how he learned this from his father, about the fact that he is a union member and has been doing this for 30 years, and about why he did what he did, not just what he did. This type of testimony will provide the jury with a complete understanding of what was done in terms of building the brick wall, and they will learn about masonry as a trade; hence, the jury will have a foundation of knowledge to prepare them for the expert witness. Your opponent may have an expert who is an expert civil engineer but may not have laid a brick in his life.

It is in this fashion that you will be able to repeat the theme of your case—through the testimony of the worker who mixed the mortar, the mason who laid up the wall, and the expert who provides opinion testimony. Try to be sure that all use the same terminology. Do not hesitate to use actual photographs of the wall in question. The witness who is a mason can provide the foundation for introducing those photographs into evidence. A videotape of that witness actually laying the brick would be helpful in allowing the jury to understand how the work was done.

An example of the questioning of the mason is the following:

Q: Good afternoon, Mr. Brown, what do you do for a living?
A: I am a brick mason.
Q: What is a brick mason?
A: Someone who builds buildings or other structures out of blocks and bricks, mostly the kind of concrete blocks and red bricks you see all over, based on specifications provided in blueprints or plans.
Q: How long have you been doing that?

A: About 30 years, ever since I was 18 years old.
Q: How did you learn to do this?
A: My father was a brick layer and when I was a teenager, I would go where he was working every once in a while and watch him work. I got interested in it and I began to work part-time on construction sites cleaning up and everything. Then I began carrying the sacks of cement and helping to shovel the sand. After a while, they let me mix the mortar, you know, I added the water and mixed the water, sand, and cement under the supervision of the master mason.
Q: What happened after that?
A: Finally, I was apprenticed to a master mason and did the same thing, but he let me actually lay the bricks or block and after a while, he taught me all the tricks of the trade. I would actually set up the leveling string and make sure that the wall was level and plumb, you know, straight up and down.
Q: How long was your apprenticeship?
A: Three years.
Q: How did you learn to read blueprints and specifications?
A: I was sent to vocational school for courses and, of course, the master mason.
Q: What were the tricks of the trade you mentioned?
A: Things that weren't in the books, like the air temperature you could lay bricks or blocks in, whether it was too hot or too cold, the proper consistency of the mortar, working with different additives to the mortar for color and stuff like that.

Specific questions relating to the area of expertise in dispute should be elicited. After the preliminary questioning, the jury should have no doubt that this witness is a highly qualified, competent tradesman, dedicated to his trade, and therefore, credible.

§ 11.12 Expert Witnesses

We discuss the use of consultants and the selection of experts and their use at trial in **Chapter 4**. This section focuses on the unique utilization of expert witnesses in construction litigation during direct examination.

Preliminarily, the trial attorney has the final word on just who will be called to testify at the trial. When it comes to expert witnesses, the trial attorney should not overlook using the client, who may be perfectly qualified and suitable to testify at the trial.

The purpose of using an expert witness is summed up in Federal Rule of Evidence 702: "If scientific, technical, or other specialized knowledge will assist the trier of fact to understand the evidence or to determine a fact in issue, a witness qualified as an expert by knowledge, skill, experience, training, or education, may testify thereto in the form of an opinion or otherwise."

The key is whether the expert's testimony will assist the jury in its job of understanding what is sought to be proved, or help them determine a material fact.

The important point is to select a scientific, technical, or other specialized expert who is a practitioner in the field and who can educate the jury using demonstrative evidence with simplicity and clarity. As previously stated, demonstrative evidence is uniquely suitable for construction litigation cases. However, that evidence must be introduced with the proper foundation and can only have its maximum impact in the hands of a skilled person. Demonstrative evidence must be explained to the jury, and this is best done by an expert.

While there are many books and articles written on the subject of expert witnesses, construction litigation presents a real challenge in the attempt to simplify the presentation to the jury. One of the problems is the esoteric nature of the scientific principles inherent in construction products, methods, and machines. The further challenge is the extensive documentation often encountered.

The solution to this problem is using the expert to create almost an exception to the hearsay rule. Federal Rule of Evidence 703 permits the expert's opinion to be based on facts or data that are not in evidence, if the facts are the type that are reasonably relied upon by experts in that field in making such opinions. Furthermore, facts can include the opinions of others, subject to the same requirement. Thus, volumes of written materials, job records, diaries, and other documentation can be marshalled and fed to the jury by the expert, either as a fact or a series of facts under Rule 702, or as the basis for the opinion under Rule 703.

For example, a young woman who dove from a county bridge sustained serious personal injuries when she struck a submerged island in the middle of a stream over which a new bridge had been constructed by the county. The plaintiff's theory of liability against the owner and designer was that the bridge design created a foreseeable hazard because the area where the old bridge was located had historically been used for recreational purposes, including swimming and diving.

The river was an alluvial stream carrying particles of sand. A civil engineer surveyed the area of the bridge, developed a profile of the cross-section of the river at the site of the accident, and conducted hydraulic studies to determine the direction and velocity of flow. He discovered the presence of an island near the middle of the bridge just below the surface of the water which was "cedar water" and highly reflective of the noonday sun; this was the direction the injured party faced when she dove off the bridge.

Another civil engineer, a soil specialist, took samples of the bed of the river and the water upstream of the bridge, and performed borings of the island. Using samples of the sandbed and sand in suspension in the water, he demonstrated that the island was formed from the deposition of sand particles held in suspension.

Another engineer, who was a mathematician, took data available in discovery from the county, the bridge designer, and the contractor, and showed mathematically that the equilibrium of the river, which was disturbed by the widening of the cross-section of the river at the bridge, would be restored within a certain number of years after construction. Thus, the formation of the island in its existing location was certain in fact and predictable in time.

A civil engineer, who was an expert in bridge design, noted that at the time the new bridge was constructed, the river was significantly widened. He opined that, based on this information and the opinions of the other experts, this widening caused the velocity of the water to slow down and deposit particles in the streambed at the center of the bridge, creating a foreseeably dangerous condition for swimmers.

Since the work-product of the surveying engineer, soil specialist, and mathematician consisted of facts or data of a type reasonably relied upon by bridge design experts in forming opinions or inferences inherent in the design and construction of bridges, it was not necessary to call each of these witnesses because of the flexibility of Federal Rule of Evidence 703. The bridge design expert was able to effectively use and convey the findings and opinions of these other professionals. Further, since the methodology they adopted was commonly used in their profession in developing their opinions, it was not necessary to introduce this data in evidence. Thus, Rule 703, or its state court equivalent, when properly utilized, can simplify complex trials both in terms of number of witnesses and introduction of data.

In presenting evidence on direct examination of expert witnesses, it should be presented in four stages. First, the experts should be qualified. This is something the judge will determine based upon the witnesses' own testimony concerning their qualifications. Second, the experts have undoubtedly gone to a lot of trouble, expense, and time in reading, studying, and analyzing the problem. This should all be spelled out to the jury to impress them with the thoroughness of the experts and to make them more amenable to accepting their opinions. Third, the experts should be asked for an opinion. Fourth, the experts should take the time to carefully, methodically, and clearly explain why they arrived at that opinion. In any but the simplest cases, the experts should try to use the terms that the attorney explained in the opening and that have been used by preceding witnesses. If the experts use different terminology in everyday work, they should be asked to explain the equivalent terminology so as to tie in the testimony of previous witnesses. It is difficult to overkill in a situation like this.

In order to insure the adequate performance of the experts, not only should they know the questions the attorney intends to ask (and, of course, the answers they intend to give), but their testimony should be rehearsed so that their performance matches the attorney's level of skill in the preparation of the case.

§ 11.13 Documents and Demonstrative Evidence

Construction litigation often involves voluminous quantities of documentation. The challenge for the trial attorney in the face of this is three-fold: (1) determine the bases for authentication and admissibility of the document sought to be introduced into evidence to the jury; (2) develop a plan for its expeditious presentation; and (3) implement the plan in such a way that the presentation is persuasive.

The problem with respect to the bases for authentication and admission into evidence is the fact that documents are hearsay and, under Federal Rule of Evidence 802, not admissible except as prescribed by court rules or statute. There are five ways to overcome this problem with other Federal Rules of Evidence. It is beyond the scope of this chapter to involve the reader in an extended discussion of the mechanics of utilizing these rules. Rather, the following chart showing the rule number, name, and witness requirements is presented as an overview.

Rule	Name	Witnesses Required
803(5)	Recorded recollection	Witness who prepared document
803(6)	Records of regularly conducted activity (business records)	Custodian or other qualified witness
803(8)	Public records	Public official (Rule 1005) or certificate (Rule 1002)
1006	Summaries	Witness who prepared chart, summary, or calculation
703	Expert testimony	Expert

For example, documentation for the pickup or delivery of material for a jobsite may be contemporaneously created and recorded by the truck driver or a clerk at the point of pickup or delivery. The person who measured the load on the truck (weight) or counted the loads (volume) could

§ 11.13 DOCUMENTS

testify to the weights or quantities. It is unlikely that the records (delivery tickets) he or others made will refresh his recollections. If he testifies that he has no personal recollection of these details but that he contemporaneously recorded the information, the document can be admitted into evidence (Rule 803(5)). However, the compilation of the consolidated records for weeks or months, if compiled regularly in the course of the trucking business or by the contractor at the point of delivery, can be introduced by the custodian of the records (Rule 803(6)). This affords the trial attorney the chance to introduce into evidence for the jury all the necessary data to support a claim with one witness.

If the claim is a delay claim caused by a slowdown in delivery of the material under a supply contract as against a predetermined schedule, this information can be expeditiously presented under Rule 1006 in a chart showing the schedule as well as the record of deliveries. The best way of presenting the case would be through an expert testifying as to the ultimate issue of delay (Rule 704) using the chart and its impact on the job to support his conclusions.

From this it can be seen that information can be presented to the jury by a witness, using documents to refresh the witness's recollection, if necessary, or introducing the document itself under Rule 803(5) by calling the witness who now has insufficient recollection to enable him to testify fully and accurately. The process of calling successive witnesses to produce increments of facts or individual documents is a time-consuming, tedious task and to be avoided unless the testimony or document is a "smoking gun."

The next most expeditious way of presenting documentary evidence is under the business records exception to the hearsay rule (Rule 803(6)), which enables one witness to authenticate and gain admission of many volumes of business records, if need be.

Another method is the public records exception (Rule 803(8)). For example, in one case tried to a judge, the critical issue was the existence of a severe thunderstorm at a particular location and time of the day some years before the trial. Certainly, lay testimony could have been produced on this issue from a number of witnesses who were present. The opponent had witnesses whose recollection was different. However, evidence of the date, time, origin, size, location, boundaries, and severity of thunderstorms in the area on the day in question, together with the nature and degree of precipitation, and accompanying lightning (and thunder), was all introduced into evidence by public records. These records were certified by the United States Department of Commerce, Information Services Division, National Climatic Center, Asheville, North Carolina, without the necessity of a witness.

This documentary evidence included:

1. Surface weather observations
2. Radar summary charts
3. Satellite photoprints
4. Radar scope photographs.

In the hands of the expert, who was really testifying as to causation, there was not the slightest doubt about the weather conditions.

Although a witness in the courtroom is not necessary for purposes of evidence introduction, the expert should be there to explain the evidence for purposes of persuasion.

Under Rule 1006, Summaries, essential information from voluminous books, records, or documents not only can be expeditiously presented to the jury, but it can be introduced in a very persuasive fashion. Labor hour overruns are generally an element of damages for delay, disruption, or acceleration cases. Data from certified payroll records can be helpful in demonstrating and documenting labor force expenditures. Introducing each page of the payroll data would be absurd. Summaries of this data, especially in a graphic time line format, provide visual appeal for very detailed records.

Use of an expert witness, as described above, does not require the trial attorney to introduce the act and documents into evidence as exhibits. On the other hand, the purpose of introducing documents into evidence is to support a particular thesis and to persuade the jury. However, it is of little consequence that the documents are not in evidence if the expert has provided testimony in the form of an opinion or otherwise under Rule 702. Under the Federal Rules of Evidence, the expert can even take the next step and testify as to the ultimate issue under Rule 704(a). For example, on construction delay cases, a scheduling expert can prepare an as-built schedule reflecting the actual progress of the project as delayed by certain events. The schedule is developed from daily reports and diaries. The jury need not examine every daily report, and indeed, this would detract from the advocate's case. The scheduling expert may testify that such daily reports are the type of documents upon which scheduling experts rely. Thus, the expert can get to the heart of the delay issues, but allow the expeditious development of a factual issue.

Documentary evidence presents problems not only in the sheer massiveness of documents, but also in the form and sequence of them. Summaries and expert testimony overcome the voluminous aspect of large numbers of documents. With appropriate demonstrative aids, they enable the trial attorney to shape the form in which the evidence is presented as well as the sequence of the documents, which may be important to an understanding of the problem in the minds of the jury.

A technique that is helpful in construction litigation is to photographically enlarge one or more important documents or reproduce them on an overhead projector. The overhead projector is preferable because it enables the trial attorney to have an expert focus on something for a short period of time, magnifying it on the screen, and then turn the switch off so that the jury is not distracted by the exhibit when moving on to the next point. Since clear plastic copying material is readily available, even opposing exhibits can be copied quickly and put up on the screen, enabling the expert to draw the jury's attention to the desired point using a crayon or working pen on the exhibit copy.

In summary, construction litigation disputes can lead to serious problems in introducing documents into evidence in a jury trial case. This problem can not only be overcome, but can be used to the benefit of the proponent whose foundation is those documents by effective trial strategies and tactics.

§ 11.14 Closing Arguments and Jury Charges

In a closing argument to the jury in a construction litigation case, the trial attorney should use the opportunity to clarify any parts of the case that were not sufficiently clear, either during the plaintiff's or defendant's presentation. Not only should "legalese" be avoided in construction litigation cases, but excessively technical terminology should be avoided to prevent the jury from just giving up in its attempts to understand the facts of the case as you present them.

Certainly, demonstrative evidence should be used in the summation if it is permitted in the jurisdiction and if it will simplify and clarify your position. Keeping in mind the theme of the case, the closing argument should tie together the remarks made in the opening, the points made during direct and cross-examinations of witnesses, and exhibits introduced into evidence. Because construction cases are often very long, the advocate should assure that the theme and theory of the case are once again explained. Further, the closing appeal should address what the advocate knows the judge will charge as far as the substantive law of the case after the closing arguments are concluded. If written interrogatories will be submitted to the jury in complex construction cases, blown-up versions, if permitted, should be referred to in the closing argument just like sample ballots are circulated before general elections.

Since the closing argument is the last time to present anything to the jury, use visual aids of your own in summing up, if permitted. Better yet, mark up exhibits introduced by your opponent to drive home your point. Use their exhibits against them as explained in the preceding section. Your expert's marked up copy of your opponent's exhibit will have, hopefully, been marked in evidence and can be used in summation.

The substantive law of the case will be read to the jury by the judge in the form of the charge to the jury. In more complicated cases, like many construction cases, written interrogatories are often submitted to the jury to assist them in thinking through the elements of particular claims or defenses and to determine on what basis they are rendering their verdict. On the one hand, the interrogatories can be helpful to the jury in discharging its obligation to the court in following the law, but on the other hand, inconsistent answers lead to confusion and more problems than they solve.

The solution to all of this in construction litigation is, again, to stick to the theme of your case right through the presentation of evidence into the closing argument and the charge to the jury. Always try to incorporate into your closing argument significant points raised by witnesses or evidence during the trial that can be tied to what you know the judge will tell the jury during the charge.[13] The principles of primacy and recency still take effect. What the jury heard first and last will be more easily remembered than what is in the middle; those things that were repeated throughout the trial will also make an impression. The process of *jury nullification* will tend to make the jurors either not hear or not see or accept evidence or other proofs that do not fit their notion of who should win, which was probably greatly decided near the beginning of the case.

On the other hand, it is difficult for the average person, no matter how biased, to write down an answer on a written interrogatory that directly conflicts with a piece of documentary or demonstrative evidence. The construction litigator should always have a draft of the jury charge prepared for the judge. The proposed charge should be prepared in such a way that the words describing the substantive law lend themselves to the evidence that the lawyer knows will be introduced during the trial of the case.

§ 11.15 Advocating a Construction Claim to a Judge

The problems facing an attorney trying a construction dispute to a judge without a jury are significantly different than with a jury. The four main points of difference are (1) the application of the Federal Rules of Evidence to admissibility, (2) oral argument, (3) drafting findings of fact and conclusions of law, and (4) the outcome of appeals.

Preliminarily, judges are no better than jurors in most cases when it comes to evaluating and analyzing scientific and technical matters involved in construction cases. A judge may be educated, trained, and experienced, and thus an expert in analyzing evidence in general. However, the

---

[13] *See* Fed. R. Civ. P. 51.

§ 11.15 ADVOCATING CLAIM TO JUDGE

judge's exposure to this evidence and type of dispute will, in most cases, come exclusively from the trial itself and not from general education, training, or experience in the construction industry. Thus, everything that was said about presenting a case to the jury in this regard applies in a bench trial.

On the other hand, without a jury, the judge occupies the dual capacity of factfinder and referee. A judge will be much more flexible in admitting evidence of probative value which may not be admissible in a jury trial. The result is a speedier resolution time as compared with the time to try the same case to a jury. In addition, certain evidence and theories may be considered by a judge, even though he or she may not allow a jury to do so. For example, judges may consider evidence of total cost type damages as discussed in **Chapter 7**, but may be reluctant to allow such evidence to be presented to a jury.

While a juror is precluded from expressing opinions during the course of a trial to the attorneys, a judge, in a normal situation, begins to exhibit feelings about a case through rulings, comments, and other indicia as the case unfolds. No matter how circumspect the judge may be, the judicial attitude begins to appear at some point. If it does not, make sure that it does.

While jurors can sit through a whole trial without understanding what is going on, the judge will be compelled at the conclusion of the case, in most instances, to specially find the facts and state conclusions of law in arriving at a decision. This means that if judges do not understand something, they are likely to tell the attorney or the witness. Judges may even question the witness to ensure an understanding of the operative facts, something jurors cannot do. Not only do such questions enlighten the judge, but they provide the attorney with indications of the judge's concerns.

While a judge may participate in settlement discussions during a jury trial, this will not normally be the case in a nonjury situation. This is unfortunate because judicial intervention has helped attorneys settle many construction cases being tried before juries. Although another judge can be assigned to help settle the case, the new judge may not be conversant with the details. However, it is possible to involve another judge in the details to facilitate settlement.

In a major construction case I tried, the supervising judge assigned the trial to one judge and assigned another judge to evaluate the case in an attempt to settle it. The "settlement judge" required the submission of settlement memoranda and exhibits from both sides on the issues of liability and damages. He then reviewed them and gave his opinion as to the issues. What occurred was a variation of a minitrial as explained in **Chapter 10**. The same judge could have also filled the role of mediator along the way.

Since the trial attorney normally cannot pick the judge, the attorney should become as familiar as possible with the trial judge on a personal basis and with as much understanding of that judge's idiosyncrasies as possible. All judges have preferences regarding oral arguments, briefs or memoranda, objections, and evidence introduction. If the trial counsel is not from the jurisdiction in which the case is to be tried, it would be wise to associate with a local attorney who can better perform this function. Even though the need of a local attorney is diminishing, the desirability of it remains.[14]

What all of this means to the trial attorney in a construction litigation context is that the attorney should get to know the judge as well as possible, plan the trial minimizing the use of technical approaches to the rules of evidence, try to engage the court in arguments in an effort to find out where the case is going in the judge's mind and, if necessary, ask the court to assign the case to another judge for purposes of settlement discussions.

Construction litigation cases tend to revolve around documentary evidence and demonstrative exhibits. Therefore, caution should be taken in connection with the appeal of a judge's decision when, under Federal Rule of Evidence 52, or its local equivalent, the judge has prepared findings of fact and conclusions of law. Every lawyer knows that judge-tried cases are harder to reverse on factual issues because of the trial judge's ability to observe a witness's demeanor and credibility. While some appellate courts still defer to the trial court's findings of fact under the "clearly erroneous" rule, many appellate courts do not, especially in cases where documents or exhibits are crucial to the decision. This is often the case with construction litigation.

The rule relating to findings by the court provides that: "Findings of fact, whether based on oral or documentary evidence, shall not be set aside unless clearly erroneous, and due regard shall be given to the opportunity of the trial court to judge of the credibility of the witnesses."[15] Nevertheless, a number of appellate courts have taken the position that trial court findings based on an evaluation of documentary proof and the drawing of inferences from that proof do not rely on the trial court's assessment of the credibility of witnesses.[16] This would eliminate the need for the appellate court's deference to the trial court's findings in such cases. If this is true, in construction litigation tried to a judge, the suggested findings of fact the attorney submits should reflect the court's findings concerning the credibility or demeanor of witnesses, as well as on the documentary proof. Many construction cases lend themselves to this type of approach. For example, in construction delay cases, the credibility of the expert witnesses and the accuracy of project schedules are distinct matters to be addressed in the proposed findings of fact.

---

[14] Frazier v. Heebe, 482 U.S. 641 (1987); Thorstenn v. Barnard, 842 F.2d 1393 (1988).
[15] Fed. R. Civ. P. 52(a).
[16] Fed. R. Civ. P. 52(a), Notes of Advisory Committee on Rules, 1985 Amendment.

In general, judges are no different than anyone else when it comes to appreciating the significance of photographs, schedules, models, summaries, and other devices to efficiently and dramatically present voluminous materials or complex construction problems. The difference is that in a jury trial, the inferences the jury draws from an exhibit are largely unknown; a judge will make them known. Some appellate courts will draw their own inferences and may arrive at completely different results.

§ 11.16 Use of Special Masters

In general, masters are professional appointees of judges to perform certain judicial duties.[17] Courts have always found inherent power to appoint and use masters for any number of purposes.[18] Many lawyers are familiar with references to masters in chancery or equity practice in complicated matters regarding accountings and other matters. Courts have extended the use of masters from chancery to courts of law. Reference by a United States district court judge to federal magistrates under Federal Rule of Evidence 53 or under United States Code § 636[19] can be done in certain circumstances that can be helpful in construction cases.

Under the statute, magistrates can decide nondispositive pretrial motions subject to review by the federal court judge. Under the rule, upon the finding of an exceptional condition, a federal magistrate can function as a master under the reporting procedures of Rule 53(e). Either way, the construction litigator should treat the magistrate just as a judge.

In many construction cases, numerous heated battles are generated by depositions, producing and inspecting documents, and the inspection of property that may divert from the effort to expeditiously and effectively resolve the matter. The construction litigator involved in a complex dispute in a court trial context should keep in mind the possibility of having the judge refer the conduct of discovery to a master for purposes of conducting these pretrial procedures. The special master can intervene in the discovery phase to expeditiously resolve and reduce the time of unusually protracted or contested procedural issues.[20]

In some construction litigation there are multiple parties, many witnesses, many attorneys, and complex issues involving the exercise of the attorney-client privilege or other privileges, as well as issues regarding confidentiality of information contained in documents. In the normal

---

[17] *Ex parte* Paterson, 253 U.S. 312–13, 40 S. Ct. 543, 64 L. Ed. 919 (1920).
[18] 8 Fed. Proc., L. E. § 20.14.
[19] 28 U.S.C. § 636 (b)(1)(A), (B) (1988).
[20] An excellent book on this subject is W. Brazil, G. Hazard & P. Rice, *Managing Complex Litigation: A Practical Guide to the Use of Special Masters* (ABA Law Foundation 1983).

course, objections raised by attorneys in the course of depositions, with attendant instructions not to answer questions or not to produce documents, will lead to numerous extensive and expensive motions. These motions must await the normal time period for the typing of transcripts or payment of expedited rates. This delays the discovery, interrupts the flow of crucial information, and adds to the cost.

The motions may necessitate the use of protective orders to limit the dissemination of information, including special provisions regarding the filing of pleadings which are open to the public. These motions are "paper heavy." Briefs must be written. Judges do not generally like to decide these cases because they are as time-consuming for them to review and decide as for the attorneys to prepare. This can extend the time and expense of already complex construction cases immeasurably.

The process of having these discovery matters decided and enforced can be fragmented and disruptive. If an objection is made to a question during deposition, and the attorney instructs the witness not to answer the question, months can pass before gaining the answer to a particular question that may be critical to complete discovery. This disrupts the discovery plan. In cases without a judge specially assigned to bring a complex matter to completion, the judge who decides a particular motion may not be the same judge who hears and decides other motions, by reason of reassignment, retirement, rotation, and the like.

In such cases, appointing a master to actually attend and supervise the taking of the deposition, with power to rule on objections as they arise, can move the matter along significantly. The cost of this person will be shared by the participants and, thus, the cost per party will be very reasonable. The proceedings can take place in the attorney's office. In the case of a recalcitrant witness, the proceedings may take place in a room in the courthouse near the courtroom of the trial judge. The point is that the construction litigator must deal effectively with discovery problems using the available power of the court.

For example, Federal Rule 16(c)(6) permits the judge or the magistrate to refer discovery matters to the magistrate or a master. **Section 11.17** contains a form of order for preliminary reference by a judge to a master to supervise discovery under the powers enumerated in Federal Rule of Civil Procedure 37.[21]

The construction litigator must identify and address potential sources of discovery delays and expenditures as much in advance as possible in order to save time and money. In our jurisdiction, a well-known case involved an explosion in a plant that resulted in extensive property damage, deaths, and injuries. On the day of the accident, the owner and designer of the plant (the future defendants), presumably with their insurance carriers,

---

[21] Manual for Complex Litigation, § 3.21 (5th ed. 1981).

rushed their attorneys and investigators to the scene, developing work-product in anticipation of litigation. Obviously, the attorneys for the deceased and injured were not able to marshal their forces until a much later date, only to be confronted with the work-product privilege, the attorney/client privilege, claims of confidentiality relating to the chemical processes involved, and other privileges.

These privileges were strenuously defended by the defendants and hotly contested by the plaintiffs. The pretrial discovery process became bogged down at every deposition, interrogatory, and document production request. Only after the appointment of a special master for purposes of hearing and ruling on discovery objections, backed up by the trial judge, was the litigation able to move ahead and bring the case to a conclusion.

§ 11.17 —Sample Order for Appointment of Special Master

SAMPLE PRETRIAL ORDER—APPOINTMENT OF SPECIAL MASTER TO SUPERVISE DISCOVERY*

A pretrial conference was held on the _____ day of _____, 19___, wherein or as a result of which the following proceedings were had:

A. The following counsel were present representing the plaintiffs: (list).

B. The following counsel were present representing the defendants: (list).

C. It appearing at such pretrial conference that both plaintiffs and defendants plan to take the depositions of numerous persons and that because of the complexity of the issues many questions will arise regarding the relevance and materiality of the testimony and exhibits; that all parties expect to request the production and inspection of documents under Federal Rule of Civil Procedure 34, and that many questions will arise concerning privilege and confidential treatment of documents; and that all parties expect to request numerous and complex interrogatories, the Court (with the consent of counsel) hereby appoints _____ as special master in this cause to supervise such discovery proceedings.

D. The special master is hereby vested with the powers enumerated in Federal Rule of Civil Procedure 37, and all proceedings had before him and appeals from his orders, if any, shall be controlled by that rule.

E. The special master shall make periodic reports to the Court, at intervals of not less than _____ days, regarding the matters committed to him under this order of reference or by subsequent Order of the Court.

---

*This sample pretrial order is based on an order by Judge George H. Boldt appointing a special master in Washington v. General Elec., Civil Action No. 5271 (W.D. Wash.). This order can be adapted to the appointment of a magistrate to supervise discovery.

Copyright is not claimed as to any part of the original work prepared by a United States government officer or employee as part of that person's official duties.

F. Compensation allowed the special master for his services shall be fixed by Order of the Court whenever it may appear appropriate to do so. At that time, the Court will allocate the special master's compensation between the parties, and such allocation shall be taxable as costs in this cause at the close of the case within the Court's discretion.

Dated this _____ day of _____, 19___.

_____
JUDGE

§ 11.18 Conclusion

Construction court trials offer the litigator an opportunity to exploit the unique aspects of construction processes and projects to the client's benefit using techniques available only in judicial proceedings. Early recognition of evidence problems that will be confronted at trial is essential to a proper presentation. Adopting available procedures to problems inherent in presenting construction matters to judge, jury, or master is essential to reduce costs, speed the judicial process, and present the client's case in its best light.

PART IV
TRIAL ISSUES

CHAPTER 12
THE AFFIRMATIVE CASE
John W. Hinchey, Esquire

John W. Hinchey is a partner in the law firm of Phillips, Hinchey & Reid, Atlanta, Georgia. He holds law degrees from Emory University, Harvard University, and Oxford University, and is admitted to practice before the Supreme Court of the United States, the United States Court of Appeals for the Eleventh Circuit, the United States District Courts in Georgia, and the Supreme Court of Georgia. He is a Division Chairman of the American Bar Association's Forum on the Construction Industry, a vice-chairman of the ABA's Fidelity and Surety Committee of the Tort and Insurance Practice Section, and a vice-chairman of the ABA's General Practice Section's ADR Committee. He is an approved arbitrator for the American Arbitration Association and concentrates his practice in the area of construction claims and litigation. Mr. Hinchey has written and lectured extensively on construction-related subjects for the American Bar Association, the American Arbitration Association, the Northwest Center for Professional Education, the University of Tulsa, various state and local bar associations and other construction-oriented groups and associations. Most recently he has published articles in *Arbitration Journal* (June 1986) and *Tort & Insurance Law Journal* (Vol. 22). A more complete biographical sketch of Mr. Hinchey appears in *Who's Who in American Law* (5th ed. 1987).

§ 12.1   Reconstructing the Past
§ 12.2   Developing the Theme
§ 12.3   Introducing the Case
§ 12.4   —Keep It Simple
§ 12.5   —Use the Dramatic Method
§ 12.6   —Reach Out and Grip Someone
§ 12.7   —Be and Appear Sincere
§ 12.8   —Develop Your Talents to Best Advantage
§ 12.9   —Be Accurate, but Don't Argue
§ 12.10 —Use Visuals
§ 12.11 —Confront Problems with the Case
§ 12.12 —Rehearse

§ 12.13 —The Best and Last Chance
§ 12.14 Presenting the Case
§ 12.15 —Proof Strategies
§ 12.16 —Typical Proof Strategy
§ 12.17 —General Tips in Witness Presentation
§ 12.18 —Expert Testimony
§ 12.19 —Real and Demonstrative Evidence
§ 12.20 —Redirect Testimony
§ 12.21 —Summarizing the Case

§ 12.1 Reconstructing the Past

> "History, with its flickering lamp,
> stumbles along the trail of the past,
> trying to reconstruct its scenes,
> to revive its echoes,
> and kindle with pale gleams
> the passion of former days."[1]

Construction litigation, like history, looks to the past. It is retrospective, not prospective. And, the past can never be seen, heard, touched, tasted, or smelled with the same full appreciation as the five senses experience the present. Rather, the past is seen "through a glass darkly," in fragments that can only suggest wholeness, and in bits and pieces that must be discovered, collected, arranged, and rearranged to reveal the original pattern. An example of a jigsaw puzzle dumped on the table is only partially apt, since a jigsaw puzzle has all of its pieces included, our task being merely to find and put them together. However, all that occurred on a completed construction project can never be fully known.

Therefore, it becomes the task of the historian and the construction litigator to reconstruct the past. It is true that neither can completely reconstruct the scenes, amplify the echoes, nor rekindle the passions of the past; but, those who do it better will win more Pulitzer prizes or construction disputes.

It may be that those who practice construction law have an advantage over attorneys in other practices. Why? Because architects, contractors, engineers, and lately, even owners, have learned to "put it on paper," or, in recent years, on audio or video tapes. They know that what they are doing now may be reexamined later. Therefore, they are increasingly more

---

[1] Winston Churchill, speaking in the House of Commons on November 12, 1940, *quoted in* W. Manchester, The Last Lion, Winston Spencer Churchill: Alone, 1932–1940 ii (1988).

§ 12.1 RECONSTRUCTING THE PAST

careful to record every event or communication of substance. Hence, the task of the construction litigator is aided by this recorded history.

But, there is frequently a problem with the reconstruction of case history. Once you take the case, you may find that key facts are missing. If so, where do you go? To whom do you talk? Suppose, for example, that the contractor claims it was damaged because of the owner's late and reduced payments toward the end of the job. The contractor says it was performing on schedule and strictly according to the contract. On the other hand, the owner's representative says that the contractor was behind schedule and that the work was defective. Where is the truth, and where do you look?

Louis Nizer, in *My Life in Court,* made use of an invaluable tool for reconstructing the past. He called that tool the rule of probability.[2] This rule is that what is likely to have happened, probably did happen. And, the flip side of his rule of probability is that if something was unlikely to have happened, most likely it did not happen. In other words, the construction litigator uses as a compass for fact finding the facts of life, which include the seven deadly sins of pride, envy, wrath, sloth, avarice, gluttony, and lust, and assumes that these sins are still alive and motivating human events.

Yet, the construction litigator's task, though aided by Nizer's rule of probability, is never easy. As Nizer put it, "facts never fly in the courtroom window," rather, "they must be dragged by their heels through the courtroom door."[3] And the parties most often involved in construction disputes (contractors, suppliers, architects, engineers, owners, and sureties) are also ordinary human beings, susceptible to all of the facts and fantasies that guide and misguide the rest of the human race. Consequently, if one is to successfully function as a construction litigator, one must have a working knowledge of what makes people tick.

F. Lee Bailey, in *To Be a Trial Lawyer,* stresses the importance of becoming a "people person":

> A "people person" is one who is comfortable with other people, getting along with them and giving them some elbow room of their own without resenting the concessions that have to be made. Some people would rather deal with things such as computers, laboratory instruments, a craft such as woodworking, or a vehicle. Others prefer to live in a world where imagination can act as a shield from the harder side of reality. Some artists, though by no means all, would fall into this category.
>
> A trial lawyer works with people every day: clients, witnesses, other lawyers, judges and the court personnel, people of every kind and description. It helps to learn early on that people vary greatly within the parameters of what is considered to be "normal human conduct" and that one must be

---

[2] *An interview with Louis Nizer,* 2 Trial Diplomacy Journal 9 (Spring 1986).
[3] *Id.* at 7.

flexible to a substantial degree to get along successfully with almost all of them.[4]

So, to be an effective construction litigator, one must become a student of the construction industry and the everyday people who make it work.

Before you can convince a factfinder to believe and sympathize with your client, you must first yourself believe in and know the client. Litigators must be willing to spend countless hours talking to their clients and key witnesses until the deepest motivations of these people become clear. Only then can litigators translate what they have learned into a claim or defense that can elicit sympathy and compassion for their clients on a basic human level. This skill is even more critical in a construction case, which is prone to be technical and, therefore, dull.

While immersing oneself in the context of construction, a caution is in order. Be yourself, or you will be perceived to be phony. Cufflinks are not necessarily incompatible with hard hats. Both the client as well as the factfinder know well that lawyers spend their days pushing a pen rather than swinging a pick. The point is that people can communicate openly and honestly from different perspectives, as long as each maintains a genuine respect for the other. Polonius spoke to all generations when he so wisely advised Laertes, his son, "This above all, to thine own self be true. And it must follow, as the night the day, thou canst not then be false to any man."[5]

So, what is "the truth" and where do we look to find the real story behind the contractor's and owner's conflicting claims? First, we look to what was probable, given what contractors typically do toward the end of the job, when the profit has already been paid and spent, and what owners frequently do when the construction loan is 98 percent gone and the work is 80 percent complete. Then, taking our "flickering lamp" and "rule of probability" as a compass, we painstakingly dig for the facts where we think they might be buried. We read through the reams of project files. We find and talk with the key parties who lived through the history we are trying to reconstruct. Then, as we dig and sift, we try to simplify and synthesize the morass of facts and events into a harmonious whole, which calls for the singlemost essential skill of a master advocate. In short, we begin to develop the theme of the case.

§ 12.2 Developing the Theme

What is a theme? A theme is like a trail leading through the forest or a skeleton giving form to a body. A theme is the essence of something. For example, DNA is the theme of an organism that dictates the form and

---

[4] F. Bailey, To Be a Trial Lawyer 17 (1982).
[5] William Shakespeare, Hamlet, Prince of Denmark, Act I, Scene III.

§ 12.2 DEVELOPING THEME

function of the biological cell. Any work of art or literature embodies a theme. In a scholarly work, we call the theme a thesis. Good music likewise is structured around a theme. Who can forget the basic theme of Beethoven's Symphony No. 5: Da-Da-Da-Dummm. . . ? It carries throughout the work and is repeated in various tones and timbres—each time reminding us that we are still listening to Beethoven's Fifth.

Similarly, every good construction claim or defense has a theme. The theme of a lawsuit serves several purposes. First, it serves to clarify and to simplify the complex. Second, a theme serves to unify and to make sense of the conflicting positions being taken by the parties to the dispute. Third, a theme serves to persuade by offering a clear, commonsensical, fair, easy-to-state solution for the problem at hand. The primary function of a theme in a lawsuit is to form the basic skeleton upon which we, as construction lawyers, will hang the evidence. If a claim or defense does not have a theme, it will likely fail because the position will not be easily understood.

Development of the theme should begin at the inception of the case. For example, during the first interview with the client, we should be turning the facts over and over in our minds, asking, "What are the possible themes?" As each participant is consulted, and as each document is read, the attorney should be testing the tentative theme against the following:

1. The applicable contract
2. The applicable law
3. The facts known to date
4. The conflicting positions being taken by the parties
5. The rule of probability
6. Common sense
7. Fairness
8. Result desired by the client.

If the tentative theme does not mesh with the above factors, then look for another theme. As they say in the Appalachian mountains, "That dog won't hunt."

As soon as a possible theme is developed, write it down. Typically, the theme evolves as the facts and law are developed. It is absolutely essential that the theme account for all sides of the issue and, therefore, be able to withstand any challenge from the opponents. Rufus Choate, reportedly second only to Daniel Webster as a trial and appellate advocate, once said, "In determining the theory of the case, I am never satisfied until I have met every supposition that could be brought against it."[6] Most great

---

[6] B. Elliott & W. Elliot, A Treatise on General Procedure, Containing Rules and Suggestions for the Work of the Advocate in the Preparation for Trial, the Trial and Preparation for Appeal 107 (1894).

advocates concentrate their efforts on the weaker points of their case and how to overcome or reconcile them with their theory of the case.

The theme of a case should be subject to statement in one simple sentence, two at most. For example, a theme might be stated as follows:

> The real reason the owner underpaid the contractor was because the owner ran out of money before the end of the job.

Note that the theme of a case differs from a theory of the case. While every case should have both a theory and a theme, the theory of the case is concerned with the legal basis for the claim or defense. For example, the case theory may be that even though the contractor failed to complete the project, the contractor is still entitled to the contract price, less the cost to complete the work, because the contractor "substantially completed" the project. On the other hand, the theme of the case focuses upon facts, logic, and emotion, rather than the applicable law. Additional sample themes might be as follows:

1. The contractor and the architect had a visceral dislike for one another which made it extremely difficult for them to cooperate.
2. The contractor experienced difficulties in controlling erosion on the site because the contractor's previous experience was in road building, and this was his first job in capping a landfill.
3. The architect/engineer joint venture team continually produced tardy and inaccurate responses to the contractor's submittals because the joint venture parties were a "shotgun marriage," forced to work together by the city's minority hiring requirements.
4. The construction manager lost control of this job because he had 15 other jobs going on at the same time and could only visit the site about once a month.

The development of a consistent and comprehensive theme is the most critical task of the modern construction advocate. Why? Because if the theme fails, the case collapses.

§ 12.3 Introducing the Case

At this point we have reconstructed past events, we have shaped and developed those events into a coherent and comprehensive theme, and so we have come to the moment of truth. It is now time to communicate the sum and substance of our case to the decision-maker—perhaps a jury, a judge, or a panel of arbitrators. But no matter who or what institution is to decide the case, the principles of presentation are essentially the same. The task is to reveal the past to the present, or, in Churchill's words, "to reconstruct the scenes . . . revive its echoes, and rekindle . . . the passion of former days." To do this effectively, one must call upon the ancient Muses.

Perhaps the oldest and most effective method for re-creating the past is the drama, and, more particularly, the story form of drama. Before humans learned to record history in script, they communicated past events verbally—in story and song. This method was highly effective. Although we now read Homer's Odyssey and the Pentateuch, consider that these earliest recountings of birth and death, victory and defeat, greed and goodness, were first passed from generation to generation while sitting around campfires or in councils of the elders. When Hamlet wanted to convict the consciences of his mother and stepfather for the murder of his father, he used the medium of the play. Why? Because drama was and still is one of the best methods for relating the past in a brief space of time. Similarly, that becomes our task as construction advocates—to take the whole of the past, not just the bare acts, omissions, and events, but also the emotions, motivations, and reasons for those acts and events, and present them to the decision-maker in a brief span of time. We call this event the opening statement.

Perhaps the best examples of effective communication in opening statements are to be found in the media. We may disagree about media motivations, morals, and content, but we can surely agree that the media message is generally effective. This is because media communication requires the assimilation of masses of facts, data, emotions, disputes, and controversial issues, followed by the synthesis of this material into a form and format that can generally be understood by a twelve-year-old in a span of minutes rather than hours. And, not only can the message be understood, it also effectively persuades, which generally is the point of the message.

What are those lessons to be learned from the ancient Muses and the media that will help the construction lawyer to make an opening statement? They are described in §§ 12.4 through 12.13.

§ 12.4 —Keep It Simple

Speak in concrete rather than abstract terms. Say, "The owner didn't do what it agreed to do," rather than "The owner failed in its primary contractual obligation to remit the agreed consideration to the contractor." Concrete, simple, Anglo-Saxon words of one or two syllables generally have greater impact and, therefore, stick better to the brains and hearts of the hearers. Consider that 70 percent of the words used in Lincoln's Gettysburg Address, the best remembered speech of all time, came from 500 of the most commonly used words in the English language. It is also helpful to apply the twelve-year-old standard; that is, if a twelve-year-old cannot readily understand what you are trying to explain, the fault lies generally with the speaker rather than the hearer. This is not to suggest that the decision-maker may have the mentality of a pre-adolescent; but it is to suggest that the best speeches, the best stories, and the best opening statements can be understood by a twelve-year-old as easily as an adult.

§ 12.5 —Use the Dramatic Method

The dramatic method is time-tested and proven effective for communication and persuasion. For example, the opening statement might begin as follows:

> At ten o'clock A.M., on a crisp Monday morning in October, 1988, Bill Matson stood alone at the corner of Elm and Main Streets. Bill was at that particular corner because that's where he had been working every Monday morning for the past 15 months. Bill was not working on that particular Monday because his job had come to a grinding stop. He was standing alone, because, on the previous Friday, he had to tell his 157 field employees that they no longer had a job—even though the job they were working on, the office tower now outlined against the October sky, was yet to be finished. The reason Bill and his 157 employees could not complete the tower is because Mr. Stiff, who hired Bill and his company to build the job, refused to pay his bills. Bill is a building contractor, has been for 47 years, and he is here today to tell his story of how his company was brought to its knees and virtually destroyed by Mr. Stiff.

There are, perhaps, a hundred variations of how to use the dramatic method, but the point is to use the form or method that best fits the facts. You might, for example, use the contrasting scenes method:

> **Scene 1.** Takes place at the construction site on the corner of Elm and Main Streets. It is September 15, 1988. Work is proceeding at a frenetic, but efficient pace. The sounds of construction fill the air: compressor motors, equipment back-up horns, grinding truck gears, steel striking upon steel, shouts of the superintendent to steel workers leaning over the tenth floor. It is 15 months after construction began. The office tower is rising, floor-by-floor. Progress is steady. The work is good. Matson Construction Company is on the job and the job is going well.
>
> **Scene 2.** Takes place at the First Fidelity Bank, just down the street from the construction site. Jack Stiff, one of the biggest developers in town, is meeting with his banker, Sylvester T. Scrooge. Mr. Scrooge is speaking to Mr. Stiff and says, "Jack, we have been doing business together for a long time, but, frankly, I am getting worried about all of these shopping center projects you are involved with. We had a meeting of the loan committee the other day, and, I am sorry, but we are going to have to reduce your credit line." Jack responds, "Sy, don't worry. I've got everything under

control. The big office tower job down the street is almost finished, and I can cut back Matson's pay requests until the job is finished and have enough cash flow to finish all the shopping centers. Besides, Matson is big enough to finish the job with his own cash flow. And, who knows, once the job is finished, we can argue for a year or two over the reduced pay requests and settle for a lower sum. Everything is going to work out."

But, do not fall into the timeworn traditional lawyer's speech; for example:

Ladies and Gentlemen. I am J. Warren Smithson, attorney at law, with offices at 14th and Main Streets. I, together with my 47 partners and associates, have been retained to represent Matson Construction Company, a building contractor, which is the complaining party in this action against Stiff & Associates, the defending party. Each of you, as a decision-maker, has an honored and awesome responsibility to decide the factual issues in this case. We will now make what is known as the opening statement, but please be cautioned that what I say is not evidence. . . . and so forth.

Because, if you do, the honored decision-makers will soon be counting the holes in the ceiling tiles.

§ 12.6 —Reach Out and Grip Someone

Although it is difficult to explain, accomplished speakers have mastered the technique of, figuratively, reaching out with mind and voice and gripping the minds of the audience. Good speakers know when it happens, because, during those brief moments, they can sense that their minds and those of the hearers are locked together in perfect communication. Mastery of the technique comes only with much practice and experience; but, it helps to: (1) have complete confidence in the thoroughness of your preparation; (2) have your case organized from beginning to end; (3) have a coherent, comprehensive theme developed; (4) feel the rightness and fairness of your position; (5) speak slowly and forcefully; and (6) look directly into the eyes of your audience.

§ 12.7 —Be and Appear Sincere

There is a Latin phrase, *esse quam vidiri,* which means, "to be rather than to seem." This is an excellent credo from a moral standpoint, but the effective construction advocate must extend this credo so as "to be *and* to seem." Why? Because to convince the decision-maker of the justice of your client's cause, you must not only be sincere, you must be perceived to be sincere. The only way to be and to appear sincere is to sincerely believe in the rightness and soundness of your cause.

§ 12.8 —Develop Your Talents to Best Advantage

A young lawyer was making a closing argument in a National Institute for Trial Advocacy (NITA) session, but had given an embarrassingly inept closing statement. A leading San Francisco trial lawyer critiqued the closing as follows:

> Jack, that was not a good closing argument. It was unclear, disjointed, and unpersuasive. You never took your eyes off your notes, you never looked at the jury or the judge. It was not good.
>
> But, Jack, I saw in it a spark—a strong indication of your belief and the righteousness of your client and of his cause. You have to blow on the spark. You have to throw off the cast of self-consciousness and self-doubt with which you are encased. If you are to become a trial lawyer, you must be prepared to make great sacrifices. You were not blessed with an imposing presence, a beautiful voice or a warm and outgoing personality; but, if you learn to take your precious spark, the feeling that, by God, you and your client are right, and build on it, you can become an advocate. You can do it if you are prepared to sacrifice.
>
> It will take some gut-wrenching effort, but remember a young Greek named Demosthenes. He was orphaned at the age of seven. He was a shattered little boy. He stuttered, he totally lacked confidence, but he had one driving ambition: to reclaim his inheritance which his guardians had wrongfully taken from him. He decided to become a great orator and to take his guardians to court. He shaved off half of his hair so that he would not be tempted to rejoin society prematurely. He went to live in a seaside cave. He put pebbles in his mouth and learned to speak over the pebbles and over the roar of the waves. He studied the masters of Athenian prose to perfect his skills. His hair grew back. He left the cave. He took his guardians to court. He won. He became the greatest orator of ancient Greece. Many of his orations are preserved, and you can read them today.
>
> He had the inner fire. I believe you may have it. He polished what he had and learned from others. Get to work, Jack.[7]

So, what can timid lawyers do to become master construction litigators? They can take an inventory of their best attributes and observe carefully the best trial advocates in action. Without trying to copy particular styles, they should try to learn what it is that makes good advocates effective and see, within their own framework, how they can adapt to them. Consider that most good trial lawyers are self-confident. This is a quality that does

---

[7] Hanley, *The Importance of Being Yourself,* in Master Advocates' Handbook 10–11 (D. Rumsey ed., 1st ed. 1986). Copyright © 1986 by National Institute for Trial Advocacy, University of Notre Dame Law School, Notre Dame, Indiana 46556. Reprinted with permission.

not come from ancestors, but rather from hours on their feet speaking to and persuading people, not just in court, but before civic associations, church groups, or, whoever asks them to speak. They may have also taken adjunct teaching jobs, participated in seminars whenever asked, or volunteered to handle CLE (continuing legal education) teaching assignments that no one else wanted. They joined amateur theatrical groups and learned to perform effectively and confidently in front of live audiences. They spoke at local chapters of the AGC, AIA, NSPE and other construction industry groups. In short, they made use of every available opportunity to master the art of effective speaking.

§ 12.9 —Be Accurate, but Don't Argue

One of the worst mistakes a lawyer can make in an opening statement is to state that something will be proven in evidence when it is not. Decision-makers are typically at their highest state of alertness during the opening statement and they remember much of what is said. It is also generally considered that juries and decision-makers decide cases based on who they think has the greatest credibility, which, like reputation, is hard to build but easy to destroy. Thus, if what is proven, or not proven, differs from what is said will be proven, credibility can be destroyed and the case will likely be lost.

Perhaps the only prohibition in opening statements is that you cannot be argumentative. There is no bright line which separates a statement of what will be proven from what has been proven. But, to paraphrase what Justice Potter Stewart said of pornography, you will know argument when you have heard it. In general terms, an opening statement permits you to state who, what, where, and when. Whereas in a closing argument, you may explain the why and how.

§ 12.10 —Use Visuals

An opening statement can be made even more effective and dramatic by the use of visual aids. This is particularly true in construction cases, because of the issues involving time and complex activities. Charts, slides and overhead projectors, blowups of photographs and documents, flip charts, and blackboards are some of the more effective visual tools.

Maps, diagrams, or photographs of the project site are always helpful to the decision-maker in perceiving the location and arrangement of the construction site. Graphs and overlays are usually effective for depicting schedules and the events causing delays to the schedules. Key documents should be shown to the decision-makers by blowups or overhead projectors.

Defective materials should be physically displayed in the courtroom, if possible.

However, the use of visual aids should be well conceived, and permission of the court or decision-maker should be obtained before attempting to use these devices. One should not conduct the entire opening statement with visual aids, because they will eventually detract from the decision-maker's concentration on your presentation of the case.

§ 12.11 —Confront Problems with the Case

Never forget that the reason you are in court or before a tribunal is that there are disputed issues to be resolved. The necessary implication of an issue is that someone, typically the opposing party, has a contrary view from that of your client. Therefore, although your case may be affirmative, in order for you to persuade you must plausibly answer, explain, reconcile, or destroy the opponent's position. The time to begin this process is during the opening statement, when you should take the opportunity to recognize the opponent's position and explain what response you will make to that position. This is where the opening statement can easily slip into argument, and the advocate must tread carefully on the right side of the line.

§ 12.12 —Rehearse

Remember that a great deal of information, emotion, and reason must be conveyed in a limited period of time. As a general rule, 30 minutes should be the maximum time limit for an opening statement. Tradition has it that preparation time should be in inverse proportion to speech time; that is, the shorter the speech, the longer the preparation time. Therefore, experienced advocates preparing for an opening statement first write the statement in full, refine and edit it, then reduce it to outline form. Next, they reduce the outline to a few key opening phrases and practice giving the statement orally. Finally, they put away the notes and stand alone with the story deeply imbedded in their minds.

§ 12.13 —The Best and Last Chance

Research and experienced opinion has confirmed that the opening statement is determinative of the outcome in 80 percent of all cases.[8] That

---

[8] L. Decof, Art of Advocacy: Opening Statement Sec. 1.01[1] (1988).

means that most decision-makers make up their mind as to who is right and who is wrong at the close of the opening statement. As common experience shows, once minds are decided, even tentatively, it is extremely difficult to change them. Therefore, the opening statement may be the best and last opportunity not only to introduce the case, but to present it as well.

§ 12.14 Presenting the Case

At this point the promises have been made, now they must be fulfilled. The affirmative case must be presented to the decision-makers. The following sections describe proof strategies and offer tips on preparing and presenting the most critical evidence in the affirmative construction case.

§ 12.15 —Proof Strategies

There are at least four strategies that can be followed, singly or in combination, in presenting the construction case:

1. Chronological
2. Topical
3. Logical
4. Emotional.

The chronological strategy is to present the proof in the same order in which it occurred in time. This method is the simplest and easiest, and, because it follows a natural course of events, is often the easiest to follow for the decision-makers. Construction takes place over time, and schedules or timelines can be used to depict key events. For the sake of simplicity and understanding, it should be the preferred strategy unless there are strong reasons to the contrary.

The topical strategy is to present the proof by topics or subjects; for example, all evidence relating to a delay claim is presented together; all evidence relating to "the roof problem" is grouped, and so on. This strategy adapts well to cases that involve a number of discrete issues, such as nonpayment, delay claims, disputed change orders, differing site conditions, and various nonconforming work categories, for example, a defective roof or a faulty heating, ventilation, and air conditioning (HVAC) system.

The logical mode is simply to adapt the order of proof to the elements of the claim. For example, to prove a claim by the total cost method, a contractor is generally required to prove the following:

1. The contractor's estimate was accurate
2. The contractor's actual costs were reasonably incurred through no fault of the contractor
3. The owner's acts or omissions were such that damages could be reasonably anticipated to occur; and
4. The nature of the contractor's claim makes it impractical or unreasonable to require a greater degree of certainty from the contractor.[9]

Therefore, the corresponding proof should be presented in the order of the elements to be proven.

The emotional strategy is to find the "gut" issue and hit it over and over again. For example, the real reason the contractor lost his shirt on this job is because the owner intentionally and fraudulently concealed the fact that the project site was sitting atop a granite mountain. Generally, the emotional strategy will be selected when the contractor's legal position is weak, both under the contract and the applicable law.

Which, or which combination, of these strategies should be followed depends upon the facts and issues making up the case, the theme of the case, and the best way to communicate the facts and theme to the decision-makers. Great sculptors have said that before they pick up a chisel and hammer, they spend many hours observing, touching, and feeling the undefined mass of stone, until they can sense the ultimate shape within. The same approach should apply to presenting the case; that is to say, the subject in hand should dictate the strategy.

§ 12.16 —Typical Proof Strategy

If there is a "typical" construction case, the typical strategy will be to present the evidence in chronological order, but by the following classes of witnesses.

Lead Witness

The first witness in the affirmative case should generally set the scene by giving an overview of the project. Ideally, this person will be the president or founder of the company, but, more often than not, will be the project manager, or, in larger companies, a major vice-president. A rule of thumb is that the lead witness should be the highest placed person in the company who is capable of setting the scene for the decision-makers. The higher status of the lead witness will serve to impress the decision-makers

---

[9] *See* J.D. Hedin Constr. Co. v. United States, 347 F.2d 235 (Ct. Cl. 1965); Moorehead Constr. Co. v. City of Grand Forks, 508 F.2d 1008 (8th Cir. 1975); G.M. Shupe, Inc. v. United States, 5 Cl. Ct. 662 (1984).

§ 12.16 TYPICAL PROOF STRATEGY

that the matters in issue are being taken seriously and are worthy of their highest attention.

In addition to setting the scene, the lead witness will focus on the key issues in terms of what was contracted for or what was planned versus what in fact occurred and what went wrong. Unusual or key terms or provisions of the contract documents in the trade or industry will be identified and explained in terms the decision-makers will readily understand. The damages sustained by the complainant will be recounted, typically in general terms, but, if the witness is qualified, in detail. Issues of causation, if and to the extent they are in issue, should also be addressed.

The lead witness's testimony should also introduce those persons, both in and out of the organization, who will later testify in greater detail about particular aspects of the case such as the schedule, home office overhead, accounting procedures, damages, calculation of damages, and causation. Each of these persons should be identified by the lead witness, and a general statement should be made about the subject of their testimony. (This summary should also have been covered by the opening statement, but the repetition will be helpful.) The purpose of this overview is to tell the decision-makers what to expect, so that when the persons do appear and testify as indicated, their expectations will be fulfilled. Generally speaking, both playgoers and decision-makers feel most comfortable when what happens is what they expect to happen. While the surprise witness is standard fare for Perry Mason, it is generally unsettling in a real-life context.

The lead witness should also make use of demonstrative exhibits. Examples include photographs and diagrams of the project site, graphic schedules, and photographs or diagrams of the problem areas. However, care should be taken that the visual props are consistent with the level of general testimony of the lead witness, and that they do not focus on details to be covered by later witnesses. If they do, the decision-makers may become confused.

In summary, the primary goals of the lead witness are to provide a backdrop for the entire case and to begin to establish credibility on behalf of the complainant.

Supporting Witnesses

The next class of witnesses for the affirmative case should typically be those persons who can paint in the colors and details on the broad canvas presented by the lead witness. Generally, these persons should be the employees, subcontractors, or agents of the complainant; for example, the project superintendent or foreman, the schedulers, the in-house accountant—in other words, the people who actually lived with or through the problems in issue. At this stage in the proceedings, it is probably better to use the in-house or project players, because you are still trying to establish credibility and trust with the decision-makers. Unless the decision-makers are convinced that the company is basically solid, competent, and honest, they will not be persuaded.

Bit Players

Following the supporting witnesses should generally come the bit players, for example, the outside, independent experts and consultants who will undertake to confirm and enhance previous testimony by focusing on such issues as validity of existing schedules, interference and causation, alternative options, if any, available to the contractor, or calculation of damages. Included within this class of witnesses are the accountants, who can confirm or establish the scope of damages, and calculate home office overhead, field overhead, and lost revenues and profits. With respect to expert testimony, and for purposes of clarity in otherwise esoteric subjects, the witness should generally state, in the following order:

1. The scope of the assignment
2. Qualifying credentials
3. Conclusions
4. Methodology and process of reasoning.

Included with the bit players is testimony or documentation with respect to special studies; for example, calculations and conclusions by various institutions with respect to learning curves and inefficiency caused by disruption, acceleration of work, or stacking of trades.

The bit players by themselves will generally convey less credibility than the company's own personnel, because they may be perceived as hired guns who are not testifying because they have a burning desire to see justice prevail in the world. Rather, they are in the business for a fee. In earlier, perhaps more naive times, it was commonly believed that outside, independent experts came with greater credibility because they were "independent." Now, however, with the proliferation of experts for hire, this assumption is questionable. But by this point in the trial, if the decision-makers are convinced that the company people are competent and credible, they will be more likely to accept as credible the testimony of the retained experts.

Concluding Witness

It is traditional and true wisdom that a case should begin and end with a strong witness. Therefore, one suggestion for a strong, concluding witness is to find one of the company employees who has been in the contracting business for at least 30 years, who has seen it all, the peaks and the valleys—the guy who can walk into the court or hearing room wearing his work boots and jeans, carrying his battered hard hat under his arm, perhaps a little dirt and oil under his fingernails, and tell his story in plain and unvarnished terms. It is this type of person, who, more than all the presidents, project managers, and independent experts, can convey to the decision-makers that the claim is credible, the claimant is right, and the damage ought to be recompensed with big bucks. Witnesses like these are often worth their weight in gold.

§ 12.17 —General Tips in Witness Presentation

General tips for presentation of the affirmative case witnesses include the following:

1. Immediately before the trial have the witnesses meet together in conference to review their testimony; this will go a long way to promote consistency. However, a caution: avoid uniformity of testimony.
2. Prepare witness notebooks before trial, including an outline of the witness's testimony, perhaps a few questions verbatim, a summary of the witness's previous testimony as contained in depositions or transcripts of previous hearings, together with the documents and exhibits to be identified by that witness.
3. Do not begin direct examination with phrases like "Please state your name for the record." This is too stilted. Rather, say: "Please introduce yourself to the [decision-makers], tell them where you live and where you work, ..."
4. Give the witness time to calm down by asking a few introductory questions.
5. As soon as the witness has been introduced and is comfortable, get to the critical part of the testimony. The attention of the decision-makers will be at its peak during early testimony.
6. Emphasize important points visually, using demonstrative evidence and exhibits. This would include schedules, enlarged copies of key documents, and models of portions of the construction work.
7. Try to vary the manner and method of asking questions; this will stimulate the audience and keep interest at a high level. For example, mix questions calling for narrative answers with short, staccato questions.
8. Vary the manner and method of presenting direct evidence.
9. Don't ask unnecessary questions; such questions have an amazing potential for causing confusion and introducing problematic testimony.

318   AFFIRMATIVE CASE

10. Disclose and respond to weaknesses in the case.
11. Anticipate and prepare for objections.
12. Consider calling opposing parties and witnesses for adverse examination.
13. Consider leaving some traps and surprises for the cross-examiner, for example, evidence that could not be elicited upon direct examination.
14. Maintain the capacity to be flexible; the flow of the case can change at any time.
15. Close the testimony with a question calling for a summary of the key facts.

§ 12.18 —Expert Testimony

Even more than "ordinary" testimony, and notwithstanding that independent consultants hold themselves out as being experts in forensics, expert testimony should be thoroughly prepared and rehearsed. In a sense, the construction litigator must treat the expert as a foreigner, whose language and manner of speaking must be translated into the native tongue of the decision-makers.

The need for simple speaking cannot be over stressed. One litigator has suggested that experts should be enjoined to "explain their theories the way they wish Einstein's theories had first been explained to them."[10] For example, persons expert in a particular discipline have a tendency to explain concepts in abstract principles, and, when challenged, to rely on professional "buzz words" to work out of their uncertainty. Instead, they should be encouraged to follow any abstract statement of principle with specific examples, down-to-earth and localized, if possible. Thus, if a waste-to-energy air emissions system using reverse air filter technology is in question, it should be compared to an ordinary household vacuum cleaner. Again, the twelve-year-old standard of comprehension should be applied, and, if the expert cannot or will not comply with this rule, another expert should be found who can. If the expert's ego is an obstacle, he or she may truthfully be advised that only the accomplished can relate their craft in simple terms, without losing anything essential in the translation.

The expert should be prepared for cross-examination as would be done by your opponent at trial. At least three goals are achieved by this exercise: First, it helps you to evaluate the reasonableness and plausibility of the expert testimony; second, it reveals how the expert will react to adverse

---
[10] Hanley, *The Importance of Being Yourself,* in Master Advocates' Handbook 10 (D. Rumsey ed. 1986).

pressure; and third, it will cause the expert to be more relaxed (thereby appearing more confident) during actual cross-examination.

Contrary to opinions held by most experts, their testimony will be suspect (because it is paid for), and it will typically carry all of the excitement of watching paint dry. Therefore, the testimony should be pared down to the essentials and presented in palatable form. In other words, keep it to the point, brief, and interesting. Visuals always help, but make sure the visuals are themselves simple and straightforward.

§ 12.19 —Real and Demonstrative Evidence

Real evidence is a thing or substance that was directly involved in the history of the case; for example, a concrete core sample. Demonstrative evidence was not directly involved in the history of the case, but rather was created to represent or depict something that was; for example, a photograph, a chart, or a map. Both can be evidence and both can and should be used in presenting the affirmative case. But, if rules of evidence are applicable, different rules may apply for laying the appropriate foundation for real or demonstrative evidence.

In addition, a few other considerations are in order. Be prepared to demonstrate that the real or demonstrative evidence is authentic under the applicable rules of evidence. In many cases this can and should be done in advance of the trial by a request for admissions, stipulation by opposing counsel, or pursuant to the tribunal's pretrial procedures.

Construction cases are notorious for involving massive numbers of documents. If large numbers of documents are involved, have them marked as exhibits in advance to save time during trial. Also, consider binding, numbering, and indexing all of the documents, perhaps in separate volumes. Then prepare several different copies of each bound volume so that the witness, the decision-maker, the opposing counsel, and you as the examiner can be looking at the same document simultaneously. Even if this procedure does not strictly comply with the local rules, ask for permission to follow it. Most decision-makers will happily agree in order to save time and avoid needless repetition.

Take the demonstrative evidence to the courtroom or hearing location long beforehand and make sure that the show will flow smoothly. For example, check for available electrical outlets, extension cords, chart supports, and adequate lighting. Make sure also that the demonstrative evidence can be readily seen. Nothing can be more embarrassing than if the presentation is interrupted because you are unfamiliar with how something works. Remember that "for want of a nail, . . . the battle was lost." It is also a good idea to rehearse the use of demonstrative evidence with witnesses, so that they can be accustomed to testifying with reference to a chart or graph, diagram, or slide projection. For the same reasons that a Broadway play would never go on without weeks of rehearsal, including exercising the stage props, a case presentation should be rehearsed.

§ 12.20 —Redirect Testimony

In general, a witness should only be called for redirect testimony if and to the extent it is necessary to: (1) clarify a confusing statement; (2) elaborate (for clarification purposes) upon a statement that became confused during cross-examination; or (3) correct an erroneous statement. Otherwise, there is no need or occasion to call the witness for redirect.

§ 12.21 —Summarizing the Case

If the construction litigator has performed well the preliminary tasks of reconstructing the past, developing the theme, and introducing and presenting the case, the decision-makers will most likely be ready to decide the case. Accordingly, the summation can play the third triad of the military method of instruction: tell them what you are going to say; say it; then tell them what you said.

The summation should, essentially, be a reflection of the opening statement, adding the why and how to the what, where, who, and when. The summary should demonstrate that the promises outlined in the opening statement have been fulfilled. Where there were conflicts or inconsistencies in the evidence, they should be reconciled with the affirmative case, the rule of probability, and the rule of reason. The applicable law should be reviewed and meshed with the facts of the affirmative case. And, finally, the recurring theme should be sounded again, which, by this time, should be reverberating in the decision-makers' minds with the same intensity as the famous four notes of Beethoven's Fifth Symphony.

CHAPTER 13

DEFENSE AND CROSS-EXAMINATION

David T. Knight, Esquire
Jeanne T. Tate, Esquire

David T. Knight is a member of the firm of Shackleford, Farrior, Stallings & Evans in Tampa, Florida. Mr. Knight received his B.A. degree from the University of South Florida and his J.D. from the University of Florida Law School. He is a member of the American, Florida, and Hillsborough County bar associations. Mr. Knight concentrates in the area of construction law and fidelity and surety practice.

Jeanne T. Tate is a partner in the law firm of Shackleford, Farrior, Stallings & Evans in Tampa, Florida. She specializes in commercial litigation, with a heavy emphasis in the construction and securities areas. Ms. Tate is admitted to practice before all state courts in Florida, the United States District Court for the Middle District of Florida, the Eleventh Circuit, the Sixth Circuit, and the United States Supreme Court. Her professional activities include serving as president of the Hillsborough County Bar Association, Young Lawyer's Section; Chairman of the Judicial Nominating Commission for the Thirteenth Judicial Circuit; and barrister in the American Inn of Court LII. She received her juris doctorate degree from the University of Florida College of Law, with honors, where she graduated in the top 10 percent of her class.

§ 13.1   Introduction

§ 13.2   Risk Allocation

§ 13.3	Perfecting Rights by Timely Notice
§ 13.4	Preserving the Facts
§ 13.5	Indemnification Clauses
§ 13.6	Do You Want a Jury?
§ 13.7	—Types of Jury Selection
§ 13.8	—Goals of Jury Selection
§ 13.9	Opening Statement
§ 13.10	—Goals of Opening
§ 13.11	—Typical Opening in a Construction Case
§ 13.12	Responding to the Plaintiff's Case
§ 13.13	—Objecting during Direct Examination
§ 13.14	Cross-Examination
§ 13.15	—Impeachment
§ 13.16	—Discrediting Direct Examination
§ 13.17	—Expert Witnesses
§ 13.18	—Records Witnesses
§ 13.19	Mounting the Attack on Damages
§ 13.20	Defendant's Case
§ 13.21	—Fact Witnesses
§ 13.22	—Expert Witnesses
§ 13.23	—Charts and Documentation
§ 13.24	Jury Instructions and Verdicts
§ 13.25	Conclusion

§ 13.1 Introduction

The objective of the defense counsel is to avoid paying any money to the plaintiff; this can be done in several ways. The most direct approach is a successful defense against the claimant. Less direct, but equally effective, strategies are to pass the claims through to another party who is primarily responsible, assert a counterclaim, or if all else fails, have an insurance carrier absorb the loss.

The degree of success that the defendant in a construction case enjoys in achieving one of these objectives at trial is frequently determined by actions taken long before the claim is filed. Even the most skilled trial advocate cannot overcome clear and dispositive contractual language, nor avoid the consequences of crucial mistakes made as the facts giving rise to the claim are being developed. The construction attorney can provide effective advice to the client in advance of litigation in an attempt to avoid the types of situations requiring extensive legal defense.

§ 13.2 Risk Allocation

The most effective technique for defense against construction claims is the proper use of the construction contract to allocate the financial risks for the various types of situations from which claims have traditionally arisen. Anticipating and shifting responsibility for all risks of construction, and thereby "bulletproofing" oneself against any claim, is not possible. However, substantial protection against known hazards can generally be avoided by employing contractual language that places the risk of loss from certain conditions on the other party. Popular risk allocation clauses include no damage for delay clauses,[1] site investigation clauses, reciprocal insurance requirements, and indemnity obligations.[2] Closely analogous provisions, frequently found in construction contracts, that limit the amount or type of recoverable damage include liquidated damage provisions, clauses capping the amount of recoverable damages for breach of the agreement, and clauses precluding recovery of consequential damages.

§ 13.3 Perfecting Rights by Timely Notice

In order to avoid hamstringing the defense at trial, care must be taken throughout the claims process to ensure that all rights are preserved for later litigation. One of the most important first steps that the counsel should take is to gather and carefully review all contract documents, insurance policies, and other relevant documents for any requirements that must be met to perfect the client's right to later assert a claim or defense. Frequently, construction contracts require that written notice of any claim be submitted within a short time after gaining knowledge of the circumstances giving rise to the claim. Otherwise, the later right to assert the claim is waived.

Similarly, most insurance policies that provide coverages for the risks of construction also contain provisions requiring the insured to submit notice of any claims under the policy, and to later file a written proof of claim within a relative short period after the facts giving rise to the claim become known. This is often true in design and other professional liability policies that may apply in defending against construction claims.

The rationale behind both requirements is to afford the party receiving notice an adequate opportunity to investigate the claim while the facts are

---

[1] For a discussion on this type of clause and a collection of the cases dealing with this topic, *see* B. Bramble & M. Callahan, Construction Delay Claims, §§ 2.42–2.47 (1987); Annotation, *Validity and Construction of 'No Damage' Clause with Respect to Delay in Building or Construction Contracts,* 74 A.L.R.3d (1976).

[2] *E.g.,* Fla. Stat. § 725.06 (1986).

still fresh and the witnesses are still available and capable of clearly recalling the events. In line with this policy, the courts will generally enforce timing requirements or notice clauses, waiving a construction claim or insurance coverage where the failure to give timely notice has prejudiced the ability of the other party to adequately investigate the claim. For this reason, it is very important that prospective defendants, who wish to visit the ultimate liability for a claim upon another contracting party or the insurance carrier, carefully comply with all applicable notice provisions.

§ 13.4 Preserving the Facts

Construction claims (for example, a delay or acceleration claim) frequently take a long time to fully develop and almost never go to trial until at least several years after the facts giving rise to the claim have passed. By the time of the trial, the project has long since been completed and many of the witnesses have left the local area. Those witnesses that can be found have a new project which is foremost in their minds, and their recollection of the facts surrounding the claims at issue has become a rapidly fading memory. Furthermore, the details of a claim and the amount of harm actually suffered by the plaintiff, if any, can only be fully understood by reviewing and comprehending a meticulous system of records. For these reasons, and others, construction litigation is often a battle of documents, with the better prepared and better documented side often the winner.

To win, therefore, the defense attorney must be prepared. This preparation should start long before the project ends and the lawsuit begins. Statements from friendly and helpful witnesses are invaluable. Every experienced practitioner knows that memories of events fade with the passage of time. This is particularly true of the details of important conversations during meetings and inspections that were not confirmed in writing.

Also, the ability to properly defend against a claim will be greatly undermined if concurrent records were not kept documenting the facts important to the claim. Establishing that a contractor's forces were doing work within the scope of the contract, and not outside the scope of contract work, during a certain period can be vital to the successful defense of a claim. In short, winning at trial is often dependent upon determining what facts will be important at trial, and taking the steps necessary to insure that those facts are documented and preserved.

There are numerous kinds of documents that can be kept to document the case. However, the most valuable documents are project schedules, project cost records, daily reports and diaries, correspondence, and minutes of job meetings. Often these records alone will dictate the success or failure of a construction case. Prudent attorneys work closely with their clients as the facts are still developing to establish a system of record-keeping to properly document the claim.

§ 13.5 Indemnification Clauses

A standard feature of most construction contracts and subcontracts is the indemnity clause, in which the contractor or subcontractor agree to indemnify the owner for any and all claims asserted against the owner on account of any acts or omissions of the contractor or subcontractor. Indemnity clauses that go no further simply place the financial exposure for a claim upon the party that is ultimately responsible.

Some indemnity clauses, however, provide the owner with more extensive protection by also shifting the liability to the contractor for claims that arise in whole or in part due to an act or omission of the owner, or one for whom the owner is responsible, such as the architect or engineer. Because of their harshness and unfairness, these clauses have been given only grudging effect by the courts, and then only when the intention is expressed in clear and unequivocal terms. Broad, general language about the contractor's responsibility to indemnify the owner will not suffice. The language must clearly express the intention that the owner is being indemnified from claims arising from its own acts. In some states, these clauses are even more strictly limited in construction contracts, by making them voidable unless a separate consideration is paid for the indemnity undertaking by the contractor, or the dollar limit of the indemnity undertaking is capped.[3]

In any event, the defense counsel will likely encounter indemnification clauses. The advice of the counsel is much more effective if applied prior to entering into the construction contract, and clients should be so advised as to existing and future transactions.

§ 13.6 Do You Want a Jury?

Another important ingredient of the ultimate success the defense counsel may enjoy at trial is the decision to have the case decided by a jury or a judge. This is a decision that must typically be made at the early stages of the litigation. Often the plaintiff's counsel will make the decision by electing a jury trial when filing the complaint. If not, the defense counsel will have the option. In electing between a bench and jury trial in a construction case, two major considerations must be addressed. First, who is the judge and what are his or her proclivities? Is the judge plaintiff-oriented? Is

---

[3] *Id.*

it someone who favors small businesses over large corporations? Ask attorneys familiar with the judge what the reasonable expectations can be at trial. Second, consider whether the construction case has "jury appeal." Most construction litigation does not have the emotional appeal of a horribly injured person in a personal injury case, and it often involves complex issues of law and fact revolving around substantial quantities of documentary proof which may confuse and bore jurors. For these reasons, many lawyers prefer a bench trial in commercial cases, although juror confusion may serve to mitigate against the plaintiff's recovery in a construction case.

Although the selection of a jury or nonjury trial can only be intelligently made on a case-by-case basis, after considering the specific facts, witnesses, parties, and lawyers involved, the following generalizations may be useful:

1. Juries are more likely to favor a small contractor over a large corporation.
2. Juries are less likely to return large verdicts against local governments, schools, hospitals, and small businesses.
3. Juries are more likely to return verdicts against sureties and insurance companies.
4. Juries are more likely to return verdicts based upon equitable factors rather than upon the strict interpretation of the construction contract.
5. Juries are more likely to be confused by highly technical and complicated evidence.
6. Jury trials are generally more expensive and progress slower than bench trials.

§ 13.7 —Types of Jury Selection

Approaches to jury selection vary widely, as do opinions as to the effectiveness of the process. There are three general methods of questioning prospective jurors, depending usually on the forum of the litigation. Under the traditional federal mode, the trial judge does all of the questioning, with the counsel participating only through submission of written questions in advance of voir dire for the court's consideration. It is often difficult to get the federal courts to understand the factors that may apply to the selection of a jury in a construction case. The state courts generally give the counsel wide leeway in questioning the jury panel, with little interference by the judge. More and more federal courts, however, are sharing the task of questioning the veniremen, with the court directing general questions to the panel, and the lawyer following with specific questions for the individual jurors. Federal Rule of Civil Procedure 47(a) gives the federal district judges discretion to employ this mixed procedure, and it should be used by the counsel whenever available; it establishes an early rapport with the jury, and gives attorneys an opportunity to frame their own questions and follow-up questions.

§ 13.8 —Goals of Jury Selection

The defense counsel should briefly acquaint the jurors with the dispute, the parties, and the counsel by making introductions all around the counsel's table, including the opposing counsel. The counsel should then provide a brief recitation of the nature and theory of the defensive case so the jurors can understand the client's position. But most importantly, the proper function of jury selection is to learn about each juror, and not to indoctrinate the panel with the theory of the case. Increasingly, judges are interrupting the counsel and admonishing them in front of the jury when they run afoul of this rule.

The construction attorney should then endeavor to ascertain any bias or other grounds for dismissal from the jury panel for cause by inquiring into (1) familial relationships with the parties, counsel, judge, and witnesses; (2) any financial ties between the respective parties; (3) any pretrial exposure to news accounts about the case; and (4) prior jury duty or personal litigation experiences of the jurors and their families. It is not unusual for prospective jurors in construction cases to have exposure to the contractors, designers, or sureties involved in a case. For example, the contractor may have repaved streets in the juror's neighborhood, or the surety may have provided homeowner's or other insurance to the juror through its related companies.

As problems with processing insurance claims become a universal experience, the potential juror may exhibit an unstated bias. Thus, the counsel should probe for subtle factors that might influence jurors to favor one side or another, including their racial, ethnic, religious, or socioeconomic prejudices, attitudes, and backgrounds. Jury studies have determined that some occupations are considered to be pro-plaintiff, including salesmen, students, social workers, teachers, writers, and small businessmen, while others are considered to be pro-defendant, such as accountants, military personnel, suburban housewives, and utility workers. Especially in construction cases, persons employed in the construction industry may carry preconceived biases into the jury room.

The defense counsel should diffuse the opponent's strong points by being candid with the jurors about the difficulties of the case, and honestly explaining why the client should be exculpated despite these difficulties.

Jury selection is the time to present the "problems" in the case, get the prospective jurors' reaction to those problems, and then use challenges to exclude those least likely to accept the client's position. Prospective jurors with bad experiences on home renovations, for example, are likely to be unfavorable jurors for a contractor.

§ 13.9   Opening Statement

The opening statement provides the first opportunity for the counsel to present a coherent preview of the proof expected to be presented at trial in defense to the plaintiff's case. It also presents the only opportunity for the defense lawyer to make an unrebutted presentation. As such, although it is probably the most overlooked part of the jury trial process, the opening statement is a critical part of the trial, and it must be carefully organized and presented. Studies have shown that jury verdicts are, in the substantial majority of cases, consistent with the initial impressions received during the opening statement.

While the opening statement may be waived by either side, it is almost never advantageous to do so, even if the opposing counsel forgoes the opportunity. In this same regard, the opening statement should generally be given before the plaintiff's case (instead of before the defendant's case) so the jury can consider the competing facts and positions when listening to the plaintiff's proof. Otherwise, the plaintiff's case can be considerably more convincing. This is especially true in construction cases where the highly technical issues, the overwhelming amount of documentation, and the length of the trial will certainly distract and confuse the jury. Providing the jury with a road map to interpret and debunk the plaintiff's case in plain, forceful language during the opening statement is vital to the jury's understanding of the defense's later efforts to impeach or discredit the plaintiff's witnesses.

§ 13.10   —Goals of Opening

A forceful, logical opening statement must clearly demonstrate the facts that entitle your client to a favorable defense verdict. The facts should be presented in a direct and positive way, instead of alluding to them in a conclusory fashion.

Another objective of the opening statement is to personalize the client so the jury can empathize with the person. Refer to the client by name, whenever possible, and if representing a corporation, refer to its representative. On the other hand, de-personalize the adversary by use of the word

§ 13.10 GOALS OF OPENING

"plaintiff," "claimant," or "the other side." If the plaintiff is an out-of-state contractor, remind the jury of this fact.

Other advice to the defense counsel can be phrased in terms of do's and don'ts. Do present the facts in a chronological way to facilitate juror comprehension and, if feasible, utilize demonstrative aids. This is very important in construction delay cases, in which a simple timeline will serve to put the case in perspective. A jury that fails to clearly comprehend the case, which is often true in complex construction disputes where the evidence comes in disjointed segments from the witnesses, cannot be persuaded. This is when a timeline can be helpful.

Do not be argumentative, since arguments are reserved for closings. Specifically avoid discussions about the credibility of witnesses, conclusions about who breached the contract, inferences from the evidence, and other issues that cannot be supported directly by a witness's testimony. It is permissible and preferable, however, to develop the theory of the case in conjunction with an overview of the factual evidence. If necessary, let the expert witness make conclusory and argumentative points in a professional and authoritative manner, while striving to avoid the perception of an advocate or hired gun.

Do not overstate. Most attorneys are familiar with values of primacy and recency. Primacy is the first thing the jury hears, and if presented reasonably and truthfully, it sells. Overstating the case at any time, especially in the opening statement, can be fatal because the jury will remember and resent the representations. Also, it will cause them to distrust other things the attorney tells them. Because of the technical aspects and long duration of construction cases, jurors may be persuaded more by counsel than by complex evidence. But overstatement is almost always recognized, despite the complex nature of the case, particularly since any competent adversary will be sure to highlight such issues to the trier of fact.

Do mention obvious weaknesses in the defendant's case and deemphasize their importance. Juries appreciate candor and it diffuses the impact of the plaintiff's presentations. Owners and designers are often guilty of administrative delays that may affect the project. Denial and over-defensive reactions are less effective than honest admissions with offsetting explanations.

Do not reserve strong points for a later point in the trial; this strategy sacrifices the most important opportunity to cripple the opposition. As previously mentioned, the opening statement is the *only* time the defense goes unrebutted. Moreover, and especially in a complex construction case, the jury's opportunity to acquire information is greatest at the start of the case, when its thinking is unencumbered. So, do not forego this crucial advantage to provide the jury with a compelling reason to deny recovery to the plaintiff. After all, the case for the defense is not presented until after the plaintiff has rested. It is, therefore, very important that the jury hear the strong points of the defense during the opening statement rather than toward the end of the trial.

Do not engage in a dull recitation of each witness's testimony, but do highlight limited testimony of major significance. Tell the jury to watch for the testimony of the architect, the scheduling expert, or the accountant who will best diffuse the claimant's position.

Do not read an opening statement; otherwise, you risk seriously undermining your rapport with the jury and the persuasive impact of your presentation. Maintain eye contact. Construction cases often prove boring to the jurors. Lively and interesting counsel are crucial in such cases to capture the jury's attention and sympathy.

§ 13.11 —Typical Opening in a Construction Case

Although no opening can be strictly adhered to in all cases, the following outline will assist in the presentation of a persuasive, organized opening statement:

1. Prepare a thematic opening paragraph that discloses the overall defensive position in a capsule form. For example, in a defective roofing case in which the installation contractor is the defendant, tell the jury that the blame lies with the manufacturer of the defective material or with the owner's maintenance staff for walking on the roof and poking holes when adding vent pipes.
2. Explain the purpose of the opening statement, setting forth what an opening statement is and why the counsel are permitted to address the jury at this point.
3. Introduce the parties and crucial witnesses by name, with a personal description of their significance to the case. As mentioned before, provide a personal touch to the defendant, even if it is a corporate owner, out-of-state contractor, or design firm.
4. Described the location of the construction site or the defective work in question, supplemented by visual aids if possible.
5. Pinpoint crucial dates, times, and site conditions. This is especially true in construction delay claims.
6. Identify the key issue in dispute by factually controverting the plaintiff's version of the facts. It is crucial that this be done forcefully and with conviction. For example, in defense to a wrongful termination case, describe the defective work and the understaffed work force that existed prior to termination, the serious delay being caused, and the catastrophic results to the owner if the plaintiff contractor had not

been removed and replaced by a competent contractor. Make the reasons for termination sound compelling.

7. Present a coherent narrative of the actual event involved, trying to make the jury visualize the event. Avoid technical terms without definition. Describe the complex construction project in everyday terms and in simple construction-related analogies such as building a house or shed.
8. Rebut damages as being overstated or not as a result of the defendant's actions. It is not unusual for plaintiffs to inflate their claims. This will not sit well with a jury, and it is a key defensive opportunity.
9. Conclude with a statement that the facts justify a defense verdict.

§ 13.12 Responding to the Plaintiff's Case

The plaintiff, of course, is given the initial opportunity to tell the jury what the case is all about in an effort to convince them that a plaintiff's verdict is warranted. The defense lawyer has two major roles during the plaintiff's case. The first is interposing objections to the plaintiff's proof, so that improper or prejudicial information is not admitted to the jury. The second is paying careful attention to the evidence so that an effective cross-examination or rebuttal evidence can be presented.

§ 13.13 —Objecting during Direct Examination

The decision to object is one of the most basic functions of a trial lawyer, and of crucial value to the defense attorney in a construction case. Instantaneous conclusions must be made as to whether the evidence is improper and, if so, whether an objection should be made. To make this decision, the construction lawyer must consider the overall effect that the proffered evidence and the potential objection will have on the judge and the jury. While this may seem impossible to do in a split second, with the degree of pretrial preparation common in construction lawsuits today, lawyers often have a good idea what testimony will be presented in the trial. Key documents have previously been identified, expert witness depositions have previewed important technical issues, and pretrial memoranda have identified important legal issues. As a consequence, trial preparation should enable the defense attorney to anticipate and be prepared for most of the evidentiary issues that arise during the trial.

Also, the purposes to be served by objecting must be considered. The purposes of making objections include the basic goals of (1) keeping damaging evidence out of the record; (2) forcing the adversary to resort to an alternative means of proof, which may be less persuasive than the proffered means; and (3) protecting the record on appeal. Although it may be unethical to make an unfounded objection solely to disrupt an examination, it is proper to make an objection whenever there is a legitimate evidentiary basis, even if the inevitable effect is to interrupt the opponent's examination or to rescue a floundering witness. The complex technical issues involved in a construction case will provide the defense counsel with ample legal and technical grounds for interposing an objection. The efforts of the plaintiff to build a proper foundation for his claim and a cohesive theory of recovery will certainly suffer by such interruptions.

Balanced against these goals are the drawbacks of making an objection. First, there are the jurors, who dislike interruptions in the flow of evidence. They resent having the already long construction trial being further extended. Worse yet, jurors view lawyers that make constant objections as trying to conceal the truth. Since the credibility of the lawyer has a considerable effect on the ultimate outcome of a construction trial, the defense attorney should anticipate evidentiary problems whenever possible and make objections before trial by way of a motion in limine, or outside of the jury's presence during recesses and side bar conferences. In addition, in the opening statement, the defense attorney might explain to the jury that objections are necessary to save time and to facilitate the search for the truth. Further, although objections are directed to the judge, some line of indirect communication can be filtered to the jury so they will understand the importance of the objection and not dismiss the defense attorney as an obstructionist.

Second, there is the judge. Most judges are already impatient at the thought of presiding over a construction case that may last several weeks or more. Once the trial is underway, the judges like to expedite the proceedings. Technical objections to matters that are harmless or not really in dispute, and repetitive objections when a continuing or single objection would suffice, should be avoided. Otherwise, the defense attorney runs the risk of antagonizing the judge, and fostering jury speculation on what the answer would have been (which is often far worse than the actual answer).

A third significant drawback to lodging an objection is that an objection can sometimes enhance the credibility of the evidence it seeks to exclude. This can happen when the objection is overruled, because the objection draws the jurors' attention to the question and corresponding answer. This may be the case with a proposed exhibit prepared by the plaintiff's expert to explain the project delays. Consequently, the defense attorney should be reasonably sure that the objection will be sustained, and should have the legal authority ready to support major objections that he or she anticipates making during the trial.

The Federal Rules of Evidence and those of most states preserve the common-law requirement that attorneys object to questions or evidence offered by their adversary. Indeed, in order to preserve the issue for appeal, specific objections must be made simultaneously with the attempted admission of the improper evidence.[4] On the timeliness issue, if a question is improper, an objection should be made before the answer is given. Since a well-prepared witness will respond promptly to questions posed by his counsel, objections cannot always be interposed in the interlude. In this instance, it is still permissible to make an objection to the question, but the objection should be followed by a motion to strike the response.

In construction litigation, questions often arise about the competency of a witness to testify in a particular field. Despite the intentions of the plaintiff's counsel, if the witness is favorable to the defense, caution should be used in articulating the basis of an objection. For example, it is far better for the jury to hear that the questions are beyond the witness's area of expertise than to announce that the questions are improper because the witness is incompetent.

§ 13.14 Cross-Examination

Without a doubt, cross-examination is the least understood and most poorly used opportunity in the trial phase of a construction case, perhaps because of the dearth of education concerning this very important process. The two global goals of cross-examination are to elicit favorable testimony by having the witnesses agree with the facts supporting one's own case, and to discredit the witnesses or their testimony so the jury will disregard or minimize it. Because of the complex nature of construction cases, the jury may not understand the technical details, but may appreciate the fact that the witness has been discredited. It is the perception of credibility that is often important in such cases. It is also a key opportunity for the lawyer, not the witness, to testify, in effect by doing most of the talking and limiting the responses of the witness. The defense attorney should avoid any questions that relinquish control of cross-examination to the witness. Several observations about cross-examination in general, with an epilogue regarding expert cross-examination, can assist the defense attorney in the enhancement of this advocacy skill.

Although cross-examination strategies vary from case to case, there are a number of basic guidelines that warrant consideration in all construction litigation. Fundamentally, of course, the defense attorney must initially

---

[4] Fed. R. Evid. 103(a).

decide whether or not to cross-examine a witness. This decision can be resolved by investigating the answer to several basic questions.

1. Has the witness hurt your case? Some witnesses may only establish a required technical element of a cause of action that you will not seriously dispute. Cross-examination in this situation is not essential. For example, in defending an acceleration case, the counsel may choose not to cross-examine a witness who testifies that the owner directed the contractor to increase its work force. Rather than contest the owner's directive, the defense counsel may focus upon the reason for the directive, for example, the delays were the contractor's fault, and the size of the work force was woefully inadequate in any event.

2. Did the witness give less than expected on direct examination? This strategical decision is one of the most crucial in determining whether to cross-examine. If a witness or the opposing lawyer forgot an important part of the testimony, cross-examination may give the opposition a second chance. This is a real possibility in construction litigation because certain witnesses are called upon to testify about several matters. Because of the length of the direct examination, the plaintiff's counsel may have purposely omitted some areas of question so as not to bore the jury. More importantly, since damaging testimony is twice as damaging if elicited during cross-examination, a witness may intentionally withhold damaging parts of his testimony so that it can be revealed in cross-examination. Do not give your adversary this tactical advantage. If you decide to cross, avoid the subject of the omitted testimony so that redirect examination is inappropriate on that issue.

3. Was the witness credible and important? Jurors have preconceived notions that lawyers should cross-examine significant witnesses, and the failure to cross will likely create negative inferences for the jury. This is especially true of expert witnesses in construction cases. For example, the failure to cross-examine the plaintiff's accountant testifying as to damages may create the impression that the defendant does not contest the amount of the claimed delay damages.

4. Do you have any real ammunition for cross-examination? Be sure you can either elicit favorable testimony from the witness or discredit his testimony given in direct examination before undertaking cross-examination. When in doubt, waive cross-examination unless you can articulate a specific purpose that justifies the risk of the witness reconfirming and strengthening the plaintiff's theory of the case. Another strategy is to conduct a safe, cursory cross-examination on a peripheral point in order to avoid the appearance that you are accepting the witness's testimony. Construction cases, because of the

volumes of documents involved, provide the defense counsel with ample ammunition to cross-examine witnesses who participated in creating the paper trail. The witness may have written certain entries in a daily log that are not crucial to the case, but may prove embarrassing to the witness.

Once again, practical advice concerning cross-examination in construction litigation can be formatted in terms of do's and don'ts.

1. Do phrase all of your questions in a manner that requires the witness to answer in a yes or no fashion. Remember that you are testifying now, not the witness. Construction superintendents, architects, and expert witnesses like to talk, and will resist yes or no answers. This will make the cross-examination even more difficult for them.
2. Don't rehash or repeat the witness's direct testimony, unless it is helpful to your case.
3. Do write down your cross-examination in advance, and have a reason for asking each question. This is possible since the liberal rules of discovery eliminate most surprises at trial. Having the cross-examination written down eliminates delays between questioning; such delays allow the witness to compose himself. Further, have your own expert review the questions to make sure you properly understand any technical matters involved.
4. Don't let the witness control you or give an alternative answer. Instead, press for the answer to the question you posed. Construction and design personnel are often masters at evasive answers in the field as well as in the courtroom.
5. Do get to your strong points early while the witness is still adjusting to you.
6. Don't ask a question you don't know the answer to, and know what not to ask. Review such matters with your own expert, because the technical nature of construction litigation provides many possible pitfalls. When in doubt, leave out the question since the plaintiff's witnesses will generally seize every opportunity to hurt your case.
7. Do end on a strong point, and since you are "testifying," stand in a way that the jury focuses on you, not the witness.
8. Don't cover the waterfront with cross-examination since it will dilute your strong points; in short, resist the temptation to continue cross once you have established your big issues. The goal is not to win the case on cross-examination, but to detract from the plaintiff's main points. Creating doubt in the validity of the plaintiff's delay claim is success in itself.

§ 13.15 —Impeachment

Impeachment of a witness in a construction case, if done effectively and forcefully, can devastate the witness's credibility in the eyes of the jury. This can be particularly effective if the witness was a key actor in the construction process. Fortunately, impeachment is one of the easiest parts of cross-examination to master as long as you follow one golden rule—use impeachment selectively and when a witness's testimony is blatantly contradictory. Juries do not appreciate subtle contradictions, especially from a daily log or a deposition that was taken many years before trial.

When impeaching a witness with prior inconsistent testimony, you should begin with a direct, leading question (as should all questions on cross-examination), and you should end with a restatement of the impeaching testimony. Avoid impeaching statements that are taken out of context, because under Federal Rule of Civil Procedure 32 and most state rules, your adversary can require you to read the entire relevant portion of the transcript. Such an exercise undermines your integrity before the jury. In addition, be sure to read questions and answers verbatim from the transcript as it is improper to summarize or paraphrase a witness's testimony. An example of impeachment questions following these guidelines is:

Q: Mr. Engineer, you state that Defendant Contractor was not entitled to compensation for installing the air compressor because it was part of the scope of the original contract, correct?

Q: Do you recall when I took your deposition on September 12, 1988?

Q: You swore to tell the truth in that deposition, correct?

Q: (I recommend furnishing copies of the deposition page to the witness even though not required by the federal rules or many state codes). Do you see that I asked you this identical question, that is, (repeat question) and you testified that Mr. Defendant was entitled to compensation for the air compressor because it was an extra?

Resist the temptation to ask for an explanation of the inconsistency, or even asking the witness if he told the truth at his deposition or at trial. This only provides an opportunity for the witness to rehabilitate himself. The technical nature of the construction and design process often provides the witness with an opportunity to explain away the inconsistency in technical jargon that may not be really understood by the attorney or the jury. Do not provide the witness with an opportunity to create a technical or weasel response.

Impeachment of a witness can also occur with unsworn written statements, oral representations, pleadings, and omissions; the impeachment technique is essentially the same for all. Yet, regardless of the impeachment attempted (except where the witness unequivocally admits making the prior statement), you must "prove up" the impeaching statement by offering proof through the appropriate document (written statement or transcript), or through a witness who was present when the inconsistent statement was made. The voluminous paper trail of the typical construction project will generally provide a wealth of documents to prove up your impeachment. Failure to prove up your impeachment will subject that portion of your cross-examination to a motion to strike.

§ 13.16 —Discrediting Direct Examination

There are three basic methods by which a defense attorney can discredit the plaintiff's direct examination: discrediting the motives, interests, and biases of the witness, discredit the testimony of the witness, or discrediting the conduct of the witness. Your emphasis should be on obtaining unlikely explanations, retractions, contradictions, inconsistencies, or implausibilities. The traditional ways to discredit witnesses include questioning their motives (revenge, greed, love), interest (financial or otherwise in the outcome of the suit), bias (family, employment, or financial relationship), and prejudice. Subtlety is essential in this area to avoid offending the jurors and invoking sympathy with the witness.

Discrediting a witness's testimony involves a challenge to the reliability of the witness's perception or memory. This is the most common type of cross-examination, particularly in construction cases that involve a high degree of testimony about occurrences. For example, consider a case where the plaintiff claimed that a nitric acid plant was damaged by a sudden turbine failure as a result of the defendant's negligent construction and engineering of the plant. In cross-examining a witness who was describing the wreck, it would be beneficial to show that the event occurred quickly and unexpectedly, and that the witness was apprehensive. If done effectively, the jury will realize that the circumstances under which the witness made his observations were not conducive to accurate recøllection.

Finally, a defense attorney can emphasize inconsistencies between a witness's testimony and his conduct in order to discredit his presentation. As an example, again consider the case involving the nitric acid plant. There, the construction manager testified that the plant was built perfectly and that the defendants were without fault. It was learned, however, that the manager was not at the plant during start-up operations. When confronted with a request to explain this absence, the manager blurted out that he never attended start-ups, just in case there was a wreck. The manager's actions and concern for his personal safety undoubtedly cast considerable doubt on the error-free nature of his work.

§ 13.17 —Expert Witnesses

Expert witnesses can be cross-examined like any other witnesses, and the ground rules for impeachment and discrediting testimony are the same. However, additional caution and pretrial preparation are required to create an effective cross-examination of experts in construction litigation. This involves a thorough investigation into the witness's qualifications and experience, the basis for the expert opinion, and the resources utilized in forming the expert's opinion. The defense counsel should always consult with its own expert about possible weaknesses of the plaintiff's expert; a defense expert is in the best position to identify and ascertain these defects.

Cross-examination of an expert has the same basic purpose as cross-examination of a lay witness, to wit: to elicit favorable concessions about the merits of the defense, and to undermine the credibility of the witness or his testimony. With expert witnesses in particular, it is more effective to elicit any favorable testimony to your client before launching an attack on their opinions or credentials.

A general checklist for cross-examining experts would include the following areas of possible inquiry: attack any weaknesses in the expert's qualifications, and highlight the absence of practical experience with the exact subject matter in question. Many experts have broadly based experience in engineering, for example, but most have little direct experience with the specific subject matter of the suit, such as high-temperature process chemical plants.

Narrow the expert's expertise, which may be unfairly exalted in the minds of the jurors following direct examination. The jury should not be left to assume, for example, that a mechanical engineer has an unassailable opinion on a civil engineering problem, or even that such an engineer is an expert in every mechanical process.

Briefly demonstrate the expert's financial interest in the case by inquiring into professional fees charged and the percent of income derived from consulting and testifying as an expert. Although this is a two-way street, if you forego the opportunity to question the plaintiff's expert about fees, you can be sure your expert will confront those questions, leaving the appearance of partiality solely with your expert.

Attack the witness's opinion by varying the assumptions in a hypothetical question. If used effectively, the hypothetical question can have great impact on the issue of causation in various kinds of construction accidents. For example, with an expert who has tested a generator for performance and efficiency, ascertain the temperature and pressure assumptions that were made, and then ask if his opinion would be different if the temperature or pressure were higher or lower. Again be sure that your own expert has discussed with you the impact of varying the assumptions. The new assumption, or course, should relate to your client's factual version of the events, so you can argue in closing that your opponent's expert essentially agrees with you. If the expert testifies that his opinion would not change, you can argue that his opinion is really not an opinion, but rather, a fixed or close-minded conclusion that would never deviate from the plaintiff's theory of the case.

Highlight any changes in the expert's opinion that are not readily explainable. This may suggest to the jury that the expert's vacillation was possibly for pecuniary advantage alone. The matter need not be a crucial point. For example, increases in the expert's calculation of delay damages always create a suspicion that the expert is a hired gun.

Attack the thoroughness of the expert's preparation by thoroughly examining the time spent, focusing on the usually small amount of time spent personally by the expert in formulating an opinion, as opposed to investigative work done by others. It may be appropriate to examine experts concerning: their knowledge of background facts, the nature and extent of tests performed (or not performed), the documents reviewed, the physical examinations made of the site, and their consideration of alternative assumptions. The expert should review and have a working knowledge of the details of all applicable blueprints, drawings, specifications, and contractual agreements pertaining to the area in question. Point out the expert's lack of first-hand knowledge about the documents or the problem, and reliance on subordinates to conduct the underlying investigation.

Force the expert to concede or corroborate selected facts or assumptions that dovetail with your own expert's opinion. For example, there may be agreement between experts on both sides as to the validity of the as-built schedule prepared by your expert in defending against a construction delay claim.

Use these witnesses to criticize their own client's conduct in selected areas. It would be unrealistic for an expert to testify that the plaintiff did everything in the safest, most efficient, and easiest way. Particularly in construction delay cases, experts may have to concede that their client contributed to project delay in some manner. This is especially true when the owner is responsible for coordinating the work of other subcontractors.

Encourage the opposing expert witness to agree that legitimate differences of opinion between qualified experts exist. If demonstrated previously by deposition, establish that this expert has sometimes been proven wrong in differences of opinion with other experts. This is often the case with design tolerances, which are subject to a great deal of debate in the design professions.

Attack any inconsistencies between the opinion of experts and any books, articles, or speeches they may have authored, or any recognized treatises or learned articles. This is especially productive if you can establish in advance that the expert accepts the treatise as authoritative.

Inconsistencies should also be exposed between the expert's testimony and recognized standards and codes, such as local building codes.

Question the reliability of the information that the expert used to formulate an opinion, remembering that under the Federal Rules of Evidence and those of most states, experts can rely on information which is itself inadmissible (such as treatises, safety codes, and the opinion of other experts). See **Chapter 11**.

Each of these areas of expert cross-examination must be scrutinized and tailored to each case, with a view toward the particular facts and, more importantly, the expert witness in question.

§ 13.18 —Records Witnesses

The trial of a construction case is often a trial based on documents. Expert witnesses base their opinions upon the construction documentation, and the lay witnesses try to explain the content and meaning of the documents. At times, a records witness may be used to qualify the records and other documentation for admission into evidence. If you are unable to exclude the documentation on grounds of relevance, hearsay, foundation, or other grounds, you may wish to cross-examine the records witness, asking him to point out any favorable material in the records, as well as any inconsistencies, errors, and incompleteness. In many instances, however, you may wish to waive cross-examination, or better yet, stipulate to the authenticity of the documentation and obviate the need for a records witness all together.

§ 13.19 Mounting the Attack on Damages

Often the most effective strategy for the defendant in a construction case is to mount a full-scale attack upon the plaintiff's damages. This is not to say that the defendant should concede liability, or even down play the liability issue. Rather, the approach is to scrutinize the claimed costs in order to demonstrate fundamental flaws, inconsistencies, and a lack of credibility that may taint the plaintiff's entire case.

The attack on damages should be multifaceted. One aspect is to find and exploit duplication in the claimant's damages. For example, in construction lost productivity claims, it is common for the plaintiff contractor to calculate losses for labor efficiency due to numerous causes. However, the aggregate productivity losses in terms of labor hours may exceed the total labor hours expended on the entire project. Obviously, duplication and overstatement are at work. The defense counsel should expose this duplication and argue that it is more than mere overstatement, but a fundamental lack of credibility and merit in the claim.

Another defense tactic is to eliminate legally insufficient elements of damage. For example, claimants routinely resort to the total cost approach to calculate damages, as we discuss in § 7.8. However, there are certain legally recognized prerequisites that must be proved in order to apply a total cost formula: (1) other methods of calculating damages are impossible or impractical; (2) the actual costs are reasonable; (3) the claimant's estimate is accurate; and (4) the claimant did not contribute to the overrun. (See § 7.8.) In some instances, the defense has been able to successfully thwart the claimant's entire damages presentation by strenuously attacking each of these legal foundations for a total cost claim. Other specific elements of damages may also be demonstrated to be legally insufficient, such as prejudgment interest, lost profits on other jobs, and expert witness fees.[5] Despite the questionable nature of these damages, they routinely appear in damages presentations in construction claims.

Even if the damages cannot be dismissed as legally insufficient, it is possible to challenge the assumptions that underlie certain elements of damages. For example, if the court allowed the plaintiff to proceed under a total cost damages theory, the defendant's counsel can attack the claimant's estimate. Revealing flaws in the estimate supporting a bid will require the claimant to modify its total cost claim, as we discuss in § 7.10. Errors and deficiencies in construction estimates are not uncommon, given the limited time and resources that are often devoted to the pre-bid estimating process by contractors. A seasoned cost estimator may assist the defense counsel by providing expert testimony in this regard.

Finally, because of the complex and intertwined aspects of construction, the defense counsel will often be able to identify cost damages related to causes that were the responsibility of the claimant. For example, the default termination or poor performance by a subcontractor will likely have a cost impact on a claimant general contractor; this would serve to reduce the defendant owner's damages. A thorough investigation of subcontractors' performance on most projects would reveal problems that could work to the benefit of the defendant owner in minimizing damages.

§ 13.20 Defendant's Case

Presentation of the defendant's case in a construction litigation often involves challenges because of the lack of fact witnesses and documentation. Further, defense experts may suffer from a perception by the finder of fact

---

[5] B. Bramble & M. Callahan, Construction Delay Claims, §§ 10.30, 10.33, 10.35 (1987).

that they were retained solely to snuff out the claim. However, an astute defense counsel can overcome these obstacles in most instances.

§ 13.21 —Fact Witnesses

Owners, who are often defendants in construction litigation, frequently do not have a cadre of their own field representatives. That is why they retain architects and construction managers to assist them. However, these groups are likely to be involved in the litigation as third parties with their own interests. Thus, the owner defendants often will not have access to first hand fact witnesses of their own. On the other hand, the plaintiff contractor will have a legion of potential fact witnesses such as project managers, superintendents, foremen, and workers.

Nevertheless, the owner defendant will generally have at least one member of its own staff who was involved in the project. One good witness is better than 40 bad witnesses. The challenge for the owner's attorney is to identify the available witnesses and help them to become credible, articulate witnesses. This can be done by working with the witnesses to be sure that they are knowledgeable about the facts and documents. The attorney can also assist witnesses to meet the onslaught of depositions and cross-examination, often by helping them overcome bias, defensiveness, and anger. A project plagued with litigation will certainly strain the owner's representatives, resulting in deep-seated emotions, and perhaps concern with their careers. The defense attorney should address these matters straightforwardly.

§ 13.22 —Expert Witnesses

The defense counsel must also address the matter of bias, or perceived bias, on the part of expert witnesses retained on behalf of the defendant owner. Objectivity and independence are crucial in maintaining credibility with the trier of fact. A hired gun expert often will not assist in the defense of a construction claim.

The defense counsel needs to obtain a realistic view of the case. This can be done by following the advice in **Chapter 1**, which concerns simplifying the complex construction claim. However, simplification is not enough. The defense counsel needs a blunt, candid evaluation of the merits of the claim in order to prepare for the case. There is a tendency for some experts to paint a rosy picture of the possible defenses. Reliance upon exculpatory clauses, late notices of claims, and vague references to contractor mismanagement will generally not withstand trial by fire. Simplistic or distorted schedule analysis techniques discussed in § 5.5 may be applied for the defense to no avail. Defense counsel should be prepared for such matters.

§ 13.23   CHARTS & DOCUMENTATION   343

The defense counsel may want to retain an expert solely to assist in the analysis of the matter, but not to testify at trial. Discovery upon such advisory experts is generally limited,[6] and the defense counsel may be able to obtain advice on technical matters for a worst-case scenario without intimidation or jeopardizing the defense case.

More importantly, the defense counsel must use a credible expert if the matter goes to trial or a hearing. Perceptions of expert bias may be reinforced by overly optimistic testimony, aggressive behavior, a smug demeanor, or any financial interest of the expert in the outcome of the case. The defense counsel should take little consolation in the fact that the plaintiff's expert also came across as a hired gun, and therefore, the battle of the experts was a wash.

§ 13.23   —Charts and Documentation

Construction projects tend to produce an overwhelming amount of documentation, such as contracts, purchase orders, daily diaries, time cards, invoices, requests for information, shop drawings, field orders, change orders, surety bonds, correspondence, schedules, and accounting records. The effective handling of the documentation at trial calls for mental and manual dexterity as well as visual acuity. As discussed in **Chapter 2**, an effective way to assemble and analyze documentary evidence is to abstract documents and key the information into a computer database program that is capable of assembling and sorting the abstracts into chronological order by subject, author, and date. This organization allows easy identification of the documents that will be used as exhibits, and the exhibits may then be assembled for introduction at trial according to the order of the witnesses.

Superior control of the documentation may be the winning factor in the successful defense of a construction case. Be sure you have gathered and reviewed all of the primary and secondary contract documents at issue. Photographs of all defects in the work and of any subsequent repairs should be taken under rigorous authentication procedures. Include frames of reference, such as scales where appropriate, and be sure to retain a reference as to the date, time, and place of the photograph. Large blowups should be made of any critical portions of the specifications or construction contract.

Much of the project documentation in a construction case is generated by parties other than the owner. The contractor will have developed volumes of daily reports, schedules, diaries, correspondence, and so forth. The architect or construction manager may also have prepared documents, but their own biases and interests may be reflected and not the owner's. But

---

[6] J. Underwood, A Guide to Federal Discovery Rules, 47 (2d ed. 1985).

this is not fatal to an owner defendant. The construction record is likely replete with documents that can be used to refute the claimant's case. For example, subcontractor records may reflect coordination problems of the general contractor, shop drawing logs may indicate submissions delayed by the contractor, and job meeting minutes may discuss contractor problems. All is not lost, especially if the documents are well organized to allow easy access to information useful to the defense.

§ 13.24 Jury Instructions and Verdicts

After a lengthy construction trial, the jury is inundated with the various tasks of recollecting the facts, determining the significance of the testimony and the documents, evaluating the demeanor of the witnesses, and trying to understand and apply the law given them by the judge. With respect to this last task, some researchers have demonstrated that juries frequently misunderstand the instructions on the law; this is painfully true in complex construction disputes. It is therefore imperative that logical, rational, and understandable instructions on the law, which support the theory of recovery as well as the theory of the defense, be prepared to guide the delicate and sometimes difficult deliberations of the jury.

With increasing regularity, judges are requiring the submission of proposed jury instructions at or before the commencement of the trial. Advance preparation of the jury instructions also serves the important goal of focusing the lawyer's attention on the legal elements of the claims and defenses. However, the instructions need to conform to the court's rulings and the nature of the proof actually presented during the trial. Accordingly, the instructions should be modified at the conclusion of the evidence, and a revised copy should be filed with the clerk to preserve rejected instructions for appellate review.

In most jurisdictions, proposed jury instructions must be accompanied by citation to legal authority. At the charge conference, the legal support for the instruction is argued in an oral presentation to the court. Although often overlooked by even the most seasoned lawyers, a court reporter should be present at the charging conference to preserve a record of the objections made concerning the instructions proposed by the adversary. It is preferable to state objections at the charge conference instead of after the instructions are given to the jury. Curative instructions should be submitted with the record.

Since jury instructions must convey complex legal concepts that are often misunderstood, they should be simple and easy to understand. Avoid technical terms and legalese. This may be difficult to do in construction cases, but use of straightforward language will help to present a clear case, and will help jury comprehension.

Instructions should not be argumentative or one-sided, because this significantly reduces your chance of getting the requested charge and, if given, increases your chance of appellate reversal. Caution must be taken to walk the line between honing instructions that subtly favor your client's position in the case, and drafting instructions that endeavor to be unfairly persuasive.

Jury instructions should explain the introductory parts of the trial; the permissible use of the evidence, as well as opening and closing arguments; the substance of the claims and defenses; and the process of deliberating and reaching a verdict. Again, straightforward explanations are more useful than construction industry jargon.

A carte blanche objection to the jury instructions will generally not be sufficient to attack specific instructions on appeal. Thus, as is true with objections during direct examination, objections should be specific, and a ruling on the objection should be obtained. This is crucial since the single largest source of reversals on appeal after trial is error in jury instructions.

Common objections to jury instructions include: ambiguous, argumentative, failure of evidentiary proof, legal standard erroneous, theory of the case or issue omitted, personal opinion stated, or appeal to juror sympathy.

Construction litigation over a single project usually involves claims by the contractor against the owner, as well as claims by the owner against the contractor. In such circumstances, it is advantageous to furnish the jury with a special verdict form that allows it to reach separate monetary verdicts on all claims, rather than being compelled to find that a single sum is due to either party. Special verdict forms may minimize an expensive, full-blown retrial on the merits after a successful appeal. Special verdicts can also be prepared in consideration of the effect that a verdict may have on insurance coverage.

§ 13.25 Conclusion

Defending against construction claims usually provides the counsel with unique challenges and opportunities. An astute attorney can generally provide the client with an effective defense for what at first appears to be a difficult case. Analysis, advocacy, and hard work often are keys for the defense in construction litigation. However, it is often the case that effective defense advocacy directs the client to settlement or alternate ways to resolve construction disputes, even when the defendant has a solid case. Effective defense is to protect the defendant's interests in resolving or litigating the case.

CHAPTER 14
SETTLING CONSTRUCTION CASES
M. Hamilton Whitman, Jr., Esquire

M. Hamilton Whitman, Jr., is a partner in the law firm of Ober, Kaler, Grimes & Shriver (Maryland, Washington, D.C., New York, and New Jersey). His litigation practice includes commercial and contract disputes; personal injury defense; and property, casualty, and insurance litigation. Areas of emphasis include construction law, customs and international trade, intermodal transportation and maritime law, and creditors' rights. Mr. Whitman is a member of the Litigation Section of the Maryland State and American Bar Associations, the Forum on the Construction Industry, the Maritime Law Association of the United States, the Association of Transportation Practitioners, and the American Waterways Operators, Inc. He has lectured on construction law, including serving as a Lecturer at the University of Virginia School of Law. Mr. Whitman is a graduate of Princeton University and the University of Virginia School of Law.

§ 14.1 Introduction
§ 14.2 Principles Underlying Settlement: Control and Cost
§ 14.3 Good Reasons to Settle
§ 14.4 Bad Reasons to Settle
§ 14.5 Considerations of Confidentiality
§ 14.6 Initiating Settlement
§ 14.7 —Offers of Judgment
§ 14.8 —Settlement Conferences
§ 14.9 Documenting Settlement
§ 14.10 —Liquidating Agreements
§ 14.11 —Mary Carter Agreements
§ 14.12 Negotiating toward Settlement

§ 14.13 —Negotiating Style
§ 14.14 —Timing of Negotiations
§ 14.15 Dealing with the Players
§ 14.16 Conclusion

§ 14.1 Introduction

Inclusion of a chapter on settlement in a book dedicated to litigation strategies and techniques may appear to be a case of providing instructions on how to close the barn door after the horse is gone. Settlement, however, is always one of the weapons in the litigator's arsenal. This chapter considers some of the ways in which construction attorneys may ensure that efforts toward settlement are employed at the appropriate time and to best effect. We consider first some of the reasons why settlement should always remain an option in construction cases, even through the trial process and on appeal. We then explore approaches to settlement and settlement techniques, including some of the pitfalls that may be encountered when insufficient attention is paid to the mechanics and documentation of settlement.

§ 14.2 Principles Underlying Settlement: Control and Cost

Two principles underlie all the benefits of settlement. The first and paramount settlement principle is that when a case is settled, the parties retain control over the outcome, denying that control to the lawyer and the court. This principle has been well stated in the address of one federal district court judge to the participants in a pretrial settlement conference before a major construction trial:

> Gentlemen, this is a case which should be settled between the parties. In present day thinking, it seems to be the idea that any problem can be cured in a Federal District Court. This, I assure you, is an erroneous approach. There is not a lawyer in this courtroom capable of operating the Providence Hospital. There is not a lawyer in this courtroom capable of running Manhattan Construction Company; there is not a lawyer in this room capable of running McCauley Associates; nor a lawyer capable of running Fairbanks-Morse; nor a lawyer capable of running Ernst, and I assure you there is not a Judge in this courtroom capable of doing so.[1]

---

[1] E.C. Ernst, Inc. v. Manhattan Constr. Co., 387 F. Supp. 1001, 1008 (S.D. Ala. 1974).

§ 14.2 UNDERLYING PRINCIPLES: CONTROL & COST

The implications of this statement, and of this first principle of settlement, should be impressed upon every party to construction litigation. When a case is settled, the outcome has been determined and controlled by the opposing parties themselves. By contrast, the decision of a jury, judge, arbitrator, or other dispute resolution forum is outside the control of the parties. One or more of the parties to a case may be unenthusiastic about the terms of settlement, if not downright dissatisfied with them, but at least the parties know what those terms will be. Leaving the matter in the hands of the court, arbitrator, or other decision-maker, by contrast, involves the real risk of rolling the dice and placing one's fate in the hands of others. And while the term "runaway jury" is perhaps most familiar, judges and arbitrators have also been known to "run away" with construction cases.

A simple yet realistic example should suffice by way of illustration. Take the case of a subcontractor who walks off the job, protesting nonpayment by the owner and general contractor, and frustrated over mismanagement of the construction project. In ensuing litigation, the general contractor sues for punitive damages, alleging bad faith dealings (or another appropriate standard for punitive damages under the applicable substantive law) by the subcontractor. In weighing the risks and benefits of proceeding to trial, the subcontractor and its attorney may believe wholeheartedly that the punitive damages claim is unlikely to be upheld by the court, and that such an opinion may be shared by the general contractor and its attorney. As a consequence, it may very well be possible to negotiate settlement without serious consideration of the punitive damages count.

On the other hand, if the case goes to trial, and the jury surprises everyone by returning an award of punitive damages, the case becomes much more difficult to settle. The attorney for the plaintiff general contractor may find the client no longer willing to settle for a reasonable figure, as the prospect of the pot of gold at the end of the punitive damages rainbow changes the client's view of the case. Complicating the situation may be questions of recoverability of the punitive damage award, the insurability of the award, and the viability of the defendant's business in the face of a massive punitive damages award.

Thus, the failure to settle, or, viewed properly, the affirmative decision not to settle, may lead the litigants down a path of uncertainties. It will certainly lead the litigants down a path of significant expense. This brings us to the second principal reason to keep settlement always in mind as a possibility, namely, the immense cost of construction litigation (both in money and in diverted resources).

With the disappearance of major antitrust cases, construction cases have come into their own as among the longest and most complex kinds of cases tried before the courts. For instance, in a construction case recently concluded in the United States District Court for the District of Delaware, it was noted on the record that the case consumed more pages of trial transcript than any other case in the history of that court, and that in terms of the number of trial days, the case was the second longest that district had ever seen. Yet the trial itself involved only five parties represented by three sets of lawyers, the remnants of the fourteen parties and nine sets of lawyers who had earlier participated in the litigation. That earlier litigation was pared down after a minitrial effort succeeded in having most of the parties settle. Had it gone to trial with all fourteen parties still involved, it might very well have set a world's record for trial time and length of transcript.

Construction cases typically involve not one incident but rather a relationship that developed over time. The presentation of such a relationship to the trier of fact necessarily involves days, weeks, or months of trial time. The preparation of the case will have already required months, if not years, of discovery. Thus, unless one has the distinctly mixed blessing of handling a case filed on an expedited trial docket such as that maintained by some courts, the participants in even a relatively modest construction dispute can look forward to years of legal expense.[2]

The costs of lost opportunities in a major piece of construction litigation can also be staggering. Construction cases have grappled for years with appropriate means of calculating underabsorbed or diverted management and overhead costs for purposes of construction delay claims, yet the very act of proceeding with litigation is likely to cause similar costs to be incurred, without any hope of their ever being recovered. During the months or years of discovery and pretrial activity, key players in the disputed construction project will be distracted from their ongoing responsibilities in order to assist in educating the lawyers and in order to respond to discovery requests. Upper level and home office management will also be involved in the efforts to document damages and in the decision-making that goes along with preparing for trial. Particularly if the case is to be tried to a jury, it will probably be necessary to have a representative of the client company present in the courtroom at trial to personalize the client before the finder of fact. This representative will be a valuable member of the client's construction team, whose presence in court will deprive the client of his services in construction activities. All of these represent opportunity costs and expenses that will not be recoverable in litigation.

---

[2] The United States District Court for the Eastern District of Virginia is perhaps the best known of these fast track courts. *See "Rocket Docket:" Federal Courts in Virginia Dispense Speedy Justice,* The Wall Street J., Dec. 3, 1987, at 1. In a construction case recently filed in that court, the complaint was filed in October, discovery cutoff and pretrial conference were the following February, and trial was in April.

Thus, cost and control are the two principles that underlie much of the rationale for settlement. These principles should be part of the decision-making calculus throughout the stages of litigation described in the other chapters of this book, from evaluating the case upon initial involvement to deciding whether to appeal. At any stage, from preliminary evaluation through discovery, pretrial motions, trial, and appeal, there may come a time when the positions of the parties are uniquely favorable to a settlement that will best promote, or will least discourage, the fortunes of all the parties. When those moments occur, the lawyer who truly has a grasp on the case will recognize the occasion and will act to dispose of the case through settlement.

§ 14.3 Good Reasons to Settle

Specific reasons why cases should be settled are as numerous as the cases themselves. However, in construction cases, certain factors reappear often enough in the decision-making process to be worth highlighting, if only briefly.

One of these factors is the desire to maintain an ongoing business relationship between the parties. It is often the case in the construction setting that parties have done, or are doing, business together apart from the one project that has fallen into litigation. It may be very much in the parties' best interest to continue to even expand those business dealings, notwithstanding the difficulties on the problem project. Prosecuting the litigation through trial, however, is likely to jeopardize those business interests. If only on account of the litigation posture, businesspersons will come to view each other as adversaries rather than as venturers both seeking a reasonable profit on their business deals. Specific documents discovered and testimony adduced at discovery depositions may contribute to a hardening of positions. As the field supervisors and office middle managers testify, their frustrations may boil over in the form of harsh, often personal criticism of their opponent and of their counterparts in the opponent's work force or office staff. Once such criticism is articulated in public and on the record, it may be impossible to continue "business as usual" with the other side.

The construction attorney can and should do the client the service of anticipating such consequences of litigation. The client who is adamant about bringing suit is well served by advice covering more than simply the chances of winning or losing and providing an understanding of the wider ranging consequences of pursuing litigation.

Another factor in settling an individual case is the opportunity that settlement provides for tailoring the outcome to the circumstances of the case and to the needs of the parties. Not every dispute can best be resolved by an exchange of money. While courts are restricted in their ability to prescribe equitable relief or imaginative alternative outcomes, the parties themselves are not so limited. Future business, shared remedial efforts, and assumption of liabilities to other parties are all among the elements that might be included in a settlement truly tailored to a particular case.

In addition to these positive inducements for settlement, there are a number of reasons to settle in order to avoid unpleasant realities of the litigation and trial process. Litigation, especially the trial itself, is a form of stylized warfare. The adage, "All's fair in love and war" may not literally apply, because the warfare is restricted by rules and procedures. It is certainly the case, however, that the attorneys will seek every reasonable advantage, and that in doing so the weaknesses of the parties will be laid bare on the public record. That public record will come to reveal a number of things that the parties, or individual actors, would much prefer had been left undiscovered.

A prime example is the discovery and use of personnel files. Most companies of any sophistication or size maintain some form of personnel evaluation system, including periodic written evaluations of job performance. Such a system enables the company to justify and document merit-based promotions and salary decisions. Such a system also provides objective support for employment decisions, so as to enable the employer to head off possible discrimination suits based on allegations of racial, sex, or age discrimination. It is important, therefore, that criticism be candidly expressed in performance evaluation and reports.

The existence of critical reports, however, can cause significant pain in discovery or at the trial of a construction case. An aggressive litigator will obtain copies of evaluations for anyone whose job performance is an issue in the case. Those evaluations can be used to undermine the opponent's witnesses and, in the right case, to disarm the opponent against a charge of incompetent performance. For instance, if proper scheduling is an issue, it will be difficult to respond to a revelation that the job scheduler was fired after a series of highly critical performance reviews. Even if the reports are not substantively damaging on the merits, a good employee may respond with anger and hurt feelings if made aware of previously confidential management criticism of his or her work.

The parties may also want to protect against discovery and publication of other confidential business information. A trade contractor may not want the world (or even the general contractor and owner) to know how it prepared its job estimate. A supplier may have proprietary design information that it wants to protect. Engaging in litigation will almost guarantee that the opponent will have the opportunity to discover, and make more or less public, information that the client would prefer to keep confidential. Settlement at an appropriate stage can avoid such damage, and tailored settlement terms that include the return of documents or the sealing of files can help contain any damage that has occurred.

§ 14.4 Bad Reasons to Settle

Commentators and authors have generated a significant body of literature extolling the virtues of settlement from the standpoint of what might be called supposed benefits to society at large. While these societal benefits may have some importance, they are not a reason for settling a particular construction case.

The foundation upon which much of this literature appears to be erected is the perception that the courts are literally overwhelmed by the number of cases they must handle; therefore, more cases should be settled because judges do not have the time to preside over all of the trials that would otherwise be necessary. Although there is something to be said for this "resource management" approach to the judicial branch of government, it should not be surprising that much of the support appears to come from judges and not from litigators or trial lawyers.[3] Within the strictures of the role as a member of the bar and as an officer of the court, the attorney has an absolute duty to represent the client zealously and to press the client's case to the best possible conclusion. Consequently, notions of whether the judicial system should be burdened with the trial of a particular case should not be part of the lawyer's approach. Rather, the lawyer should recognize and fulfill the job as advocate, leaving questions of resource management to other people or to other occasions.

Another bad reason to settle a case is the client's or the lawyer's cold feet in the face of uncertainty as trial of the construction case draws near. If the case has been properly prepared and the risks have been weighed at some length, there should rarely be reason for a last-minute reassessment that results in settlement for an amount quite different from the earlier agreed upon figure. Yet such settlements are not uncommon in construction cases. The client is entitled to demand, and the lawyer should be prepared to provide, a good reason why the evaluation of the case has changed suddenly. If either client or attorney senses uncertainty, it may be that the cold feet syndrome has set in, and a rigorous analysis may renew the determination of both client and attorney to carry the case forward through trial.

This cold feet syndrome can have a drastic effect upon construction litigation, with its typical multiparty posture. In such cases, it is not at all

---

[3] *See, e.g.,* W. Brazil, Effective Approaches to Settlement (1988); H. Will, R. Merhige, & A. Rubin, The Role of the Judge in the Settlement Process (Federal Judicial Center, 1977).

unusual for co-parties to have spread the burden of trial preparation, relying on each other to prepare fact witnesses and shared experts. If one party develops cold feet, his reluctance to go to trial may drag down the value of his co-party's case. Especially in states where the plaintiff is entitled to one dismissal without prejudice up to the eve of trial, a co-plaintiff can find that all the thorough trial preparation is for naught. To avoid this outcome, attorneys should keep themselves abreast of the progress of all co-parties during trial preparation, and should demand rigorous justification for any maneuver that suggests cold feet.

§ 14.5 Considerations of Confidentiality

With these principles of settlement in mind, there is one important issue to consider before turning to specific settlement devices. The confidentiality of settlement negotiations always should be of concern in construction cases. Very often, a case can be settled, in whole or in part, during the course of litigation. This may reflect on the merits of the cases against various defendants or among various parties. Discovery may have revealed the truth about a subcontractor's delay claim or an owner's loss of use/lost profit claim, or the merits of the case may otherwise have become clear. It may also reflect a number of different tactical elements, including the plaintiff's need to avoid financing further litigation or a defendant's desire to avoid being caught in a crossfire. The general contractor may want to settle with a subcontractor in order to pursue claims against the owner without having to look over his shoulder.

Whatever the impetus for settlement with some party or parties, it is likely that the other parties will have an interest in learning the terms of the settlement. It may also be the case that settlement efforts fall through, and litigation continues. One party may then desire to admit evidence of the negotiations during trial. It may also be the case that someone not a party to a particular case may later want to learn the terms upon which a settlement was effected. All of these issues raise a concern for the confidentiality of settlement efforts.

Criminal defendants are read *Miranda* rights and are thereby put on notice that what is said can and will be used against them. Parties to civil actions are put on notice as to what may and may not be used against them regarding what was said and done during settlement negotiations by Rule 408 of the Federal Rules of Evidence. Rule 408 addresses the admissibility of statements and conduct made during or related to settlement negotiations. For state actions, the attorney must become familiar with each state's rules or common law of evidence to the extent that they are different from the federal rules. Even if worded the same, state rules may be interpreted differently by that state's case law.

§ 14.5 CONFIDENTIALITY CONSIDERATIONS

Admissibility of Evidence of Settlement Negotiations

The most important aspect of confidentiality of settlement efforts is the admissibility of such evidence at trial. Federal Rule 408 bars the admission of evidence pertaining to offers to "compromise a claim" when such a claim is "disputed" and the evidence is offered "to prove liability for or invalidity of the claim or its amount." This means that there must first be a dispute between the parties before compromise negotiations will be protected by the rule. For example, the Advisory Committee Notes state that the protection of Rule 408 is not afforded to a debtor who does not deny the amount or size of the debt owed but is merely trying to reduce the amount the creditor will accept in full satisfaction of the debt. Without a dispute as to the existence of the claim or the amount of the claim, the rule offers no protection.

An important additional element of the federal rule is the second sentence, offering protection to communications and conduct made during the course of compromise negotiations. Thus, under Rule 408, it is not only the offer of settlement itself which is protected, but also the various efforts which led to and surrounded the offer itself. This is a distinct broadening of the protection provided to settlement negotiations by common law, and therefore may not be a protection available under the law of states without evidence rules, or with rules that differ significantly from the federal rules.

These two levels of protection are provided by Rule 408 to fulfill the policy of "favoring the compromise and settlement of disputes." A major concern in the application of Rule 408 is the issue of when a dispute is deemed to have arisen, such that the protection of the rule is invoked. Some courts have suggested that a dispute may not have arisen for purposes of Rule 408 until after a lawsuit has been filed, although that is not the majority rule.[4] Another court made a technical distinction between business communications and offers of compromise, with the former not protected by Rule 408.[5]

These two cases do not appear to conform to the purpose of Rule 408, promoting settlement negotiations. If a party must wait to file a lawsuit, or threaten to file, the atmosphere then is likely to be less conducive to settlement negotiations. Other courts have used a more reasonable standard to determine when a dispute has arisen, holding that a dispute arises under Rule 408 when the plaintiff reasonably "contemplated that litigation might be necessary" and the other party concedes "that litigation was possible."[6]

---

[4] *See* United States v. Hooper, 596 F.2d 219, 225 (7th Cir. 1979).

[5] Big O Tire Dealer, Inc. v. Goodyear Tire & Rubber Co., 561 F.2d 1365 (10th Cir. 1977).

[6] Olin Corp. v. Insurance Co. of North Am., 603 F. Supp. 445, 450 (S.D.N.Y. 1985).

Under this standard there is no requirement to threaten to file suit, or to actually file suit. This may have an important application to construction disputes. Often claims arise during the course of construction, and are handled as part of the contract administration process rather than litigation. The parties to construction claims do not always threaten or contemplate the necessity of litigation. However, once litigation has commenced there is no doubt that a Rule 408 dispute exists.

It must be remembered that Rule 408 is not a complete bar to use of settlement evidence at trial, but only a partial bar pertaining to proving "liability for or invalidity of the claim or its amount." When evidence of settlement negotiations is offered for any other purpose it may be admissible. The rule itself states that evidence is not required to be excluded if offered to prove "bias or prejudice of a witness, negativing a contention of undue delay, or proving an effort to obstruct a criminal investigation or prosecution."

It is important to note, however, that evidence is not automatically admissible just because opposing counsel finds another purpose to offer the evidence. When evidence of settlement negotiations is offered for a purpose which is not barred by Rule 408, then Rule 403 of the Federal Rules of Evidence should come into play. Under Rule 403, the court must balance the probative value of the evidence against the likely harm of admitting the evidence. The court must give great concern to the public policy against inhibiting freedom of communication in the context of compromise negotiations, especially in the area of construction claims, because of the frequency with which disputes arise on construction projects. Such a policy would surely be jeopardized if evidence of settlement could easily be admitted by finding any convenient purpose not specifically barred under Rule 408.

Showing bias is a permissible purpose under the rules and is not barred by Rule 408. One common way to show bias is to introduce evidence of a settlement agreement between the contractor and a former defendant subcontractor who has testified against the remaining defendant owner and architect. The nonsettling defendants will want to offer evidence of the settlement agreement between the contractor and the subcontractor to show that the subcontractor is biased in favor of the plaintiff contractor. However, the general contractor may have many reasons for settling with a subcontractor for a much lower amount early on in negotiations. Offers of compromise often are not relevant, even for a permitted purpose, "since the offer may be motivated by a desire for peace rather than from any concession of weakness of position."[7] Under Rule 403 the plaintiff can argue that admitting such evidence is prejudicial because: (1) revealing evidence from settlement negotiations goes against the weighty public policy of

---

[7] Fed. R. Evid. 408 advisory committee's note.

favoring settlement negotiations and (2) revealing the amount of the settlement may imply to the jury that the settlement amount is the value of the claim against the nonsettling defendant.

Therefore, if precluded from using Rule 408 to protect confidential settlement negotiations, counsel should look to Rule 403, arguing irrelevancy and prejudicial effect of the evidence. On this issue, the courts have gone both ways.[8]

Discoverability of Evidence of Settlement Negotiations

The second aspect of confidentiality is the discoverability of evidence of settlement negotiations. There is no bar under federal procedure to the discoverability of settlement negotiations. Rule 408 "does not require the exclusion of any evidence otherwise discoverable simply because it is presented in the context of settlement negotiations."[9] Federal Rule of Civil Procedure 26(b), which defines the scope and limits of discovery, states "[i]t is not ground for objection that the information sought will be inadmissible at the trial if the information sought appears reasonably calculated to lead to the discovery of admissible evidence." This makes it explicit that counsel cannot rely on Rule 408 to prevent discovery of settlement negotiations.

Discoverability may lead to abuse, however, as parties seek to discover settlement negotiations in hopes of finding a permissible purpose for later having the evidence admitted at trial. This, in effect, undermines and diminishes the protection offered under Rule 408. To protect against discoverability, some have argued that settlement communications should be privileged and barred from discovery under Rule 26(b). However, that is not the apparent intent of the Federal Rules of Evidence. Rule 408 does not rise to the level of a "privilege" in its wording, nor were settlement communications considered as one of the nine nonconstitutional privileges originally submitted by the Supreme Court to Congress as Article V of the proposed Federal Rules of Evidence.[10] Prior to the effective date of the Federal Rules of Evidence, courts were not disposed to treat settlement negotiations as privileged. Whether under Federal Rule of Evidence 501 (a general rule about common-law privileges) such a privilege will ever evolve is yet to be determined.

---

[8] *See* John McShain, Inc. v. Cessna Aircraft Co., 563 F.2d 632 (3rd Cir. 1977) (nonsettling defendant allowed to introduce the terms of the settlement agreement to show that the plaintiff's expert witness was biased); Kennon v. Slipstreamer, Inc., 794 F.2d 1067 (5th Cir. 1986) (trial judge committed reversible error by disclosing to the jury the nominal consideration of the settlement).

[9] Fed. R. Evid. 408.

[10] Proposed Federal Rules of Evidence, art. V, Privileges, 51 F.R.D. 315, 356–83 (Mar. 1971).

Parties to construction cases should be especially concerned about protecting against the discoverability of the settlement negotiations. First, there are usually many parties involved, and one party may try to settle with another one without exposing the discussions and considerations to the other side. Second, because construction cases are so highly technical and complex, experts are often called upon to assist in the negotiations. The findings and opinions of the parties' experts are important considerations that can later be turned against the experts.

There are, however, means available to keep evidence of settlement negotiations from being discovered. First, Federal Rule of Civil Procedure 26(c) allows for a protective order whereby a party may petition the court to limit the scope of discovery. By means of such a motion, a party can ask the court to analyze the discovery request and balance the public policy stated in Rule 408 against the requesting parties' need for the requested information. This adds a level of protection and guards against routine discovery requests.

A second means to protect the confidentiality of settlement negotiations is to approach settlement by way of a private settlement conference hosted by a judge or magistrate. The judicial host can require that counsel reveal the reasoning for and the strengths and weaknesses of the client's claims directly to the judge, in private, before the judge sits down with the opposing counsel. Therefore, the opposing counsel does not know directly what the other counsel has revealed to the judge, nor, without compelling reason, can the judge be required to divulge that which was revealed in private.

Third, the parties to settlement negotiations can contract to guarantee the confidentiality of their communications and conduct before, during, and after negotiations. The contract can be worded so as to bar all parties to the agreement from introducing at trial or attempting to discover any evidence relating to the settlement negotiations, for *any* purpose. Unfortunately, such contracts only bind those who sign the agreement, and any other nonsigning party may make discovery requests or introduce at trial communications covered by the contract. Thus, to minimize the danger of discovery in multiparty construction litigation, the contractor, owner, subcontractor, designer, and other parties must sign the confidentiality agreement. This may be difficult in such a construction case, because of the multitude of parties and their divergent interests.

Whether confidentiality contracts between those who participate in settlement negotiations are enforceable is not settled in the law.[11] Because the agreement is a contract it is subject to all the constraints imposed by the law of contracts. A confidentiality contract that is contrary to law or public policy may not be enforceable. Also, there is always the risk that a judge

---

[11] *See* Grumman Aerospace Corp. v. Titanium Metate Corp., 91 F.R.D. 84 (1981).

will determine the policy of ascertaining the truth to outweigh that of private contract. Nevertheless, a confidentiality agreement may be of significant assistance whenever there is a concern for privacy.

§ 14.6 Initiating Settlement

Having considered questions of policy and principle, it is appropriate to examine some devices that may be employed for initiating settlement of construction cases. Two such devices, offers of judgment and settlement conferences, are discussed in the following sections.

§ 14.7 —Offers of Judgment

A significant mechanism for precipitating settlement of a construction case is the offer of judgment provided for in Rule 68 of the Federal Rules of Civil Procedure. Rule 68 allows a party who is defending a claim to have an offer served upon the adverse party "to allow judgment to be taken against him for the money or property or to the effect specified in his offer, with costs then accrued." The offer is served only on the opposing party and is not filed with the court unless and until it is accepted.

An offer of judgment has the advantage of formalizing the settlement negotiations by invoking the powers of the court, as well as letting the opposing party know of the seriousness of the offer. The rule imposes a strict time frame in which to work. A defending party must make its offer of judgment "more than 10 days before the trial begins." After the offer has been served it remains valid and cannot be withdrawn for 10 days. An offer that is not accepted within the 10-day time period is deemed withdrawn.

The party offering must be willing to have judgment entered against itself. The offeror must be "a party defending against a claim," which in most cases is the defendant. A plaintiff may make an offer of judgment only to a counterclaim, and such an offer can only relate to the counterclaim and not to the plaintiff's complaint.[12] Also, the plaintiff cannot make a counteroffer to the defendant's offer; the plaintiff may only accept or reject the defendant's offer.

Rule 68 stipulates that the offer of judgment must be for "money or property or to the effect specified in his offer, with costs then accrued." When making an offer of judgment the offeror must be careful to understand the implications of "with costs then accrued." An offer is valid even if it fails to recite that costs are included.[13] Unless the offer explicitly

---

[12] *See* Delta Air Lines, Inc. v. August, 450 U.S. 346, 350 n.5 (1981).
[13] Marek v. Chesny, 473 U.S. 1, 6 (1985).

excludes costs, in which case the offer would be invalid as not in compliance with Rule 68, costs will be assumed to be a part of the offer.

The most important aspect of Rule 68 is the leverage it provides to the offeror. The Rule states that "[i]f the judgment finally obtained by the offeree is not more favorable than the offer, the offeree must pay the costs incurred after the making of the offer." The costs referred to are twofold. First, the plaintiff must pay the post-offer costs of the defendant, which in and of themselves can be substantial, and second, the plaintiff is denied recovery of its post-offer costs. As a result, even though the plaintiff wins on the merits and recovers some damages, the plaintiff will not be as big a winner as first thought.

This device can be used effectively in construction delay cases. It is not unusual for a contractor to win on the entitlement issues but not recover extensive damages. A contractor that has experienced this dilemma in the past may be receptive to an offer of judgment from the owner. If the contractor is recalcitrant, the owner may take some satisfaction from a subsequent unfavorable verdict, if the judgment deprives the contractor of a portion of its costs and deducts the owner's post-offer costs.

A significant anomaly in the operation of Rule 68 is that the rule does not apply when the plaintiff fails to recover but instead the defendant prevails at trial.[14] This may happen in construction delay cases where instead of the contractor plaintiff prevailing, the defendant owner recovers its delay costs. Delay claims are often risky in this regard. Under this scenario, the plaintiff does not recover its costs or attorney fees, but the offer of judgment does not operate to require the plaintiff to pay the defendant's post-offer costs. Instead, the defendant's recovery of costs is then discretionary with the judge, under Federal Rule of Civil Procedure 54(d).

Rule 68 allows a defendant to make more than one offer of judgment. The Rule states "The fact that an offer is made but not accepted does not preclude a subsequent offer." However, the closer the offer is made to the time of trial, the more the defendant will have to include to cover costs accrued to the plaintiff, and the less risk to the plaintiff, who would only be responsible to pay the post-offer costs.

§ 14.8 —Settlement Conferences

The use of settlement conferences has become more common in construction cases, as both state and federal courts employ this device to dispose of cases on their dockets. Rule 16 of the Federal Rules of Civil Procedure stipulates that the court may require the parties and their attorneys to

---

[14] Delta Air Lines, Inc. v. August, 450 U.S. 346, 351–52.

appear for a pretrial conference for, among other purposes, "facilitating the settlement of the case." Among the subjects to be discussed is "the possibility of settlement." Out of this and similar state rules, or out of the courts' inherent powers to control their own dockets, has grown what has come to be known as the judicially hosted settlement conference.

The settlement conference can be initiated by counsel or by the court, and may be hosted by judge or magistrate. If a case is to be tried to the court, and not to a jury, it is most appropriate for the host of the settlement conference to be someone other than the judge to whom the case will be tried. In many federal courts, such cases are referred to the magistrates for settlement conferences. In some state systems, a retired judge serves as the settlement judge, performing this valuable service on a part-time basis and thereby freeing active judges of this burden.

There are divergent views as to whether active participation as settlement negotiator is a proper role for the judicial branch. There is a strong advocacy among the civil trial judges for the active employment of judges to help facilitate settlement.[15] Many judges have found their dockets so crowded that they feel compelled to help settle cases out of court so that "justice" may proceed. Judges express their frustration that "non-meritorious" cases are consuming precious court time and prefer holding pretrial conferences in order to attempt to settle those cases without trial.

It must be noted that this is a relatively new role for judges. To be sure, judges have been helping cases settle since time immemorial, but never has the judicial branch taken such a concerted and active role in settlement negotiations as it has in recent years. This trend has been a cause of some concern for many judges and commentators. One early and thoughtful critic, Professor Judith Resnick, observes that judges no longer decide cases but rather merely "process" or "manage" caseloads.[16] A guiding focus of the judicial branch has always been that judges not only decide cases between the parties, but also settle important societal issues in doing so. There is concern that this focus is blurring, and that judges are becoming more preoccupied with clearing their dockets than with filling a role that only the judicial branch can fill.

Another critic, Professor Dale Oesterle, posits that judges who engage in settling their cases do not clear their dockets any faster than if they did not engage in pretrial settlement negotiations.[17] Professor Oesterle also argues that overzealous judges may misuse their influence to settle cases

---

[15] Brazil, *Settling Civil Cases: What Lawyers Want from Judges,* Judges' J., Summer 1984.

[16] Resnick, *Managing Judges,* 96 Harv. L. Rev. 374 (1982).

[17] Oesterle, *Dangers of Judge-Imposed Settlements,* 9 Litigation Mag., No. 3, Spring 1983.

on improper grounds. Professor Oesterle questions the quality of decisions reached by judges acting as negotiators and asks for a more thorough analysis.

Despite these theoretical and practical criticisms, the judicial settlement conference can be a useful occasion for moving a construction case toward settlement. Frequently, large construction cases take on a life of their own. Construction cases are often so complex that judicial involvement and even threats may be necessary to get the parties and counsel to begin to talk about settlement in a serious way.

The format of such a conference depends upon the judge or other judicial host. The judge may have standing orders that describe the requirements for settlement conferences. Many judges require a written settlement conference statement to be received prior to the conference. Such statements are often required on a confidential basis from each party. In the alternative, a joint statement in the nature of a pretrial order may be required. The contents of such a document may include a brief factual setting of the case, legal and factual arguments that support each side's position, procedural dates such as when trial is scheduled and which motions have been considered, and a description of the relief being sought. Confidential statements may include estimated costs if the case goes to trial, and an opening figure that the client has agreed to. The judge may meet with all participants, including both attorneys and client representatives vested with settlement authority. More often, the judge may prefer to meet with each party and its attorney separately and then shuttle back and forth between both sides. Another alternative is to meet with counsel for both sides together without the presence of the parties.

A primary advantage of the judicially hosted settlement conference is the presence of an authority figure to make recalcitrant clients feel more comfortable in accepting assessments of their weaknesses and the other party's strengths. The judge may be able to deflate extreme positions taken by recalcitrant owners and contractors, as well as by exaggerated legal and evidentiary arguments of inexperienced or aggressive counsel. When voluntary negotiations have failed to result in settlement, the presence of a respected third party may break the impasse.

Another advantage is that a judicially hosted settlement conference is relatively inexpensive, especially when compared to hiring a private mediator or holding a minitrial in a construction case, as we discuss in **Chapter 10.** In this regard, a full-blown judicial settlement conference can acquire many of the attributes and advantages of a minitrial. Each side has the opportunity to present its case in condensed fashion, and the presentation can be made to representatives of the parties, or at least to a neutral person who can immediately convey a reaction to the parties. This can provide the impetus for successfully reaching a settlement that had earlier been elusive.

§ 14.9 Documenting Settlement

Despite the obvious attributes of settlement conferences and offers of judgment as precipitating factors, most settlements of construction cases are still the result of extended hard negotiation. Possible approaches to that negotiation are considered in § 14.13. Before they reach agreement, however, the attorneys involved in negotiations of construction cases must be aware of possible ways to document settlement, ways that may be dictated by the relationships of the parties and the settlement strategies employed. In that light, this section of the chapter will examine liquidating agreements and Mary Carter agreements as possible devices for documenting settlement of construction cases.

§ 14.10 —Liquidating Agreements

One of the best mechanisms for achieving settlement of construction delay claims is the liquidating agreement. In such a document, the general contractor agrees to press the subcontractor's delay claim against the owner, while the subcontractor agrees to accept some limited recovery as full satisfaction of its delay claim. The rationale for entering into such a document is, typically, the general contractor's agreement that delay was caused by the owner or by the design professionals. In theory, this rationale could also apply in reverse, to an owner's delay claim against a general contractor, when both agree that delay was actually caused by a particular subcontractor.

There are two principal reasons for the popularity of the liquidating agreement as a device for settling part of a construction case. First, it is often in the general contractor's best interest to avoid being caught in a crossfire of claims by the owner and by subcontractors. Second, the substantive law of contracts often precludes suit directly between owner and subcontractors, as they are not in privity with each other. If the general contractor liquidates the claim of one or more subcontractors, the general contractor can then present the claim to the owner, including litigating against the owner, while relying upon support from the subcontractor.

There tend to be two polarized views of the usefulness of the liquidating agreement. The general contractor typically views the liquidating agreement as a means to obtain the tactical benefits of the subcontractor's support in exchange for a modest, up-front payment and a promise to pay the subcontractor its fair share of any future recovery from the owner. The subcontractor, however, may view the liquidating agreement as a means of getting nearly full payment on its claim up front, postponing only a small portion of its claim pending the outcome of the general contractor's claim against the owner. Such an extreme subcontractor's view is unrealistic, and is likely to defeat efforts to liquidate the claim. By way of example, in a recent negotiation the general contractor proposed an up-front payment of $50,000, while the subcontractor proposed that the up-front payment be $900,000. No matter what the tactical benefits of enlisting the subcontractor's support, few general contractors will be willing to make such an up-front payment.

The substantive governing law and the language of the construction contracts will determine in great measure the terms of the liquidating agreement. For instance, in some jurisdictions the general contractor is held not to be liable to the subcontractor for delay damages caused by the owner unless there is specific contractual language to that effect.[18] The effectiveness of a liquidating agreement may be open to question in such a jurisdiction. Under federal contract law, however, it is common practice for such agreements to be entered into, and for the general contractor to then present claims of its subcontractor against the government.[19]

The heart of the liquidating agreement is to be found in the provisions for the general contractor's liability to the subcontractor, provisions that typically operate together to establish, but limit, that liability. Examples of such provisions follow.

A first provision establishes liability and simultaneously lays the groundwork for its limitation:

> General and Sub acknowledge that the liability for the Sub's claim is the ultimate responsibility of Owner and that Sub's claim is against and through General by reason of lack of privity; by reason thereof, General acknowledges liability to Sub for Sub's claim as set forth and shall and does hereby liquidate such liability as hereinafter provided.

A following provision addresses the extent of any up-front payment by the general contractor to the subcontractor:

> General recognizes that Sub's claim as will be presented by General to Owner is meritorious, and General agrees to pay the sum of $_____ to Sub as a nonrefundable advance payment on the recovery of Sub's claim.

Typically, the agreement will provide that additional payment to the subcontractor will be based upon some proportionate share of the general contractor's recovery from the owner. Such a clause should address and

---

[18] *See* Doyle & Russell, Inc. v. Welch Pile Driving Corp., 213 Va. 698, 194 S.E.2d 719 (1973); Walter Kidde Constr., Inc. v. Connecticut, 37 Conn. Supp. 50, 434 A.2d 962 (1981).

[19] U.S. Indus., Inc. v. Blake Constr. Co., 671 F.2d 539, 550 (D.C. Cir. 1982); *see* United States v. Blair, 321 U.S. 730 (1944).

allow for possible alternative methods of recovery by the general contractor. For instance, if the court or arbitrator awards a specific dollar amount representing the subcontractor's claim, the amount to be paid by the general contractor to the subcontractor is easy to determine. If only an undifferentiated lump sum award is made, however, it may be necessary to calculate the subcontractor's share based on the percentage of the subcontractor's claim to the general contractor's overall claims.

Another essential provision establishes the downside protection to the general contractor, who is relieved of further liability if prosecution of the claim does not succeed.

> In the event that there is no recovery by General with respect to Sub's claim, or that Sub's share of recovery is less than or equal to the advance payment, then General's advance payment and General's efforts to collect and recover Sub's claim each, independently, shall constitute payment, settlement and discharge of Sub's claim, and General thereby will be discharged fully of any and all liability for Sub's claim.

Many other subjects should be covered by a comprehensive liquidating agreement. Among the other points to clarify are the subcontractor's obligation to participate at trial and/or pay attorneys' fees, the method by which the general contractor and subcontractor will agree on the contents of the subcontractor's claims, and the manner of handling any liability of the subcontractor for owner-asserted claims. All these details need to be closely attended to if the liquidation of the delay claim is to be successful.

§ 14.11 —Mary Carter Agreements

A form of partial settlement commonly used in tort cases involving joint tortfeasors is the so-called Mary Carter agreement.[20] The crux of the Mary Carter agreement is that it guarantees the plaintiff a minimum recovery, which is paid by the settling tortfeasor contingent upon the amount the plaintiff ultimately recovers from the nonsettling tortfeasor.[21] Hence, the amount the settling tortfeasor actually pays is inversely related to the size of the judgment against the nonsettling tortfeasor. In addition, the settling tortfeasor is ensured of a maximum liability, absent any allowable action for contribution.

---

[20] *See* Booth v. Mary Carter Paint Co., 202 So. 2d 8 (Fla. Dist. Ct. App. 1967). Mary Carter agreements are referred to in some states as Gallagher agreements, loan receipt agreements, or sliding scale recovery agreements.

[21] Entman, *Mary Carter Agreements: An Assessment of Attempted Solutions,* 38 U. Fla. L. Rev. 521 (1986).

For example, a settling tortfeasor in a construction personal injury claim might agree to pay the plaintiff $50,000, to be reduced dollar for dollar by the amount of any judgment against the nonsettling tortfeasor. Therefore, if the nonsettling defendant paid the plaintiff a judgment in the amount of $40,000, the settling defendant would pay only $10,000. A judgment for $50,000 or more against the nonsettling defendant would free the settling party from paying any amount under the Mary Carter agreement.

As the Mary Carter agreements only have application to tort claims, their application to construction cases may be primarily in cases involving the liability of multiparty personal injury or professional malpractice cases. For example, the Kansas City Hyatt collapse involved designers, contractors, subcontractors, and other actors in the construction process. Another example involves major hotel fires where personal injury plaintiffs allege that a conflagration resulted from negligent design and construction practices. In some cases, the owner may have a design malpractice case against two or more design firms involved in a project that resulted in substantial economic or property damages.

The nature of the agreement produces strong incentive for the parties to the agreement to maximize the absolute size of the judgment as well as to increase the proportion of the judgment that the nonsettling tortfeasor is liable for. The larger the judgment the less the settling tortfeasor will have to pay the plaintiff. Also, the larger the comparative share of the judgment attributed to the nonsettling tortfeasor, the less the plaintiff will have to rely upon the settling defendant for payment.

The perceived unfairness of this type of agreement, as pointed out by many commentators, is that the nonsettling tortfeasor is not dismissed from the suit, but remains a party-defendant to the action and participates "collusively" with the plaintiff at trial. This is unlike a conventional settlement, where the settling tortfeasor is dismissed from the litigation.

The pattern of "collusion" can take many forms. The parties to the Mary Carter agreement may cooperate during discovery by sharing documents and information. During voir dire the parties may use their challenges to find jurors most favorable to the plaintiff or who are predisposed against the nonsettling defendant.[22] At trial, the plaintiff and the settling defendant can refrain from vigorous cross-examination of each other's witnesses, while energetically cross-examining the witnesses of the other, nonsettling defendant.[23] The settling defendant may even buttress the claims of the plaintiff by conceding liability on behalf of all

---

[22] *See, e.g.,* Griener v. Zinker, 573 S.W.2d 884 (Tex. Civ. App. 1978).

[23] *See, e.g.,* General Motors Corp. v. Lahocki, 286 Md. 714, 724–26, 410 A.2d 1039, 1044–455 (1980).

the defendants, or maintaining that the nonsettling defendant is completely at fault.[24] Under a Mary Carter agreement the plaintiff is free to concentrate all effort against the nonsettling tortfeasor. Together, the plaintiff and the settling defendant can work to see that the nonsettling defendant is found completely liable or found responsible for the greater proportion of the judgment. For example, this can be disastrous for the designer of a collapsed building if the defendant contractor settles with the plaintiffs, and then recounts all of the design problems and deficiencies it encountered when constructing the project. The defendant designer and its professional liability insurance carrier will face a greater exposure with a contractor detailing the events to a jury, if the contractor is secure hiding behind a Mary Carter agreement.

Before drafting a Mary Carter agreement, counsel must research the applicable state law, both statute and judge-made. Counsel must be aware not only of the basic joint tortfeasor law of the state, but also must look closely at the state's handling of Mary Carter agreements. At one extreme, Nevada has ruled that Mary Carter agreements are void, concluding that they contravene professional ethics, constitute maintenance and champerty, and produce trial irregularities and unfairness.[25] Other jurisdictions have tried to curb the use of Mary Carter agreements by other means.[26] One common means is to allow the agreement to be admissible at trial, showing that the settling defendant's real interest is to favor the plaintiff and aid the plaintiff in receiving a substantial verdict.[27] Several jurisdictions allow the trier of fact to be informed, usually by means of a limited instruction, of the existence of the agreement and its terms.[28] All jurisdictions require that a Mary Carter agreement be disclosed to the unsettling defendant, either as an affirmative duty or in response to a properly framed discovery request. Without such disclosure the likelihood of trial unfairness is assured, for without such knowledge the nonsettling defendant will not be able to challenge the feigned posturing of the settling defendant.

Some jurisdictions have determined that even admission of a Mary Carter agreement into evidence and requiring its disclosure are not sufficient to address the unfairness inherent in such agreements. These

---

[24] *See, e.g.,* Ponderosa Timber & Clearing Co. v. Emrich, 86 Nev. 625, 632, 472 P.2d 358, 362 (1970) (contained terms discussed here).

[25] *See* Lum v. Stinnett, 87 Nev. 402, 488 P.2d 347 (1971).

[26] *See, e.g.,* General Motors Corp. v. Lahocki, 286 Md. 714, 728, 410 A.2d 1039, 1046 (1980).

[27] *See, e.g.,* Hegarty v. Campbell Soup Co., 214 Neb. 716, 725–26, 336 N.W.2d 758, 764–65 (1983).

[28] *See, e.g.,* General Motors Corp. v. Lahocki, 286 Md. 714, 728, 410 A.2d 1039, 1046 (1980).

jurisdictions require that either the settling defendant be dismissed[29] from the case or require severance[30] of the plaintiff's claim against the settling defendant.

Despite these restraints, a carefully drafted Mary Carter agreement can be a useful tool to structure partial settlement in the proper case.

§ 14.12 Negotiating toward Settlement

Treatises and articles on approaches to negotiation have in the last decade become something approaching a cottage industry, as lawyers, academics, judges, and others have published their analyses of negotiation techniques.[31] The subject has even achieved best seller status for authors associated with the Harvard Negotiation Project.[32] It is beyond the scope of this chapter to survey the literature on negotiation, or to attempt to reconcile the disparate positions taken by many of the authors. Rather, it is appropriate to describe briefly some of the various approaches that have been identified as an aid to developing a settlement awareness in construction cases.

§ 14.13 —Negotiating Style

Every negotiator comes to the bargaining table with his or her own negotiating style. Generally, negotiating styles and strategies have been viewed as falling into one of two camps: hard or soft. Negotiators who employ the hard style may be characterized as tough, intolerant, quarrelsome, demanding, engaging in strategic gamesmanship so as to trip up the opponent, and seeking to gain an advantage, no matter how small, by intimidation. The hard style is often employed by contractors in the field, and is also frequently employed by counsel for those same contractors. Soft negotiators, on the other hand, are often viewed as nice, easygoing, cautious, forgiving, and attempting to seek reconciliation and agreement at any cost as long as confrontation and hostility can be avoided. We have all met people across the negotiating table who exemplify one or the other of

---

[29] *See, e.g.,* Popovich v. Ram Pipe & Supply Co., 82 Ill. 2d 203, 210, 412 N.E.2d 518, 522 (1980).

[30] *See, e.g.,* Burkett v. Crulo Trucking Co., 171 Ind. App. 166, 177, 355 N.E.2d 253, 259 (1976).

[31] *See* by way of a small sampling, H. Cohen, You Can Negotiate Anything (1980); T. Schelling, The Strategy of Conflict (1981); Thensted, *The Negotiation Alternative,* 59 Tul. L. Rev. 7 (1984).

[32] R. Fisher & W. Ury, Getting to Yes (1981) (described on the cover of the Penguin Book edition as "the National Bestseller").

§ 14.13 NEGOTIATING STYLE

these extremes. More likely, however, the opposing negotiator will have a blended style, encompassing some of both styles in a muted form.

The negotiator should not focus on whether to use a hard or soft approach, but should focus on being useful and effective in the short and long term. Of course, for some negotiations this may mean badgering the opponent until he concedes on your terms. Although this may work for that particular settlement negotiation, it may come back to haunt you when you attempt to negotiate for another client. Being an effective negotiator takes some thought and planning.

One negotiation style has been made popular by Professor Roger Fisher and William Ury of the Harvard Negotiation Project.[33] Their "principled negotiations" approach stresses deciding the issues based on the merits, or principle, rather than on personality and dogmatism. Some commentators contend that this approach has a "wonderful application in the negotiation of construction claims."[34]

An important aspect of the principled approach is that the parties should, as is practicable, look to their mutual gains. When conflicts do arise, the parties should look to the interests behind the positions which are in conflict. Instead of haggling over "$50,000 and not a penny less," the parties should look to why $50,000 is necessary. Is there $50,000 in current remedial expenses for the roof, or perhaps is there $25,000 in immediate repair expenses but the negotiator's client fears there may be $25,000 more in future roofing repairs? If the latter is true, then that party may be willing to settle for $25,000 now with a guarantee of $25,000 more contingent upon future repair expenses that actually arise, or a roofing guarantee or bond. Fisher and Ury urge that determining one another's interests allows for creative and meaningful solutions rather than dogged positional bargaining. In addition, any result achieved should be based on an objective and fair standard rather than a contest of wills. Or, as Fisher and Ury put it, a solution should be based on "principle, not pressure."

Another commentator offers what he terms a "New Strategic Model."[35] This model of negotiating fuses the "moderate versions" of the hard and soft negotiation styles into a hybrid. It bases bargaining both on an objective standard, such as legal precedent and established principles, and on internal standards of individual conduct, local customs and procedures, and rules of common courtesy. Despite the often litigious nature of the construction industry, there are trade practices, standards of workmanship, and local differences that should be respected in negotiations. The model rejects the extreme principled approach and recognizes that a firm negotiating position may have its advantages. For instance, a high opening

---

[33] *Id.*

[34] B. Bramble & J. O'Connor, Avoiding and Resolving Construction Claims 8–9 (1987).

[35] Thensted, *The Negotiation Alternative,* 59 Tul. L. Rev. 7 (1984).

demand by a contractor has the advantage of providing the psychological boost the owner receives from "wringing" concession from the contractor. Also, a high opening position hedges against any miscalculation and leaves the door open for the possibility that the owner may be willing to settle for higher than originally believed.

Adopting only one negotiating style from the many that have been identified in the literature may be both impossible and unwise in attempting to settle construction cases. In the construction industry, clients' needs and demands change, opposing clients and their negotiators change, and the facts and legal issues are also never the same. Each dynamic will require a difference in style, perhaps subtle, perhaps drastic. Effective negotiation of construction disputes requires flexibility and a willingness to adopt one's style to each particular setting.

§ 14.14 —Timing of Negotiations

There are a number of factors that militate toward beginning (or continuing) settlement negotiations early in the course of the litigation of a construction dispute. The sooner a case can be settled, the less money is spent on lawyers, with the result that both plaintiff and defendant can take a more reasonable approach to the dollars in settlement. The plaintiff will have spent less in seeking recovery, and therefore will need less to feel made whole. The defendant, who has spent less on attorneys' fees, may therefore have more available resources with which to contribute toward settlement. Similarly, the sooner the case is settled, the less "dirty linen" is likely to be aired in public. Yet it may not be possible to settle early because, for example, the public owner is controlled by political processes. Alternatively, the nature of the case may make early settlement overtures inadvisable, as in the case of a design malpractice case where the professional liability carrier does not want to get the reputation for being an "easy mark." In such cases, the attorney should be aware of potential turning points in the litigation that offer the potential for settlement. Such turning points typically have to do with events that will significantly affect the cost and inconvenience of the litigation, or with informational developments (either in terms of facts or law) that may change the complexion of the case.

Despite the adage, "Nothing quite focuses the mind like being sued," it is often the case that the defendant (and the defendant's attorney) will not really focus attention on a lawsuit until forced to do so. Service of the complaint and the process of directing an attorney to file a relatively pro forma answer will probably not galvanize the defendant. The construction industry is sufficiently litigious such that there is often little shock value from the filing of a suit. However, service of discovery requests, especially broad document demands and numerous demands for depositions, will probably alert the defendant to the time, effort, and cost likely to be required if the lawsuit is to be defended. This is especially true in a construction case because of the extensive number of potential witnesses and volumes of documents. Shortly after the service of the plaintiff's discovery requests is, therefore, a time to be alert for settlement possibilities.

Another possible time when the construction case may be at a turning point is the stage just before significant expert discovery is conducted. Preparing for expert discovery requires a large investment in expert and attorney fees. The actual conduct of expert discovery may also be the time when one party is surprised to learn how very weak (or strong) the opponent's case is.

The stage before final pretrial conference submissions must be prepared and filed is also a moment to consider settlement of a construction case. The opponent may suffer from the cold feet syndrome discussed in § **14.4**. It may well be the case that a thorough pretrial effort (involving legal briefs, exhibit marking, and summarization of fact and expert testimony) will require the expenditure of so much effort that the cost of trial will become less intimidating once that pretrial process is complete. From that standpoint, the final pretrial conference itself may be too late to maximize pressure (and chances) for settlement. A formal effort at settlement, by means of a settlement conference or at least a negotiation session, is often therefore appropriate before the final pretrial stage arrives.

Informational developments may also signal a turning point at which settlement efforts should be begun, or renewed. An important example is a pretrial legal ruling that settles one of the issues in the case. If the parties know that punitive damages are in (or out) of the case, or that certain other causes of action like a constructive acceleration claim will (or will not) go to the jury, or that certain evidence like expert testimony will (or will not) be permitted, that news may provide the leverage to move the parties off dead center in negotiations.

§ 14.15 Dealing with the Players

In attempting to settle a construction case, the attorney must give some consideration to dealing with the other players in the settlement setting, especially the lawyer's own client and the opposing lawyer and client. This discussion does not focus on personalities, but rather on techniques for interacting with each of these three major players.

In dealing with the opposing attorney, there is a certain divergence of approach between construction cases that are likely to settle early and cases that are likely to go to trial. A construction lawyer is always at an advantage when he knows more about the case than does the opposing lawyer. It follows that, for purposes of trial, the less the opposing attorney knows about the case, the better off one is.

If a case is to be settled, however, it is necessary to make sure that the opposing lawyer knows the case well enough to assess the risks realistically and to make reasonable recommendations to the opposing party. The lawyer who does not yet have a grasp on the facts, the issues, and the law will in all likelihood not feel comfortable making a recommendation to the client, not knowing whether the figure is too high or too low. The unprepared attorney will surely have difficulty persuading the client to accept a recommendation that cannot be backed up with reasoned support.

When settlement is the goal, therefore, the attorney should take steps to educate the opponent. Discovery should be crafted so that the factual weaknesses in the opponent's case become evident as interrogatories are answered and requests for admission are responded to. Sensitive documents should be highlighted, not buried in discovery responses. A deposition of a well-prepared and persuasive expert witness may be very helpful in this regard. Dispositive motions should be filed at an early date, even if the court is not likely to rule promptly, in order to put before the opponent well-reasoned argument exposing the weaknesses of the case on the law.

While taking steps to educate the opposing lawyer, one must also consider what incentives may be operating on that attorney in a particular construction case. If the case involves some degree of contingent recovery to the attorney (as is often the case with specialty construction litigation firms), the incentive to the plaintiff's lawyer will be to avoid the investment of great amounts of time, thereby maximizing the "premium" represented by the contingency fee. Such an attorney may well be brought to early settlement when it becomes apparent that tremendous resources will have to be used to cope with discovery requests and motion practice initiated by the other side. At the other extreme, the lawyer with numerous associates and legal assistants generating large hourly billings may have an incentive to prolong pretrial maneuverings and avoid serious discussions of settlement.

Bringing the appropriate incentives to bear on the opposing lawyers is only half the battle, however, for it is the opposing lawyer's client who must, in the end, be persuaded to settle. All one's excellent legal and factual argument may be to no avail unless those lessons are brought home to the opposing party. There are a number of techniques for ensuring that this is done on a construction case.

Discovery devices provide one such technique. Answers to interrogatories typically must be subscribed to by a party representative, not just the attorney. The drafting of answers, or at least the providing of raw information to convert into answers, is also usually done by the client. Interrogatories should be posed, therefore, so that the responding party representative is forced to confront the weaknesses in the case. Requests for admission

§ 14.15   DEALING WITH THE PLAYERS   373

can serve the same purpose, as the opposing attorney will, in all likelihood, seek the client's input to and approval of the responses to such requests.

Another opportunity to educate the opposing party is a deposition of the individual or the decision-maker within the party's organization. Such a deposition should not be conducted prematurely, but should only go forward after the deposing attorney has conducted sufficient other discovery to be able to lay out, in detail, the inconsistencies and weaknesses in the opposing party's case.

In preparing for the deposition of the opposing party, the attorney should give careful consideration to his or her behavior at such a deposition. Efforts to intimidate the opposing party deponent are likely to backfire, causing the deponent to become more rigid in the defense of his actions and less receptive to later overtures of settlement. The better approach is, often, to permit the deponent an early opportunity to tell his side of the story, at least in capsule form, in an unchallenged, unfettered way. This should be followed by methodical, detailed examination to impress upon the deponent the grasp which the examining lawyer has on the case, and to lay bare, through questioning, the weaknesses in the deponent's case.

For example, in opposing a contractor's delay claim, the attorney representing the owner should depose the president of the contracting firm. Let the contractor's CEO discuss the delays that it allegedly suffered. Then ask about delays for which the contractor may be responsible, such as a subcontractor's default, lack of manpower, and bid errors. By your questioning, let the contractor know that you are aware of significant problems with the claim. The contractor's president will appreciate the weaknesses of the case, and perhaps make a business decision to settle.

The third significant opportunity that the attorney has to impress the opposing party is with a properly drafted letter demanding settlement. In drafting such a letter, the attorney must consider how hard the tone of the letter should be. For example, a letter intended only to be seen by the opposing owner's lawyers, which is accusatory in tone and describes the negligence, incompetence, or other failings of the opposing owner and architect, may cause disastrous hardening of positions if the opposing lawyer passes it on to the owner. Instead of posturing, therefore, the demand letter of the contractor's attorney should be a concise explanation of the factual and legal bases for the reasonableness of the contractor's claim. The opposing counsel may simply pass the letter along with his own commentary, thus providing an unmatched opportunity to put one's own case before the decision-maker on the other side.

Dealing with one's own client is the final consideration in this chapter on settlement. It is the client who has the financial stake, and who is likely to have the emotional stake, in the outcome of the case. The attorney must fulfill the role as a neutral, objective advisor in order to serve the client properly. The attorney must find a way to communicate to the client the view of the case likely to be taken by a judge and jury. This is true whether representing the owner, architect, or contractor. All of these parties frequently take a hardened and often unrealistic view of the facts in their cases.

The importance of frequent, direct personal contact cannot be overemphasized. The client must be advised of unfolding developments in the pleadings and in discovery in order to make educated decisions about the conduct, and possible settlement, of the trial. If the client contact is a businessperson, and not an insurance claims handler or an in-house attorney, the reporting must be in language so simple, short, and direct that the client will take the time to read, or listen to, what is being told.

The main problem the attorney often faces is deflating the client's expectations in the case. One technique for laying the groundwork is to review documents and actual deposition testimony with the client, rather than relying on the client to read the lawyer's reports and absorb the flavor of the case from them. Another is to have the client attend selected depositions, where the strength of the opponent's witnesses can be seen firsthand. Perhaps the client should sit in on the deposition of the experts for both sides. This will give the client a feeling for the merits of the case. Once such efforts at education have been made, having the client participate in a settlement conference or in a minitrial will provide the best possible opportunity for the client to see presentations from both sides and the reaction of a neutral observer to those presentations. In that way, the client may be aided toward understanding how the case will be viewed by the court, and the further expenses of actual trial may well be averted.

§ 14.16 Conclusion

Because of the magnitude and complexity of construction cases, attorneys would be well advised to incorporate settlement devices and opportunities throughout the entire litigation process. The best resolution may be achieved by the parties, rather than an imposed decision by the judge, jury, or arbitrators.

Settlement of construction claims does not evolve naturally. The construction attorney must work to provide the client with the opportunities to achieve a favorable resolution through settlement. This does not mean that the attorney should force or even advise the client to settle every construction case. But settlement is one option that must be seriously considered by the client and developed by the attorney to achieve the best result in a construction claim.

CHAPTER 15

THE DECISION TO APPEAL

Albert E. Phillips, Esquire

Albert E. Phillips is a senior partner of Phillips, Hinchey & Reid, an Atlanta law firm specializing in construction matters. Mr. Phillips is a frequent seminar speaker and lecturer on the prevention, handling, and resolution of construction disputes. He currently serves as a member of the Forum Committee on the Construction Industry of the American Bar Association, the Public Contract Law Section, and the Construction Litigation Committee. He is vice-chairman of its Committee on Fidelity and Surety Law. Mr. Phillips is an advisor to the National Association of Attorneys General Committee on Construction Contracts and is chairman of the National Institute of Municipal Law Officers Section on Public Contracts. Mr. Phillips also serves as a member of the American Arbitration Association's panel of Construction Arbitrators.

§ 15.1 Introduction
§ 15.2 Is the Decision Appealable?
§ 15.3 Should the Case Be Appealed?

§ 15.1 Introduction

The decision whether to appeal always comes at a bad time. The construction case has just been tried and lost. The client has likely expended large sums for trial preparation, trial, and related costs; emotions may be running high while resources are diminishing. Is this the end of the road or just a low point along the path to ultimate victory? As with many of the other issues discussed in previous chapters, there are usually no hard and fast rules to follow in answering this question. But a few points are worthy of consideration.[1]

§ 15.2 Is the Decision Appealable?

The immediate reaction to the adverse result may be, "We'll appeal!" But it is first well to consider whether an appeal will lie and, if so, what grounds are available?

Today, the vast majority of construction contracts are evidenced by standard forms of agreement promulgated by various groups involved in the construction process. For example, the American Institute of Architects (AIA) has long published a series of standard forms of agreements for the various parties to the construction process. These agreements are now so widely accepted that even agreements that appear to be custom-made may, upon closer scrutiny, be found to be almost identical to the AIA documents. Virtually all standard forms of agreement call for binding arbitration of all disputes under the Construction Industry Rules of the American Arbitration Association.[2] Thus, it is likely that the initial question of appeal will arise from an adverse arbitration award and not a jury verdict or a judge-rendered decision. While enforcement of the award requires that it first be made the judgment of a court having jurisdiction, the matter of appeal therefrom may be a different issue altogether. Under the Federal Arbitration Act,[3] as well as the arbitration acts adopted by many states, grounds of appeal from an adverse award are extremely limited.[4] Moreover, there is often no transcript of the testimony during arbitration and the award itself is seldom accompanied by any written findings and reasoning. As a result, even those courts that are inclined to inquire into an award may have little to review.

Even in those cases where major construction disputes are not arbitrated, they may be bifurcated by the trial judge for an initial determination as to liability only, or even as to only certain aspects of liability. Or, the trial judge may, under certain circumstances, refer the entire case to a special master for an initial hearing and findings.[5] In each of these

---

[1] We are not concerned in this chapter with the usual appellate issues such as whether the verdict is contrary to the weight of the evidence or whether various rulings by the trial judge during a lengthy trial were sufficiently prejudicial to constitute reversible error. Rather, this chapter focuses on a few issues which may be uniquely germane in construction cases.

[2] *See, e.g.,* AIA Doc. A201, ¶ 4.5, 14th ed.

[3] 9 U.S.C. § 1 (1947).

[4] *See, e.g.,* 9 U.S.C. §§ 1–14 (1947); and **ch. 8.**

[5] *See, e.g.,* Fed. R. of Civ. P. 53; and **§ 11.16.**

situations, the right of appeal, if present at all, may be substantively eliminated or significantly curtailed.

Under these and similar circumstances, it is incumbent upon trial counsel to make a preliminary determination of whether the decision is appealable and, if so, whether it is subject to a substantive review on its merits.

§ 15.3 Should the Case Be Appealed?

The result at the trial level may, in the view of the losing party, be so extreme in terms of money, precedent, or otherwise as to leave no real choice but to pursue every possible avenue of reversal. For example, if a subcontractor suffers a multimillion dollar judgment against it, which approaches the value of the subcontract, the subcontractor may have no real choice but to appeal.[6] Most adverse decisions do not reach this extreme, even in the view of the losing party, and thus a more reasoned approach may be taken.

The trial attorney should, of course, review the record to determine whether the evidence properly adduced during the trial supports the result, and whether interim rulings along the way might be fairly said to have adversely impacted the client's position. The attorney is also well advised to carefully consider whether the trial court erred in its interpretation of the applicable law, or whether it improperly interpreted the pertinent contract requirements to the prejudice of the client. While this advice may be sound in any contract litigation, it is particularly relevant to the litigation of construction disputes.

Numerous appellate battles have been fought over such issues as the legality of a no damages for delay clause or the applicability of exceptions thereto.[7] What constitutes a materially changed site condition has been the focus of more than a few appellate battles.[8] At this writing, a number of jurisdictions are yet to be heard from as to their interpretation of the meaning of "pay when paid" clauses encountered by subcontractors in many subcontracts. Is the general contractor liable to pay the subcontractor only if the owner pays the general contractor? Further, is a termination for convenience clause totally for the owner's convenience, or does the contractor have certain limited protection against termination?

---

[6] *See* Pierce Assocs., Inc. v. The Nemours Found., 865 F.2d 530 (3d Cir. 1988).

[7] *See* Giammetta Assocs., Inc. v. J.J. White, Inc., 573 F. Supp. 112 (E.D. Pa. 1983); Corinno-Civetta Constr. Co. v. City of New York, 67 N.Y.2d 297, 493 N.E.2d 905, 502 N.Y.S.2d 681 (1986); Coatesville Contractors & Eng'rs., Inc. v. Borough of Ridley Park, 509 Pa. 553, 506 A.2d 862 (1986); Edward J. Dobson, Jr., Inc. v. Seite, 218 N.J. Super. 123, 526 A.2d 1150 (1987).

[8] *See* Acchione & Canuso, Inc. v. Commonwealth, Dep't of Transp., 501 Pa. 337, 461 A.2d 765 (1983); Grow Constr. Co. v. State, 56 A.D.2d 95, 391 N.Y.S.2d 726 (1977); Welch v. State, 139 Cal. App. 3d 546, 188 Cal. Rptr. 726 (1983).

Other appealable issues may include the method of calculating and establishing damages. Numerous appeals have involved the use of the total cost method of calculating damages.[9] As we discuss in **Chapter 7,** the method may be subject to concerns for fairness and reasonableness, and appellate courts tend to be reasonable and fair. Further, the unsuccessful claimant using the total cost method may find that it is a winner take all proposition. One of the four premises in establishing the right to use the method is that other methods of calculating damages are impossible. Should the claimant fail on one of the other three premises (see **Chapter 7**), then the claimant may be unable to utilize another method to establish damages. In such cases, the appellate remedy may be fruitless.

Our purpose here is not to attempt to definitively answer each of these questions, but rather to point out that it is in situations such as these that appeals by the losing litigant are frequently successfully waged.

When an apparently viable issue of contract interpretation or law is found, it is important that the attorney meticulously review the trial record for facts that may bear upon that issue. Appellate courts do not rule in a vacuum and the application of pertinent facts to a given set of contract terms may depend in large measure upon the cumulative weight of all of the facts bearing upon a particular issue.

A noteworthy example of the decision to appeal is found in *Pierce Associates, Inc. v. The Nemours Foundation.*[10] Here, a 79-day jury trial resulted in a judgment of more than $29 million against a mechanical subcontractor, of which more than $22 million was also awarded against the subcontractor's surety. Predictably, the subcontractor and its surety decided to appeal. In reversing the judgment entered by the trial court, the court of appeals addressed two primary issues earlier decided in the trial court. The first issue was whether, under the contract documents executed by and among the parties, the owner was a third-party beneficiary of the subcontract between the owner's general contractor and its mechanical subcontractor. Second, the court considered whether, absent privity of contract, a party might maintain a cause of action sounding in negligence to recover for purely economic loss under the law of Delaware.

After reviewing the general contract between Nemours and the general contractor, the "flow-down" provisions contained therein, and the subcontract provisions agreed by and between the general contractor and Pierce, the court concluded that it was not the intent of the parties that a third-party beneficiary status should be created and, accordingly, reversed

---

[9] Huber, Hunt & Nichols v. Moore, 69 Cal. 3d 278, 136 Cal. Rptr. 603 (1977); WRB Corp. v. United States, 183 Ct. Cl. 409 (1968); Chicago College of Osteopathic Medicine v. Fuller, 719 F.2d 1335 (7th Cir. 1983); John F. Harkins Co. v. School Dist. of Philadelphia, 313 Pa. Super. 425, 460 A.2d 260 (1983).

[10] 865 F.2d 530 (3d Cir. 1988).

Nemours's recovery on the theory of being a third-party beneficiary. Having eliminated any issue involving privity of contract, the court of appeals then went on to predict that the Delaware Supreme Court would deny Nemours any recovery in negligence for purely economic loss.

The result in the *Pierce* case affords a classic example of a successful appeal being prosecuted on the basis of improper interpretation of contract provisions and applicable law.

Thus, when considering whether to appeal an adverse result in a construction case, deliberate and clear thought should be given to the traditional grounds of appeal, and those noted in this chapter should receive special attention to the extent that circumstances warrant and permit.

TABLE OF CASES

Case	Book §
Abbett Elec. Corp. v. United States, 162 F. Supp. 772 (Ct. Cl. 1958)	§ 6.9
Acchione & Canuso, Inc. v. Commonwealth, Dep't of Transp., 501 Pa. 337, 461 A.2d 765 (1983)	§ 15.3
Acousti Eng'g Co. of Fla. v. United States, 15 Cl. Ct. 698 (1988)	§ 9.4
Aeronautics Div., AAR Brooks & Perkins Corp. v. United States, 12 Cl. Ct. 132 (1987)	§ 9.6
Afro-Lecon, Inc. v. United States, 820 F.2d 1198 (Fed. Cir. 1987)	§ 9.14
AGH Distribs., Inc. v. Silvertone Fasteners, Inc., 105 A.D.2d 648, 481 N.Y.S.2d 706 (1984)	§ 3.7
Alan J. Haynes Constr. Sys., Inc. v. United States, 10 Cl. Ct. 526 (1986)	§ 9.13
Alliance Oil & Ref. Co. v. United States, 13 Cl. Ct. 496 (1987)	§ 9.5
Allstate Ins. Co. v. Fioravanti, 451 Pa. 108, 299 A.2d 585 (1973)	§ 8.29
Alvin, Ltd. v. United States, 816 F.2d 1562 (Fed. Cir. 1987)	§ 9.14
American Abrasive Metals Co., ASBCA Nos. 35198, 35410, 88-1 B.C.A. (CCH) ¶ 20,287 (1987)	§ 9.21
American Steel Prod. Corp. v. Penn Central Corp., 110 F.R.D. 151 (S.D.N.Y. 1986)	§ 3.7
Anteri v. NRS Constr. Corp., 117 A.D.2d 696, 498 N.Y.S.2d 435 (1986)	§ 3.15
Arabian Am. Oil Co. v. Schartone, 119 F.R.D. 488 (M.D. Fla. 1988)	§ 10.22
A&R Constr. Co. v. Gorlun-Okum, Inc., 41 A.D.2d 876, 342 N.Y.S.2d 950 (1973)	§ 8.24
Ascrone v. City of Union City, 77 N.J. Super. 542, 187 A.2d 193 (1962)	§ 11.4
Assurance Co. v. United States, 813 F.2d 1202 (Fed. Cir. 1987)	§§ 6.17, 6.22
Astoria Medical Group v. Health Ins. Plan, 11 N.Y.2d 128, 182 N.E.2d 85, 227 N.Y.S.2d 401 (1962)	§ 8.11
Bagwell Coatings, Inc. v. Middle S. Energy, Inc., 797 F.2d 1298 (5th Cir. 1986)	§§ 6.10, 6.16, 6.22
Baise v. Alewel's, Inc., 99 F.R.D. 95 (W.D. Mo. 1983)	§ 3.12
Baltimore Contractors, Inc. v. Albro Metal Prod. Corp., Nos. 79-4231 & 81-3887 (E.D. Pa., filed Sept. 13, 1984)	§§ 6.11, 6.22

Case | *Book §*

Beiny, In re, 129 A.D.2d 126, 517 N.Y.S.2d 474 (1987) | § 3.15
Belcher v. Bassett Furniture Indus., 588 F.2d 904 (4th Cir. 1978) | §§ 3.9, 3.12
Big O Tire Dealer, Inc. v. Goodyear Tire & Rubber Co., 561 F.2d 1365 (10th Cir. 1977) | § 14.5
Black Star Sec., Inc. v. United States, 5 Cl. Ct. 110 (1984) | § 9.6
Blake Constr. Co. v. C.J. Coakley Co., 431 A.2d 569 (D.C. 1981) | §§ 1.3, 6.4, 6.10
Booth v. Mary Carter Paint Co., 202 So. 2d 8 (Fla. Dist. Ct. App. 1967) | § 14.11
Boutique Fabrice, Inc. v. Bergdorf Goodman, Inc., 129 A.D.2d 529, 514 N.Y.S.2d 380 (1987) | §§ 3.4, 3.7
Boyajian v. United States, 423 F.2d 1231 (Ct. Cl. 1970) | § 6.22
Brandeis Intsel Ltd. v. Calabrian Chem. Corp., 656 F. Supp. 160 (S.D.N.Y. 1987) | § 8.28
Brookfield Constr. Co. v. United States, 228 Ct. Cl. 551, 661 F.2d 159 (1981) | § 9.16
Bruce Constr. Corp. v. United States, 324 F.2d 516 (Cl. Ct. 1963) | § 6.22
Burkett v. Crulo Trucking Co., 171 Ind. App. 166, 355 N.E.2d 253 (1976) | § 14.11

Casson Constr. Co., GSBCA No. 4884, 83-1 B.C.A. (CCH) ¶ 16,523 (1983) | § 6.8
Casson Constr. Co. v. Armco Steel Corp., 91 F.R.D. 376 (D. Kan. 1980) | § 3.15
Central Mechanical Constr., ASBCA No. 29434, 86-3 B.C.A. (CCH) ¶ 19,240 (1986) | § 6.12
Chicago College of Osteopathic Medicine v. Fuller, 719 F.2d 1335 (7th Cir. 1983) | §§ 7.8, 15.3
Cincinnati Gas & Elec. v. General Elec. Co., 854 F.2d 900 (6th Cir. 1988) | § 10.25
Cipriano v. Righter, 100 A.D.2d 923, 474 N.Y.S.2d 839 (1984) | § 3.15
Citizens Assocs., Ltd. v. United States, 12 Cl. Ct. 599 (1987) | § 9.13
Clark Mechanical Contractors, Inc. v. United States, 12 Cl. Ct. 411 (1987) | § 9.6
Claude E. Atkins Enters., Inc. v. United States, 15 Cl. Ct. 644 (1988) | § 9.13
Coatesville Contractors & Eng'rs, Inc. v. Borough of Ridley Park, 509 Pa. 553, 506 A.2d 862 (1986) | § 15.3
Cochran Constr. Co., ASBCA No. 34378, 87-3 B.C.A. (CCH) ¶ 19,993, *aff'd on reconsideration,* 87-3 B.C.A. ¶ 20,114 (1987) | § 9.6
Color Dynamics, Inc., ASBCA No. 33686, 87-3 B.C.A. (CCH) ¶ 19,996 (1987) | § 9.5
Commonwealth Coatings Corp. v. Continental Casualty, 393 U.S. 145 (1968) | § 8.29

CASES

Case	*Book §*
Conoc Constr. Corp. v. United States, 3 Cl. Ct. 146 (1983)	§ 9.6
Consolidated Edison Co. v. NLRB, 305 U.S. 197 (1938)	§ 9.14
Consolidated Pac. Eng'g Inc. v. Greater Anchorage Area Borough School Dist., 563 P.2d 252 (Alaska 1977)	§ 8.14
Contract Cleaning Maintenance, Inc. v. United States, 811 F.2d 586 (Fed. Cir. 1986)	§ 9.5
Contract Servs. Co., ASBCA No. 34438, 87-2 B.C.A. (CCH) ¶ 19,850 (1987)	§ 9.11
Corinno-Civetta Constr. Co. v. City of N.Y., 67 N.Y.2d 297, 493 N.E.2d 905, 502 N.Y.S.2d 681 (1986)	§ 15.3
Cosmic Constr. Co. v. United States, 697 F.2d 1389 (Fed. Cir. 1982)	§§ 9.11, 9.12
Coughlin v. Capitol Cement Co., 571 F.2d 290 (5th Cir. 1978)	§ 3.5
Craig v. New York Tel. Co., 123 A.D.2d 580, 507 N.Y.S.2d 154 (1986)	§ 3.8
Crow-Crimmins-Wolff & Munier v. County of Westchester, 126 A.D.2d 696, 511 N.Y.S.2d 117 (1987)	§ 3.12
Crow-Crimmins-Wolff & Munier v. County of Westchester, 123 A.D.2d 813, 507 N.Y.S.2d 428 (1986)	§§ 3.1, 3.9, 3.12
Crow-Crinimins-Wolff & Munier v. County of Westchester, 110 A.D.2d 877, 488 N.Y.S.2d 429 (1985)	§§ 3.4, 3.8
Crown Cork & Seal Co. v. Chemed Corp., 101 F.R.D. 105 (E.D. Pa. 1984)	§ 3.4
Davis-Eckert v. State of N.Y., 118 A.D.2d 375, 504 N.Y.S.2d 874 (1986), *aff'd,* 70 N.Y.2d 632, 518 N.Y.S.2d 957 (1987)	§ 3.13
Delco Wire & Cable, Inc. v. Weinberger, 109 F.R.D. 680 (E.D. Pa. 1986)	§ 3.12
Delta Air Lines, Inc. v. August, 450 U.S. 346 (1981)	§ 14.7
Dewey Elecs. Corp. v. United States, 803 F.2d 650 (Fed. Cir. 1986)	§ 9.14
D. Moody & Co. v. United States, 5 Cl. Ct. 70 (1984)	§ 9.11
Donald M. Drake Co. v. United States, 231 Ct. Cl. 954 (1982)	§ 9.6
Door Pro Sys., Inc., ASBCA No. 34114, 87-3 B.C.A. (CCH) ¶ 19,997 (1987)	§ 9.4
Dowlitt v. City of N.Y., 113 A.D.2d 722, 493 N.Y.S.2d 560 (1985)	§ 3.7
Doyle & Russell, Inc. v. Welch Pile Driving Corp., 213 Va. 698, 194 S.E.2d 719 (1973)	§ 14.10
Durham Medical Search, Inc. v. Physicians Int'l Search, Inc., 122 A.D.2d 529, 504 N.Y.S.2d 910 (1986)	§ 3.8

384   TABLE

Case	Book §
Dykowsky v. New York City Transit Auth., 124 A.D.2d 465, 507 N.Y.S.2d 626 (1986)	§ 3.15
Dyson & Co., ASBCA No. 21673, 78-2 B.C.A. (CCH) ¶ 13,482 (1978), *aff'd on reconsideration,* 79-1 B.C.A. (CCH) ¶ 13,661 (1979)	§ 6.12
E.C. Ernst, Inc. v. Koppers Co., 520 F. Supp. 830 (W.D. Pa. 1981), *on remand from* 626 F.2d 324 (3d Cir. 1980)	§ 6.22
E.C. Ernst, Inc. v. Manhattan Constr. Co., 387 F. Supp. 1001 (S.D. Ala. 1974)	§ 14.2
E.C. Morris & Son, Inc., ASBCA No. 30385, 86-2 B.C.A. (CCH) ¶ 18,785 (1986)	§ 9.8
E.C. Schleyer Pump Co., ASBCA No. 33900, 87-3 B.C.A. (CCH) ¶ 19,986 (1987)	§ 9.6
E.D.S. Fed. Corp. v. United States, 2 Cl. Ct. 735 (1983)	§ 9.29
Edward J. Dobson, Jr., Inc. v. Seite, 218 N.J. Super. 123, 526 A.2d 1150 (1987)	§ 15.3
Eichleay Corp., ASBCA No. 5183, 60-2 B.C.A. (CCH) ¶ 2688 (1960)	§§ 4.8, 7.16
Electronics & Missile Facilities, Inc. v. United States, 416 F.2d 1345 (Ct. Cl. 1969)	§§ 6.10, 6.13, 6.22
Emily Malone v. United States, 849 F.2d 1441 (Fed. Cir. 1988)	§ 9.13
Episcopal Hous. Corp. v. Federal Ins. Co., 273 S.C. 181, 255 S.E.2d 451 (1979)	§ 8.12
Erickson Air Crane Co. of Washington, Inc. v. United States, 731 F.2d 810 (Fed. Cir. 1984)	§ 9.4
Esprit Corp. v. United States, 6 Cl. Ct. 546 (1984), *aff'd mem.,* 776 F.2d 1062 (Fed. Cir. 1985)	§ 9.5
Federal Trade Comm'n v. Grolier, 462 U.S. 19 (1983)	§ 3.11
Ferris Constr. Co. v. Lasker, 51 A.D.2d 1081, 381 N.Y.S.2d 352 (1976)	§ 8.28
F.H. McGraw & Co. v. United States, 82 F. Supp. 338 (Ct. Cl. 1949)	§ 6.9
Fidelity Constr. Co. v. United States, 700 F.2d 1379 (Fed. Cir. 1985)	§§ 9.3, 9.6, 9.16
Fidelity & Deposit Co. of Md. v. United States, 2 Cl. Ct. 137 (1983)	§ 9.6
Fireman's Fund/Underwater Constr., Inc., ASBCA No. 33018, 87-3 B.C.A. (CCH) ¶ 20,007 (1987)	§ 9.4
First Baptist Church v. George A. Creed & Sons, Inc., 276 S.C. 597, 281 S.E.2d 121 (1987)	§ 8.2
Frazier v. Heebe, 482 U.S. 641 (1987)	§ 11.15
Fulford Mfg. Co., ASBCA Nos. 2143, 2144 (May 20, 1955), 6 Cont. Cas. Fed. (CCH) ¶ 61,815 (May 20, 1955) (digest only)	§ 9.11

CASES

Case	*Book §*
Gallagher v. Schernecher, 60 Wis. 2d 143, 208 N.W.2d 437 (1973)	§§ 8.18, 8.29
Garrity v. Lyle Stuart, 40 N.Y.2d 354, 353 N.E.2d 793, 386 N.Y.S.2d 831 (1976)	§ 8.27
Garver v. Ferguson, 76 Ill. 2d 1, 389 N.E.2d 1181 (1979)	§ 8.29
Gauntt Constr. Co., ASBCA No. 33323, 87-3 B.C.A. (CCH) ¶ 20,221 (1987)	§§ 9.5, 9.6
General Motors Corp. v. Lahocki, 286 Md. 714, 410 A.2d 1039 (1980)	§ 14.11
Giammetta Assocs., Inc. v. J.J. White, Inc., 573 F. Supp. 112 (E.D. Pa. 1983)	§ 15.3
Glendale Joint Venture v. United States, 13 Cl. Ct. 325 (1987)	§ 9.29
Glenn v. United States, 858 F.2d 1577 (Fed. Cir. 1988)	§ 9.6
G.M. Shupe, Inc. v. United States, 5 Cl. Ct. 662 (1984)	§§ 5.6, 6.15, 7.8, 12.14
Great Lakes Dredge & Dock Co. v. United States, 96 F. Supp. 923 (Ct. Cl. 1951), *cert. denied,* 342 U.S. 953 (1952)	§ 6.22
Gregory Lumber Co. v. United States, 229 Ct. Cl. 762 (1982)	§ 9.11
Griener v. Zinker, 573 S.W.2d 884 (Tex. Civ. App. 1978)	§ 14.11
Griffin Servs., Inc., GSBCA No. 8876, 88-1 B.C.A. (CCH) ¶ 20,305 (1987)	§ 9.13
Groves-Black, ENGBCA No. 4557, 85-3 B.C.A. (CCH) ¶ 18,398 (1985)	§ 6.14
Grow Constr. Co. v. State, 56 A.D.2d 95, 391 N.Y.S.2d 726 (1977)	§ 15.3
Grumman Aerospace Corp. v. Titanium Metate Corp., 91 F.R.D. 84 (1981)	§ 14.5
G. Schneider, ASBCA No. 333021, 87-2 B.C.A. (CCH) ¶ 19,865 (1987)	§ 9.4
G.S.&L. Mechanical & Constr., Inc., DOT BCA No. 1856, 87-2 B.C.A. (CCH) ¶ 19,882 (1987)	§§ 9.3, 9.5
GTE Prod. Corp. v. Gee, 115 F.R.D. 67 (D. Mass. 1987)	§ 3.7
Gunn-Williams v. United States, 8 Cl. Ct. 531 (1985)	§ 9.13
Haehn Management Co. v. United States, 15 Cl. Ct. 50 (1988)	§ 9.4
Havens Steel Co. v. Randolph Eng'g Co., 613 F. Supp. 514 (W.D. Mo. 1985)	§ 6.8
Hegarty v. Campbell Soup Co., 214 Neb. 716, 336 N.W.2d 758 (1983)	§ 14.11
Herbert v. Lando, 441 U.S. 153 (1979)	§ 3.4
Hickman v. Taylor, 329 U.S. 495 (1947)	§§ 3.1, 3.12
Hoffman Constr. Co. v. United States, 7 Cl. Ct. 518 (1985)	§ 9.5
Holiday Inns, Inc. v. Robertshaw Controls Co., 560 F.2d 856 (7th Cir. 1977)	§ 3.6

Case	Book §
Huber, Hunt & Nichols v. Moore, 69 Cal. 3d 278, 136 Cal. Rptr. 603 (1977)	§ 15.3
Huntington Builders, ASBCA No. 33945, 87-2 B.C.A. (CCH) ¶ 19,898 (1987)	§ 9.5
Industrial Coatings, Inc. v. United States, 11 Cl. Ct. 161 (1986)	§ 9.13
Ingalls Shipbuilding Div., Litton Sys., Inc., ASBCA No. 17579, 78-1 B.C.A. (CCH) ¶ 13,038 (1978)	§ 6.12
J.D. Hedin Constr. Co. v. United States, 347 F.2d 235 (Ct. Cl. 1965)	§§ 6.22, 12.14
J.F. Shea Co. v. United States, 4 Cl. Ct. 46	§ 9.6
JMJ Contract Management, Inc. v. Ingersoll-Rand Co., 100 A.D.2d 291, 475 N.Y.S.2d 528 (1984)	§ 3.7
John F. Harkins Co. v. School Dist. of Philadelphia, 313 Pa. Super. 425, 460 A.2d 260 (1983)	§§ 7.8, 15.3
John McShain, Inc. v. Cessna Aircraft Co., 563 F.2d 632 (3d Cir. 1977)	§ 14.5
John McShain, Inc. v. United States, 412 F.2d 1281 (Ct. Cl. 1969)	§ 6.13
John Price Assocs. v. Davis, 588 P.2d 713 (Utah 1978)	§ 6.12
Johnson & Gordon Sec., Inc. v. United States, 857 F.2d 1435 (Fed. Cir. 1988)	§ 9.13
Joseph L. Muscarelle, Inc. v. Two Univ. Plaza Corp., No. A-3658-78 (N.J. Super. Ct. App. Div. 6/17/80) (unreported decision)	§ 8.14
Joseph Morton Co. v. United States, 757 F.2d 1273 (Fed. Cir. 1985)	§ 9.8
J.R. Stevenson Corp. v. Dormitory Auth. of State of N.Y., 112 A.D.2d 113, 492 N.Y.S.2d 385 (1985)	§§ 3.9, 3.15
Kalman Floor Co. v. Joseph L. Muscarelle, Inc., 196 N.J. Super. 16, 481 A.2d 553 (1984), *aff'd,* 98 N.J. 266, 486 A.2d 334 (1985)	§ 8.14
Kansas City Bridge Co. v. Kansas City Structural Steel Co., 317 S.W.2d 370 (Mo. 1958)	§ 7.4
Kennon v. Slipstreamer, Inc., 794 F.2d 1067 (5th Cir. 1986)	§ 14.5
Koehring Co. v. Hyde Constr. Co., 254 Miss. 214, 178 So. 2d 838 (1965)	§ 6.22
Kozlowski v. Sears, Roebuck & Co., 73 F.R.D. 73 (D. Mass. 1976)	§ 3.8
Kunz Constr. Co. v. United States, 12 Cl. Ct. 74 (1987)	§ 9.6
Kyle Eng'g v. Kleppe, 600 F.2d 226 (9th Cir. 1979)	§§ 3.4, 3.7
LDG Timber Enters., Inc. v. United States, 8 Cl. Ct. 445 (1985)	§ 9.6
Lebow-Bogner-Seitel Realty, Inc., *In re,* 55 A.D.2d 695, 389 N.Y.S.2d 51 (1976)	§ 8.23

CASES

Case	Book §
Lerma Co. & Assocs., *In re,* ASBCA No. 34012, 87-3 B.C.A. (CCH) ¶ 19,958 (1987)	§ 9.3
Lewitinn v. Loventhal Management Co., 109 A.D.2d 629, 486 N.Y.S.2d 209 (1985)	§ 3.15
Lichter v. Mellon-Stuart Co., 305 F.2d 216 (3d Cir. 1982)	§ 6.22
Lighting Unlimited, Inc. v. Unger Constr. Co., 217 Pa. Super. 252, 269 A.2d 368 (1970)	§ 8.24
Livingston v. Allis-Chalmers Corp., 109 F.R.D. 546 (S.D. Miss. 1985)	§ 3.12
Lum v. Stinnett, 87 Nev. 402, 488 P.2d 347 (1971)	§ 14.11
Luria Bros. & Co. v. United States, 369 F.2d 701 (Ct. Cl. 1966)	§§ 6.2, 6.4, 6.9, 6.12, 6.16–6.18, 6.22
MacDougald Constr. Co. v. United States, 122 Ct. Cl. 210 (1952)	§ 6.22
Maki v. United States, 13 Cl. Ct. 779 (1987)	§ 9.7
Marek v. Chesny, 473 U.S. 1 (1985)	§ 14.7
Mars Assoc., Inc. v. Facilities Dev. Corp., 111 A.D.2d 581, 489 N.Y.S.2d 646 (1985)	§ 3.1
Martin J. Simko Constr., Inc. v. United States, 852 F.2d 540 (Fed. Cir. 1988)	§ 9.8
Martin Mechanical Corp. v. City of N.Y., 100 Misc. 2d 1107, 420 N.Y.S.2d 537 (Sup. Ct. 1979)	§ 3.11
Marvin Lumber & Cedar Co. v. Norton Co., 113 F.R.D. 588 (D. Minn. 1986)	§§ 3.2, 3.4, 3.6
Maryland Sanitary Mfg. Corp. v. United States, 119 Ct. Cl. 100 (1951)	§ 6.8
Master Key, *In re,* 53 F.R.D. 87 (D. Conn. 1971)	§ 3.6
McCarty Corp. v. Pullman-Kellogg, 571 F. Supp. 1341 (M.D. La. 1983)	§§ 6.7, 6.18
McMillin Bros. Constructors, Inc., EBCA No. 328-10-84, 86-3 B.C.A. (CCH) ¶ 19,179 (1986)	§ 9.4
Mega Constr. Co. v. United States, 14 Cl. Ct. 555 (1988)	§ 9.13
Megin v. State, 181 Conn. 47, 434 A.2d 306 (1980)	§ 8.14
Merrill Lynch Realty Commercial Servs., Inc. v. Rudin Management Co., 94 A.D.2d 617, 462 N.Y.S.2d 16 (1983)	§ 3.7
Merritt-Chapman & Scott Corp. v. United States, 429 F.2d 431 (Ct. Cl. 1970)	§ 6.13
Metric Constr. Co. v. United States, 14 Cl. Ct. 177 (1988)	§ 9.5
Metric Constr. Co. v. United States, 1 Cl. Ct. 383 (1983)	§§ 9.5–9.7
Metro Eng'g, AGBCA No. 6069, 1962 B.C.A. (CCH) ¶ 16,143 (1962)	§ 6.8
M. Farbman & Sons, Inc. v. New York City Health & Hosp. Corp., 62 N.Y.2d 75, 476 N.Y.S.2d 69 (1984)	§ 3.11

Case	*Book §*
Miles Constr., VABCA No. 1674, 84-1 B.C.A. (CCH) ¶ 16,967 (1983)	§ 6.13
Milmark Servs. Corp. v. United States, 731 F.2d 855 (Fed. Cir. 1984)	§ 9.14
Milmark Servs., Inc. v. United States, 231 Ct. Cl. 954 (1982)	§ 9.7
Mingus Constructors, Inc. v. United States, 812 F.2d 1387 (Fed. Cir. 1987)	§ 9.5
Minmar Builders, Inc., GSBCA No. 3430, 72-2 B.C.A. (CCH) ¶ 9599 (1972)	§§ 5.4, 5.7
Misco, Inc. v. United States Steel Corp., 784 F.2d 198 (6th Cir. 1986)	§§ 3.4, 3.10
Moorehead Constr. Co. v. City of Grand Forks, 508 F.2d 1008 (8th Cir. 1975)	§§ 5.6, 12.14
Morris County Land Improvement Co. v. Parsippany-Troy Hills Township, 40 N.J. 549, 193 A.2d 232 (1962)	§ 11.4
Moses H. Cone Hosp. v. Mercury Constr. Corp., 460 U.S. 1, 103 S. Ct. 927 (1982)	§ 8.13
Multi-Roof Sys. Co. v. United States, 5 Cl. Ct. 245 (1984)	§ 9.29
National Neighbors, Inc. v. United States, 839 F.2d 1539 (Fed. Cir. 1988)	§ 9.12
Natkin & Co. v. George A. Fuller Co., 347 F. Supp. 17 (W.D. Mo. 1972)	§§ 5.4, 5.7
Nebraska Pub. Power Dist. v. Austin Power, Inc., 773 F.2d 960 (8th Cir. 1985)	§§ 6.18, 6.22, 7.18
Nelco Corp. v. Slater Elec., Inc., 80 F.R.D. 411 (E.D.N.Y. 1978)	§§ 3.4, 3.12
Newhall Ref. Co., EBCA Nos. 363-7-86, 364-7-86, 365-7-86, 366-7-86, 367-7-86, 368-7-86, 87-1 B.C.A. (CCH) ¶ 19,340 (1987)	§ 9.6
New Pueblo Constructors, Inc. v. State, 144 Ariz. 95, 696 P.2d 203 (1985)	§ 6.22
Northbridge Electronics, Inc. v. United States, 444 F.2d 1124 (Ct. Cl. 1971)	§ 6.17
North Hempstead, Town of v. Wiedersum, 131 A.D.2d 661, 516 N.Y.S.2d 743 (1987)	§ 3.9
Novak & Co. v. Facilities Dev. Corp., 116 A.D.2d 891, 498 N.Y.S.2d 492 (1986)	§ 7.16
Nuclear Research Corp. v. United States, 814 F.2d 647 (Fed. Cir. 1987)	§ 9.13
Olin Corp. v. Insurance Co. of N. Am., 604 F. Supp. 445 (S.D.N.Y. 1985)	§ 14.5
Oliver-Finnie Co. v. United States, 279 F.2d 498 (Ct. Cl. 1960)	§ 6.22
Omaha Pub. Power Dist. v. Foster Wheeler Corp., 109 F.R.D. 615 (D. Neb. 1986)	§ 3.7

CASES

Case	*Book §*
Opalack v. United States, 5 Cl. Ct. 349 (1984)	§ 9.9
Oppenheimer v. Sanders, 437 U.S. 340 (1978)	§ 3.8
Oremland v. Miller Minutemen Constr. Corp., 133 A.D.2d 816, 520 N.Y.S.2d 397 (1987)	§ 3.9
Palmer & Sicard, Inc. v. United States, 4 Cl. Ct. 420 (1984)	§ 9.6
Paragon Energy Corp. v. United States, 227 Ct. Cl. 176, 645 F.2d 966 (1981)	§§ 9.5, 9.6
Parrino Enters. v. United States, 230 Ct. Cl. 1052 (1982)	§ 9.6
Paterson, *Ex parte,* 253 U.S. 312–313, 40 S. Ct. 543, 64 L. Ed. 919 (1920)	§ 11.16
Pathman Constr. Co. v. United States, 817 F.2d 1573 (Fed. Cir. 1987)	§§ 9.7, 9.11
Paul E. Lehman, Inc. v. United States, 230 Ct. Cl. 11, 673 F.2d 352 (1982)	§§ 9.6, 9.10
Penn York Constr. Corp. v. State, 92 A.D.2d 1086, 462 N.Y.S.2d 82 (1983)	§ 3.11
Peoples Trust Co. v. Board of Adjustment Borough of Hasbrouck Heights, 60 N.J. Super. 569, 160 A.2d 57 (1959)	§ 11.4
Pierce Assocs., Inc. v. The Nemours Found., 865 F.2d 530 (3d Cir. 1988)	§ 15.3
Pinkerton & Laws Co. v. Roadway Express, Inc., 650 F. Supp. 1138 (N.D. Ga. 1986)	§§ 3.7, 3.15
Pittman Constr. Co. v. United States, 2 Cl. Ct. 211 (1983)	§§ 5.6, 6.12, 6.13
Placeway Constr. Corp. v. United States, 713 F.2d 726 (Fed. Cir. 1983)	§ 9.14
Ponderosa Timber & Clearing Co. v. Emrich, 86 Nev. 625, 472 P.2d 358 (1970)	§ 14.11
Popovich v. Ram Pipe & Supply Co., 82 Ill. 2d 203, 412 N.E.2d 518 (1980)	§ 14.11
Powlak v. General Motors Corp., 112 A.D.2d 725, 492 N.Y.S.2d 216 (1985)	§ 3.7
P.R. Post Corp. v. Maryland Casualty Co., 68 Mich. App. 182, 242 N.W.2d 62 (1976)	§ 8.2
Puerto Rico Aqueduct & Sewer Auth. v. Cion Corp., 108 F.R.D. 304 (D.P.R. 1985)	§ 3.6
Puerto Rico Elec. Power Auth., *In re,* 687 F.2d 501 (1st Cir. 1982)	§ 3.8
Raisler Corp. v. 101 Park Ave. Assoc., 102 A.D.2d 794, 477 N.Y.S.2d 153 (1984)	§ 3.8
Raymond Kaiser Eng'rs, Inc./Kaiser Steel Corp., ASBCA No. 34133, 87-3 B.C.A. (CCH) ¶ 20,140 (1987)	§ 9.6
R.E. Bean Constr. Co. v. Middlebury Ass'n, 139 Vt. 200, 428 A.2d 306 (1981)	§ 8.22

Case — *Book §*

Case	Book §
Rider v. United States, 7 Cl. Ct. 770 (1985)	§§ 9.5, 9.6
Rios v. Donovan, 21 A.D.2d 409, 250 N.Y.S.2d 818 (1964)	§ 3.1
Rodgers Builders, Inc. v. McQueen, 76 N.C. App. 16, 331 S.E.2d 726 (1985)	§ 8.27
Romala Corp. v. United States, 12 Cl. Ct. 411 (1987)	§ 9.6
Rozier v. Ford Motor Co., 573 F.2d 1332 (5th Cir.), *reh'g denied,* 578 F.2d 871 (5th Cir. 1978)	§§ 3.6, 3.12
Russell Corp. v. United States, 15 Cl. Ct. 760 (1988)	§ 9.13
Sanford Constr. Co. v. Kaiser Aluminum & Chem. Sales, Inc., 45 F.R.D. 465 (E.D. Ky. 1968)	§ 3.9
Santa Fe Int'l Corp. v. Potashnick, 83 F.R.D. 299 (E.D. La. 1979)	§ 3.9
Sarbo, Inc., ASBCA No. 34292, 88-2 B.C.A. (CCH) ¶ 20,550 (1988)	§ 9.6
Schachar v. American Academy of Opthamology, Inc., 106 F.R.D. 187 (N.D. Ill. 1985)	§ 3.12
SCM Corp. v. Fisher Park Lane Co., 40 N.Y.2d 788, 358 N.E.2d 1024, 390 N.Y.S.2d 398 (1976)	§ 8.26
Securities & Exch. Comm'n v. Cymaticolor Corp., 106 F.R.D. 545 (S.D.N.Y. 1985)	§ 3.11
Shank-Artukovich v. United States, 13 Cl. Ct. 346 (1987)	§ 9.13
Shaw v. Kuhnel Assocs., Inc., 102 N.M. 607, 698 P.2d 880 (1985)	§ 8.27
Skelly & Loy v. United States, 231 Ct. Cl. 370, 685 F.2d 414 (1982)	§ 9.3
S. Leo Harmonay, Inc. v. Binks Mfg. Co., 597 F. Supp. 1014 (S.D.N.Y. 1984)	§§ 6.6, 6.11, 6.16, 6.22
Soeder v. General Dynamics Corp., 90 F.R.D. 253 (D. Nev. 1980)	§ 3.12
South Corp. v. United States, 690 F.2d 1368 (Fed. Cir. 1982)	§ 9.1
Southern New Eng. Contracting Co. v. State, 165 Conn. 644, 345 A.2d 550 (1974)	§ 7.16
Southland Corp. v. Keating, 465 U.S. 1, 104 S. Ct. 852 (1984)	§ 8.13
Specialty Assembling & Packing Co. v. United States, 355 F.2d 554 (Ct. Cl. 1960)	§ 6.22
State v. Schmidt-Tiago Constr. Co., 108 F.R.D. 731 (D. Colo. 1985)	§§ 3.6, 3.8, 3.12
Statue of Liberty-Ellis Island Found. v. International United Indus., Inc., 110 F.R.D. 395 (S.D.N.Y. 1986)	§ 3.15
Stef Shipping Corp. v. Norris Greenco, 209 F. Supp. 249 (S.D.N.Y. 1962)	§ 8.11
Story Parchment Co. v. Paterson Parchment Paper Co., 282 U.S. 555 (1931)	§ 6.22
Strandell v. Jackson County, 838 F.2d 884 (7th Cir. 1988)	§ 10.21

CASES

Case	*Book §*
Sugarhill Records Ltd. v. Motown Record Corp., 105 F.R.D. 166 (S.D.N.Y. 1985)	§ 3.7
Summit Contractors v. United States, 15 Cl. Ct. 806 (1988)	§ 9.11
Swager Tower Corp. v. United States, 12 Cl. Ct. 499 (1987)	§ 9.3
Systron Donner, Inertial Div., ASBCA No. 31148, 87-3 B.C.A. (CCH) ¶ 20,066 (1987)	§ 9.13
Technassociates, Inc. v. United States, 14 Cl. Ct. 200 (1988)	§§ 9.3, 9.5
Tecom, Inc. v. United States, 732 F.2d 935 (Fed. Cir. 1984)	§§ 9.5, 9.6
Teller Envtl. Servs., Inc. v. United States, 802 F.2d 1385 (Fed. Cir. 1986)	§ 9.14
Tempo, Inc. v. Rapid Elec. Sales & Servs., 132 Mich. App. 93, 347 N.W.2d 728 (1984)	§ 7.18
Thoen v. United States, 765 F.2d 1110 (Fed. Cir. 1985)	§§ 9.3, 9.6
Thomas Funding Corp. v. United States, 15 Cl. Ct. 495 (1988)	§ 9.4
Thorstenn v. Barnard, 842 F.2d 1393 (1988)	§ 11.15
T.J.D. Servs., Inc. v. United States, 6 Cl. Ct. 257 (1984)	§§ 9.3, 9.6
T&M Properties v. ZVFK Architects, 661 P.2d 1040 (Wyo. 1983)	§ 8.29
Tom Warr, IBCA No. 2360, 88-1 B.C.A. (CCH) ¶ 20,231 (1987)	§ 9.11
Tuttle/White Constructors, Inc. v. United States, 228 Ct. Cl. 354, 656 F.2d 644 (1981)	§ 9.12
United States v. American Tel. & Tel. Co., 83 F.R.D. 323 (D.D.C. 1979)	§ 3.4
United States v. Blair, 321 U.S. 730 (1944)	§ 14.10
United States v. Centex Constr. Co., 638 F. Supp. 411 (W.D. Va. 1985)	§ 6.12
United States v. General Elec. Corp., 727 F.2d 1567 (Fed. Cir. 1984)	§§ 9.6, 9.14
United States v. Hooper, 596 F.2d 219 (7th Cir. 1979)	§ 14.5
United States v. Johnson Controls, Inc., 713 F.2d 1541 (Fed. Cir. 1983)	§ 9.4
United States v. Lockheed Corp., 817 F.2d 1565 (Fed. Cir. 1988)	§ 9.14
United States v. Turner Constr. Co., 827 F.2d 1554 (Fed. Cir. 1987)	§ 9.6
United States v. United States Gypsum Co., 333 U.S. 364 (1948)	§ 9.14
Universal Sur. Co. v. United States, 10 Cl. Ct. 794 (1986)	§ 9.4
University of Alaska v. Modern Constr. Co., 522 P.2d 1132 (Alaska 1974)	§ 8.23
Upjohn v. United States, 449 U.S. 383 (1981)	§ 3.12

Case	Book §
Urban Elec. Supply & Equip. Corp. v. New York Convention Center Dev. Corp., 105 F.R.D. 92 (E.D.N.Y. 1985)	§ 3.15
U.S. Indus., Inc. v. Blake Constr. Co., 671 F.2d 539 (D.C. Cir. 1982)	§§ 6.2, 6.4, 6.14, 6.22, 14.10
Walter Kidde Constr., Inc. v. Connecticut, 37 Conn. Supp. 50, 434 A.2d 962 (1981)	§ 14.10
Warchol Constr. Co. v. United States, 2 Cl. Ct. 384 (1983)	§ 9.6
Welch v. State, 139 Cal. App. 3d 546, 188 Cal. Rptr. 726 (1983)	§ 15.3
Wheeling v. Underwriters, 81 F.R.D. 8 (N.D. Ill. 1978)	§ 3.7
Wheeling-Pittsburgh Steel Corp. v. Underwriters Laboratories, Inc., 81 F.R.D. 8 (N.D. Ill. 1978)	§ 3.7
White v. Martins, 100 A.D.2d 805, 474 N.Y.S.2d 733 (1984)	§ 3.7
W.H. Moseley Co. v. United States, 230 Ct. Cl. 405, 677 F.2d 850, *cert. denied,* 459 U.S. 836 (1982)	§§ 9.3, 9.6
William F. Klingensmith, Inc. v. United States, 731 F.2d 805 (Fed. Cir. 1984)	§ 9.14
Willoughby Roofing & Supply Co. v. Kajima Int'l, Inc., 598 F. Supp. 353 (D. Ala. 1984), *aff'd,* 776 F.2d 269 (11th Cir. 1985)	§ 8.27
Wimberly v. City of Patterson, 75 N.J. Super. 584, 183 A.2d 691 (1962)	§ 11.4
W.M. Schlosser & Co. v. United States, 705 F.2d 1336 (Fed. Cir. 1983)	§§ 9.3, 9.6
Wolff & Munier, Inc. v. Diesel Constr. Co., 41 A.D.2d 618, 340 N.Y.S.2d 455 (1974)	§ 8.28
Woods Hole Oceanographics Inst. v. United States, 677 F.2d 149 (1st Cir. 1982)	§ 9.8
WRB Corp. v. United States, 183 Ct. Cl. 409 (1968)	§ 15.3
Wunderlich Contracting Co. v. United States, 351 F.2d 956 (Ct. Cl. 1965)	§§ 6.12, 6.15, 6.17, 6.22
Zambelis v. Nicholas, 92 A.D.2d 936, 460 N.Y.S.2d 360 (1983)	§ 3.8
Zinger Constr. Co., ASBCA No. 28788, 86-2 B.C.A. (CCH) ¶ 18,920 (1986)	§ 9.6

INDEX

ABUSE OF DISCOVERY
  Discovery devices §§ 3.1, 3.4
ACCELERATED APPEALS
  Federal contract disputes §§ 9.15, 9.24
ACCELERATION
  Claims. See DELAY AND ACCELERATION CLAIMS
  Lost productivity claims § 6.11
ACTS OF GOD
  Delay and acceleration claims § 5.4
ACTUAL COST METHOD OF DAMAGES DETERMINATION
  Lost productivity claims § 6.22
ADEQUATE WORK FORCE
  Delay and acceleration claims §§ 5.4, 5.12
ADJOURNMENTS
  Arbitration advocacy § 8.25
ADMISSIBILITY
  Affirmative case § 12.19
  Alternative disputes resolution, minitrials § 10.13
  Arbitration advocacy § 8.18
  Court trials §§ 11.13, 11.15
  Settlements § 14.5
ADMISSIONS REQUESTS
  Discovery devices § 3.10
ADR
  See ALTERNATIVE DISPUTES RESOLUTION
ADVERSE WEATHER
  Lost productivity claims §§ 6.1, 6.9
AFFIDAVITS
  Arbitration advocacy § 8.20
AFFIRMATIVE CASE
  Opening statement
  –Generally § 12.3
  –Accuracy § 12.9
  –Best and last chance § 12.13
  –Confronting problems with case § 12.11

AFFIRMATIVE CASE *(Continued)*
  –Dramatic method § 12.5
  –Hooking audience § 12.6
  –Rehearsal § 12.12
  –Simplicity § 12.4
  –Sincerity § 12.7
  –Talent development § 12.8
  –Visuals § 12.10
  Presentation of case
  –Generally § 12.14
  –Evidence, real and demonstrative § 12.19
  –Expert testimony § 12.18
  –Proof strategies §§ 12.15, 12.16
  –Redirect testimony § 12.20
  –Summarizing case § 12.21
  –Witness presentation § 12.17
  Reconstructing past § 12.1
  Theme development § 12.2
AGENCY BOARDS OF CONTRACT APPEALS
  Federal contracts. See FEDERAL CONTRACT DISPUTES AND FORUMS
AGREEMENT TO ARBITRATE
  Arbitration advocacy § 8.2
AIA STANDARD FORMS
  Arbitration advocacy § 8.2
ALTERNATIVE DISPUTE RESOLUTION
  Generally § 10.1
  Benefits § 10.2
  Criticism § 10.3
  Federal contract disputes §§ 9.27, 9.31
  Mediation
  –Benefits § 10.16
  –Case study § 10.19
  –Definition § 10.15
  –Role of mediator § 10.18
  Minitrial agreement
  –Generally § 10.7

INDEX

ALTERNATIVE DISPUTE
RESOLUTION *(Continued)*
–Confidentiality § 10.13
–Discovery § 10.9
–Information exchange §§ 10.10, 10.11
–Neutral's role § 10.12
–Status of pending dispute § 10.8
Minitrials
–Agreement, see Minitrial agreement, this heading
–Case study § 10.14
–Elements § 10.4
–History § 10.5
–Types of disputes resolved by § 10.6
Summary jury trial
–History § 10.15
–Jury selection and presentation § 10.23
–Post-trial discussion and negotiation § 10.24
–Pretrial conference § 10.22
–Public right to access § 10.25
–When to use § 10.21
AMERICAN ARBITRATION ASSOCIATION
Arbitration selection. See ARBITRATION ADVOCACY
ANNOYANCE
Discovery § 3.7
APPEALS
Generally § 15.1
Can decision be appealed § 15.2
Court trials § 11.15
Defense § 13.13
Delay and acceleration claims § 5.6
Should opinion be appealed § 15.3
APPOINTMENT OF ARBITRATORS
Arbitration advocacy, arbitrator selection § 8.8
ARBITRATION
Alternative disputes resolution. See ALTERNATIVE DISPUTES RESOLUTION
Appealability § 15.2
Case management § 2.12
Delay and acceleration claims §§ 5.6, 5.7
Identification of key parties § 1.3

ARBITRATION ADVOCACY
Generally § 8.1
AAA arbitration
–Generally § 8.4
–Categories of arbitrators § 8.6
–Disclosure and disqualification of arbitrators § 8.9
–Panel lists, selection for § 8.5
–Right arbitrators, getting § 8.8
–Sole arbitrator selection § 8.7
–Special selection procedures § 8.10
Adjournments § 8.24
Advocacy style § 8.15
Agreement to arbitrate § 8.2
Award
–Generally § 8.26
–Elements of § 8.26
–Vacating § 8.29
Briefs, post-hearing § 8.22
Closing statements § 8.19
Conclusion § 8.30
Conduct at hearings § 8.16
Consolidation
–Generally § 8.12
–Alternatives to § 8.14
–Elements of § 8.13
Demonstrative evidence § 8.25
Evidence § 8.18
Hearing format § 8.20
Opening statements § 8.17
Punitive damages § 8.27
Site visits § 8.23
Transcript § 8.21
Tripartite arbitration § 8.11
Types of arbitration § 8.3
ARGUMENTATION
Affirmative case § 12.9
Defense § 13.10
AS-BUILT CPM TECHNIQUE
Delay and acceleration claims § 5.5
AS-PLANNED CPM TECHNIQUE
Delay and acceleration claims § 5.5
ASSIGNEES
Federal contract disputes § 9.4
ATTORNEY-CLIENT PRIVILEGE
Court trials § 11.16
Discovery § 3.12
Settlements § 14.15
ATTORNEYS
See LAWYERS

INDEX

ATTORNEYS' FEES
Case management § 2.15
Federal contract disputes § 9.30
Settlements §§ 14.7, 14.10
AUDIT REPORTS
Discovery § 3.9
AUTHORITY
Alternative disputes resolution § 10.4
AWARDS
Arbitration. See ARBITRATION ADVOCACY

BACKGROUND
Arbitration advocacy, arbitrator selection § 8.5
BAD FAITH
Discovery § 3.7
BAR CHART SCHEDULES
Delay and acceleration claims § 5.4
BEHAVIOR
Arbitration advocacy § 8.16
BENCH TRIALS
Court trials § 11.15
Defense §§ 13.6–13.8
Delay and acceleration claims § 5.6
BIAS
Alternative disputes resolution, minitrials § 10.13
Arbitration advocacy, arbitrator selection § 8.9
Arbitration awards, vacating § 8.29
Court trials §§ 11.6–11.8
Defense §§ 13.8, 13.21, 13.22
Settlements § 14.5
BIDS
Damages, establishing § 7.10
BIFURCATION
Federal contract disputes §§ 9.14, 9.28
BIOGRAPHIES
Arbitration advocacy, arbitrator selection § 8.5
BREACH OF CONTRACT
Discovery § 3.6
Lost productivity claims §§ 6.10, 6.12, 6.22
BRIEFS
Arbitration advocacy § 8.22
BOARD OF CONTRACT APPEALS
Delay and acceleration claims § 5.6

BUDGETS
Case management. See CASE MANAGEMENT
BUILDING CODE VIOLATIONS
Discovery § 3.6
BUSINESS RECORDS
Court trials § 11.13
BUT-FOR CPM TECHNIQUE
Delay and acceleration claims § 5.5

CALCULATING DAMAGES
Appealability § 15.3
CASE MANAGEMENT
Budget and cost control
–Generally § 2.13
–Litigation budgets § 2.15
–Predicting litigation costs § 2.14
–True litigation cost § 2.16
Designing support system
–Generally § 2.3
–Developing key phrases § 2.5
–Key phrases v. full text § 2.4
–Review process § 2.6
Litigation support systems
–Generally § 2.1
–Advantages of use § 2.2
–Designing, see Designing support system, this heading
–Updating system § 2.7
–Uses of § 2.8
Trial resources
–Generally § 2.9
–Document availability § 2.11
–Location of trial § 2.12
–Witness availability § 2.10
CAUSATION
Consultants and experts, use § 4.1
Court trials § 11.9
Damages, establishing § 7.4
Experts, use § 1.5
Lost productivity claims. See LOST PRODUCTIVITY CLAIMS
CAUSE AND EFFECT METHOD
Damages, establishing § 7.9
CERTIFICATION
Federal contract disputes, contractor claims § 9.6
CHALLENGES
Arbitration advocacy, arbitrator selection § 8.9

INDEX

CHALLENGES TO CLAIMED
  DAMAGES
  Delay and acceleration claims § 5.12
CHAMPERTY
  Settlements § 14.11
CHANGED SITE CONDITION
  Appealability § 15.3
  Consultants, use § 4.5
  Discovery § 3.3
  Lost productivity claims §§ 6.1,
    6.12, 6.13, 6.17
CHANGE ORDERS
  Court trials § 11.2
  Damages, establishing § 7.13
  Delay and acceleration claims § 5.5
  Lost productivity claims § 6.12
CHARTS
  Arbitration advocacy § 8.25
  Consultants and experts, use § 4.4
  Defense § 13.23
CLARITY
  Damages, establishing § 7.6
  Delay and acceleration claims § 5.1
CLAUSES
  Arbitration advocacy §§ 8.2, 8.4
CLOSING ARGUMENTS
  Court trials § 11.14
CLOSING STATEMENTS
  Arbitration advocacy § 8.19
COLD FEET
  Settlements §§ 14.4, 14.14
COLLAPSED AS-BUILT METHOD
  Delay and acceleration claims § 5.5
COLLUSION
  Settlements § 14.11
COLOR
  Delay and acceleration claims § 5.10
COMMUNICATION
  Alternative disputes resolution,
    mediation § 10.18
COMPENSATION
  Consultants and experts, use § 4.10
COMPLAINT
  Federal contract disputes § 9.26
COMPLEXITY
  Court trials § 11.5
  Damages, establishing § 7.2
COMPLEX MADE SIMPLE
  Generally § 1.1
  Central parties, identifying § 1.3
  Challenges for attorney § 1.2
  Conclusion § 1.8

COMPLEX MADE SIMPLE
  (Continued)
  Explanations, developing
    straightforward § 1.6
  Key issues, focusing on § 1.4
  Procedures § 1.7
  Technical issues § 1.5
COMPUTER PRINTOUTS
  Discovery § 3.8
COMPUTER PROGRAMS
  Defense § 13.23
  Discovery §§ 3.8, 3.13
COMPUTERS
  Litigation support systems. See
    CASE MANAGEMENT
CONCURRENT DELAYS
  Delay and acceleration claims §§ 5.5,
    5.7, 5.8
CONDUCT
  Arbitration advocacy § 8.16
CONFERENCES
  Settlements §§ 14.5, 14.8
CONFIDENTIALITY
  Alternative disputes resolution
    §§ 10.2, 10.17
  Settlements §§ 14.3, 14.5, 14.8
CONSEQUENTIAL DAMAGES
  Defense § 13.2
CONSOLIDATION
  Arbitration advocacy. See
    ARBITRATION ADVOCACY
  Federal contract disputes § 9.29
  Identification of key parties § 1.3
CONSTRUCTION INDUSTRY
  RULES FOR ARBITRATION
  Arbitration advocacy § 8.4
CONSTRUCTIVE CHANGES
  Lost productivity claims §§ 6.10,
    6.13
CONSULTANTS AND EXPERTS
  Generally § 4.1
  Conclusion § 4.12
  Cross-examination of opposing
    experts
  –Background of expert § 4.6
  –Compensation § 4.10
  –Expert v. staff time § 4.9
  –Foundations of expert's opinion
    § 4.7
  –Learned treatises § 4.11
  –Prior opinions § 4.8
  Decision to retain expert § 4.2

INDEX

CONSULTANTS AND EXPERTS
(Continued)
   Interrogatories and depositions of opposing experts § 4.5
   Roles § 4.4
   Selection process § 4.3
CONTINGENCY FEES
   Settlements § 14.15
CONTRACT BALANCE
   Discovery § 3.3
CONTRACT DISPUTES ACT OF 1978
   See FEDERAL CONTRACT DISPUTES AND FORUMS
CONTRACT DRAFTING
   Court trials § 11.1
CONTRACT INTERPRETATION
   Appealability § 15.3
CONTRACTS
   Arbitration advocacy § 8.2
   Complexity § 1.1
CONTROL
   Settlements § 14.2
CONVENIENCE
   Court trials § 11.3
COORDINATION
   Court trials § 11.2
COORDINATION OF PRIMES
   Lost productivity claims § 6.13
COORDINATION OF SUBCONTRACTORS
   Delay and acceleration claims § 5.4
COPIES
   Discovery § 3.4
CORPORATION CLIENTS
   Court trials § 11.6
   Defense § 13.10
   Discovery § 3.7
CORRESPONDENCE
   Discovery § 3.11
CORROBORATION
   Lost productivity claims § 6.18
CORRUPTION
   Arbitration awards, vacating § 8.29
COST DAMAGES
   Defense § 13.19
COST OVERRUNS
   Damages, establishing §§ 7.10, 7.17
COSTS
   Alternative disputes resolution §§ 10.11, 10.16, 10.21

COSTS *(Continued)*
   Case management. See CASE MANAGEMENT
   Court trials § 11.1
   Discovery §§ 3.4, 3.8
   Federal contract disputes § 9.30
   Settlements §§ 14.2, 14.7
COUNSEL
   Arbitration advocacy § 8.1
COUNTERCLAIMS
   Federal contract disputes §§ 9.26, 9.27
   Settlements § 14.7
COURT TRIALS
   Generally § 11.1
   Advocating construction claim to judge § 11.15
   Advocating construction claim to jury § 11.5
   Closing argument § 11.14
   Conclusion § 11.18
   Construction claims, unique characteristics § 11.2
   Demonstrative evidence § 11.13
   Direct examination § 11.10
   Documents § 11.13
   Expert witnesses § 11.12
   Fact witnesses § 11.11
   Forum selection §§ 11.3, 11.4
   Jury charges § 11.14
   Jury selection §§ 11.6, 11.7
   Opening statement § 11.9
   Site visit § 11.4
   Special masters, use §§ 11.16, 11.17
   Voir dire § 11.8
CPM SCHEDULING
   Delay and acceleration claims §§ 5.1, 5.5, 5.7
CREDENTIALS
   Consultants and experts, use § 4.6
CREDIBILITY
   Consultants and experts, use § 4.3
   Defense §§ 13.13–13.17
CRITICAL PATH METHOD SCHEDULING
   Delay and acceleration claims §§ 5.1, 5.5, 5.7
   Lost productivity claims § 6.3
CROSS-EXAMINATION
   Consultants and experts. See CONSULTANTS AND EXPERTS

INDEX

CROSS-EXAMINATION *(Continued)*
  Defense and cross-examination. See
    DEFENSE AND
    CROSS-EXAMINATION

DAILY REPORTS
  Discovery devices § 3.2
DAMAGED WORK
  Lost productivity claims § 6.14
DAMAGES
  Alternative disputes resolution
    § 10.5
  Appealability § 15.3
  Consultants and experts, use §§ 4.2,
    4.4
  Defense §§ 13.11, 13.19
  Identification of key issues §§ 1.4, 1.5
  Lost productivity claims § 6.22
DAMAGES CALCULATIONS
  Discovery §§ 3.6, 3.7
DAMAGES, ESTABLISHING
  Generally § 7.1
  Conclusion § 7.20
  Presentation of damages
  –Basic elements § 7.2
  –Documentation § 7.5
  –Liability and damages linked § 7.4
  –Quantifying incremental impacts
    § 7.3
  –Simplicity and clarity § 7.6
  Specific types of damages
  –Generally § 7.12
  –Change orders and extra work
    § 7.13
  –Cost overruns and documentation
    § 7.17
  –Defective work § 7.14
  –Delay and disruptions § 7.15
  –Interest § 7.18
  –Labor, material and equipment
    escalation during construction
    § 7.19
  –Overhead § 7.16
  Theories of damages
  –Generally § 7.7
  –Modified total cost claims § 7.10
  –Quantum meruit claims § 7.11
  –Specific cost claims § 7.9
  –Total cost claims § 7.8
DEFAULT, TERMINATION FOR
  Federal contract disputes §§ 9.11,
    9.13

DEFECTIVE WORK
  Damages, establishing § 7.14
DEFENSE AND
  CROSS-EXAMINATION
  Generally § 13.1
  Conclusion § 13.25
  Cross-examination
  –Generally § 13.14
  –Discrediting direct examination
    § 13.16
  –Expert witnesses § 13.17
  –Impeachment § 13.15
  –Records witnesses § 13.18
  Damages, attacking § 13.19
  Defendant's case
  –Generally § 13.20
  –Charts and documentation § 13.23
  –Expert witnesses § 13.22
  –Fact witnesses § 13.21
  Delay and acceleration claims §§ 5.6,
    5.12
  Discovery § 3.3
  Fact preservation § 13.4
  Indemnification clauses § 13.5
  Jury instructions § 13.24
  Jury trials
  –Decision § 13.6
  –Selection of jury §§ 13.7, 13.8
  Objections during direct examination
    § 13.13
  Opening statements §§ 13.9–13.11
  Responding to plaintiff's case
    §§ 13.12, 13.13
  Risk allocation § 13.2
  Timely notice, perfecting rights § 13.3
  Verdicts § 13.24
DELAY AND ACCELERATION
  CLAIMS
  Generally § 5.1
  Acceleration delineated § 5.3
  Analysis §§ 5.4, 5.5
  Conclusions § 5.13
  CPM scheduling § 5.7
  Defenses to delay claims § 5.12
  Delay delineated § 5.2
  Explaining acceleration § 5.9
  Explaining delays § 5.8
  Forum § 5.6
  Graphics § 5.10
  Scheduling techniques to
    demonstrate delay § 5.5
  Themes for presentation § 5.11

INDEX

DELAY CLAIMS
  Consultants and experts, use § 4.1
  Court trials §§ 11.13, 11.15
  Defense § 13.17
  Identification and understanding issues §§ 1.4, 1.5
  Settlements § 14.7
DELAY DAMAGES
  Consultants and experts, use § 4.5
  Establishing § 7.15
DELAYS
  Discovery devices § 3.2
  Federal contract disputes § 9.7
  Lost productivity claims §§ 6.1, 6.10
DEMAND LETTER
  Settlements § 14.15
DEMONSTRATIVE EVIDENCE
  Affirmative case §§ 12.10, 12.16, 12.18, 12.19
  Alternative disputes resolution, minitrials § 10.10
  Arbitration advocacy § 8.26
  Court trials §§ 11.5, 11.9, 11.12–11.15
  Defense §§ 13.10, 13.23
DEPOSITIONS
  Case management §§ 2.6, 2.11
  Consultants and experts, use §§ 4.4, 4.5
  Court trials § 11.16
  Discovery devices §§ 3.7, 3.14
  Federal contract disputes §§ 9.22, 9.27
  Settlements § 14.15
DESIGN ERRORS
  Lost productivity claims §§ 6.1, 6.13
DIFFERING SITE CONDITIONS
  Appealability § 15.3
  Consultants and experts, use § 4.5
  Discovery § 3.3
  Lost productivity claims §§ 6.1, 6.12, 6.13, 6.17
DIRECT EXAMINATION
  Court trials § 11.10
DISCLOSURE
  Alternative disputes resolution, mediation § 10.17
  Arbitration advocacy, arbitrator selection § 8.9
  Settlements § 14.11

DISCOVERY
  Generally § 3.1
  Abuse of §§ 3.1, 3.4
  Alternative disputes resolution §§ 10.2, 10.9, 10.13, 10.22
  Arbitration advocacy § 8.17
  Conclusion § 3.16
  Consultants and experts, use §§ 4.4, 4.5
  Court trials, special masters §§ 11.16, 11.17
  Defense § 13.22
  Devices
  –Generally § 3.5
  –Admissions requests § 3.10
  –Depositions § 3.7
  –Document production § 3.8
  –Inspection requests § 3.9
  –Interrogatories § 3.6
  Federal contract disputes §§ 9.22, 9.24, 9.27
  Motion practice § 3.15
  Organization and management § 3.13
  Plan § 3.3
  Privileges § 3.12
  Purpose § 3.2
  Scope § 3.4
  Settlements §§ 14.3–14.5, 14.11, 14.14, 14.15
  Targeting information § 3.11
  Witness targeting § 3.14
DISPUTES RESOLUTION CLAUSE
  Alternative disputes resolution § 10.6
DISQUALIFICATION
  Arbitration advocacy, arbitrator selection § 8.9
DISRUPTIONS
  Damages, establishing § 7.15
  Lost productivity claims §§ 6.3, 6.4, 6.10, 6.14, 6.18
DOCUMENTATION
  Complexity §§ 1.2, 1.5
  Court trials §§ 11.12, 11.13
  Damages, establishing §§ 7.5, 7.8, 7.9, 7.17
  Delay and acceleration claims § 5.12
  Delays, discovery devices § 3.2
  Settlements. See SETTLEMENTS

DOCUMENTS
Affirmative case § 12.19
Case management. See CASE MANAGEMENT
Consultants and experts, use §§ 4.3, 4.4, 4.9
Court trials §§ 11.13, 11.15
Defense §§ 13.18, 13.23
Discovery § 3.7
Discovery devices § 3.8
Federal contract disputes §§ 9.22, 9.27

DUTY OWED
Lost productivity claims § 6.15

EDUCATION
Jury selection, court trials § 11.6

EICHLEAY FORMULA
Consultants and experts, use § 4.8
Damages, establishing § 7.16

ELECTION DOCTRINE
Federal contract disputes § 9.12

EMBARRASSMENT
Discovery § 3.7

EQUAL ACCESS TO JUSTICE ACT
Federal contract disputes § 9.30

EQUIPMENT
Court trials § 11.2
Damages, establishing § 7.19

EQUIPMENT DOWNTIME
Lost productivity claims § 6.1

EQUITY
Damages, establishing §§ 7.2, 7.8

ERRORS AND OMISSIONS
Defense § 13.19

EVIDENCE
Affirmative case § 12.19
Alternative disputes resolution, minitrials §§ 10.10, 10.23
Arbitration advocacy §§ 8.18, 8.26
Court trials § 11.10
Federal contract disputes §§ 9.14, 9.23
Lost productivity claims § 6.22
Settlements §§ 14.5, 14.11

EXCESSIVE CHANGES
Lost productivity claims § 6.1

EXCUSABLE DELAY
Delay and acceleration claims §§ 5.3, 5.4, 5.7, 5.8
Lost productivity claims § 6.6

EXECUTIVE AGENCY
Federal contract disputes § 9.2

EXHIBITS
Consultants and experts, use § 4.4
Court trials § 11.14

EXPERTS
Arbitration advocacy, arbitrator selection §§ 8.5, 8.8
Consultants and experts. See CONSULTANTS AND EXPERTS
Discovery §§ 3.12, 3.14
Jury selection, court trials § 11.7
Lost productivity claims § 6.18
Technical issues, understanding § 1.5
Witnesses. See EXPERT WITNESSES

EXPERT WITNESSES
Affirmative case § 12.18
Case management §§ 2.8, 2.10
Court trials §§ 11.10–11.13, 11.15
Damages, establishing § 7.8
Defense §§ 13.10, 13.22
Delay and acceleration claims § 5.7
Federal contract disputes § 9.30
Lost productivity claims §§ 6.6, 6.15, 6.18

EXTENSIONS
Delay and acceleration claims § 5.9
Discovery § 3.3

EXTRAJUDICIAL PROCEDURES
Minitrial as § 10.8
Summary jury trial as § 10.21

EXTRA WORK
Damages, establishing § 7.13
Discovery § 3.3

FACT WITNESSES
Court trials § 11.11
Defense § 13.21

FALSE CLAIMS ACT
Federal contract disputes § 9.18

FEDERAL ARBITRATION ACT
Arbitration advocacy § 8.13

FEDERAL CONTRACT DISPUTES AND FORUMS
Generally § 9.1
Agency boards of contract appeals
–Generally § 9.19
–Bringing an appeal § 9.21
–Discovery, prehearing procedures, and motions § 9.22
–Hearings and post-hearing matters § 9.23

FEDERAL CONTRACT DISPUTES
AND FORUMS *(Continued)*
  –Practice before boards § 9.20
  –Small claims procedures § 9.24
  Appeal of contracting officer's
      decision
  –Generally § 9.9
  –Election doctrine § 9.12
  –Necessity of decision § 9.10
  –Nonmoney claim decisions § 9.13
  –Time for § 9.11
  Attorneys' fees § 9.30
  Boards of Contract Appeals and
      Claims Court, review of § 9.14
  Consolidation of cases § 9.29
  Contract Disputes Act of 1978, scope
      § 9.2
  Contracting officer
  –Appeals, see Appeal of contracting
      officer's decision, this heading
  –Defined § 9.5
  Contractor claims
  –Generally § 9.3
  –Certification § 9.6
  –Contracting officer's decision § 9.7
  –Contracting officer's decision
      appeal, see Appeal of contracting
      officer's decision, this heading
  –Submitting claims, persons allowed
      § 9.4
  –What constitutes claim § 9.5
  Forum selection §§ 9.12, 9.31, 9.32
  Fraudulent claims § 9.18
  Government claims § 9.8
  Interest § 9.16
  Miller Act § 9.32
  Payment of claims § 9.17
  Small claims § 9.15
  Transfer of cases § 9.29
  US Claims Court
  –Generally § 9.25
  –Bringing suit § 9.26
  –Discovery, pretrial procedures, and
      motions § 9.27
  –Trials and post-trial matters § 9.28
FEES
  Consultants and experts, use §§ 4.3,
      4.10
FINANCIAL RECORDS
  Discovery § 3.11
FIRST IMPRESSIONS
  Court trials § 11.9

FORESEEABILITY
  Court trials § 11.12
  Lost productivity claims §§ 6.2,
      6.12, 6.14
FORUM SELECTION
  Court trials § 11.3
  Delay and acceleration claims § 5.6
  Federal contract disputes §§ 9.12,
      9.31, 9.32
FOUNDATION
  Lost productivity claims § 6.18
FRAUD
  Arbitration awards, vacating § 8.29
FRAUDULENT CLAIMS
  Federal contract disputes § 9.18
FREEDOM OF INFORMATION
    REQUESTS
  Discovery § 3.11
FULFORD DOCTRINE
  Federal contract disputes § 9.11

GAG ORDERS
  Alternative disputes resolution
      § 10.25
GLOBAL IMPACT METHOD
  Delay and acceleration claims § 5.5
GOOD FAITH
  Federal contract disputes § 9.6
GOVERNMENT CLAIMS
  Federal contract disputes § 9.8
GRAPHICS
  Damages, establishing § 7.6
  Delay and acceleration claims
      § 5.10

HARASSMENT
  Discovery § 3.7
HARVARD NEGOTIATION
    PROJECT
  Settlements §§ 14.12, 14.13
HEARINGS
  Arbitration advocacy § 8.20
  Federal contract disputes § 9.23
HEARSAY
  Arbitration advocacy § 8.18
  Court trials § 11.13
HISTORICAL DATE
  Lost productivity claims § 6.20
HISTORY
  Court trials § 11.9
HUMOR
  Delay and acceleration claims § 5.7

IDENTIFICATION WITH CLIENT
  Jury selection, court trials § 11.6
IMPEACHMENT
  Consultants and experts, use
    §§ 4.6, 4.7
IMPLIED CONTRACTUAL DUTIES
  Lost productivity claims § 6.16
IMPLIED WARRANTY
  Lost productivity claims § 6.16
INCONSISTENT TESTIMONY
  Defense §§ 13.15, 13.17
INCORPORATION BY REFERENCE
  Arbitration advocacy § 8.2
INCREASED LABOR FORCES
  Lost productivity claims § 6.6
INCREMENTAL IMPACTS
  Damages, establishing § 7.3
INDEMNIFICATION CLAUSES
  Defense § 13.5
INFORMATION EXCHANGE
  Alternative disputes resolution,
    minitrials §§ 10.10, 10.11
INJURY
  Lost productivity claims. See LOST
    PRODUCTIVITY CLAIMS
INSPECTION
  Discovery § 3.9
INSPECTION REQUESTS
  Discovery devices § 3.9
INTEREST
  Arbitration awards § 8.28
  Damages, establishing § 7.18
  Federal contract disputes §§ 9.3,
    9.6, 9.16
INTERFERENCE WITH
  PERFORMANCE
  Discovery § 3.3
INTERROGATORIES
  Case management § 2.6
  Consultants and experts, use § 4.5
  Court trials § 11.14
  Discovery devices § 3.6
  Federal contract disputes §§ 9.22,
    9.27
INTERVIEW
  Consultants and experts, use § 4.3
INVESTIGATION
  Arbitration advocacy § 8.23
  Court trials § 11.5
  Defense § 13.19
IRRATIONALITY
  Arbitration awards, vacating § 8.29

ISSUE IDENTIFICATION
  Consultants and experts, use § 4.4

JARGON
  Eliminating § 1.6
JOB SITE
  Discovery § 3.9
JOB SITE CLEAN-UP
  Damages, establishing § 7.3
JOB SITE CONDITIONS
  Lost productivity claims § 6.14
JOB SITE VISITS
  Arbitration advocacy § 8.24
  Consultants and experts, use § 4.3
  Court trials § 11.4
  Defense § 13.2
JOB-SPECIFIC DATA
  Lost productivity claims § 6.21
JOINDER
  Arbitration advocacy § 8.13
JOINT PRELIMINARY STATUS
  REPORT
  Federal contract disputes § 9.27
JOINT TORTFEASORS
  Settlements § 14.11
JUDGES
  Court trials § 11.15
  Settlements § 14.8
JURISDICTION
  Agency boards of contract appeals
    § 9.19
  Court trials § 11.3
JURY CHARGES
  Court trials § 11.14
  Defense § 13.24
JURY SELECTION
  Alternative disputes resolution,
    summary jury trials § 10.23
  Court trials §§ 11.6, 11.7
JURY TRIALS
  Court trials. See COURT TRIALS
  Damages, establishing § 7.6
  Defense. See DEFENSE AND
    CROSS-EXAMINATION
  Delay and acceleration claims § 5.6
  Lost productivity claims § 6.22

KEY PHRASES
  Litigation support systems §§ 2.4, 2.5

LABOR COSTS
  Damages, establishing § 7.19

LAWYERS
Arbitration advocacy, arbitrator selection § 8.5
LEARNED TREATISES
Consultants and experts, use § 4.11
LETTERS
Federal contract disputes § 9.5
LIABILITY
Alternative disputes resolution §§ 10.5, 10.21
Damages, establishing §§ 7.4, 7.8
Lost productivity claims §§ 6.3, 6.16
Settlements §§ 14.10, 14.11
LIMITATIONS ON DISCOVERY
Generally § 3.4
LIMITATIONS PERIOD
Federal contract disputes § 9.11
LIQUIDATED DAMAGES
Defense § 13.2
LIQUIDATING SETTLEMENTS
Settlements § 14.10
LITIGATION SUPPORT SYSTEMS
Case management. See CASE MANAGEMENT
LOSSES
Identification of key issues § 1.4
LOST PRODUCTIVITY CLAIMS
Generally § 6.1
Causation and injury
–Generally § 6.17
–Experts § 6.18
–Historical data § 6.20
–Job-specific date § 6.21
–Trade publications § 6.19
Causes
–Generally § 6.5
–Acceleration § 6.11
–Adverse weather § 6.9
–Constructive changes § 6.12
–Disruption § 6.14
–Increased labor forces § 6.6
–Out-of-sequence work § 6.10
–Overtime § 6.8
–Trade stacking § 6.7
Conclusion § 6.23
Damages § 6.22
Defense § 13.19
Delay and acceleration claims § 5.3
Judicial recognition § 6.4
Liability § 6.16
Loss of efficiency, definition § 6.2

LOST PRODUCTIVITY CLAIMS
(Continued)
Proving claim § 6.15
Recovery, obstacles to § 6.3

MAGISTRATES
Settlements § 14.8
MAINTENANCE
Settlements § 14.11
MANUAL FOR COMPLEX LITIGATION
Discovery § 3.4
MARY CARTER AGREEMENTS
Settlements § 14.11
MATERIAL
Damages, establishing § 7.19
MEASURING PRODUCTIVITY
Lost productivity claims § 6.21
MECHANIC'S LIEN
Damages, establishing § 7.11
MEDIATION
Alternative disputes resolution. See ALTERNATIVE DISPUTES RESOLUTION
Delay and acceleration claims § 5.6
MILLER ACT
Federal contract disputes § 9.32
MINITRIALS
Alternative disputes resolution. See ALTERNATIVE DISPUTES RESOLUTION
Delay and acceleration claims § 5.6
Federal contract disputes § 9.27
Settlements §§ 14.2, 14.8
MISCONDUCT OF ARBITRATOR
Arbitration awards, vacating § 8.29
MISMANAGEMENT
Delay and acceleration claims § 5.12
MISREPRESENTATION
Federal contract disputes § 9.18
MODELS
Arbitration advocacy § 8.25
MODIFICATION OF AWARD
Arbitration awards § 8.28
MODIFIED TOTAL COSTS APPROACH
Damages, establishing § 7.10
Lost productivity claims § 6.22
MOTIONS
Federal contract disputes §§ 9.22, 9.27

MULTIPLE PARTIES
Complexity §§ 1.1, 1.2
Identification of key parties § 1.3
Case management § 2.14

NEGOTIATIONS
Settlements. See SETTLEMENTS

NET IMPACT TECHNIQUE
Delay and acceleration claims §§ 5.5, 5.6

NETWORK SCHEDULES
Delay and acceleration claims § 5.4

NEUTRAL
Alternative disputes resolution §§ 10.4, 10.12

NEW STRATEGIC MODEL
Settlement negotiations § 14.13

NO DAMAGES FOR DELAY CLAUSES
Appealability § 15.3
Defense § 13.2
Delay and acceleration claims § 5.12
Lost productivity claims § 6.10

NONSETTLING TORTFEASOR
Settlements § 14.11

NOTICE
Defense § 13.1
Delay and acceleration claims § 5.12
Federal contract disputes §§ 9.21, 9.24
Settlements § 14.4

NOTICE TO PRODUCE DOCUMENTS
Discovery § 3.8

OATHS
Arbitration advocacy § 8.18

OBJECTIONS
Alternative disputes resolution § 10.23
Defense §§ 13.12, 13.13, 13.24

OFFERS OF JUDGMENT
Settlements § 14.7

OMISSIONS
Discovery § 3.3

ONE-TIME COSTS
Damages, establishing § 7.3

OPENING STATEMENTS
Affirmative case. See AFFIRMATIVE CASE
Arbitration advocacy § 8.17
Court trials § 11.9
Defense §§ 13.9–13.11

OPINIONS
Arbitration awards § 8.28
Consultants and experts, use §§ 4.1, 4.7, 4.8
Court trials § 11.12
Defense § 13.17
Lost productivity claims § 6.18

OPPRESSION
Discovery § 3.7

ORAL ARGUMENT
Court trials § 11.15

ORDER OF WITNESSES
Affirmative case § 12.16

OUT-OF-SEQUENCE WORK
Lost productivity claims § 6.10

OVERHEAD
Damages, establishing § 7.16

OVERSTATEMENT
Defense § 13.10

OVERTIME
Lost productivity claims §§ 6.8, 6.19

PARTIES
Identification of key parties § 1.3

PAST RE-CREATION
Affirmative case §§ 12.1, 12.3

PAYMENT BONDS
Federal contract disputes, Miller Act § 9.32

PAYMENTS
Federal contract disputes, claims § 9.17

PERFECTING RIGHTS
Defense § 13.1

PERFORMANCE EVALUATION
Settlements § 14.3

PHOTOGRAPHS
Arbitration advocacy § 8.25
Court trials § 11.1

PHYSICAL EXAMINATIONS
Discovery § 3.9

PLEADINGS
Case management § 2.6

POST-HEARING BRIEFS
Arbitration advocacy § 8.23

PRECLUSION ORDERS
Discovery § 3.15

PREHEARING PROCEDURES
Federal contract disputes § 9.22

PREJUDICE
Arbitration advocacy §§ 8.13, 8.14

INDEX

PRETRIAL ACTIVITY
  Case management. See CASE MANAGEMENT
  Complex made simple. See COMPLEX MADE SIMPLE
  Consultants and experts. See CONSULTANTS AND EXPERTS
  Discovery. See DISCOVERY

PRETRIAL CONFERENCES
  Alternative disputes resolution, summary jury trials § 10.22

PRETRIAL ORGANIZATION
  Discovery § 3.13

PRIMACY
  Court trials, closing arguments § 11.14
  Defense, opening statement § 13.10

PRIME CONTRACT
  Arbitration advocacy § 8.2

PRIME CONTRACTORS
  Federal contract disputes §§ 9.4, 9.32

PRINCIPLED NEGOTIATIONS
  Settlement negotiations § 14.13

PRIOR OPINIONS
  Consultants and experts, use § 4.8

PRIVILEGES
  Discovery devices § 3.12

PRIVITY
  Federal contract disputes § 9.4
  Identification of key parties § 1.3
  Settlements § 14.10

PROBABILITY
  Affirmative case § 12.1

PROCEDURES
  Complexity § 1.7

PRODUCTIVITY
  Lost productivity claims. See LOST PRODUCTIVITY CLAIMS

PROOF
  Affirmative case §§ 12.15, 12.16
  Damages, establishing §§ 7.8, 7.18
  Delay and acceleration claims § 5.3
  Lost productivity claims §§ 6.15, 6.17, 6.20, 6.22

PROTECTIVE COURT ORDERS
  Alternative disputes resolution, minitrials § 10.13
  Discovery § 3.15
  Settlements § 14.5

PROVING LOSSES
  Lost productivity claims § 6.3

PSYCHOLOGICAL EXAMINATION
  Discovery § 3.9

PUBLIC POLICY
  Alternative disputes resolution § 10.3

PUBLIC RECORDS EXCEPTION
  Court trials § 11.13

PUBLIC RIGHT TO ACCESS
  Alternative disputes resolution, summary jury trials § 10.25

PUNITIVE DAMAGES
  Arbitration advocacy § 8.27

QUANTUM
  Federal contract disputes §§ 9.14, 9.23, 9.28

QUANTUM MERUIT CLAIMS
  Damages, establishing § 7.11

REASONABLENESS
  Damages, establishing §§ 7.2, 7.8

REASONABLE VALUE
  Damages, establishing § 7.11

RECENCY
  Court trials, closing arguments § 11.14
  Defense, opening statement § 13.10

RECIPROCAL INSURANCE REQUIREMENTS
  Defense § 13.2

RECORDS
  Defense §§ 13.4, 13.18
  Discovery devices §§ 3.1, 3.3

RECOVERY THEORIES
  Discovery § 3.6

RECURRING PROBLEMS
  Identification of key issues § 1.4

REDIRECT TESTIMONY
  Affirmative case § 12.20

REGISTRATION
  Consultants and experts, use § 4.6

REHEARSALS
  Affirmative case § 12.12

REMEDIES
  Settlements, money alternatives § 14.3

REPORTS
  Consultants and experts, use § 4.7

REQUESTS FOR ADMISSIONS
  Court trials § 11.9
  Federal contract disputes §§ 9.22, 9.27

RÉSUMÉ
Consultants and experts, use §§ 4.3, 4.6
RETAINAGE
Discovery § 3.3
RETROACTIVE CURE OF DEFECT CERTIFICATION
Federal contract disputes § 9.6
RISK ALLOCATION
Defense § 13.1
RISK FACTORS
Court trials § 11.2
RULE OF PROBABILITY
Affirmative case § 12.1
RULES OF EVIDENCE
Arbitration advocacy § 8.18

SAFETY
Lost productivity claims § 6.14
SANCTIONS
Discovery § 3.15
SCHEDULE ANALYSIS
Defense § 13.22
SCHEDULES
Consultants and experts, use § 4.4
Delay and acceleration claims §§ 5.5, 5.7
SEGREGATED DAMAGES
Damages, establishing § 7.5
Lost productivity claims § 6.22
SEPARATION OF CLAIMS
Federal contract disputes § 9.6
SERIATUM ARBITRATION
Arbitration advocacy § 8.13
SERVICES
Consultants and experts, use § 4.3
SETTLEMENTS
Generally § 14.1
Alternative disputes resolution §§ 10.2, 10.24
Conclusion § 14.16
Confidentiality § 14.5
Control and cost § 14.1
Court trials § 11.15
Dealing with parties § 14.15
Documenting settlement
–Generally § 14.9
–Liquidating agreements § 14.10
–Mary Carter agreements § 14.11
Initiating settlement
–Generally § 14.6
–Conferences § 14.8

SETTLEMENTS *(Continued)*
–Offers of judgment § 14.7
Negotiations
–Generally § 14.12
–Style § 14.13
–Timing § 14.14
Reasons to settle §§ 14.3, 14.4
SEVERANCE
Settlements § 14.11
SEVERE WEATHER
Delay and acceleration claims § 5.4
SIGNATURES
Arbitration advocacy § 8.26
Federal contract disputes § 9.6
SIMPLICITY
Affirmative case §§ 12.4, 12.18
Damages, establishing § 7.6
SIMPLIFICATION
Defense § 13.22
Delay and acceleration claims § 5.1
SINCERITY
Affirmative case §§ 12.1, 12.7
SITE
See JOB SITE
SMALL CLAIMS
Federal contract disputes §§ 9.15, 9.22–9.24, 9.31
SMOKING
Arbitration advocacy § 8.16
SPECIAL MASTERS
Court trials § 11.16
SPECIALTY TRADE CONTRACTORS
Lost productivity claims § 6.20
SPECIAL VERDICTS
Defense § 13.24
SPECIFIC COST CLAIM
Damages, establishing § 7.9
STANDARD FORMS
Appealability § 15.2
Arbitration advocacy §§ 8.2, 8.12
STARE DECISIS
Arbitration advocacy § 8.1
STIPULATIONS
Federal contract disputes § 9.27
STRIKES
Court trials § 11.2
Delay and acceleration claims § 5.4
Lost productivity claims §§ 6.1, 6.14

INDEX

STRUCTURED SETTLEMENT PROCESS
　See ALTERNATIVE DISPUTES RESOLUTION
SOIL SAMPLES
　Discovery § 3.9
SPECIAL MASTERS
　Court trials § 11.17
STIPULATIONS
　Alternative disputes resolution §§ 10.8, 10.9
　Court trials § 11.9
SUBCONTRACTORS
　Discovery devices § 3.2
　Federal contract disputes §§ 9.4, 9.32
　Settlements § 14.10
SUMMARIES
　Affirmative case § 12.21
　Court trials §§ 11.13, 11.15
SUMMARY JUDGMENTS
　Federal contract disputes § 9.27
SUMMARY JURY TRIAL
　See ALTERNATIVE DISPUTES RESOLUTION
SUPPLIERS
　Federal contract disputes § 9.32
SUPPORTING DATA
　Federal contract disputes § 9.6

TECHNICAL KNOWLEDGE
　Jury selection, court trials § 11.6
　Understanding § 1.5
TERMINATION FOR CONVENIENCE CLAUSE
　Appealability § 15.3
TERMINATION FOR DEFAULT
　Federal contract disputes §§ 9.11, 9.13
TERMS
　Court trials § 11.9
TEST RESULTS
　Discovery § 3.9
THEME
　Affirmative case § 12.2
　Court trials §§ 11.6, 11.11, 11.14
　Defense § 13.11
　Delay and acceleration claims § 5.11
THEORY OF CASE
　Defense § 13.8
THEORY OF RECOVERY
　Court trials § 11.5

THIRD-PARTY ACTIONS
　Lost productivity claims § 6.1
TIME
　Federal contract disputes §§ 9.7, 9.9, 9.11, 9.14, 9.21, 9.24
TIME EXTENSIONS
　Delay and acceleration claims § 5.3
TIME IMPACT ANALYSIS
　Consultants and experts, use § 4.4
　Delay and acceleration claims § 5.5
TIMELY NOTICE
　Defense § 13.1
TOTAL COST METHOD OF DAMAGES DETERMINATION
　Lost productivity claims § 6.22
　Shortcuts § 1.6
TOTAL COSTS CLAIMS
　Damages, establishing § 7.8
TRADE PUBLICATIONS
　Lost productivity claims § 6.19
TRADE SECRETS
　Alternative disputes resolution, minitrials § 10.13
　Discovery § 3.11
TRADE STACKING
　Lost productivity claims § 6.7
TRANSCRIPTS
　Arbitration advocacy § 8.21
TRANSFER OF CASES
　Federal contract disputes § 9.29
TRIAL PREPARATION
　Consultants and experts, use § 4.4
TRIAL RESOURCES
　Case management. See CASE MANAGEMENT
TRIPARTITE ARBITRATION
　Arbitration advocacy, arbitrator selection § 8.11

UNDUE BURDEN OR EXPENSE
　Discovery § 3.8
UNDUE MEANS
　Arbitration awards, vacating § 8.29
UNSEGREGATED DAMAGES
　Lost productivity claims § 6.22
US CLAIMS COURT
　Federal contracts. See FEDERAL CONTRACT DISPUTES AND FORUMS

VACATING AWARD
　Arbitration advocacy § 8.29

VERDICTS
  Defense § 13.24

VIDEOTAPE
  Alternative disputes resolution, minitrials § 10.10
  Court trials § 11.1

VISUAL AIDS
  Affirmative case § 12.10

VOIR DIRE
  Alternative disputes resolution §§ 10.22, 10.23
  Court trials §§ 11.3, 11.8

WAIVER
  Defense § 13.3
  Federal contract disputes, hearing § 9.22

WEATHER
  Court trials § 11.2
  Delay and acceleration claims § 5.4

WITNESSES
  Arbitration advocacy § 8.20
  Affirmative case §§ 12.16–12.18
  Alternative disputes resolution §§ 10.10, 10.23
  Case management §§ 2.3, 2.10
  Court trials §§ 11.5, 11.10–11.12
  Discovery devices §§ 3.1, 3.7, 3.14

WORK PRODUCT
  Case management § 2.3
  Discovery §§ 3.7, 3.11, 3.12